Preaching to Nazi Germany

Preaching to Nazi Germany

The Pulpit and the Confessing Church

William Skiles

LEXINGTON BOOKS/FORTRESS ACADEMIC
Lanham • Boulder • New York • London

Published by Lexington Books/Fortress Academic
Lexington Books is an imprint of The Rowman & Littlefield Publishing Group, Inc.
4501 Forbes Boulevard, Suite 200, Lanham, Maryland 20706
www.rowman.com

86-90 Paul Street, London EC2A 4NE, United Kingdom

Copyright © 2023 by The Rowman & Littlefield Publishing Group, Inc.

Portions of chapter 8 were taken from William Skiles, "Franz Hildebrandt on the BBC: Wartime Broadcasting to Nazi Germany" in the *Journal of Ecclesiastical History*, 74, no. 1 (January 2023), pp. 90–115. Copyright © 2022. Reprinted with permission of Cambridge University Press.

Portions of chapter 7 were taken from William Skiles, "'The Bearers of Unholy Potential': Confessing Church Sermons on the Jews and Judaism." *Studies in Christian-Jewish Relations*, 11, no.1 (2016): 1–29. Reprinted with permission.

Portions were taken from William S. Skiles, "Protests from the Pulpit: The Confessing Church and the Sermons of World War II." *Sermon Studies* 1.1 (2017) : 1–23. Reprinted with permission.

All rights reserved. No part of this book may be reproduced in any form or by any electronic or mechanical means, including information storage and retrieval systems, without written permission from the publisher, except by a reviewer who may quote passages in a review.

British Library Cataloguing in Publication Information Available

Library of Congress Cataloging-in-Publication Data

Names: Skiles, William, 1976– author.
Title: Preaching to Nazi Germany : the pulpit and the confessing church / William Skiles.
Description: Lanham : Lexington Books/Fortress Academic, [2023] | Includes bibliographical references and index. | Summary: "In Preaching to Nazi Germany, William Skiles argues that clergy expressed various messages that aimed to limit Nazi interference in church affairs and at times even to undermine the Nazi state and its leaders and policies"— Provided by publisher.
Identifiers: LCCN 2023024627 (print) | LCCN 2023024628 (ebook) | ISBN 9781978700635 (cloth) | ISBN 9781978700642 (epub)
Subjects: LCSH: Church and state—Germany—History—1933–1945. | Germany—Church history—1933–1945. | Germany—Politics and government—1933–1945. | Pastoral theology—Germany—History—19th century. | Preaching—Germany—History. | National socialism and religion. | Holocaust, Jewish (1939–1945)—Religious aspects—Christianity.
Classification: LCC BR856.R65 S55 2023 (print) | LCC BR856.R65 (ebook) | DDC 322/.10943—dc23/eng/20230710
LC record available at https://lccn.loc.gov/2023024627
LC ebook record available at https://lccn.loc.gov/2023024628

Contents

Acknowledgments	vii
Chapter 1: Introduction	1
Chapter 2: The Church Divided: The Rise of National Socialism and the Question of Divine Revelation	27
Chapter 3: A Fettered Gospel	63
Chapter 4: The Confessing Church and the "New School" of Homiletics	85
Chapter 5: Challenging Nazi Ideology	115
Chapter 6: Against the Nazi Persecution of the Churches	145
Chapter 7: "The Bearers of Unholy Potential"	173
Chapter 8: In the Defense of Jews and Judaism	209
Chapter 9: Spying in God's House	235
Chapter 10: Conclusion	255
Selected Bibliography	261
Index	285
About the Author	295

Acknowledgments

I have been tremendously encouraged and inspired by many individuals throughout the process of writing this book, and it is my pleasure to acknowledge them here. From my days at the University of California at San Diego, I wish to thank Richard Biernacki, Patrick Patterson, Cynthia Truant, and my doctoral chairs, Frank Biess and Deborah Hertz. They provided an abundance of guidance, encouragement, and wisdom, without which this project would never have gotten off the ground. I am grateful to friends and colleagues through the years whose conversations have helped me to develop and refine my ideas and arguments, including Ryan Zroka, Amy Zroka, Suzanne Hillman, and Kevin Grimm. Special thanks especially to Victoria Barnett, Josh McMullen, Michael Pregitzer, and Robert Schwarzwalder for reading chapters of the book and offering thoughtful and invaluable comments. I also wish to thank two mentors who have gone out of their way to support me and the publication of this book. Kyle Jantzen and Richard Weikart have shown extraordinary support in offering keen insights and criticisms that helped me refine the argument. Both have read the entire manuscript and offered incisive comments and feedback. I am grateful for their investment in me and this project. It goes without saying (but must be said) that I am responsible for any shortcomings and errors that remain.

Several institutions have generously supported my research. The Leo Baeck Institute, the Deutscher Akademischer Austausch Dienst, the University of California, San Diego, and Regent University provided research grants that allowed for extended stays in Germany. Special thanks also to the archivists and staff at the Evangelisches Zentralarchiv (EZA) in Berlin and the Landeskirchliches Archiv der Evangelischen Kirche von Westfalen in Bielefeld, especially Dr. Peter Beier at the former and Dr. Jens Murkens at the latter. I am deeply grateful for their assistance. Thanks to Michael Gibson, Neil Elliott, Gayla Freeman, and the team at Fortress Academic and Lexington Books, for their commitment to this project and their keen editorial insights (as well as patience). I would also like to thank the editors at *Church*

History and Religious Culture, the *Journal of Christian-Jewish Relations*, the *Journal of Ecclesiastical History*, and *Sermon Studies* for permission to reprint articles I had written and included, in whole or in part, in this book.

Thanks most of all to my family for their continual support and inspiration. My mom and dad, Dorothy and Bill Skiles, have instilled in me a love for books and history, and they have read numerous drafts of the chapters through the years. Thanks to my twin brother and his wife, George and Dena Skiles, who have likewise read drafts and consistently encouraged me along the way. Thanks to my children, Liam, Marie, and Theodore, for keeping me grounded and inspiring me with your curiosity about how the world works and why things are the way they are. I dedicate this book to my wife Renee, whose love and companionship sustain me.

Chapter 1

Introduction

The last sermon Martin Niemöller preached as a free man in Nazi Germany demanded a "decision of faith" from his congregation in the Dahlem suburb of Berlin. He called for a condemnation of the Nazi persecution of the German churches. On Sunday, June 27, 1937, at the Jesus Christus Kirche, he turned to a familiar New Testament text, Acts 5:34–42. It was the story of an "upright and pious" Jew, the Pharisee Gamaliel, who advised his community after the crucifixion of Jesus, to wait and observe the work of the early Christian leaders. Do not judge them too quickly, Gamaliel advised. If they succeed in spreading their message and the Jesus movement thrives, then they can affirm that God's hand is at work.[1] Like any skilled preacher, Niemöller then explicitly applied the ancient text to his own situation in Nazi Germany. The time for waiting and observing is over, he argued. It is time to render judgment about whether God's hand is at work in the Nazi regime.

Niemöller, the former submarine captain in World War I, had voted for the Nazi Party in the Prussian elections of 1924 and the Reichstag elections on March 5, 1933, hoping for the spiritual rejuvenation of Germany.[2] But now, just four years later, he proceeded to lay out to his whole congregation the recent actions of the Nazi state against the German churches. Niemöller condemned the secret police arrest of eight church leaders the Wednesday prior. He condemned the arrest just the day before of six women and a man in Saarbrücken who circulated church-wide election leaflets supporting Confessing Church candidates. Remarkably, Niemöller even condemned the three Gestapo agents who crashed his communion service the previous Friday "to inform upon the activities of the community of Jesus."[3] And he continued to offer a laundry list of the most recent Nazi persecutions of the German churches. Niemöller's message was clear: Gamaliel was pious and wise to wait to see the hand of God at work, yet Germans have witnessed the enemies of God at work for four long years. "Make a decision of faith," he advised his congregation. And then echoing Jesus' words, he marked a clear contrast, "He who is not with me is against me."[4]

It is not surprising given the boldness of this sermon that two days later, on Tuesday morning at 8:30 am, two Gestapo agents paid a visit to the Niemöller residence. Niemöller left in the custody of the agents and headed to the police headquarters at Alexanderplatz. He waited for hours until he was taken again, this time to the remand prison in the neighborhood of Moabit.

Certainly, Niemöller was not surprised by his arrest. He had been arrested five times previously due to his bold preaching, and he was usually detained for only a few hours each time.[5] That early summer, he suspected the Nazi regime would soon arrest him as he preached against the persecution of the German churches. In fact, a contact informed him in the spring of 1937 that the Public Prosecutor was preparing charges against him.[6] This was just two months before the Gestapo paid a visit that Tuesday morning.

While waiting at the police headquarters in Alexanderplatz, nine Gestapo agents returned to Niemöller's home and conducted a thorough search of the premises. They even arrested visiting Confessing Church pastors who had stopped by for a scheduled meeting.[7] From that day to the end of the Second World War, Niemöller persevered in prison and later in a concentration camp.

Niemöller's record of speaking out from the pulpit against Nazi persecution of the German churches raises the question about the nature and frequency of pastors' criticisms from the pulpit against the regime. The German pastor and historian Wolfgang Gerlach's ground-breaking 1970 dissertation, *Als die Zeugen schwiegen*, argued that Confessing Church leaders failed to bear witness in word and deed about the persecution and extermination of Jews and "non-Aryan" Christians in the Nazi period. They remained silent, he argued. Gerlach's critics at the time condemned his account as unfair and ungrateful for the courage these men demonstrated in confronting the Nazi threat to Germany and the churches. His work remained unpublished until the historiographical tides shifted in his favor in the late 1980s. Today, Gerlach's arguments predominate in the historiography of the Protestant churches in Nazi Germany, and they have been corroborated and supplemented by historians for nearly three decades.[8]

While historians have used select sermons, whether from Catholic or Confessing Church clergymen, to argue that pastors at times expressed support for the Nazi regime, criticism of Nazi persecution of the churches, or even the rare occurrence of the condemnation of specific Nazi policies—there has to date been no in-depth treatment of the wide variety of messages pastors expressed from the authority of the pulpit in response to the Nazi regime. This study seeks to address this lacuna in the scholarship. Sermons abound in the historical record, and they reveal a range of pastors' messages, including support, acquiescence, and opposition. Pastors preached every Sunday and on holidays and special events throughout the year. Frequently, in Germany in the early- and mid-twentieth century, their sermons were written down and even published. While it is not possible to provide a representative body of Confessing Church sermons given the unknown number and locations of extant sermons (certainly ranging in the thousands), this book is based on a study of over 900 of them.

This research on Confessing Church sermons will be situated in the context of early-twentieth-century German Protestant homiletics (i.e., the art of preaching). An examination of German Protestant biblical interpretation and practical theology is required to appreciate how counter-cultural many of the messages were. The genre of the sermon and the constraints of the pulpit must be explored before the pastors' messages can be fully understood.

This study is long overdue contribution to the history of the Protestant churches in Nazi Germany. Historians have called for a thorough analysis of Nazi-era sermons to see how and to what degree German pastors supported the Nazi regime and its nationalist, racist, and antisemitic values through their preaching, and if and how they spoke truth to power, defended the oppressed, and demonstrated love to their neighbors in need.[9] I will provide an extensive analysis of sermons throughout the Nazi period to understand better how Confessing Church pastors responded to Nazi ideology, its policies, and persecutions, especially of the Jewish people. In short, I ask: If a German were to walk into a Protestant church on any given Sunday in Nazi Germany and listen attentively to a Confessing Church pastor deliver a sermon, what kinds of messages might he or she hear about the Nazi regime? In this introductory chapter, I will briefly present the context of the Church Struggle (*Kirchenkampf*) in Nazi Germany, lay the historiographical and methodological groundwork necessary for this study, and elucidate the contributions of this research to the field.

THE CHURCH STRUGGLE

As will be discussed in the following chapters, the German Protestant churches fractured along theological fault lines when Hitler and the Nazi regime came to power in January 1933. This struggle played out in the pulpits. The popularity of the pro-Nazi faction within the German Protestant churches, the German Christian Faith Movement (*Glaubensbewegung Deutsche Christen*), encouraged Hitler to create a Reich Church (*Reichskirche*) to unite all Protestant churches under German Christian leadership in the summer of 1933, though the regime never gained complete control of the church (as will be examined in chapter 2).[10] Approximately 600,000 people aligned themselves with the German Christians by the mid-1930s.[11] This religious movement sought to align Christianity with National Socialist principles, to praise Hitler as Germany's savior, to strip Christianity of its Jewish elements, to apply racialist ideology to Christianity, and to deny leadership or even membership in the German churches to Christians of Jewish descent.[12] For many, the German Christian movement went too far, and in September 1933, the Berlin-Dahlem pastor Martin Niemöller organized the Pastors' Emergency League (*Pfarrernotbund*, henceforth PEL), which, not a year later, would become the Confessing Church. The PEL was specifically constituted to assist "non-Aryan" clergy.[13] The single issue that united members of the Confessing Church was simply that they wanted to halt any National Socialist infringements—whether by the regime or German Christians—in Christian theology and practice.[14] To clarify, the Confessing Church did not become a new church, but rather was a faction within the German Evangelical Church, as was the German Christian movement. As will be discussed in chapter 2, this division in the churches concerned the nature and identity of Protestantism in Nazi Germany. The Confessing Church asserted that the Reich Church had become a corrupted church, and subsequently claimed to be the true church, faithful to Scripture and its interpretation by the Reformation confessions.[15] Yet, even then, as will be discussed in Chapter 2, the unity of the Confessing Church would be short lived as members vehemently disagreed about how to engage with state churches. Furthermore, along with the German Christians and the Confessing Church members, there were also "neutrals" who simply wished to stay out of the fray and not take a stand one way or the other in relation to the Nazi regime.

Yet the division of the German Protestant churches was by no means inevitable. Ever since the early days of the *Nationalsozialistische Deutsche Arbeiterpartei* (National Socialist German Workers Party), Hitler and the Nazis sought to placate Christians concerned about the Party's stance on religion. They asserted that Nazism was not opposed to Christianity so long as it served the nation's interests. Thus, the Nazi Party Platform of 1920 states,

> We demand liberty for all religious denominations in the state, so far as they are not a danger to it and do not militate against the moral feelings of the German race.
>
> The party as such stands for positive Christianity, but does not bind itself in the matter of creed to any particular confession. It combats the Jewish materialist spirit within us and outside of us.[16]

While the statement explicitly endorsed the religious freedom of Protestants and Catholics, it threatened persecution for Jews as a people of a "foreign spirit." Yet it assured Germans that the Nazis would not side with either Catholics or Protestants but rather maintain neutrality in support of what they called "positive Christianity," a term conveniently left undefined. Yet by defining a "Christian" historically as someone who has faith in and follows

Jesus Christ, and "Christianity" as the content of that disciple-faith, one can more easily see the contours of religious conflict in Nazi Germany.

In the early 2000s scholars such as Emilio Gentile and Michael Burleigh argued that National Socialism may best be understood as a form of political religion, an ideology in competition with Christianity, and one which likewise demands the commitment of the whole person.[17] Nazism presented the German people with a new savior, belief system, rituals, liturgies, and eschatological hope for the "Aryan" race. This argument is consonant with common interpretations of Hitler and other Nazi leaders as directly opposed to Christianity, wishing to stamp it out entirely (if only over time), or as cynical and opportunistic when dealing with the churches.[18] In response to the argument that Nazism is a "political religion," Richard Steigmann-Gall published *The Holy Reich*, in which he asserted that "many leading Nazis in fact considered themselves Christian (among other things) or understood their movement (among other ways) within a Christian frame of reference."[19] Further, he argued that "many Christians of the day believed Nazism to be in some sense a Christian movement" that would unify Germans across confessional lines on the basis of the *Volksgemeinschaft* (people's community).[20] While scholars have criticized various aspects of Steigmann-Gall's argument, the scholarship since has explored how Germans understood the relationship between Christianity and National Socialism.[21] For example, the work of Kyle Jantzen has demonstrated that Protestant pastors in Nauen, Pirna, and Ravensburg "believed that supporting Nazism was consistent with their practice of Christianity and raise the possibility that they too believed that Hitler and the Nazis were engaged in a movement that complemented, if not flowed out of, their faith."[22]

More recently, Samuel Koehne's insightful research on the Nazis' use of the term "positive Christianity" demonstrates that this was not a specific "type of Christianity" with an "inner logic," as Steigmann-Gall has argued, but rather a term that had no clear meaning.[23] Prior to the Nazis, Germans used this term to mean the "dogmatic Christian faith" of the Catholic and Protestant churches, yet the Nazis used it to advance their nationalist, racist, and *völkisch* views, often as a political ploy.[24] Thus, Hitler and the Nazis used the term "positive Christianity" contrary to its common usage in a way that asserted their neutrality between Catholics and Protestants and also placated Christians concerned about their orthodoxy.[25] As Koehne argues, "Officially, the Nazis were simultaneously supporting traditional Christianity and completely undermining it. Members of the Nazi Party could apparently adhere to the existing creeds of the Christian faith so long as the doctrines of their faith were 'Germanic' or Aryanized—which destroyed traditional Christian faith."[26] Nazism contravened numerous Christian beliefs, including the universality of the gospel for all people, the unity of the body of Christ as the

Church, the sinful nature of all human beings (and thus the need for Jesus Christ as Savior), and the ethic to love one's enemies.[27] Yet by using the term "positive Christianity," Nazism appealed not just to advocates of an "Aryan" Christianity and German paganism but also to orthodox Christians as well. The Nazis appeared to support the creeds yet subjected them to Nazi ideology, and in this way they gained favor in a nation in which 97% of citizens self-identified as Christian.[28]

National Socialism grew from a Bavarian provincial party in the early- to mid-1920s into a national party by the late 1920s for a couple of important reasons. The Weimar Republic never gained the full trust or support of conservative Protestants because it sundered the connection between throne and altar, and it was led by the socialists of the Social Democratic Party (*Sozialdemokratische Partei Deutschlands*, henceforth SPD), the largest and most dominant political party in the Reichstag.[29] The clergy of the Evangelical Churches were by and large conservative and patriotic, and indeed, would have preferred the old system of monarchy to the democracy of Weimar.[30] Moreover, as Kyle Jantzen has argued, the ideological confusion early in the Nazi era meant that "patriotic, nationally minded Germans did not yet understand that National Socialists who used national and social language would invest it with more radical, revolutionary meaning than traditional conservatives . . . could ever imagine."[31] In the early 1930s, clergy increasingly opted for the authoritarian National Socialist Party in the hope that a strong and powerful leader might lead Germany to prosperity.

Moreover, many Protestants perceived the National Socialist Party as the best option to oppose the threat of a communist revolution in Germany. Just 16 years prior, the Bolsheviks succeeded in establishing a communist state in the former Russian Empire. At the end of the First World War, communists attempted to seize control in Germany, first, in the Spartacist Uprising in January 1919, and later in the Munich Soviet Republic, both of which were toppled by the nascent Weimar Republic and Freikorp troops. Even then, there were localized communist uprisings in the early 1920s, in Saxony and Thuringia, for example. Christians feared communism as an atheistic ideology that threatened the church and the Christian faith, as well as the social order and private wealth and property. There were no more vocal or determined opponents of communism in Weimar Germany than Adolf Hitler and the Nazis.

The Nazi Party made tremendous progress throughout the later 1920s and into the early 1930s. In the elections of May 1928, only 2.6% of the votes went to the Nazis.[32] But in September 1930, the Nazis had 18.3% of the votes. The Weimar government's inability to govern effectively during the economic depression that started in 1929 led many Germans to support Hitler and the Nazis. In the national elections of July 1932, 37.4% of the votes went to the Nazi Party, making it the largest party in the Reichstag. Though the percentage took a dip in the elections of November 1932, the Nazis still had 33.1% of the vote and remained the largest in parliament. After a series of chancellors failed to lead Germany through the turmoil of the Weimar Republic, President Paul von Hindenburg appointed Adolf Hitler as chancellor on January 30, 1933. Just two months later, the Nazis gained 17 million votes, 43.9% of the votes cast. Hitler and the Nazi Party had succeeded in coming to power legally and democratically in Germany, though they would subsequently dismantle the democratic system with the Enabling Act of March 23 after the Reichstag fire, paving the way for the Nazi dictatorship.

By the time of the establishment of the Confessing Church in the spring of 1934, Confessing Church pastors had arrived at a wide range of perceptions about the Nazi regime. As Victoria Barnett has argued, "The only thing all Confessing Church Christians had in common was their opposition to the absolute demands of Nazi ideology on their religious faith."[33] As she and others have demonstrated, Confessing Church pastors could even be found in the ranks of Nazis or pro-Nazi supporters.[34] And one would not need to look far to find anti-Jewish comments in their sermons. In fact, in early 1933, many German Protestants were optimistic about the Nazi rise to power, seeing in it an opportunity for the growth of the German Protestant churches.[35] For example, just weeks after Easter 1933, Martin Niemöller preached a sermon in Berlin-Dahlem entitled, "We Would See Jesus!" on John 12:20–27, a passage that underscores the necessity of following Christ and the possibility of eternal life.[36] In this sermon, he observed that the German people had awakened from the spiritual malaise of the Weimar years (the political and economic instability of Weimar had coincided with a significant decline in church membership).[37] Just months after Hitler's rise to power, Niemöller believed he was witnessing a spiritual awakening in progress. He started his sermon in celebration:

> Rejoice! Make a joyful noise, all ye lands!
> Yes, that is what we feel like doing, for outside we see the verdant, blossoming spring, and around us we see the people of our nation awakening; and in spite of all its storm and stress, in spite of all its effervescence and fermentation, that awakening tells us that we are still a young nation which does not wish to be drawn into the collapse of Western Civilization: we wish to live! May God speed us on our way![38]

Niemöller appears genuinely hopeful about the changes occurring in his nation, but his emphasis is not on the political changes brought by the Nazi regime; rather, his excitement is due to a spiritual "awakening" that has rejuvenated the German people.[39] Indeed, the German Protestant churches staunched the numbers of those leaving to approximately 50,000 in 1933, while nearly 325,000 joined. Steigman-Gall argues, "There could have been no clearer sign that national renewal and religious renewal were believed to be deeply connected."[40]

Yet the optimism among many Christians quickly faded as the regime meddled in church affairs and persecuted its pastors. After the Reich Church failed to achieve organizational unity in the Protestant churches, Hitler established the Ministry of Church Affairs in 1935 under the leadership of Hanns Kerrl, hoping to lessen tensions and bring the factions together under the Nazi state. Church-state relations intensified because of ongoing Nazi interference in church affairs, the harassment and mass arrests of Confessing Church pastors for minor infractions such as taking "illegal" collections of funds to support pastors, and pastors reading from the pulpit *Fürbittenliste* (intercessory lists), lists of names of pastors persecuted by the Nazi state.[41] Church leaders had been harassed and arrested in attempts to silence criticism of the state.[42] Martin Niemöller is a case in point: he was arrested by the Gestapo in July 1937 for reading the names of persecuted clergymen and for criticizing the regime from the pulpit; this was followed by the arrest of 700 pastors for various infractions against the Nazi state by November of that same year.[43]

Conflict and debates within the German Protestant churches played out in the public arena, in church elections, synods, sermons, and public pronouncements. The pro-Nazi German Christian movement continued its relentless attack on the Jewish foundations of Christianity, seeking to adapt the religion to a new modern age. They argued themes consonant with National Socialist principles, such as the racial superiority of the "Aryan" race, the destiny of the German nation, the greatness of Germany's "savior," Adolf Hitler, and the perniciousness of the Jewish people.[44]

Confessing Church pastors took the debate to the pulpit and often directly responded to these assertions by looking to the Christian scriptures: Christ is the only savior; the gospel is a universal message, for all people regardless of race or ethnicity; Christians and Jews are spiritual cousins, who share values, traditions, and sacred texts; and Judaism and its Scripture are the foundation of Christianity and thus cannot be excised from the German churches.

The Church Struggle of the Third Reich should be understood therefore not to refer simply to the churches' stance vis-à-vis the regime (the churches presented a divided and fragile front), but also to the struggle within the churches against each other.[45] Scholars have examined the histories of the rival factions within the German churches over the problem of how to deal with the Nazi regime: the Catholic Church signed a Concordat with Hitler's regime; the German Christian movement wished to align Christianity with Nazi ideology; the Confessing Church protested the Nazi regime's infringements in church governance and attempts to nazify Christian theology and practice. But many Protestant churches remained neutral and acquiesced to the demands of the Nazis, hoping to preserve the rights, ministries, and traditions of the Church.[46] As Doris Bergen writes, "The so-called church struggle was less an expression of political opposition to Nazism than a competition for control within the Protestant church."[47] My research promises to offer a new perspective of the Church Struggle as Confessing pastors took the fight to the pulpits against the German Christian movement and even, at times, the Nazi state, to inform, inspire, and challenge their own congregations. Let us now turn to a consideration of how historians have explored this struggle and developed helpful categories to understand the nature and varieties of non-conformity to the Nazi state.

METHODOLOGICAL CONSIDERATIONS

Scholars of Nazi Germany have long grappled with the question of the German people's engagement with the regime. Not surprisingly, the historiography of the Church Struggle coincides with broader trends in the historiography of the Nazi state.[48] From the late 1940s into the early 1960s, historians in West Germany such as Friedrich Meinecke and Gerhard Ritter took a defensive posture in regard to the Nazi era, arguing that Nazism was an aberration in the otherwise healthy development of the German state.[49] The crimes of Nazi Germany were attributed largely to the "demonic" figure of Adolf Hitler, whose desire for war, conquest, and the extermination of the Jews led to catastrophic defeat.[50] At the same time, historians of the Confessing Church also took a defensive posture, emphasizing its staunch and consistent resistance against the Nazi regime and the pro-Nazi German Christian movement.[51] For example, in 1948 the pastor and historian Wilhelm Niemöller, the younger brother of Martin Niemöller, published the earliest history of the Confessing Church, the ground-breaking and sympathetic account, *Kampf und Zeugnis der Bekennenden Kirche*.[52] In this period a number of biographies and critical studies were published commemorating church heroes, men and women, who took extraordinary and courageous action in the context of a totalitarian society.[53] Yet the early historiography created the impression that much more resistance took place than actually occurred.[54] One effect of these studies that were sympathetic to the Confessing Church was that it kept the failures of its pastors and the shortcomings of its theology at arm's length, away from careful scrutiny.[55]

The late 1950s and early 1960s mark the beginning of a second stage in the historiography of the German Church Struggle, coinciding with a broader trend among German historians toward social history and a revisionist perspective of the Nazi past. A concern for historical accuracy motivated historians to challenge the presentation of the German churches as untainted bastions of resistance to the Nazi dictatorship.[56] One of the earliest was Friedrich Baumgärtel, who published *Wider der Kirchenkampf-Legenden* in 1959. He pointed out that various Confessing Church pastors had not always been steadfast opponents of the Nazis—Martin Niemöller is a case in point.[57] At the same time, this new generation of historians demonstrated that while Confessing Church members might have voiced support for Christians of Jewish descent, they very rarely supported Jews as Jews in their own communities.[58] The Confessing Church and the pro-Nazi German Christian movement actually had "more similarities than differences" in how they responded to Nazi antisemitism.[59]

By the late 1960s, historians posed new and challenging questions meant to revise the prevailing view of the German churches and their resistance to the Nazis. John Conway's *The Nazi Persecution of the Churches* is a seminal work in this revisionist phase of Church Struggle historiography, underscoring the common aim of church leaders to protect their churches and maintain influence, yet in so doing, undermining their ability to oppose the regime. What emerged in the historiography was a far more nuanced view of the German churches, which no longer appeared as enclaves of opposition to Nazi ideology and policies, but rather as institutions replete with leaders who were in equal measure fearful, faithful, acquiescent, and yes, even at times courageous, all the while struggling to decide the best course of action.

Until the early 1990s, the historiography of the Church Struggle focused predominantly on the German churches' institutions, the leading figures, and the churches' public responses to the Nazi regime. Much is known about the heroic and timid responses of select high-profile members of the church leadership and the failure and meager successes of the German churches as institutions capable of galvanizing opposition against Hitler and the Nazis.

But the latest phase of Church Struggle historiography has shied away from comprehensive analyses of the churches and instead emphasized the diversity of its members, their actions and motivations, "everyday" forms of dissent, and widespread expressions of antisemitic prejudice. For example, Victoria Barnett's *For the Soul of the People* is a people's history of the Protestant churches that underscored not only the moral courage of Christian men and women in opposing the Nazi regime, but also the complexity of responses to the Nazi regime, including simultaneous membership in the Confessing Church and the Nazi Party.[60] Through the use of new sources, such as oral histories, Barnett emphasized the problems Christians had in trying to remain steadfast in their commitments to their churches and the gospel and also to give due loyalty to the state as dutiful Christians. Pastors' religiously motivated protests against Nazi infringements in church affairs often had considerable political implications—they could be persecuted as disloyal to the state, even if they considered themselves unequivocally loyal.[61]

Despite the developments in Church Struggle historiography through the decades, there has remained widespread agreement among scholars that the churches were among the only institutions in Nazi Germany generally successful in withstanding the Nazi process of *Gleichschaltung*, the "co-ordination" or nazification of institutions, organizations, and private associations.[62] Within the first year of the Nazis' rise to power, the regime outlawed oppositional political parties, rounded up and imprisoned political dissidents and communists, disbanded trade unions, and submitted schools, universities, and cultural organizations to Nazi leadership. Quickly and pervasively, the Nazi regime successfully nazified Germany's institutions, all except the German churches. As this research demonstrates, the churches could become sites in Nazi Germany to present non-conformist messages to challenge National Socialism, that is, if a pastor had the theological insight and moral courage necessary in the moment. As Klaus Scholder has argued, Hitler's decision to relent on the "co-ordination" of the German Protestant churches "brought into being—amidst the ideological totalitarianism of the Third Reich—a kind of free space, a place where things could be said that could be uttered nowhere else in the Third Reich."[63]

Yet this question of non-conformity raises another question about the variety and meaning of critical responses to the Nazi regime. Even from the pulpit, critical messages are not all the same. Preaching on a hero from the Hebrew Bible, such as Abraham, Moses, or Elijah, for example, is different in meaning and impact than an explicit criticism of Nazi persecution of the Jewish people. Pastors often expressed non-conformity in subtle or inconspicuous ways. The Nazi regime was a totalitarian state, and pastors knew that any opposition could be reported by the Gestapo or its spies or informants. Messages could be articulated with purposeful ambiguity and multiple meanings. As Beate Ruhm von Oppen has argued, "It is a feature of despotic times that things have to be said deviously and even by silence . . . In those times those messages *are* understood."[64] She mentions the choice of wording for soldiers' obituaries at the end of the war who "died for Volk und *Vaterland*, rather than for the *Führer*."[65] Pastors' word choices can be similarly understood. I will explore how pastors may have offered dissent and opposition that may not have explicitly undermined the National Socialist regime, but that clearly drew boundaries that set the Confessing Church apart from the German Christian movement.

To better appreciate the pastors' motivations and behaviors (and associated risks), it will be helpful to distinguish the types of actions and speech they expressed. Martin Broszat distinguished opposition (*Resistenz*), the criticism of specific aspects of Nazi rule or ideology (even from a position of support for the regime), from resistance (*Widerstand*), the fundamental rejection of the regime concurrent with action to seek its destruction.⁶⁶ Historians such as Detlev Peukert and Ian Kershaw have refined Broszat's distinctions. Peukert has argued, "In a strict methodological sense we should speak of 'resistance' only where the motives and actions of the people involved were directed towards the overthrow of the Nazi regime as a whole."⁶⁷ To classify other acts as resistance would diminish the meaning of the term itself and add confusion to an understanding of the behaviors in question and the consequences of those behaviors.

For the purposes of precision and clarity, I will draw from categories that Ian Kershaw offers in his now classic book, *Popular Opinion and Political Dissent in the Third Reich*.⁶⁸ Kershaw carefully distinguishes the responses of resistance, opposition, and dissent under the Nazi regime. "Resistance" (*Widerstand*) refers to the active participation in an organized attempt to undermine the regime or plan for its termination.⁶⁹ This term connotes a fundamental rejection of the Nazi regime, a desire to replace it, and an organized approach to achieve its demise.

Acts of resistance were high-risk and predominantly politically motivated, though religious motivations also often played a role.⁷⁰ Examples of resistance include the assassination attempt of Adolf Hitler by Georg Elser, the non-conformist loner with communist sympathies. Taking months of preparation, Elser painstakingly stole into Munich's Bürgerbräukeller at night and carved out a niche in a stone pillar in which to place a homemade bomb to detonate as Hitler gave a commemorative speech on November 8, 1939, the anniversary of the Beer Hall Putsch of 1923. The bomb exploded as planned, killing eight and wounding 62. Yet Hitler was not among them. He had cut his speech short and left early to catch a train back to Berlin rather than fly back in inclement weather.

The most well-known assassination attempt was the bomb plot conspiracy of July 20, 1944, by members of the German military leadership.⁷¹ Led by Colonel Claus Schenk von Stauffenberg, the resisters put in place a sophisticated bomb plot codenamed Operation Valkyrie. Operation Valkyrie called for Stauffenberg, who had access to Hitler, to plant a bomb and assassinate Hitler at a military meeting held at the Wolfsschanze headquarters in East Prussia. At the appointed time Stauffenberg's bomb detonated, but for a variety of reasons Hitler survived the attempt on his life and the Nazis put down the coup d'état, executing Stauffenberg and other conspirators that night. Nearly 5,000 Germans would be arrested in the following months in the Nazi hunt for conspirators.⁷²

There are no sermons from the Confessing Church that provide evidence of resistance akin to Elser's bomb plot or the conspiracy of July 20, 1944.

As far as I have been able to uncover, no pastor in the Nazi dictatorship ever ascended the pulpit and advocated for an organized attempt to overthrow Adolf Hitler or the National Socialist regime. That would have been virtually unthinkable. Acts of resistance were planned in secret, not publicly proclaimed before action was taken. The sermons reveal oppositional efforts that were far more restrained and subtle.

Limited acts of opposition, as Kershaw notes, can be found in all segments of society.[73] Thus, Kershaw's second term, "opposition," is used to refer to any action, including acts of resistance that at least partially aimed at challenging the dominance of the Nazi state.[74] One could have been or actually be a supporter of the Nazis or some of their policies and have still acted in opposition.[75] Opposition is a much larger category and it includes a wide range of actions that challenge an aspect of the Nazi system, including workplace sabotage of factories and farms, delivering sermons with implicit subversive content, ignoring bans on race relations, as well as other "small[er] principled acts of defiance," such as refusing to give the Hitler salute.[76] Acts of opposition were by nature temporary, limited in effect, and in direct response to specific Nazi policies or aspects of its ideology.

It is in this sense that Confessing Church pastors occasionally opposed the Nazi regime and its ideology in their sermons. As this study will show, the evidence clearly indicates that Confessing Church pastors were most critical of National Socialism as a perceived false "belief," "ideology," or "worldview," and its promotion of the worship of "false idols," such as race, blood, and nation. In the sermons, National Socialism is often condemned as a "false proclamation," as corrupt or contrary to the gospel. It is also condemned as "neo-paganism." Thus, when critical of National Socialism, Confessing Church pastors' sermons most often critique it as a competing ideology or system of belief, while also at times condemning the leaders who espouse this ideology as redemptive in German history. Only rarely does one find critical expressions of the Nazi regime's governing policies or military aggression, except as they relate to the German churches. Kershaw's observation holds true: the German churches' "considerable efforts and energies consumed in opposing Nazi interference with traditional practices and attempts to ride roughshod over Christian doctrine and values were not matched by equally vigorous denunciation of Nazi inhumanity and barbarism."[77]

And lastly, the third type of response that Kershaw outlines is "dissent," an even broader category than opposition. It refers to the "voicing of attitudes, frequently spontaneous and often unrelated to any intended action, which in any way whatsoever ran counter to or were critical of Nazism."[78] Confessing Church sermons include various examples, from a sermon on a Hebrew hero of the faith to the preferred word choice of *das Vaterland* ("the fatherland") rather than *der Führerstaat* ("the Führer state"). Dissent is not meant to undermine the Nazi regime, work toward its downfall, or limit its dominance in any way, but merely to express non-conformity or dissatisfaction. It may be a spontaneous critical comment, an entertaining joke, or a word choice that signals non-conformity, but essentially it reflects criticism of the Nazi dictatorship.[79]

Despite its advantages, this analytical framework is not without problems. Critics argue that these categories lump together disparate actions that occurred in a variety of contexts.[80] As Martyn Housden has argued, "Kershaw and Peukert risk imposing artificial structures on a morass of actions rendered incomparable and entirely distinct by the unique life experiences and character of each actor."[81] The uniqueness of the act in its context is lost. For example, resistance for a Jewish person under the oppression of the Nazi state could mean ensuring one's survival (thus, resisting the Nazis' murderous policies), contributing to cultural events or the preservation of Jewish culture in a ghetto or concentration camp (thus, resisting Nazis' aim to eradicate Jewish culture), or even choosing the terms of one's death in the act of suicide (thus, resisting Nazi execution by bullet, gas, or another method).[82]

These criticisms are valid and offer a needed correction to an uncritical acceptance of Kershaw's analytical framework. Yet, Kershaw's categories help to clarify and nuance our understanding of various forms of critical expression in the specific context of a pastor's sermon in a religious service. In using the terms "dissent" and "opposition" to describe pastors' expressions rather than "resistance," I wish to underscore the limited nature of their responses to the Nazi regime. Moreover, this framework highlights the impact of sermons in German society. As will be demonstrated in chapter 9, the Nazi *Geheime Staatspolizei* (Secret State Police, or *Gestapo*) and *Sicherheitsdienst* (Security Service, or SD) only reported pastors who made oppositional statements against the Nazi regime (that is, statements that undermined the regime or its ideology) from the pulpit. As far as I have been able to uncover, expressions of dissent (as defined here) are absent from secret police files.

To approach the question of Confessing Church pastors' expressions in the pulpit, I have scoured German archives, libraries, and used bookstores, and I have located over 900 sermons by ninety-five Confessing Church pastors. These are all the sermons I could confirm were delivered by pastors affiliated with the Confessing Church.[83] Almost all the sermons were preached in Nazi Germany, in small towns and large cities throughout the various regions, from Schleswig-Holstein in the north, to Bavaria in the south; from Westphalia in the west, to Saxony in the east. While most were preached "out in the open" in German society, others were preached in concentration camps, an underground seminary, and even over the radio via the British Broadcasting Corporation (BBC). A small percentage of them (10%) were delivered by

Confessing pastors in lands of exile, offering a unique perspective on the messages they wished to convey to Christian communities of faith abroad.[84]

Of all the sermons, approximately 700 were found in book or pamphlet collections published either during or shortly after the Nazi period. The remaining 200 were unpublished sermons found in archives.[85] Some of the sermons are dated, while others lack dating or time references. Many can only be categorized generally as pre-war, or within a certain time frame (e.g., 1941–1943). Thus, it is virtually impossible to determine how many sermons were delivered in any given year or month.

While the space limitations of this study will not allow for a discussion of all, or even most of the ninety-five pastors' sermons, I will explore the varieties of non-conformist messages they expressed in response to the Nazi regime. This study will focus on those sermons that most clearly illustrate key themes in Confessing Church preaching, as well as sermons that align with specific historical developments, such as the *Kristallnacht* pogrom of November 1938 or the outbreak of the Second World War. The aim is not so much to provide an in-depth review of what each pastor said in the pulpit but to demonstrate the extraordinary possibilities for oppositional preaching in Nazi Germany.

In examining these sermons, I wish not simply to note *what* the pastors said in their sermons but to explore *why* they said it. The pastors' motivations for publicly criticizing the Nazi regime reveal points of conflict that can illuminate our understanding of the varieties of responses evident in the sermons. I will demonstrate that in these sermons Confessing Church pastors opposed the Nazi regime on three fronts from the authority of the pulpit. First, some condemned National Socialism as a false ideology that worships false gods. Second, some expressed harsh criticism of Nazi persecution of Christians and the German churches. And third, some challenged Nazi antisemitic ideology by supporting Jews as the chosen people of God and Judaism as a historical foundation of Christianity. Yet, it should be noted, a pastor who felt compelled to speak out against Nazi ideology may not necessarily have felt equally compelled to speak out against the Nazi persecution of the Jews or the persecution of the churches, and vice versa. These are quite different though interrelated concerns. Moreover, the historian cannot fully understand a subject's motivations for a given action. Nevertheless, the sermons indicate significant debate within the churches about how pastors should respond to the Nazi regime and its ideology and policies.

Yet, it must be acknowledged that the vast majority of the sermons do not explicitly criticize the German Christian movement, Nazi regime or National Socialism. Most of the 900 sermons focused on a clear exposition of a biblical text and a theological reflection for the Christian life, without any overt political or social commentary. Thus, it is important at the start to emphasize that this research supports the consensus among historians that German Protestantism failed to resist or oppose the Nazi regime effectively or to stand in defense of Jews as Jews in Nazi Germany.[86] Pastors did not explicitly call for Hitler's removal from office or the overthrow of the National Socialist government, nor would one expect pastors to do so, ministering in a totalitarian state. Likewise, Confessing Church pastors did not call for Germans to sabotage or otherwise fight against the Nazi state, the German military, or the police. This study will explore mitigating factors that may have contributed to Confessing pastors limiting political or social commentary in their sermons. Nevertheless, this research promises to shed light on the sometimes blurred relationship between the religious and political dimensions of the pastors' protests. As Victoria Barnett has demonstrated, Confessing pastors only gradually realized the political implications of their religious protests for institutional autonomy.[87] Their orientation and language are religious, even when speaking about politics or society.

Having said this, all the criticisms—implicitly and explicitly—of the Nazi regime, its leadership, and ideology are framed in short, concise statements within a sermon on a biblical (not political) theme. In other words, the pastors' criticisms are most often not thorough or fully developed; rather, they are usually briefly stated in the larger context of a biblical story or theological reflection. As such, it is easily conceivable that an inattentive congregant sitting in a pew might miss the critical statement in a moment's distraction.

CONTRIBUTIONS

This study aims to contribute to the research on the Church Struggle in four specific ways. First, in contrast to much of the historiography that focuses on the public actions and proclamations of church leaders and pastors outside the walls of the German churches, this study examines speech from within the walls of the churches and from the rank and file of the Confessing Church. The primary source base of this research is the German Protestant sermon, a word for the community of faith specifically composed to educate and inspire men and women to godliness. The Lutheran and Reformed traditions made the sermon central in their liturgies, as will be shown; the sermon was an event in which God's Word was proclaimed to communities of faith. And yet in these sermons pastors also gave expression to their views of the Nazi regime, its ideology, and its policies. I have incorporated an analysis of both the well-known leaders of the movement, such as Martin Niemöller and Dietrich Bonhoeffer, as well as parish pastors who are more unfamiliar, such as the Kolberg pastor Paul (Paulus) Hinz and the Berlin pastor Gerhard Ebeling. The preachers included in this study held a variety of titles, such as superintendent, licensed pastor, professor, director of a social or charitable institution, provost, and lecturer. Yet each was a spiritual leader of his faith community, given the authority to preach from the pulpit.[88] Their unique perspectives allow for a much greater understanding of the work of Confessing Church pastors, as well as how they led their worship services and the values they sought to convey to their congregations.

Second, the sermons demonstrate the significance of the sermon as a potential marker of the identity of Confessing pastors and their congregations. The fracturing of the German Protestant churches had tremendous implications on preaching. This division was apparent behind the pulpit as Confessing Church pastors became increasingly influenced by a "new school" of homiletics led by the Swiss theologian Karl Barth, a professor of theology at the University of Bonn, but also advanced by three younger theologians, Dietrich Bonhoeffer of Finkenwalde Seminary, Wolfgang Trillhaas of the University of Erlangen, and Friedrich Wilhelm (Wilfried) Lempp, the Lutheran pastor of the Leonhardkirche in Stuttgart.[89] Confessing Church pastors refused to allow other sources of knowledge, such as natural theology and a providential reading of history, to compromise their commitment to Scripture as God's revelation. Scripture was the sole authority for the life of the Church in judging claims to divine knowledge.[90] While pastors associated with the German Christian movement often commented on race, the fatherland, and Hitler as a savior-figure, Confessing Church pastors asserted that the Christian faith is based upon Scripture alone and not a party platform or its propaganda machine. Thus, the sources of authority in preaching the gospel of Christ became a critical point of contention between Confessing Church and German Christian pastors. The conflict over divine revelation directly impacted church politics.

Third, this research contributes to the ongoing debate about the relationship between the Christian faith and National Socialist ideology.[91] In the context of a worship service, Confessing Church pastors at times sought to dissuade their congregants of Nazi "false beliefs" and values, at least insofar as they conflicted with Christian tenets of faith. Confessing Church pastors occasionally attacked National Socialism as a political religion and at other times as neo-pagan. Pastors occasionally spoke out when the ultimate issue of one's faith was at stake—clarifying and correcting perceived heretical beliefs. On the one hand, they would condemn the practice of worshiping Hitler as an ersatz savior or seeking redemption through service to the Third Reich, and yet on the other hand, they would also warn their congregants of the Nazis' emphasis on Nordic mysticism and the idolization of blood, race, and nation.[92] The sermons demonstrate that the issue of Nazism as a competing belief system was not simply regarded as a matter of church identity but also of liturgy, as pastors introduced the debate into the walls of the sanctuary in the form of the sermon, placed after the reading of Scripture and, when it was celebrated, the reception of the Lord's Supper. The German churches became places where public criticism of Nazi ideology from a distinctly religious perspective was possible, though not utilized nearly enough.

Lastly, as far as I am aware, *Preaching to Nazi Germany* is the only study to extensively treat sermons as the primary source base for the history of the Protestant churches in Nazi Germany, and specifically, in understanding Christian protests against the Nazi regime as well as Christian perspectives of the Jews and Judaism. The utilization of this rich source base allows us to explore the religious milieu of the Confessing Church, as well as to provide a window into the mundane and extraordinary messages pastors expressed publicly to their congregants from week to week, whether in subdued or cryptic terms or in explicit and bold language. In short, the sermons provide a unique opportunity to "listen in" to see how communities of faith expressed what was most important to them in Nazi Germany.

A central question I ask throughout this work is how and to what extent German Protestantism provided a platform for pastors to challenge the ideology and policies of the Nazi regime, in particular, as they conflicted with the interests of the German churches. The fact is that the Nazi regime was placed in power by a population that overwhelmingly self-identified as Christian. Christianity in the late-nineteenth and early-twentieth century in Germany had become tied to the concept of nation, and in this way, had become susceptible to racial antisemitism that excluded Jews from German life.[93] In short, it is fair to conclude that in some ways German Protestantism by the Nazi era was a compromised Christianity, weakened by ethnic and racial considerations that were alien to the religion, yet meant to unify and give distinct meaning to the German nation. Faith became misdirected and people followed other messiahs. Thus, to recall one of Jesus of Nazareth's great commands, a German in Nazi Germany—and even a pastor in the oppositional Confessing Church—had trouble actually identifying his "neighbors," let alone loving them as himself.[94] This situation in Germany produced a crisis in the Protestant churches that too few pastors were theologically equipped or willing to navigate.

NOTES

1. Martin Niemöller, *Here Stand I!*, translated by Jane Lymburn (New York: Willett, Clark & Co., 1937), 222.

2. Matthew D. Hockenos, *Then They Came for Me: Martin Niemöller, the Pastor Who Defied the Nazis* (New York: Basic Books, 2018), 64, 76.

3. Niemöller, *Here Stand I*, 226.

4. Niemöller, *Here Stand I*, 222.
5. Hockenos, *Then They Came for Me*, 124.
6. Dietmar Schmidt, *Martin Niemöller: Eine Biographie* (Stuttgart: Radius-Verl, 1983), 101.
7. Dietmar Schmidt, *Martin Niemöller*, 103; see also Hockenos, *Then They Came for Me*, 125.
8. Wolfgang Gerlach, *And the Witnesses Were Silent: The Confessing Church and the Persecution of the Jews*, translated and edited by Victoria J. Barnett (Lincoln: University of Nebraska, 2000), vii–ix. One pioneer in this sea change in the historiography of the Church Struggle was the American Franklin Hamlin Littell, whose *The Crucifixion of the Jews*, originally published in 1962, argued that Christians must accept responsibility for centuries of anti-Judaism and that Nazi crimes must be understood in the context of this history. In 1970s, Littell partnered with another esteemed American historian, Hubert Locke, and organized an influential "Scholar's Conference" on Christians and Jews at Wayne State University, a conference that was repeated annually for decades. See Franklin Hamlin Littell, *The Crucifixion of the Jews* (New York: Harper & Row, 1975); and Littell, Franklin Hamlin and Hubert Locke, eds. *The German Church Struggle and the Holocaust* (Detroit: Wayne State University Press, 1974).

J.S. Conway also had an enormous impact on the field. His work, especially *The Nazi Persecution of the Churches, 1933–1945*, published in 1968, influenced a new generation of North American scholars, including Robert Erickson, Doris Bergen, Kyle Jantzen, and Matthew Hockenos, among many others.

At the vanguard in Germany was the clergyman and scholar Eberhard Bethge, the biographer and best friend of Dietrich Bonhoeffer. In the late 1960s, after much inter-religious dialogue with students and Jewish scholars, such as Emil Fachenheim and Eva Fleischner, he came to reconsider his own views of anti-Judaism in the Christian tradition. See for example, "Nichts scheint mehr in Ordnung," in *Ethik im Ernstfall: Dietrich Bonhoeffers Stellung zu den Juden und ihre Aktualität*, edited by Wolfgang Huber and Ilse Tödt (Munich, 1982). See also Robert Ericksen and Susannah Heschel, "The German Churches Face Hitler," *Tel Aviver Jahrbuch für deutsche Geschichte* 23 (1994), 450.

9. See Arthur Cochrane, *The Church's Confession Under Hitler* (Philadelphia: Westminster Press, 1962); Walter Zvi Bacharach, *Anti-Jewish Prejudices in German-Catholic Sermons*, translated by Chaya Galai (Lewiston: Edwin Mellon Press, 1993); and Robert Ericksen and Susannah Heschel, "The German Churches Face Hitler."

10. I will refer to members of this movement as German Christians. Whenever I use this phrase, I mean to indicate specifically members of this movement, not all Germans who identify themselves as Christians.

11. Doris Bergen, *Twisted Cross: The German Christian Movement in the Third Reich* (Chapel Hill, NC: University of North Carolina Press, 1996), 7. Ernst Christian Helmreich cites a police report dated in May 1934 indicating 2,000 pastors belonged to the German Christian movement; see Helmreich, *German Churches*

under Hitler: Background, Struggle and Epilogue (Detroit: Wayne State University Press, 1979), 492.

12. See Bergen, *Twisted Cross*; Kurt Meier, *Die Deutschen Christen: Das Bild einer Bewegng im Kirchenkampf des Dritten Reiches* (Göttigen: Vandenhoeck & Ruprecht, 1964); and Hans-Joachim Sonne, *Die politische Theologie der Deutschen Christen* (Göttigen: Vandenhoeck & Ruprecht, 1982).

13. Victoria Barnett, *For the Soul of the People: Protestant Protest against Hitler* (New York: Oxford University Press, 1992), 35.

14. Barnett, *For the Soul of the People*, 5.

15. See Helmreich, *German Churches Under Hitler*, 162; Barnett, *For the Soul of the People*, 4; and Schilling, *Contemporary Continental Theologians*, 22. Article IV of the Barmen Declaration states, "The present Reich Church administration has abandoned this unimpeachable basis [the gospel of Jesus Christ as testified in Scripture] and has been guilty of numerous violations of the law and the constitution. It has thereby forfeited the claim to be the legitimate administration of the German Evangelical Church." See "The Declarations, Resolutions, and Motions Adopted by the Synod of Barmen, May 29–31, 1934," translated by Arthur Cochrane in *The Church's Confession Under Hitler* (Philadelphia: Westminster Press, 1962), 242.

16. Anton Kaes, Martin Jay, and Edward Dimendberg, eds., *The Weimar Republic Sourcebook* (Los Angeles: University of California Press, 1994), 126.

17. See, for example, Emilio Gentile, "The Sacralization of Politics: Definitions, Interpretations and Reflections on the Question of Secular Religion and Totalitarianism," translated by Natalia Belozentseva, in *Totalitarian Movements and Political Religions* 1(1), (2000); Emilio Gentile, "Fascism, Totalitarianism and Political Religion: Definitions and Critical Reflections on Criticism and Interpretation," translated by Natalia Belozentseva, in *Totalitarian Movements and Political Religions* 6(1) (June 2005); Michael Burleigh, *The Third Reich: A New History* (New York: Hill and Wang, 2000); and Michael Burleigh, "National Socialism as a Political Religion," *Totalitarian Movements and Political Religions* 1(2), (2000), 1–26.

18. Richard Steigmann-Gall, *The Holy Reich: Nazi Conceptions of Christianity, 1919–1945* (New York: Cambridge University Press, 2003), 3–4.

19. Steigmann-Gall, *The Holy Reich*, 3.

20. Steigmann-Gall, *The Holy Reich*, 5.

21. For more on the debate, see Doris Bergen, "Nazism and Christianity: Partners and Rivals? A Response to Richard Steigmann-Gall, *The Holy Reich: Nazi Conceptions of Christianity, 1919–1945*," *Journal of Contemporary History* 42(1) (2007), 25–33; Manfred Gailus, "A Strange Obsession with Nazi Christianity: A Critical Comment on Richard Steigmann-Gall's *The Holy Reich*," *Journal of Contemporary History* 42(1) (2007), 35–46; and Irving Hexham, "Inventing 'Paganists': A Close Reading of Richard Steigmann-Gall's The Holy Reich," *Journal of Contemporary History* 42(1) (2007), 59–78; and Richard Steigmann-Gall, "Christianity and the Nazi Movement: A Response," *Journal of Contemporary History* 42(2), 185–211.

22. Kyle Jantzen, *Faith and Fatherland: Parish Politics in Hitler's Germany* (Minneapolis: Fortress Press, 2008), 13.

23. See Samuel Koehne, "Reassessing 'The Holy Reich': Leading Nazis' Views on Confession, Community and 'Jewish Materialism,'" in *Journal of Contemporary History* 48(3) (2013), 423–445; "Nazism and Religion: The Problem of 'Positive Christianity,'" in *Australian Journal of Politics and History* 60(1) (2014), 28–42; and "Were the National Socialists a 'Völkisch' Party? Paganism, Christianity, and the Nazi Christmas," in *Central European History* 47(4) (2014), 760–790. See also Steigmann-Gall, *The Holy Reich*, 14–15; and "Christianity and the Nazi Movement: A Response," in *Journal of Contemporary History* 42(2) (2007), 185–211.

24. Koehne, "Nazism and Religion," 28.

25. Koehne, "Nazism and Religion," 29.

26. Koehne, "Nazism and Religion," 41.

27. See Jantzen, *Faith and Fatherland*, 2.

28. Helmreich, *The German Churches under Hitler*, 93.

29. See J.R.C. Wright, *"Above Parties": The Political Attitudes of the German Protestant Church Leadership, 1918–1933* (London: Oxford University Press, 1974), 10–16.

30. Conway, *The Nazi Persecution of the Churches*, 9.

31. Jantzen, *Faith and Fatherland*, 57.

32. The figures in this paragraph are based on Richard Evans' research in *The Coming of the Third Reich* (New York: Penguin, 2003), 446.

33. Barnett, *For the Soul of the People*, 5.

34. See Barnett, *For the Soul of the People*, 39–40; Steigmann-Gall, *The Holy Reich*, 223.

35. Steigmann-Gall, *The Holy Reich*, 114–116.

36. James Bentley, *Martin Niemöller, 1892–1984* (New York: The Free Press, 1984), 42–45.

37. Klaus Scholder, *The Churches and the Third Reich, vol. 1, Preliminary History and the Time of Illusions, 1918–1934*, translated by John Bowden (Philadelphia: Fortress Press, 1977), 520–521. Scholder asserts that "many signs seemed to point to a great future for the church in the Third Reich." He breaks down the numbers by region: for example, in Saxony, 10,000 people "returned to the church" in 1933, while the numbers of those leaving the church decreased from 28,000 in 1932 to 8,000 in 1933.

38. Martin Niemöller, *Here Stand I* (Chicago: Willett, Clark, & Co.), 29.

39. Bentley, *Martin Niemöller*, 43.

40. Steigmann-Gall, *The Holy Reich*, 114. See also Scholder, *The Churches and the Third Reich, vol. 1*, 520–521. Scholder agrees that "many signs seemed to point to a great future for the church in the Third Reich"; he breaks down the numbers by region, for example, in Saxony, 10,000 people "returned to the church" in 1933, while the numbers of those leaving the church decreased from 28,000 in 1932 to 8,000 in 1933.

41. Helmreich, *German Churches under Hitler*, 162; Edwin Robertson, *Christians against Hitler* (London: SCM Press, 1962), 35. Robertson also notes that many congregations openly supported their pastors if they were disciplined or lost state sanction, and so they did not need to petition their regional brotherhood council for

financial assistance. Also, Barnett notes that by 1936 the *Fürbittenliste* included lay people as well as pastors. See Barnett, *For the Soul of the People*, 81.

42. See for example, Barnett, *For the Soul of the People*, 80; Conway, *The Nazi Persecution of the Churches*, 208–211.

43. Conway, *The Nazi Persecution of the Churches*, 208–211.

44. See Bergen, *Twisted Cross*, 9–11, 31–34, 48–50, and 159.

45. See, for example, Bergen, *Twisted Cross*, 12; Conway, *Nazi Persecution of the Churches*, xxvii–xxx; and Ericksen, *Complicity in the Holocaust*, 26.

46. Conway, *Nazi Persecution of the Churches*, 331.

47. Bergen, *Twisted Cross*, 12.

48. Robert P. Ericksen provides a superb overview of these changes in "Christian Complicity? Changing Views on German Churches and the Holocaust, the Joseph and Rebecca Meyerhoff Annual Lecture," dated 8 November 2007, United States Holocaust Memorial Museum, Center for Advanced Holocaust Studies, accessed February 20, 2023, https://www.ushmm.org/m/pdfs/20091110-ericksen.pdf.

49. Kershaw, *Nazi Dictatorship*, 6. See for example, Friedrich Meinicke, *Die deutsche Katastrophe* (Weisbaden, 1946); and Gerhard Ritter, *Europa und die deutsche Frage. Betrachtungen über die geschichtliche Eigenart des deutschen Staatsdenkens* (Munich: Münchener Verlag, 1948).

50. Richard Evans, *In Hitler's Shadow: West German Historians and the Attempt to Escape from the Nazi Past* (New York: Pantheon Books, 1989), 11–12.

51. Three excellent historiographical introductions to the German churches under the Nazi dictatorship are John Conway, "The Historiography of the German Church Struggle," *Journal of Bible and Religion* 32, no. 3 (July 1964), 221–230; Robert Ericksen and Susannah Heschel, "The German Churches Face Hitler," and their more recent work, "The German Churches and the Holocaust," in *The Historiography of the Holocaust*, edited by Dan Stone (New York: Palgrave, 2004).

52. Wilhelm Niemöller, *Kampf und Zeugnis der Bekennenden Kirche* (Bielefeld: L. Bechauf, 1948).

53. While some scholars object to using the term "totalitarian" because it may seem to infer total and unified power in a dictatorship, I would agree with scholars who find the term useful to refer to political systems based on a "total" ideology that sought to explain all of human life and that was the foundation for the state's total claims on the individual. Michael Burleigh puts it succinctly when he argues that the term is helpful to refer to systems that have "*aspired* to, and fantasized about, levels of control unprecedented in history's autocracies and tyrannies, but which are familiar from the world of religion with its concerns with minds and rites." Michael Burleigh, *Earthly Powers: The Clash of Religion and Politics in Europe, from the French Revolution to the Great War* (New York: HarperCollins, 2005), Kindle version, location 129. This notion of National Socialism as a "total" ideology was one that pastors responded to, as will be explored in subsequent chapters.

54. Robert Ericksen. "A Radical Minority: Resistance in the German Protestant Church," in *Germans Against Nazism: Nonconformity, Opposition and Resistance in the Third Reich: Essays in Honour of Peter Hoffmann*, edited by Francis R. Nicosia and Lawrence D. Stokes (Oxford: Berg Publishers, 1990), 116.

55. Ericksen and Heschel, "The German Churches Face Hitler"; and Conway, "The Historiography of the German Church Struggle."
56. Conway, "Historiography of the German Church Struggle," 225.
57. Conway, "Historiography of the German Church Struggle," 226; see also John Conway, "The Present State of Research and Writing on the Church Struggle," in *The German Church Struggle and the Holocaust*, edited by Franklin Littell and Hubert Locke (Detroit: Wayne State University Press, 1974), 32–33.
58. Ericksen and Heschel, "German Churches Face Hitler," 433.
59. Ericksen and Heschel, "German Churches Face Hitler," 433.
60. Ericksen and Heschel, "The German Churches Face Hitler: Assessment of the Historiography," 447. See also Theodore Thomas' *Women against Hitler: Christian Resistance in the Third Reich* (Westport, CT: Praeger, 1995).
61. Barnett, *For the Soul of the People*, 92. See also, for example, Manfred Gailus, *Protestantismus und Nationalsozialismus. Studien zur nationalsozialistischen Durchdringung des protestantischen Sozialmilieus in Berlin* (Köln: Böhlau Verlag, 2001); Andreas Kersting, *Kirchenordnung und Widerstand: Der Kampf um den Aufbau der Bekennenden Kirche der Altpreußischen Union aufgrund des Dahlemer Notrechts von 1934 bis 1937*, Heidelberger Untersuchungen zu Widerstand, Judenverfolgung und Kirchenkampf im Dritten Reich 4 (Gütersloh: Christian Kaiser, 1994); and Shelly Baranowski, *The Confessing Church, Conservative Elites, and the Nazi State*, Texts and Studies in Religion 28 (New York: Edwin Mellon, 1986).
62. See Barnett, *For the Soul of the People*, 181–185; Hoffmann, *The History of German Resistance*, 13; Ian Kershaw, *Hitler, the Germans, and the Final Solution* (New Haven: Yale University Press, 2008), 166; Tim Kirk, *Nazi Germany* (New York: Palgrave, 2007), 108.
63. Scholder, *The Churches and the Third Reich, vol. 1*, 566–567.
64. Beate Ruhm von Oppen, "Nazis and Christians," in *World Politics 21*(3) (April 1969), 409.
65. Ruhm von Oppen, "Nazis and Christians," 410.
66. Martin Broszat, "Resistenz und Widerstand," in *Bayern in der NS-Zeit, IV*, pp. 691–709; *Nach Hitler: Der schwierige Umgang mit unserer Geschichte* (München: Oldenbourg, 1986); and "A Social and Historical Typology of German Opposition to Hitler," in D.C. Large (ed.), *Contending with Hitler: Varieties of Resistance in the Third Reich* (Cambridge 1991).
67. Detlev Peukert, *Inside Nazi Germany: Conformity, Opposition and Racism in Everyday Life*, translated by Richard Deveson (New Haven: Yale University Press, 1987), 119.
68. Kershaw, *Popular Opinion and Political Dissent in the Third Reich: Bavaria 1933–1945* (Oxford University Press, 1983), 2–4. See also his work, *The Nazi Dictatorship: Problems and Perspectives of Interpretation, Third Edition* (New York: Arnold, 1993), 170–171.
69. Kershaw, *The Nazi Dictatorship*, 170. On this point Kershaw is in general agreement with Peter Hoffmann and his argument that resistance entails "ideological commitment, clandestine networks, and armed action." See Peter Hoffmann classic work on the subject, *The History of the German Resistance, 1933–1945, Third Edition*

(Ithaca: McGill-Queen's University Press, 1996). See also John M. Cox, *Circles of Resistance: Jewish, Leftist, and Youth Dissidence in Nazi Germany* (New York: Peter Lang, 2009); Joachim Fest, *Plotting Hitler's Death: The Story of the German Resistance*, translated by Bruce Little (New York: Metropolitan, 1996); Michael Ceyer and John W. Boyer, eds., *Resistance against the Third Reich, 1933–1990* (Chicago: University of Chicago Press, 1994); Hans Mommsen, *Germans Against Hitler: The Stauffenberg Plot and Resistance under the Third Reich*, translated by Angus McGeoch (New York: I.B. Tauris, 2009); Roger Moorhouse, *Killing Hitler, The Plots, the Assassins, and the Dictator Who Cheated Death* (New York: Bantam, 2006); Louis Eltscher, *Traitors or Patriots? A Story of the German Anti-Nazi Resistance* (Bloomington, IN: iUniverse, 2013).

70. The political motivations of resisters are nearly always recounted in the historiography, but not so often the religious motivations. For more on the religious motivations, see especially Nechama Tec, *Resistance: Jews and Christians Who Defied the Nazi Terror* (New York: Oxford University Press, 2013); Barnett, *For the Soul of the People*; Annette Dumbach and Jud Newborn, *Sophie Scholl and the White Rose* (Oxford: One World, 2006); David Gushee, *Righteous Gentiles of the Holocaust: Genocide and Moral Obligation, Second Edition* (St. Paul, MN: Paragon House, 2003).

71. See Philip Freiher von Boeselager and Florence and Jerome Fehrenbach, *Valkryrie: The Story of the Plot to Kill Hitler, by Its Last Member* (New York: Vintage, 2011); Hans Bernd Gisevius, *To the Bitter End: An Insider's Account of the Plot to Kill Hiter, 1933–1944*, translated by Richard and Clara Winston (New York: Da Capo Press, 1998); Pierre Galante, *Operation Valkyrie: The German General's Plot Against Hitler* (Cooper Square, 2012); Peter Hoffmann, *Stauffenberg: A Family History, 1905–1944* (Ithaca: McGill-Queen's University Press, 2008); and Nigel Jones, *Countdown to Valkyrie: The July Plot to Assassinate Hitler* (Pen and Sword, 2013).

72. Ian Kershaw, *The Luck of the Devil: The Story of Operation Valkyrie* (New York: Penguin, 2009), 67.

73. See Kershaw, *Nazi Dictatorship*, 151–156.

74. Kershaw, *Nazi Dictatorship*, 170.

75. Barnett, *For the Soul of the People*, 71–72; see also Kershaw, *Nazi Dictatorship*, 170.

76. Kirk, *Third Reich*, 149.

77. Kershaw, *Nazi Dictatorship*, 174. See also Barnett, *For the Soul of the People*, 71–72.

78. Kershaw, *Popular Opinion and Political Dissent*, 3–4.

79. John Cox does well to warn against "rigid, static definitions" of various categories of resistance. From the perspective of the Nazis, a citizen who "relayed an anti-government joke or surreptitiously listened to foreign radio on occasion became . . . a political opponent." See Cox, *Circles of Resistance*, 6.

80. See Jo Fox, "Review Article: Resistance and the Third Reich," in *Journal of Contemporary History* 39(2) (2004).

81. Martyn Housden, *Resistance and Conformity in the Third Reich* (London: Routledge, 1997), 166.

82. Tec, *Resistance*.

83. The sermons were delivered by pastors from a variety of positions, including newly ordained pastors, superintendents, and theologians. Many well-known Confessing Church leaders contributed sermons to the source base for this research, such as Hans Asmussen (58), Karl Barth (30), Dietrich Bonhoeffer (56), Friedrich von Bodelschwingh (39), Helmut Gollwitzer (nine), and Hans Iwand (18).

84. In short, the breakdown in numbers is as follows: 770 were delivered "out in the open" in German society; 22 in concentration camps; 13 over the BBC; 16 in a Confessing Church underground seminary at Finkenwalde; and 89 in exile abroad.

85. The archives I utilized were the *Evangelisches Zentralarchiv* in Berlin, the *Landeskirchliches Archiv der Evangelischen Kirche von Westfalen* in Bielefeld, the *Archiv der Evangelischen Kirchen im Rheinland* in Düsseldorf, the archive of the National Library of Scotland in Edinburgh, and the University of Iowa Libraries, Special Collections in Iowa City.

86. See for example Gerlach, *And the Witnesses were Silent*, vii–viii; Barnett, *For the Soul of the People*, 198–199; and Ian Kershaw, *The Nazi Dictatorship*, 174.

87. Barnett, *For the Soul of the People*, 92.

88. Thus, when I speak of Confessing Church pastors, I refer to a broad definition in the Christian tradition of one called by a congregation to lead in instruction and worship. I do not mean that every individual who delivered a sermon was a licensed pastor in the German Protestant Church, though most, of course, were.

89. Old, *Reading and Preaching of the Scriptures*, 763.

90. This position is clearly expressed in the Barmen Confession, which states, "We reject the false doctrine, as though the Church could and would have to acknowledge as a souce of its proclamation, apart from and besides this one Word of God, still other events and powers, figures and truths, as God's revelation." See "The Declarations, Resolutions, and Motions Adopted by the Synod of Barmen," on May 29–31, 1934, in Cochrane, *Church's Confession under Hitler*, 239. While Confessing Church pastors viewed Scripture as the highest authority for divine knowledge, many certainly accepted other forms of divine knowledge, such as natural theology, insofar as they did not conflict with Scripture.

91. See notably Steigmann-Gall, *Holy Reich*; Doris Bergen, "Nazism and Christianity: Partners and Rivals? A Response to Richard Steigmann-Gall, *The Holy Reich: Nazi Conceptions of Christianity, 1919–1945*," *Journal of Contemporary History* 42(1) (2007), 25–33; Manfred Gailus, "A Strange Obsession with Nazi Christianity: A Critical Comment on Richard Steigmann-Gall's *The Holy Reich*," *Journal of Contemporary History* 42(1) (2007), 35–46; Gentile, "Fascism, Totalitarianism and Political Religion"; Gentile, "The Sacralization of Politics"; Irving Hexham, "Inventing 'Paganists': A Close Reading of Richard Steigmann-Gall's *The Holy Reich*," *Journal of Contemporary History* 42(1) (2007), 59–78; and Richard Weikart, *Hitler's Religion: The Twisted Beliefs that Drove the Third Reich* (Washington, DC: Regnery Publishing, 2016).

92. In the Christian tradition, the term "redemption" means simply "deliverance from some evil by payment of a price," and this "price" has commonly been

understood as the death of Christ on the cross. See J.D. Douglas, ed., et. al., *New Bible Dictionary, Second Edition* (Leicester: Inter-Varsity, 1982), 1013.

93. See Helmut Walser Smith, *German Nationalism and Religious Conflict: Culture, Ideology, Politics, 1870–1914* (Princeton: Princeton University Press, 1995); Ericksen, *Theologians under Hitler*; Alon Confino, *A World without Jews: The Nazi Imagination from Persecution to Genocide* (New Haven, CT: Yale University Press, 2014); Wolfgang Altgeld, "Religion, Denomination and Nationalism in Nineteenth-Century Germany," in *Protestants, Catholics, and Jews in Germany, 1800–1914*, edited by Helmut Walser Smith (New York: Oxford, 2001); and Günter Brakelmann, "Nationalprotestantismus und Nationalsozialismus," in *Von der Aufgabe der Freiheit: Politische Verantwortung und bürgerliche Gesellschaft im 19. und 20. Jahrhundert* (Berlin, 1995), 337–350.

94. The reference is to Mark 12:28–34.

Chapter 2

The Church Divided

The Rise of National Socialism and the Question of Divine Revelation

In early April 1945, as the war drew to an end and as Allied forces swiftly progressed through Nazi Germany in a race to Berlin, Victor Klemperer found refuge in the small village of Unterbernbach in Bavaria.[1] A Jewish convert to Christianity and a professor of French literature at Dresden University, he survived the Nazi persecutions because of his marriage to an "Aryan," Eva, his beloved wife of 39 years. He and Eva fled Dresden the night before the Allied firebombing, amid a throng of refugees, and made their way south to Bavaria, waiting and hoping for the end of the war to come soon. Even many German soldiers knew the end was only a matter of time. As individual soldiers, and even as troops, they began returning from the front lines, remnants of a dying army.

Klemperer, ever the keen observer of human behavior, witnessed a remarkable scene as he and a group of citizens and soldiers waited for the Americans to arrive. Klemperer sat at a table eating a sparse meal with four German soldiers who had just left the front. At the table one older Bavarian soldier, a carpenter in an earlier life, bitterly criticized Adolf Hitler for the destruction he brought to their Fatherland. Two younger soldiers from northern Germany heartily agreed. They were students who left university to join the war effort, and now they waited for its inevitable end. But the fourth soldier, an older man, an upholsterer from Storkow, slammed his fist down upon the table, rattling the table and startling his comrades. He shouted at them all, "You should be ashamed of yourselves. You are behaving as if we had lost the war. Just because the Yanks have broken through here!"[2]

"Oh, yes," one of them replied, "and what about the Russians? . . . And the Tommys . . . And the French?"[3] The other three were incredulous that this old soldier could possibly entertain the belief that Nazi Germany would still win the war, that Hitler could snatch victory out of the jaws of certain defeat.

But the old soldier from Storkow said that the facts of the invasion were irrelevant and that they simply lacked faith. He continued, "The Führer won't give in, and the Führer can't be defeated, and he has always found a way when others have said there is no way out. No, damn it, no, understanding is useless, you have to have faith. I believe in the Führer."[4] Klemperer heard of this Nazi-faith many times before, this profession of belief in Hitler, even since 1933, and he found it deeply troubling. He heard such professions of faith in Hitler from the old and the young, from educated and uneducated, from all strata of society. And he was convinced that these professions were sincere and not merely lip service.

As a Jewish convert to Christianity in Nazi Germany, Klemperer may have been particularly sensitive to the use of religious language in reference to Hitler and the Nazis. He knew that Hitler and the Nazis purposely appropriated Christian religious language to great effect to appeal to the German masses, inspire support of Nazi policies, support the war effort, and eliminate the Jews from the German nation.[5]

The faith of the Storkow soldier illustrates a religious problem that struck to the heart of the Protestant churches in Nazi Germany. What happens when Christians adopt faith in Hitler and the Fatherland? It was not a mere accident or a happenstance that the Storkow soldier developed a fanatical faith by the end of the war, despite all evidence to the contrary. For 12 years, indeed, since the inception of the National Socialist Party, Hitler and Nazi leaders inculcated this faith and stoked its flames to a fever pitch.

This chapter will explore the nature of the religious conflict with the Nazi state and the churches, and between the churches themselves. In particular, I will argue that the heart of the conflict between the pro-Nazi German Christian movement and the oppositional Confessing Church was a profound disagreement about the nature of divine revelation. While the German Christians argued that Christians can determine divine revelation through a reading of history and racial science, Confessing Church members adamantly disagreed, contending that the Christian scripture alone is the standard, God's special revelation, against which all divine knowledge must be measured. This conflict over divine revelation was the catalyst that caused the fragmentation of German Protestantism in Nazi Germany.

Only in understanding this theological controversy can one make sense of how Confessing Church pastors actively contributed to this debate in the pulpits. The foundations of divine knowledge for the Confessing Church and the German Christian movement were fundamentally different, and indeed, at odds. In fact, the Confessing Church leadership proclaimed itself the "true" German Evangelical Church because of the German Christians' refusal to acknowledge Scripture as the sole measure of divine knowledge, in accordance with the Reformation Confessions. An attentive congregant sitting in a German Christian service might be able to tell the difference between a Confessing Church and a German Christian movement sermon based on this difference in understanding divine revelation.

ADOLF HITLER AND THE NAZI MESSAGE

Adolf Hitler found meaning and purpose as the preacher of a new message in the days after the First World War, a message of salvation for a devastated fatherland and a disillusioned populace. After the war, Hitler stayed on with the army as an instructor and informant, reporting on the activities of political parties that emerged in the wake of Germany's defeat, the right-wing German Workers' Party (*Deutsche Arbeiterpartei*) among them. Led by Anton Drexler, the party espoused a nationalist and antisemitic program. Hitler found a political party he could pour his energy and talents into. Hitler, too, hoped to one day see a Greater Germany that united all Germans, and he also argued that Jews must lose their rights and citizenship in the nation if Germany were to be great again.

With passion and conviction, Hitler preached this new message and gained favor within the party, rising through the ranks. Hitler proved his mettle by drawing crowds to his beer hall speeches, proclaiming a strident nationalist and racist message with confidence and intensity that inspired Germans with his vision. Within half a year as a member, Hitler became the head of propaganda. He even played an integral role in changing the name of the DAP to the National Socialist German Workers' Party (NSDAP) in 1920 to better reflect their ideology. On July 29, 1921, Hitler displaced Drexler to become the undisputed leader of the party. Throughout the 1920s, Hitler transformed the Nazi Party from a provincial Bavarian party with little influence to a national movement that was poised to seize the reins of governance from the Weimar Republic.[6]

Hitler preached an unequivocal message of aggression, hatred, and German dominance, yet in a manner that gave the German people hope that they will again have their day in the sun. He demanded that the Versailles Treaty of 1919 be abolished, with its war guilt clause, outrageous reparations, and dictated peace. He preached the end of the Weimar Republic, with its gross inefficiency and impotence. His anti-gospel decried liberalism, democracy, Marxism, communism, international cooperation, and pacifism as poisons that weaken the *Volksgemeinschaft* in Germany. He preached the message that all of life is a struggle for survival and domination, a struggle against neighbors and foreigners, and peoples of different races. From time immemorial, he argued, the races have been struggling against each other. As Timothy Snyder has written, for Hitler, "Eden was not a garden but a trench."[7] Struggle was the one constant in Hitler's worldview. To be victorious, Hitler preached, Germans as the superior "Aryan" people must unite and struggle together against external and internal enemies.

Hitler placed his faith in nature and its exorable law of struggle, which then legitimized his aggressive nationalism and virulent antisemitism.[8] Historians have mined his writings and speeches for the sources of his faith.[9] Clearly, he adopted Social Darwinism to explain the law of struggle among people groups.[10] For Hitler, the races must inevitably struggle over limited land and resources in order to survive.[11] To aid in survival, a race must remain pure, and indeed become purer by eliminating "weaknesses," never mixing with other races.[12] For Hitler, then, a race does not evolve, but it persists to emerge victorious over other races. Humanitarian concerns for mercy, toleration, or charity have no role in nature's struggle. If a race were to deny nature's laws and resist the struggle for survival by engaging in these "weak" actions, they would certainly become the prey to stronger races and eventually be eliminated.[13] The laws of nature, according to Social Darwinism, are sacred truth and became the basis of Hitler's faith and the foundation of National Socialist ideology.

But his faith also relied upon nineteenth-century prophets to expound on the struggle of the races in human history. It has been notoriously difficult for historians to clearly distinguish the sources of racial ideology in Hitler's thinking, but two figures stand out from the rest, if only because of their broader cultural impact on the rise of antisemitism in Germany. The most important racial theorist of the nineteenth century was the French philosopher Joseph-Arthur de Gobineau, whose book, *An Essay on the Inequality of the Human Races* (1852) sparked debate. While it is unclear whether Hitler read Gobineau for himself or imbibed his racial theory from other sources, Gobineau's philosophy influenced the rise of racial ideology in the nineteenth century more than any other thinker.[14] Gobineau argued that all of humanity can be divided into races according to biological characteristics, and that these races can be hierarchized in degrees of superiority and inferiority. Moreover, Gobineau explained that the fall of all empires throughout history was the result of racial deterioration, the mixing of "Aryan" blood with non-white blood. Hence, the racial purity of a nation is required for its survival.

But the most prominent racial theorist in early twentieth-century Germany, and a direct source of Nazi racial ideology, was Houston Stewart Chamberlain.[15] English-born and a son-in-law of the Bayreuth composer Richard Wagner, Chamberlain's main work of racial theory, *Foundations of the Nineteenth Century* (1899), argued for "Aryan" supremacy, virulent antisemitism, and the constant of racial struggle throughout human history.[16]

In contrast to all other races, he argued, the "Aryan" race is alone capable of creating higher culture, a view that Hitler would espouse in his 1925 political treatise *Mein Kampf*.[17] The similarities in their racial thinking are striking. On a speaking tour in Bayreuth in the autumn of 1923, Hitler actually met Chamberlain. Remarkably, Chamberlain was so impressed with Hitler that he became a devoted follower until his death in January 1927.[18] Intellectuals such as Chamberlain and Gobineau were racial theorists who peddled hatred in scientific terms, and they formulated a "sacred truth" that inspired Hitler and National Socialists to unify "Aryans" and exclude Jews from German public life.

But to make Nazism palatable and easily understandable to a people that overwhelmingly identified as Christian, Hitler appropriated the language of Christianity. As Klemperer argued, "Nazism was accepted by millions as gospel because it appropriated the language of the gospel."[19] The devastation of the First World War undermined and disrupted the "web of meaning through which Western societies made sense of their world."[20] For many, the war undermined liberalism, conservatism, and even Christianity as failed ideologies or belief systems that could not prevent a catastrophic war. Fascism and communism became more and more popular as alternatives. In this context, amid the political and economic troubles of the post-First World War years, Hitler and the Nazis utilized dramatic but familiar religious language—that of a coming apocalypse, a glorious millennial kingdom, and the "purifying" Germany of Jews—to create a new "web of meaning," one that coincided with the populace's need for social harmony.[21] These were promises for a better future.

Hitler believed the Jews had led Germany into chaos and that by the time of the Weimar era, Germany had reached the proverbial fork in the road: one way led to eternal salvation and the other to eternal damnation.[22] According to Hitler and National Socialist ideology, the world needed to be redeemed from the domination of the Jews—the source of evil—and thus Hitler and the Nazis ultimately determined to eradicate this evil, leading to the extermination of the Jews.[23] Only in this way could Germans be free. This is what Saul Friedländer refers to as "redemptive anti-Semitism."[24] In this way, Hitler and the Nazis created meaning amid chaos and paved the way forward to a "harmonious" future for the *Volksgemeinschaft*.[25] The Nazis then utilized millennial language to express their own self-understanding, prejudices, and vision for the future. Nazis commonly used religiously infused words, such as messiah (or savior), Reich, destiny, faith, annihilation, and salvation, to express the apocalyptic complex.[26] Klemperer concluded, "[Nazism] permeated the flesh and blood of the people through single words, idioms and sentence structures which were imposed on them in a million repetitions and taken on board mechanically and unconsciously."[27]

As Hans Maier has argued, "without this religious enthusiasm, or enthusiasm similar to religion," it is "impossible to explain" the faith of many Germans in Hitler, even in the midst of the collapse of the Nazi state.[28] "The extreme loyalty and obedience of many cannot be accounted for by terror and angst alone, nor can the insensitivity to critique and doubt, the sense that a mission was being fulfilled, or the loyalty to the group and willingness to suffer."[29] The outburst of the Storkow soldier is difficult to explain without reference to a profound religious-like faith in Adolf Hitler. Some might argue that calling Nazism a political religion can confuse our understanding of what actually constitutes a religion and that Nazis themselves did not refer to Nazism as a religion.[30] These are points well taken. While, as Maier admits, the concept of a "'political religion' is . . . a necessary if somewhat ill-defined conceptual category," it helps to make sense of Nazism as a belief system that made truth claims upon all aspects of the human person.[31]

THE CHURCH DIVIDED

Upon becoming chancellor, Hitler quickly began the suppression of all political opposition and dissent, eliminating opposing political parties such as the *Kommunistische Partei Deutschlands* (German Communist Party) and *Sozialdemokratische Partei Deutschlands* (German Social Democratic Party), among others. He also initiated a process called *Gleichschaltung*, or "coordination," aligning social and professional institutions and organizations to Nazism.[32] Yet Hitler understood that he had to be cautious in dealing with the German churches. Even in the late 1920s, Hitler understood that any attempt at meddling with the German Protestant churches could be fraught with conflict, considering the preexisting differences between the German confessions (Catholic, Lutheran, Reformed, and United churches) and the complexity of church affairs in Germany's 28 *Landeskirchen* (or state churches).[33] And as will be seen throughout this examination of sermons, many Confessing Church pastors increasingly viewed Nazism as a competing ideology to Christianity.[34] Yet even before 1933, Hitler intended to keep the Nazi Party focused on political, and not religious, objectives; religious controversy could divide the nation like nothing else.[35]

Nevertheless, even before the Nazis assumed power in January 1933, pro-Nazi Christians within Protestantism began to form organizations that attempted to align Christianity to Nazi ideology, and thus to broaden the appeal of Christianity to the German masses. The most influential of these groups was the German Christian movement, as previously mentioned.[36] Three main currents contributed to the growth of this movement.[37] In the late 1920s, two Thüringen pastors and Nazi Party members, Siegfried Leffler and Julius Leutheuser, preached a combination of nationalism and religious renewal, and they named themselves "German Christians." Another group sprouted up in Berlin in the summer of 1932, headed by the Nazi Gauleiter of Brandenburg, Wilhelm Kube. Consisting mainly of pastors, politicians, and a concerned laity, they hoped to revitalize the German Protestant churches by harnessing the popularity of Nazi ideology. They too called themselves "German Christians." Lastly, a variety of small and disconnected Protestant associations throughout Germany emerged in the 1920s that appealed to German culture in an effort to revive the Protestant churches. These three groups found common cause under Nazi support and joined together to transform German Protestant Christianity from within.

A newly amalgamated German Christian movement published its "Guiding Principles" on June 6, 1932, a "living Confession" designed to inspire sincere "believing Germans" to achieve a thorough reformation of the church consistent with Nazi ideology.[38] This document is a call to a unified Protestant state church "that will express all the spiritual forces of our people."[39] This was to be a national church, in service of a "national mission" to battle against Marxism, Freemasonry, the Jews, and any interfering international powers.[40] It called members of the German Christian movement to a "heroic piety" like that of Luther, and to make the church once again a "vital force" in rebuilding the German nation.[41] The movement placed itself front and center of the struggle for the vitality of the German people in Europe, stating in its "Guiding Principles," "We want our Church to be in the forefront of the crucial battle for the existence of our people."[42] Furthermore, in a succinct statement that highlights the German Christian movement's close association with National Socialism, the document states: "We recognize in race, ethnicity [*Volkstum*], and nation orders of life given and entrusted to us by God, who has commanded us to preserve them. For this reason race-mixing must be opposed."[43] The document does not make any apparent attempt to support these aims with scriptural evidence, to reconcile them with contradictions in Christian theology, or even to gain their formal approval by the German Evangelical Church—all necessary tasks if this were, in fact, a true confession in the historical sense.

In the summer of 1933, Hitler took a risk and established a unified Protestant church in Germany—for the first time in Germany's history. This newly constituted *Deutsche evangelische Kirche* (German Evangelical Church) became known as the *Reichskirche*, and included the 28 Lutheran, Reformed, and United state churches in Germany.[44] To lead the new *Reichskirche*, Hitler sought the appointment of an unlikely choice in Ludwig Müller, a military chaplain since the First World War, a regional leader in the German Christian movement, and an *Alte Kämpfer*, an "old fighter" in the Nazi Party.[45]

Yet Protestant leaders demanded to nominate their own candidate, as was their historic right. They chose the clergyman Friedrich von Bodelschwingh, a widely respected Westphalian leader and administrator of Bethel, a hospital for the disabled and mentally ill.[46] After intense debate, representatives from the regional churches met in May 1933 and elected von Bodelschwingh Reich Bishop by a margin of 91 to 8.[47] Barnett writes of the aftermath, "With Müller's defeat, August Jäger, a lawyer from the Ministry of Culture, stepped in and placed the entire Prussian Church under police jurisdiction. A number of pastors were fired, suspended, or arrested, and the 'German Christians' and Nazi Party mounted a vicious campaign against von Bodelschwingh. Under this pressure, the leader of Bethel resigned."[48] This controversy indicates that pressure on the German Protestant churches came from below as well as above. From the start of Hitler's administration, the Nazi government attempted to undermine the independence of the German Protestant churches by coordinating it to Nazi ideology. But more than this, it was willing to use its power to overturn the will of the German clergy to appoint their own institutional leader and representative.

Nevertheless, the Nazi regime called for church elections for the month of July to elect regional representatives who would then select the new Reich bishop.[49] Any Protestant man or woman, aged 24 or older, could vote for their church leaders.[50] The Nazi Party supported German Christian movement candidates, with Hitler himself providing endorsements on a radio broadcast on July 22, 1933, right before the elections.[51] In the broadcast he said, "The strong state must welcome the chance to lend its support to those religious groupings which, for their part, can be useful to it."[52] Uniformed SA members stood outside churches wearing German Christian candidate sandwich boards, hoping to persuade voters at the last minute.[53]

All the campaigning worked. The German Christian movement won the July elections with two-thirds of the vote, the majority in Germany's regional synods, and the power to appoint Ludwig Müller the new Reich Bishop.[54] The synod (or assembly) of the Evangelical Church of the Old Prussian Union appointed Müller regional bishop on 5–6 September 1933. Detractors called it the "brown synod" because of the significant number of delegates who appeared wearing SA uniforms.[55] Müller was formally elected Reich Bishop by the national synod later that September. As for the infamous "Aryan Paragraph," the synod of the Old Prussian Union passed the measure, though it failed to pass in the national synod.[56]

For many German pastors, this was the moment when the German Christian movement's uncritical acceptance of Nazi ideology crossed the point of no return. The "Aryan Paragraph" stated that only clergymen of "Aryan" descent, and none married to Jewish women, could remain clergymen or serve in church government.[57] This meant the effective forced retirement of an estimated 37 German pastors of "full" Jewish descent (of a total 18,000 German pastors), an extraordinary act of discrimination within the modern Church.[58] The German-Christians hoped to apply this paragraph to all Protestant churches throughout the Reich. While most Protestant leaders were more concerned about the implications of the Aryan Paragraph for the autonomy of the church than its antisemitism, those who objected had three main problems with this proposal.[59] First, by establishing a standard by which to judge ministers, it directly challenged an elemental aspect of the Christian tradition, the equality of all believers based on faith.[60] Second, it uncritically accepted the Nazi racial categorization of Jews as distinct from Germans, regardless of religious affiliation.[61] This racial distinction meant very little to Christians convinced that faith levels ethnic, class, and gender divisions. Third, and perhaps most significant, the "Aryan Paragraph" subverted the traditional definition of who could be a true Christian. The German Christian movement argued that Jews could not be true Christians because they could not overcome the distinctions of race, and therefore, could not serve as clergymen or church officials. To many German pastors, this was an affront to the Christian tradition that made baptism the only sign of belonging to the community of faith.[62] Essentially, the German Christian movement denied the effects of baptism for a select group.

By the end of July 1933, it seemed to many that the German Protestant churches were already in the process of becoming "coordinated" to the National Socialist regime.[63] As Bergen concludes, "Affirmed by the biggest voter turnout ever in a Protestant church election and soon ensconced in the bishops' seats of all but three of Germany's Protestant regional churches, in mid-1933 the movement seemed unstoppable."[64] The elections demonstrated the widespread popularity of the new *Reichskirche* and gave it legitimacy.[65]

As previously mentioned, the best figures available for membership in the German Christian movement indicate approximately 600,000 members by the mid-1930s.[66] Laypeople greatly outnumbered clergy in terms membership; in fact, the movement claimed only one-third of the 18,000 total Protestant clergy as members.[67] This means that only 1% of the total German-Christian membership were clergymen. Though figures are not available for the proportion of men and women members, "accounts from the Confessing Church and from state and party offices consistently show that, contrary to German Christian claims [that it was a 'manly' movement], women outnumbered men at the movement's events, often by a wide margin."[68] So, while the movement represented only about 2 percent of the Protestant population in Germany, it still managed to exert a disproportionate influence over German churches and theology throughout the twelve years of the Nazi regime.[69] And though the movement lost some popularity in late 1933, it still managed to advance a popular blend of Christianity and Nazi ideology from the pulpit throughout the Nazi era.[70]

The problem for many Christians throughout Germany, however, was that the movement actually so transformed the theology, practice, and ethics of Christianity through the racial principle of "Aryan" supremacy and an aggressive nationalism that it substantively altered the meaning and message of the faith. In other words, the movement engaged in a process of changing the fundamental elements of Christianity, transforming the religion into a Nazi-based organization. In fact, to many Christians in Nazi Germany the German Christian movement was "barely recognizable as Christian."[71]

First, the movement introduced theological innovation. Fundamentally, the movement denied the "universal claims of Christianity" and instead insisted that claims of redemption and salvation are limited to the scope of the *Volksgemeinschaft*.[72] The movement sought to "dejudaize" Christianity, discard the Hebrew Bible, overhaul the New Testament, and even revise Christian hymns.[73] For example, to the German Christians, Jews cannot convert to Christianity and be welcomed into the German Christian movement; race restricts acceptance. Furthermore, the German Christian movement argued that the doctrine of the German churches must take second place to the unity of the German people; an emphasis on doctrine can lead to theological disputes, which can then result in disunity among the German people.[74] The German Christian movement shifted their sources of authority from the tenets of the Christian faith and Scripture to the Nazi state and racial convictions.[75] In short, the German Christian movement was theologically "hollow," having whittled out the doctrines of the faith.[76]

In addition to its revisions of Christian theology, the German Christian movement also transformed Christian practice. The German Protestant churches had a long tradition of established practices and regulations. For example, they had to adhere to stipulated regulations regarding who could receive the sacraments and wedding or funeral services.[77] The German Christians considerably revised these regulations. German Christian pastors would hold confirmation classes and yet not conclude with an examination or a rite to include the teenagers as members in the church—and they did this to attract more youth participants.[78] German Christian pastors violated regulations prohibiting funerals for non-Protestants when family members wanted to bury a lapsed Protestant or a Catholic according to the Protestant rite.[79] They married couples outside the Protestant faith and permitted pastors to preach and perform sacraments without theological education or ordination.[80] The militarist style of the German Christians manifested in changes in the appearance of some of the clergy—the "black jacket, riding breeches, and knee-high boots"—as well as provocations in outbursts and violence in church meetings with oppositional factions (whether Confessing Church members or neutrals).[81] The results of the consistent violation of Protestant church regulations was, as one presbytery in the village of Soest described, "the weakening and crumbling [of] the order of the church."[82]

THE QUESTION OF REVELATION

The success of the German Christian movement placed front and center for the German churches the issue of interpreting knowledge of God. Hitler and the Nazis presented a thoroughly religious political ideology—one the German Christian movement adopted—that propagated belief in a German messiah sent by Providence to redeem Germany and a racial hierarchy that intractably pit a "good" race against an "evil" race in an apocalyptic struggle that would determine the trajectory of history. The people of Germany had to confront and evaluate these Nazi religious claims on the basis of reason, history, and common sense. Yet Christians had available to them a traditional source of authority, the biblical texts. Given the conflicts, some set out to test the compatibility between National Socialism and Christianity.

In theological terms, this is an issue about the interpretation of general and special revelation. The question for the Church was (and is) essentially, how may humanity know God so that it may preach God? What are the reliable sources of the knowledge of God? On the one hand, general revelation refers to God's self-disclosure, which is in nature and thus available to all people. General revelation is found through nature, its laws, and the spiritual and moral nature of the human being.[83] Those in the German Christian movement believed that racial hierarchy was evident in nature—a source of knowledge available to all people—and therefore part of God's self-disclosure. A case in point is the "The Guiding Principles of the Faith Movement of the 'German Christians,'" mentioned above, which states that the preservation of "race, folk, and nation," as understood through history and the natural world, was a law of God given to the Germans.[84] Their reading of history assured them that God indeed chose Hitler to lead Germany to greatness once again. More will be said of the German Christian movement's reliance on general revelation as it relates to preaching in chapter 3, specifically concerning the theology of the orders of creation. Their interpretation of revelation profoundly differed from the approach of Confessing Church homiletics, as will be discussed in chapter 4.

On the other hand, special revelation refers to that knowledge that is "supernatural" and available to a specific people, the Jews, for instance. In the Christian tradition, this revelation has been preserved and passed down from generation to generation in the biblical texts. The theologian Stanley Grenz elaborates on this idea, "Special revelation, in contrast [to general revelation], is communicated supernaturally, whether directly by God or indirectly through God's messengers. Consequently, the employment of our natural powers of reason cannot put us into contact with it."[85] In short, general revelation is available to all people, and humankind may gain knowledge of God through the use of observation and reason; special revelation is the direct communication of God to humanity, for example, in the Jewish and Christian canons.

The eventual fracturing of the German Protestant churches came down to a conflict over how to interpret the rise of National Socialism according to the standards of general and special revelation. Is one source of revelation enough to legitimize the Nazi regime in the eyes of Christians, or must the two standards apply? Can general revelation be used independently of special revelation, and what happens if the two conflict? Just how authoritative is general revelation compared to special revelation? To answer these questions and to gain a deeper appreciation of why this issue was so controversial for the German Protestant churches in the Nazi period—and particularly the Confessing Church's break with the German Christian movement—it is necessary to step back for a moment and gain a broader historical perspective.

The importance of special revelation in the history of the Church has never seriously been challenged—for Christianity is a religion based on the life and ministry of Jesus as testified by the apostles.[86] But the same cannot be said of general revelation.[87] Though not greatly emphasized in the patristic era (ca. 100–451 AD), medieval scholastics developed what has become known as natural theology, a field of study which received perhaps its greatest champion in the thirteenth-century Roman Catholic monk and theologian Thomas Aquinas. Basing his work on Aristotle's arguments for causation, Aquinas developed five proofs for God's existence: God as prime unmoved mover, God as first cause, the various degrees of perfection in beings, the cause of order in the universe, and the teleological argument.[88] As Aquinas' five proofs for God's existence indicate, one can, through the use of reason, examine the natural world, history, and personal experiences, and come to a general knowledge about the existence of God. As the theologian Stanley Grenz argues, the purpose of developing a theology independent of the biblical texts was

> To articulate a universal knowledge of God, a natural theology, on which to build the specifically revealed dogmas of the church. [The medieval scholastics] argued, therefore, that God's self-disclosure in nature and in the human person provides the basis for the construction of a limited, but nevertheless true, knowledge of God available to all humans through the use of our natural powers of reason.[89]

Thus, the Christian concepts of general and special revelation assert that God has revealed God's self to the world in nature and to specific human beings (as recorded and preserved in the biblical texts) and that these two forms of revelation provide valid and trustworthy knowledge of God.[90]

The Reformation occasioned the first great challenge to natural theology as reformers throughout Europe objected to the notion that a sinful human race is capable of interpreting God's general revelation properly.[91] The argument was that sin obscures the human perception of God's revelation in nature; in other words, corrupted human beings cannot see rightly. The Swiss reformer John Calvin eloquently explicates this point:

> But though we are deficient in natural powers which might enable us to rise to a pure and clear knowledge of God, still, as the dullness which prevents us is within, there is no room for excuse . . . Wherefore, when we wander and go astray, we are justly shut out from every species of excuse, because all things point to the right path. But while man must bear the guilt of corrupting the seed of divine knowledge so wondrously deposited in his mind, and preventing it from bearing good and genuine fruit, it is still most true that we are not sufficiently instructed by their bare and simple, but magnificent testimony which the creatures bear to the glory of their Creator. For no sooner do we, from a survey of the world, obtain some slight knowledge of Deity, than we pass by the true God, and set up in his stead the dream and phantom of our own brain, drawing away the praise of justice, wisdom, and goodness, from the fountain-head, and transferring it to some other quarter.[92]

The unavoidable danger that reformers like Calvin warned against was the tendency of a "corrupted" human reason to interpret the natural world in a way that served its own interests, such as supporting unjust political and religious hierarchies, maintaining social inequalities and power structures, and sustaining burdensome institutions.[93] In sum, the reformers acknowledged that God revealed himself in nature, but they became suspicious of humanity's ability to interpret this revelation rightly.[94] This explains the great reformation emphasis on the Bible and its translation into the vernacular languages across Europe.[95]

The Enlightenment breathed new life into natural theology as philosophers and theologians promoted reason and nature as ultimate authorities on matters of truth.[96] For many Enlightenment thinkers such as John Toland and Matthew Tindal, general revelation gained pride of place ahead of special revelation, which was perceived as valid only insofar as it confirmed the truth established by the intellect and the natural world.[97] Thinkers in the age of reason were quite optimistic of the human ability to know God as revealed in the universe and in human nature. For example, the philosopher Immanuel Kant asserted that the moral imperative necessitated a divine origin of values and an afterlife where justice would be consummated.[98] Enlightenment thinkers achieved great leaps in developing the fields of natural theology, biblical criticism, and historical criticism, and in the process, they established a rational basis upon which to evaluate the biblical texts and the life of faith.

The emergence of Pietism in the late seventeenth century tempered Enlightenment thinkers' emphasis on rationalism as a means of knowing God while relying on emotion and experience.[99] Sharing similarities with Quakerism and Methodism in England and Jansenism in France, Pietism, as an inter-confessional movement, emphasized an emotional enthusiasm for the gospel message; a focus on practical Christianity and the development of a personal spirituality rather than a concentration on matters of dogma; and an appreciation of the Lutheran notion of the priesthood of all believers.[100] The movement breathed new life into the Lutheran and, to a lesser extent, the Reformed confessions, encouraging men and women not simply to intellectually assent to religious dogma but to engage in spiritual development through exercises of devotion and service to God.[101]

The romantics of the late-eighteenth and nineteenth centuries also challenged the Enlightenment's stress on reason in gaining knowledge of God and human nature, and instead explored the range of human emotions. One scholar notes, romanticism "looked to break through the confines of desiccated, well-tempered reasonableness (they called it mediocrity) in the name of individual genius, inspiration, and feeling."[102] Unlike Pietism, romanticism did not emphasize intimacy with God or even the belief in or knowledge of God, yet both movements were concerned with exploring the emotions to develop the spirit and to gain a clearer perception of the world and one's place in it.[103] In Pietism and romanticism, pastors had a new language to explore the relationship between God and humanity, one that relied upon feeling, experience, and, to a lesser extent, the biblical texts.

The most influential German thinker to address the Enlightenment's critiques of Christianity from a Pietist and romantic perspective was the Reformed pastor and theologian Friedrich Schleiermacher (1768–1834). He developed an approach that located truth not in the biblical texts but in religious feeling and experience—a realm impervious to the rational critique of others.[104] Known as the father of modern liberal Protestant theology, he emerged as a profound religious thinker who breathed new life into the Christianity of his day.[105] Schleiermacher became an immensely popular preacher at Berlin's Church of the Holy Trinity, as well as an influential theologian and educator who co-founded the University of Berlin, serving as the head of the School of Theology. No work better captures his approach and popular appeal than *On Religion: Speeches to Its Cultured Despisers*, wherein he argues that "true religion" is simply the "sense and taste for the Infinite," underscoring the dependence of finite man upon the infinite God.[106] In the feeling of dependence one is aware of the infinite, as when one walks beneath the starry skies or experiences the wonder of transcendence in a work of art: one feels unity with the infinite.[107] As Schleiermacher argued, "In the midst of finitude to be one with the Infinite and in every moment to be eternal is the immorality of religion."[108] Schleiermacher thus locates knowledge of God in the self, in feeling, beyond the realm of scientific and rational inquiry.

This emphasis of general revelation over special revelation in knowing God held sway in Protestant Germany until after the turn of the twentieth century and the outbreak of the First World War, when the Swiss pastor and theologian Karl Barth presented a sharp and widely influential critique against it.[109] Given his central role in the history of the Confessing Church, a short introduction is in order. Barth was born on May 10, 1886, in Basel, Switzerland, and by the time of his death on December 10, 1968, he was widely acknowledged as one of the greatest Protestant theologians of the twentieth century. He is perhaps most well-known for his contribution to Protestant theology, his magnum opus, the *Church Dogmatics*, a thirteen-volume systematic theology published in parts over thirty-five years. Barth was raised in a Swiss Reformed household, and discovered early in life a passion for theology, which he studied first at the University of Bern, and then in Germany at the universities of Berlin, Tübingen, and Marburg. After graduation Barth accepted an appointment as the pastor of a parish in the small town of Safenwil, Switzerland, and though he enjoyed his pastoral work immensely, he decided after ten years to begin a teaching career. He accepted a position at the University of Göttingen, and then later transitioned to the universities of Münster and Bonn. It was at the University of Bonn in the early 1930s that Barth, a member of the Social Democrat Party, recognized National Socialism as a dangerous movement in German politics. Moreover, as will be discussed, he recognized the German Christians as a grave threat to the unity and mission of the German Protestant churches.[110]

But decades prior, Barth was stunned at the outbreak of the First World War when he recognized in pro-war advocates in the church what he perceived to be an arrogant and dangerous reading of God's providence in German history.[111] These pro-war advocates included many of Barth's university of professors of theology. When they, along with other German intellectuals, signed a statement in support of Kaiser Wilhelm II's war policy, Barth began to seriously question the merits of liberal Protestantism.[112] What is more, "he saw a theology which focused attention not on the gospel but on statements concerning Christian self-awareness, depriving men of a reliable norm and inviting uncritical adjustment to passing human opinions and changing social forces."[113]

Barth perceived danger in the inability of liberal theology to provide a basis for the knowledge of God and to guide human beings to an ethical life. He wrote,

> For me personally, one day in the beginning of August of that year [1914] stands out as a black day, on which ninety-three German intellectuals, among whom I was horrified to discover almost all of my hitherto revered theological teachers, published a profession of support for the war policy of Kaiser Wilhelm II and his counselors. Amazed by their attitude, I realized that I could no longer follow their ethics or dogmatics, or their understanding of the Bible and history, and that the theology of the nineteenth century no longer had any future for me.[114]

Liberal theology was flawed, Barth argued, and he set out to convince others why.[115] Barth's answer came just a year after the end of the First World War while he served as a pastor in the small Swiss village of Safenwil. He published a ground-breaking work of biblical exposition on the Apostle Paul's Epistle to the Romans, "*Der Römerbrief*," a work that emphasized the utter inability of humankind to bridge the vast distance to God. One may attempt to know God through a providential reading of history—for example, God's favor toward Germany, given its dramatic rise and dominance in Europe—but such a view is myopic and short-sighted. Interpreters are necessarily limited by experiences, ambitions, and prejudices. Barth follows his Reformed predecessor Calvin in highlighting the problem of a sin-corrupted human mind attempting to gain untainted knowledge of God and the world. Human reason can never be fully trusted because it is tainted by original sin.

Furthermore, Barth argued that reason and science have their advantages but blind trust in them can lead down dangerous roads, for example, in the "sciences" of eugenics and phrenology. Barth advanced a "theology of crisis" (*Theologie der Krisis*), otherwise known as dialectical theology, which recognized the inadequacy of a liberal Protestantism optimistic about the potential of human reason and scientific inquiry to solve the problems of the modern world and to lead humanity to religious truth.[116] He argued that revelation is not a truth that humankind must discover, nor did he assert that it lies hidden in history, nature, or human experience; rather, revelation is a divine activity that communicates "other-worldly" faith in the person of Jesus Christ to humanity.[117]

Barth argued that God's revelation, because of its very nature, works in the soul to make it holy. Thus, the sermon is an instrument of sanctification. This is a common theme stressed in the Christian tradition, and particularly since the Protestant Reformation. As Melanchthon once said, "To know Christ . . . is to know his benefits."[118] To know Christ is to know God's grace and mercy, and this revelation is possible only through special revelation, not general revelation. General revelation, then, is altogether insufficient to gain a sanctifying understanding of God. For Barth, human beings are totally incapable of knowing God apart from God's revelation, which exists exclusively in Jesus Christ.[119] The theologian Millard Erickson writes, "Behind this position lies (probably unrecognized by Barth) an existentialist conception of truth as person-to-person and subjective, going back to both Søren Kierkegaard and Martin Buber. The possibility of the knowledge of God outside the gracious revelation in Christ would eliminate the need for Christ."[120] In Barth's theology, revelation is Christ and Christ is the "Word of God." Thus, for a Christian, according to Barth, revelation occurs when one encounters the Word of God.

Barth inspired a rejuvenation of evangelical faith in the tradition of the Protestant Reformation. He called Christians to acknowledge the *euangelion* (the gospel) as the sole basis of Protestant faith.[121] After the First World War the question of God's revelation took on new importance as Christians across Germany sought to rebuild their religious, social, and political institutions on a secure foundation. This excursus into the historical background of general and special revelation underscores the variety of ways Protestants have relied upon these two sources of religious knowledge into the early twentieth century.

FROM THEOLOGICAL DEBATE TO ECCLESIASTICAL FIRESTORM

When the German Christian movement sought a synthesis between Christianity and National Socialism, even introducing racial qualifications on who can or cannot be members of the German Protestant churches, an open debate began about what qualified as divine revelation. Should the German Protestant churches alter their theology and praxis based upon the perceived natural revelation advanced by National Socialist ideology?

Under the leadership of prominent Berlin pastors Gerhard Jacobi and Martin Niemöller, clergymen all across Germany banded together in the *Pfarrernotbund* (Pastors' Emergency League, henceforth PEL) on September 21, 1933.[122] All members had to sign a four-point pledge that explicitly grounded members in a reliance upon special revelation, the revelation of Scripture. The pledge is as follows:

> 1. I pledge myself to fulfill my office as a servant of the Word, bound only by Holy Scripture and by the confessions of the Reformation as the correct exposition of the Holy Scripture.

2. I pledge myself to protest unreservedly against every infringement upon such a confessional position.
3. I realize that I share responsibility to the extent of my powers together with those who are persecuted on account of such a confessional position.
4. In making this pledge I bear witness that the application of the Aryan paragraph in the area of the church of Christ is an infringement upon such a confessional position.[123]

The pledge underscored in its very first point that the Christian biblical texts—this special revelation—would remain the principal authority in determining the loyalties and activities of the PEL pastor.

When these pastors met at the first national synod a few days later on September 27, 1933, in Wittenberg, they issued a statement of protest. The document argued "against the ruthless silencing of the minorities in deliberative bodies, and against the adoption of the Aryan paragraph—which was contrary to Holy Writ and historic confessions."[124] As one historian put it, the pastors demanded "the unfettered preaching of the gospel."[125]

To be clear, the aim of establishing the PEL was not to form a distinctive oppositional movement to the Nazi Party, but to formally separate from the perceived heresy of the German Christian movement and thus to preserve the integrity and moral authority of the German Protestant churches. Clergymen all over Germany quickly rallied to support the Pastors' Emergency League, and by January 1934, approximately 7,000 of the 18,000 German clergymen joined.[126]

Karl Barth pinpointed the critical issue at stake for pastors concerned about the German Christian movement's reforms under the auspices of the Nazi regime. The election of the Reich Bishop, the establishment of a *Reichskirche*, and the passage of the "Aryan paragraph" rested on the ambition to align the church to the state, not on the traditional source of Christian authority, the biblical texts.[127] In the hopes of drawing attention to this fundamental problem in the contemporary church, Barth issued a pamphlet entitled, *Theological Existence Today*, in the summer of 1933. He writes,

> For the mighty temptation of this age, which appears in every shape possible, is that we no longer appreciate the intensity and exclusiveness of the demand which the Divine Word makes as such when looking at the force of other demands: so that in our anxiety in face of existing dangers we no longer put our whole trust in the authority of God's Word, but we think we ought to come to its aid with all sorts of contrivances, and we thus throw quite aside our confidence in the Word's power to triumph. And this means that under the stormy assault of "principalities, powers, and rulers of this world's darkness," we seek for God elsewhere than in Jesus Christ, and seek Jesus Christ elsewhere than in the Holy Scriptures of the Old and New Testaments.[128]

For Barth and a growing number of concerned pastors, the primary concern was not simply the loss of institutional autonomy or oppression by the German Christian movement, but, as the historian Arthur Cochrane puts it, "the freedom of the Word of God in preaching and theology."[129] The question was not simply how the church would administer its affairs, select its leadership, or organize itself, but upon what authority it would preach and express its theology. Barth reminded the church that the only basis could be the biblical texts if it was to remain faithful to God and the Reformation tradition.

Tensions in the German Protestant churches ratcheted up several notches later that fall at the German Christian movement's rally at the Berlin Sports Palace on November 13, 1933. Approximately 20,000 gathered together at the call of Dr. Reinhold Krause, a forty-year-old high school teacher and the Greater Berlin district leader (*Gauobmann*) of German Christians.[130] At the Sports Palace Krause gave a speech entitled, "The Tasks of a German Reich Church in the Spirit of Dr. Martin Luther," in which he underscored the basis upon which the church must be formed, organized, and governed: the German *Volk*.[131] Amid loud shouts of applause, Krause argued for a purified German Christianity:

> . . . We now need but one mission: to remold our German people—without exception and to the depths of their souls—into German National Socialists. (Very loud applause. [stenographer's note]) Our struggle has to do with nothing less than the spiritual awakening of our Volk. Our religion is the honor of the nation in the spirit of a combative, heroic Christianity.
>
> . . . The host of those who are coming back to the church must first be won over. Indispensable to this is a feeling of coming home, and the first step in this direction is liberation from everything in the worship service and our confession of faith that is not German, liberation from the Old Testament with its Jewish reward-and-punishment morality, with its stories of cattle-dealers and pimps.
>
> . . . The pure teaching of Jesus must again become the foundation of the church. If we take from the gospels what speaks to our German hearts, then what is at the heart of Jesus' teaching comes clearly and brilliantly to light and coincides—and we can take pride in this—completely with the demands of National Socialism.[132]

Krause's provocative language aside, the speech clarified for German Christians the ultimate authority that determined who could be pastors, which texts could remain in Scripture, and the end goal of the Christian formation: the health and well-being of the German *Volk*.

The speech was printed in newspapers and read by millions of Germans.[133] It sparked a strong reaction, as well as confusion, among Protestants. Krause called for highly controversial steps for the "completion of the German Reformation in the Third Reich": the removal of all pastors hostile to National

Socialism, the institutionalization of the "Aryan paragraph," the establishment of a segregated "Jewish Christian Church" for non-Aryan Christians, and "Aryanized" worship services and liturgy.[134] In the short term, the speech resulted in the fragmentation of the German Christian movement and led to many members withdrawing their memberships, leaving the movement, including Reich Bishop Ludwig Müller.[135] Nevertheless, as Doris Bergen argues, "By the late 1930s, Krause's ideas had become common currency in German Christian circles."[136] In fact, by 1939, pro-Nazi theologians such as Walter Grundmann established the Institute for the Study and Eradication of Jewish Influence on German Religious Life, which disseminated propaganda to advance a nazified Christianity and an Aryan Jesus.[137] Susannah Heschel writes, "As Germany became increasingly accepting of racial politics during the course of the 1930s, its Christians grew more accepting of racial theology."[138] And the racial theology then "functioned as a moral sanction for the racism of the Nazis."[139]

The Sports Palace controversy underscores not simply that *völkish* religious ideas had support among German Protestants, but also that these ideas had gained respectability in the Protestant churches in the autumn of 1933, so much so that Krause promoted them as the future of the German churches and as entirely consistent with Reformation values.[140] The irony, of course, is that Krause's argument for the authority of the German *Volk* in the life of the church (as opposed to *sola scriptura* [Scripture alone]) severely undermined Luther's principle of reform, that the authority for the reform of the church stands outside "us" in Scripture. Krause wanted to "complete" Luther's reformation while swapping the standard of reform. While Luther used Scripture to judge the authority and tradition of the Roman Catholic Church, Krause used the German *Volk* to judge Scripture and the German churches.

Not surprisingly, given the Sports Palace controversy, the PEL gained momentum through the winter and spring of 1934. On May 29–31, 1934, PEL pastors met at the Barmen Conference and officially inaugurated *die Bekennende Kirche* (the Confessing Church), in acknowledgment that it remained true to the historic creeds and confessions of the Protestant faith (principally the Augsburg Confession and the Heidelberg Catechism).[141] Rather than an institutional church, the Confessing Church was more of an association of Protestant pastors and laypeople who resisted National Socialist infringement on the theology, liturgical practice, and institutional integrity of the German Evangelical Church.[142] Most significant, Confessing Church pastors claimed that the German Christian movement adulterated the gospel message with Nazi ideology, and therefore forsook its identity as a legitimate Protestant church. The Confessing Church thus declared itself the one true German Evangelical Church, though, as we will see shortly, this unity did not last long.[143]

The delegates at the Barmen Conference also affirmed a new confession of faith, known as the Barmen Confession. Confessions (or proclamations) of faith had proliferated in the early 1930s. Scores of confessions had been composed by various factions, including *völkish* groups espousing a nazified Christianity to centrists arguing for a balanced approach to integrating special and general revelation in the churches.[144] Kurt Dietrich Schmidt, for example, collected seventy-five confessions from the year 1933 alone in his work, *The Confessions and Fundamental Statements on the Church Question of 1933*.[145] Representatives of the German Christian movement repeatedly asserted the conviction that God can speak through race and nation and that the churches can alter worship, liturgy, and traditional beliefs based on general revelation. Yet Krause's speech at the Sports Palace controversy demonstrated for all to see where the German Christian position could lead and the danger it posed to the identity and mission of the church.[146] Thus, a growing awareness that a new confession, one supported by Lutheran, Reformed, and United Christians throughout Germany, was needed, one that specifically denied general revelation the authority to contravene special revelation.

The delegates at the Barmen Synod agreed on six theses in the confession, which was primarily written by Karl Barth, but also with the assistance of Hans Asmussen and Thomas Breit.[147] The document clearly articulated the Confessing Church's opposition to the German Christian movement and its *völkish* Christianity, establishing the organization's independence from the *Reichskirche*.[148] The first article provides the basis for the Confessing Church's position:

> Jesus Christ, as he is attested for us in Holy Scriptures, is the one Word of God which we have to hear and which we have to trust and obey in life and death.
>
> We reject the false doctrine, as though the Church could and would have to acknowledge as a source of its proclamation, apart from and besides this one Word of God, still other events and powers, figures, and truths, as God's revelation.[149]

The issue at stake for Confessing Church pastors was the primacy of God's revelation in Christ, as revealed in Scripture—special revelation—against the general revelation advanced by the German Christian movement. They believed that the German Evangelical Church was at risk, but even more problematic, so also was the integrity of the gospel message.

As Klaus Scholder has insightfully argued, the intentional placement of this issue of the sources of divine knowledge in the first point of the declaration "established that the controversies with the German Christians were first and foremost concerned with a theological problem."[150] The first article of the declaration explicitly affirms that divine knowledge is gained through

Christ alone, even quoting Jesus from the Gospel of John, "I am the way and the truth and the life. No one comes to the Father except through me" (14:6, ESV). The first article speaks to the problem of uncritically accepting general revelation that had gained ground in German Protestantism since the early eighteenth century and the Enlightenment.[151] This emphasis on special revelation in the first point of the Barmen Declaration further demonstrates that the newly formed Confessing Church did not set out to politically oppose the Nazi regime, but to address a profound theological threat to the German churches.

The first thesis of the Barmen Declaration presents the foundation upon which the church stands: "the one Word of God," meaning, "Jesus Christ, as he is attested for us in Holy Scripture."[152] As Eberhard Busch argues, "These first five words must be seen as the center and the provocation of the thesis—that is, that which provides the church in the situation of that time, which calls out to it to stand and not to fall, to resist and not to conform, to confess and not to remain silent."[153] This thesis binds the church to God rather than to the various idols of the world.[154] The church's "confession of God is at the same time its binding to Holy Scripture."[155] As this first thesis asserts, Christians must "hear," "trust," and "obey" the Word of God, three actions that together describe the life of faith.[156] This acknowledgement in the first thesis of "the one Word of God" forms the basis upon which the next five theses rest. Thus, the Barmen Confession is not simply a statement of faith, but a call for Christians to hear, trust, and obey the Word of God—a call for action—in the context of Nazi Germany and beyond.

Fundamentally, for Confessing Church pastors this understanding of the church's authority was an issue of identity. The pastors at Barmen charged the administration of the newly united *Reichskirche*, under Bishop Müller, with forsaking its historic and sacred foundation, the biblical texts. The Barmen Declaration reads:

> The unimpeachable basis of the German Evangelical Church is the gospel of Jesus Christ as it is testified to in Holy Scripture and brought to light again in the Confessions of the Reformation. The present Reich Church administration has abandoned this unimpeachable basis and has been guilty of numerous violations of the law and the [Church] constitution. It has thereby forfeited the claim to be the legitimate administration of the German Evangelical Church.[157]

This resolution reflects an identity that is based on the biblical text and its traditional interpretation. The Confessing Church's response highlighted the novel character of the German Evangelical Church as an institution subservient to the state, organized and administered by state functionaries, and guided by state ideology.[158] To Confessing Church pastors, this adaptation of the church to the state compromised its identity and commission to preach the gospel.

Yet it is important to note that the Confessing Church pastors walked a fine line in delineating the relationship between the church and state. On the one hand, while the Confessing Church challenged the German Christian movement's subservience to the Nazi regime, it still acknowledged the Lutheran doctrine of the two kingdoms: first, that God instituted the state to rule over the mundane lives of men and women, to preserve order and establish peace; and second, that God instituted the church to govern the spiritual lives of men and women, to preach the gospel, to instruct in matters of morals and tradition, and to provide the sacraments.[159] Though the Barmen Declaration acknowledged the state's "divine appointment" to "[provide] justice and peace," through force if need be, it "[rejected] the false doctrine, as though the State, over and beyond its special commission, should and could become the single and totalitarian order of human life, thus fulfilling the Church's vocation as well."[160] Likewise, the Confessing Church rejected the idea that it "should or could appropriate the characteristics, the tasks, and the dignity of the State, thus itself becoming an organ of the State."[161]

The church leaders and pastors at Barmen took a definitive stand on the issue of general revelation and the German Christian movement's assertion that God's truths can be known through history, nature, and race.[162] As the first article makes clear, they explicitly denied reliance on any source outside the biblical texts. In other words, the biblical texts became the standard of truth by which all claims—National Socialist or otherwise—must be measured. Again, the purpose was to maintain the historic identity of the Church as defined by the biblical texts and affirmed in the Reformation confessions, and more importantly, to preserve the integrity of the gospel.

All of these fine points of theology had a direct impact on the manner of preaching in the Confessing Church. The church would not accept politically based limitations on who could or could not preach the gospel; it was the church's affair to call and ordain pastors to preach. It would not accept sources of authority on Christian theology or practice beside the biblical texts. All knowledge of God must be verified and measured against the biblical texts. Preaching, then, must be based on this "one Word of God." Furthermore, the Confessing Church recognized preaching as the fundamental commission of the Church, its historic purpose and mission in the world. The Barmen Declaration states:

> The Church's commission, upon which its foundation is founded, consists in delivering the message of the free grace of God to all people in Christ's stead, and therefore in the ministry of his own Word and work through sermon and sacrament.

> We reject the false doctrine, as though the Church in human arrogance could place the Word and work of the Lord in the service of any arbitrarily chosen desires, purposes, and plans.[163]

In no uncertain terms, the Barmen Declaration denied the German Christian movement's reliance on general revelation and Nazi ideology, as well as its agenda in furthering the nazification of modern Christianity.

To be clear, one cannot assert that German Christian pastors only accepted general revelation as authoritative and denied special revelation. Certainly, German Christian clergy preached from Scripture, too, yet their exposition was guided by the racial and nationalist principles of National Socialism.[164] The attempts of the German Christian movement to mold Christianity into a more Aryan, masculine, and aggressive faith demonstrate which source of authority—general or special revelation—had pride of place. Their attempts to de-judaize Scripture and "Aryanize" Jesus demonstrate that their standard of truth was not Scripture itself but the German *Volk*. In a short pamphlet written in 1937 for a popular audience, entitled, "What do the German Christians Want?" the German Christian pastor Otto Brökelschen sums up the movement's position on religious authority. He explicitly states that God's revelation is not "locked into the book that is the Bible and its letters." Rather, he states, "[German Christians] believe that God reveals himself today in the history of the German Volk through Adolf Hitler. The Führer, who calls Germans to faith and unifies them in love, is the instrument of God's revelation, the German prophet."[165] The pamphlet was published by Deutsche Christen Verlag. Thus, German Christian preachers used Scripture in sermons but exposited its meaning in accordance with Nazi racist and nationalist principles.[166]

At the same time, one cannot assert that Confessing Church pastors denied general revelation altogether in their preaching. As will be discussed in later chapters, in early 1933, many Confessing Church pastors interpreted the rise of Adolf Hitler as a gift of God to the German people. And as the Second World War came to its end, some pastors interpreted Germany's battlefield losses as God's judgment on their nation. One can find examples of general revelation in Confessing Church sermons. Yet the issue that fundamentally separated German Christian pastors from Confessing Church pastors was about which source of authority—general or special revelation—had primacy in interpreting knowledge of God. The question was about which source was the standard of truth. This disagreement between the German Christian movement and the Confessing Church was a major fault line in the Protestant churches in Nazi Germany, and it is evident throughout Confessing Church preaching.

The Barmen Declaration drew an unmistakable line in the sand and demanded that German pastors pick sides in the debate.[167] The gospel message was not to be hindered, altered, or put to political service. Confessing Church pastors reflected on Jesus' great commission, to preach the gospel to the four corners of the world (Matthew 28:20), and they confronted the German Christian movement's apparent compromise. They took to heart the Apostle Paul's teaching that "the word of God is not fettered," that no Christian could accept restrictions or limitations on the gospel (2 Timothy 2:9).[168] The importance of preaching for the identity of the Confessing Church only underscores the necessity of examining its sermons to see how they applied these principles.

While many pastors aligned themselves with the Confessing Church in separating from the *Reichskirche*, this step was too far for others who might have been critical of the Nazi regime and its interference in church affairs. For example, Pastor Rudolf Peter from the Pirna district was drawn to the Confessing Church but decided to remain loyal to the German Evangelical Church.[169] He argued that the church is still the church, even when led by an "un-Christian church government."[170] Christian ministers did not have the freedom to split the church, the body of Christ. It would be better to wait, Peter argued, and to persevere amid the internal and spiritual conflict in the church.[171] Peter's position indicates that even many pastors outside the bounds of the Confessing Church were deeply critical of the Nazi regime and the leadership of the German Evangelical Church. Nevertheless, thousands of Protestant pastors felt compelled to separate from the *Reichskirche* to preserve the "true" German Evangelical Church, yet with a new framework and organization.

THE STRUCTURE OF THE CONFESSING CHURCH

Without trudging too deep in the weeds of ecclesiastical governance, it will be helpful to outline the Confessing Church's organizational structure, administration, and its relationship with the *Reichskirche*. In most of the 28 *Landeskirchen* (state churches), members of the German Christian movement took over leadership in 1933. The Confessing Church referred to these provincial churches as "disturbed churches" because their traditions and administrations had been overturned, and their leadership instituted the policies of the national church administration.[172] Yet in a few state churches, the old authorities remained in place, and they invariably sided with the Confessing Church—though to varying degrees.[173] These state churches were called "intact churches" because their traditions and administrations had remained unobstructed. Among them were the state churches of Bavaria, the Hanover-Lutheran and Reformed churches, as well as the state church of Württemberg. Of course, individual churches in either "intact" or "disturbed" provinces could align themselves with the Confessing Church, the German Christian movement, or neither and remain neutral.

From its inception in May 1934, the Confessing Church was a self-governing organization of churches, established by province throughout Nazi Germany.[174] This was accomplished through a series of tiers of brotherhood councils coordinated at the congregational, district, and provincial levels, and this structure assured a degree of representation for individual congregations.[175] Each of the 28 state churches had provincial brotherhood councils, and each sent delegates to Confessing synods; yet the Land Church of the Old Prussian Union led the way in organizing and structuring the Confessing Church—partly because of its size and membership, but also because of its location, headquartered in Berlin. As Helmreich argues, the brotherhood council of the Land Church of the Old Prussian Union "actually became the working executive and directing body of the Confessing Church in the Old Prussian Union and furnished the militant leadership for the Confessing Church of all Germany."[176]

At the inception of the Confessing Church, congregations that wished to join the organization put the question to their members: If an individual wished to join the Confessing Church, then they had to sign a red card.[177] One could become a member of the Confessing Church and yet still retain their membership in the state church.[178] The obvious problem was that it was rare for an entire congregation to align itself with either the Confessing Church or the German Christian movement; many simply remained neutral. Congregations would often be split between Confessing members, German Christians, and those who wished to remain neutral, a reality that led to conflicts within the church. In fact, in a predominantly neutral church or one aligned with the German Christian movement, there could be a small group of Confessing members who met together alone in Bible studies or other classes.[179] As one historian writes, "the dualism came to be recognized, and pastors and laity accommodated themselves to it."[180] This indicates that while churches could split over the issue of revelation, congregants found ways to cope and to worship with like-minded congregants. Nevertheless, some 2,000 congregations throughout Nazi Germany identified with the Confessing Church, and in just the regions of the Rhineland and Westphalia alone, there were approximately 800,000 card-carrying members by 1935.[181]

The Confessing Church asserted the historical right of the church to tax revenue from the state.[182] Thus, Confessing Church pastors continued to receive their paychecks from the Nazi government, which no doubt was a consideration (at least for some) to curb criticisms of the state, lest they risk biting the hand that fed them.[183] Yet as the Nazi regime increasingly harassed, arrested, or imprisoned Confessing pastors—or as leaders of German

Christian movement ousted them from their positions—the Confessing Church took up collections from their congregations in their support, which would be dispersed by the provisional brotherhood councils by region.[184] Thus, the Confessing Church established a safety net to care for pastors who fell afoul of the regime.

By the mid-1930s, however, the unity of the Confessing Church would fracture among members of the "intact" churches who were willing to cooperate with the state churches and the new Reich Ministry of Church Affairs, and others, like the more radical Dahlemites under the leadership of Martin Niemöller (from the Berlin suburb of Dahlem), who desired no conciliation with the state churches or the new ministry, declaring them to be illegitimate.[185] Despite a promising start to opposing the Nazi state's infringements in church affairs and theology in late 1933 and into 1934, culminating in the work at Barmen, the Confessing Church could not resolve internal disputes about how to engage Nazi interference in ecclesiastical affairs. Thus, the Confessing Church failed to become a united and resolute oppositional movement.

The Confessing Church was essentially a loose collection of intact churches, congregations, smaller groups within congregations, as well as brotherhood councils. As Helmreich argues, "The Confessing church never had a clear-cut structure. It was unique in its organizational complexity; it had no constitution, no elaborate system of laws and ordinances comparable to the usual German church administration. It always claimed to be the true German Evangelical Church, and thereby did not cut itself off from the legalistic maze created by the past. Instead, it made use of these laws, customs, and traditions to protect itself."[186] The Confessing Church was a church that emerged in crisis and that allowed for adaptation in the face of persecution, yet its lack of clear organization and structure would in time impede its ability to unify Confessing pastors in steadfast opposition to the Nazi regime.

The division of the German Protestant churches erupted over the fault line of the sources of authority for divine knowledge. The sermons of the Confessing Church demonstrate evidence of pastors' convictions about the meaning of Jesus Christ as revealed in Scripture as "the one Word of God," and they must be understood in the context of German Christian assertions of divine knowledge found in "race, ethnicity, and nation," as their "Guiding Principles" state. But before turning to an analysis of the sermons themselves, one should first consider how this debate over divine knowledge impacted the parameters and purpose of the sermon and the shifts in emphasis and corrections in practice of early-twentieth century homiletics in the German Protestant churches.

NOTES

1. Victor Klemperer tells this story in his insightful study, *The Language of the Third Reich* (New York: Continuum, 2000), 102.
2. Klemperer, *Language of the Third Reich*, 102.
3. Klemperer, *Language of the Third Reich*, 102.
4. Klemperer, *Language of the Third Reich*, 102.
5. See Klemperer, *Language of the Third Reich*, 97–111.
6. For a few of the best and most recent accounts of the rise of Hitler and the Nazi Party, see Richard Evans, *The Coming of the Third Reich* (New York: Penguin, 2003); Ian Kershaw, *Hitler: 1889–1936: Hubris* (New York: W.W. Norton & Company, 1999); Peter Longerich, *Hitler: A Biography* (New York: Oxford University Press, 2019); Volker Ulrich, *Hitler: Ascent: 1889–1939* (New York: Vintage Books, 2016); and Thomas Weber, *Becoming Hitler: The Making of a Nazi* (New York: Basic Books, 2017).
7. Timothy Snyder, *Black Earth: The Holocaust as History and Warning* (New York: Tim Duggan Books, 2015), 3.
8. Richard Weikart, *Hitler's Religion: The Twisted Beliefs that Drove the Third Reich* (Washington, DC: Regnery Publishing).
9. A few significant treatments include Rainer Bucher, *Hitlers Theologie* (Würzburg: Echter, 2008); Michael Hesemann, *Hitlers Religion: The fatale Heilslehre des Nationalsozialismus* (Augsburg: Sankt Ulrich, 2012); Lars Lüdicke, *Hitlers Weltanschauung: Von "Mein Kampf" bis zum "Nero Befehl"* (Paderborn: Ferdinand Schöningh, 2006); William McGovern, *From Luther to Hitler: The History of Fascist-Nazi Political Philosophy* (Cambridge, MA: Riverside Press, 1941); George L. Mosse, *The Crisis of German Ideology: Intellectual Origins of the Third Reich* (New York: Grosset and Dunlap, 1964) and *Toward the Final Solution: A History of European Racism* (New York: Howard Fertig, 1985); Michael Rissmann, *Hitlers Gott: Versehungsglaube und Sendungsbewusstsein des deutschen Diktators* (Zürich: Pendo, 2001); Anton Grabner-Haider and Peter Strasser, *Hitlers mythische Religion: Theologische Denklinien und NS-Ideologie* (Vienna: Böhlau Verlag, 2007); Richard Weikart, *Hitler's Ethic: The Nazi Pursuit of Evolutionary Progress* (New York: Palgrave Macmillan, 2009) and *Hitler's Religion*.
10. Wolfgang Bialas, "The Eternal Voice of the Blood: Racial Science and Nazi Ethics," in *Racial Science in Hitler's New Europe, 1938–1945*, eds Anton Weiss-Wendt and Rory Yeomans (Lincoln: University of Nebraska Press, 2013), 351; Richard Evans, *Third Reich in Power* (New York: Penguin, 2006), 259; and Eberhard Jäckel, *Hitler's World View: A Blueprint for Power* (Cambridge: Harvard University Press, 1981), 87–107. Weikart argues, "[So] many historians have argued that social Darwinism was a central tenet of Nazi ideology that this idea is considered commonplace." Weikart, *Hitler's Religion*, 248.
11. For example, see the Four-Year Plan (1936), in which politics is described as the "conduct and the course of the historical struggle" for "survival"; and the Hossback Memo (1937), which describes Germany's "right to a greater living space" for its preservation and security. See "Hitler's Confidential Memo on Autarky (August

1936)," in German History in Documents and Images, Volume 7, Nazi Germany, 1933–1945, accessed June 13, 2023, https://germanhistorydocs.ghi-dc.org/pdf/eng/English61.pdf; and "Summary of Hitler's Meeting with the Heads of the Armed Services on November 5, 1937 (Hossbach Protocol of November 1937)," in German History in Documents and Images, Volume 7, Nazi Germany, 133–1945, accessed June 13, 2023, https://ghdi.ghi-dc.org/sub_document.cfm?document_id=1540.

12. Weikart, *Hitler's Religion*, 235.
13. Weikart, *Hitler's Religion*, 237.
14. Mosse, *Toward the Final Solution*, 42–43.
15. Weikart, *Hitler's Religion*, 31.
16. Weikart, *Hitler's Religion*, 32.
17. Weikart, *Hitler's Religion*, 32.
18. Weikart, *Hitler's Religion*, 31.
19. Klemperer, *The Language of the Third Reich*, 110.
20. Furedi, *First World War*, 14–15.
21. Redles, *Hitler's Millennial Reich*, 45.
22. Redles, *Hitler's Millennial Reich*, 45. The term "salvation" simply means "rescue." This is an example of the Nazis appropriating Christian theological terms for propagandistic uses.
23. Friedländer, *Nazi Germany and the Jews: Vol. 1*, 3.
24. Friedländer, *Nazi Germany and the Jews: Vol. 1*, 3.
25. Redles, *Hitler's Millennial Reich*, 45.
26. Redles, *Hitler's Millennial Reich*, 5.
27. Klemperer, *The Language of the Third Reich*, 14.
28. Maier, "Political Religion: A Concept and Its Limitations," *Totalitarianism Movements and Political Religions* 8(1) (March 2007), 13. On this debate, see Emilio Gentile, "The Sacralization of Politics: Definitions, Interpretations and Reflections on the Question of Secular Religion and Totalitarianism," translated by Robert Mallett, *Totalitarian Movements and Political Religions* 1, no. 1 (2000), 18–55; Michael Burleigh, "National Socialism as a Political Religion, *Totalitarian Movements and Political Religions* 1, no. 2, (2000), 1–26; Richard Steigmann-Gall, "Nazism and the Revival of Political Religion Theory," *Totalitarian Movements and Political Religions* 5, no. 3, (2004), 376–96; Emilio Gentile, "Political Religion: A Concept and its Critics—A Critical Survey," translated by Natalia Belozertseva, in *Totalitarian Movements and Political Religions* 6, no. 1 (June 2005), 19–32; Klaus Vondung, "National Socialism as a Political Religion: Potentials and Limits of an Analytical Concept," in *Totalitarian Movements and Political Religion* 6, no. 1 (June 2005), 87–95; Milan Babík, "Nazism as a Secular Religion," in *History and Theory* 45, no. 3 (Oct. 2006), 375–396; Richard J. Evans, "Nazism, Christianity and Political Religion: A Debate," in the *Journal of Contemporary History* 42, no. 1 (January 2007), 5–7.
29. Maier, "Political Religion," 13.
30. See for example, Stanely Stowers, "The Concepts of 'Religion,' 'Political Religion' and the Study of Nazism" in the *Journal of Contemporary History* 42, no. 1 (Jan. 2007), 9–24.
31. Maier, "Political Religion: A Concept," 15.

32. See Barnett, *For the Soul of the People*, 30–38; Evans, *The Coming of the Third Reich*, 381–90; Tim Kirk, *Nazi Germany* (New York: Palgrave, 2007), 108; and Peukert, *Inside Nazi Germany*, 97–103.

33. Kirk, *Nazi Germany*, 108.

34. This was a widespread view in the Confessing Church that we'll see expressed often in sermons. For more on this conflict, see Frank Hamlin Littell, *The German Phoenix: How the German Churches' Resistance to Hitler Gave Birth to the Massive Lay Movements of the Kirchentag and the Academies* (New York: Doubleday & Company, 1960), 3; John S. Conway, "The German Church Struggle: Its Making and Meaning," in *The Church Confronts the Nazis: Barmen Then and Now*, edited by Hubert Locke (New York: The Edwin Mellon Press, 1984), 135; and Siegfried Hermle, "Predigt an der Front: Zur Tätigkeit der Kriegspfarrer im Zweiten Weltkrieg," in *Blätter für württembergische Kirchegeschichte* (Verlag Chr. Schleufele in Stuttgart, 2002), 145, 155. Doris Bergen notes that even most "hard core Nazis leaders"—including Martin Bormann, Heinrich Himmer, and Adolf Hitler—were also convinced of a fundamental opposition between Christianity and National Socialism. See Bergen, *Twisted Cross*, 1.

35. See Conway, *Nazi Persecution of the Churches*, 4–8, 13; and Helmreich, *German Churches under Hitler*, 79.

36. See Barnett, *For the Soul of the People*, 25–27; Helmreich, *German Churches under Hitler*, 121–28; Kirk, *Nazi Germany*, 109. See Albert S. Lindemann and Richard S. Levy, eds., *Antisemitism: A History* (New York: Oxford, 2010), Kindle edition, location 4454.

37. Doris Bergen, *Twisted Cross*, 5.

38. "The Guiding Principles of the Faith Movement of the 'German Christians,'" translated by Cochrane in *The Church's Confession under Hitler*, 222–23; 82.

39. Cochrane, *Church's Confession under Hitler*, 222.

40. Cochrane, *Church's Confession under Hitler*, 222.

41. "Guiding Principles," in Cochrane, *Church's Confession under Hitler*, 222.

42. "Guiding Principles," in Cochrane, *Church's Confession under Hitler*, 222.

43. "The Original Guidelines of the German Christian Faith Movement," in *A Church Undone: Documents from the German Christian Faith Movement, 1932–1940*, edited and translated by Mary Solberg (Minneapolis: Fortress Press, 2015), 49–50.

44. Barnett, *For the Soul of the People*, 33–35; Bergen, *Twisted Cross*, 5–7, 15; Lowell Green, *Lutherans against Hitler: The Untold Story* (Saint Louis: Concordia Publishing House, 2007), 370.

45. Bergen, *Twisted Cross*, 15–16; Green, *Lutherans against Hitler*, 84; see also Solberg, *A Church Undone*, 150.

46. Gutteridge, *German Evangelical Church and the Jews*, 134; Green, *Lutherans against Hitler*, 84; and Helmreich, *German Churches under Hitler*, 135

47. Barnett, *For the Soul of the People*, 34; Helmreich, *German Churches under Hitler*, 135–36; Robertson, *Christians against Hitler*, 29.

48. Barnett, *For the Soul of the People*, 34.

49. Helmreich argues that the July church elections were actually illegal as the state had no right to call them, a point that apparently no one made before the elections, but only after. See Helmreich, *German Churches under Hitler*, 140–43; Bergen, *Twisted Cross*, 15–16; and Barnett, *For the Soul of the People*, 34.

50. This information was included in an article in the Völkischer Beobachter supporting German Christian movement candidates. See "Völkischer Beobachter on the Church Elections, 19 July 1933," in Peter Matheson, *The Third Reich and the Christian Churches: A Documentary Account of Christian Resistance and Complicity During the Nazi Era* (Grand Rapids, MI, 1981), 27.

51. Bergen, *Twisted Cross*, 5–6; and Barnett, *For the Soul of the People*, 34.

52. "Radio Broadcast by Hitler on the Church Elections, 22 July 1933," in Matheson, *The Third Reich and the Christian Churches: Documents*, 28.

53. Bergen, *Twisted Cross*, 6.

54. Bergen, *Twisted Cross*, 64; Barnett, *For the Soul of the People*, 34; Gutteridge, *German Evangelical Church and the Jews*, 94; Helmreich, *German Churches under Hitler*, 140–43. A synod refers to a meeting of a governing council of a church, usually called to make a decision regarding doctrine or administration.

55. Barnett, *For the Soul of the People*, 34; Green, *Lutherans against Hitler*, 270; Gutteridge, *German Evangelical Church and the Jews*, 94; and Helmreich, *German Churches under Hitler*, 144.

56. Amid the chaos and disunity of the German Evangelical Church, this church law would actually be repealed, and then the repeal would be repealed, and back and forth, multiple times between September 1933 and August 1934, "illustrating the bankruptcy of the church leadership." The law would remain in effect from August 1934 onwards. Gerlach, *And the Witnesses Were Silent*, 65, and 78.

57. See Barnett, *For the Soul of the People*, 128–29; Bergen, *Twisted Cross*, 88–93; Gutteridge, *German Evangelical Church and the Jews*, 91–96; and Helmreich, *German Churches under Hitler*, 144–47.

58. Bergen, *Twisted Cross*, 88–93; Helmreich, *German Churches under Hitler*, 148; and Gerlach, *And the Witnesses Were Silent*, 30.

59. See Barnett, *For the Soul of the People*, 35, 128–29; Bergen, *Twisted Cross*, 88–89; Cochrane, *The Church's Confession under Hitler*, 107–10; Green, *Lutherans against Hitler*, 130–34; and Helmreich, *German Christians under Hitler*, 144–46.

60. Gerlach, *And the Witnesses Were Silent*, 35.

61. Barnett, *For the Soul of the People*, 35

62. Gerlach, *And the Witnesses Were Silent*, 24.

63. See Conway, *Nazi Persecution of the Churches*, 42–44; Helmreich, *German Churches under Hitler*, 169–75; and Kirk, *Nazi Germany*, 109.

64. Bergen, *Twisted Cross*, 5.

65. See Barnett, *For the Soul of the People*, 34; Bergen, *Twisted Cross*, 5; Kirk, *Nazi Germany*, 109.

66. Bergen, *Twisted Cross*, 7. According to Bergen, this figure was accepted by the movement itself, the Nazi regime, and even the movement's opponents.

67. Bergen, *Twisted Cross*, 178.

68. Bergen, *Twisted Cross*, 73

69. Bergen, *Twisted Cross*, 8.
70. Bergen, *Twisted Cross*, 18.
71. Bergen, *Twisted Cross*, 2.
72. Bergen, *Twisted Cross*, 45; Michael, *Holy Hatred*, 175.
73. Bergen, *Twisted Cross*, 143.
74. Bergen, *Twisted Cross*, 46. Bergen even asserts that "One searches their utterances in vain for any attempt to grapple with theological concerns that have shaped Christian discourse since the time of Paul" (p. 45).
75. Bergen, *Twisted Cross*, 47.
76. Bergen, *Twisted Cross*, 45.
77. Bergen, *Twisted Cross*, 183.
78. Bergen, *Twisted Cross*, 188.
79. Bergen, *Twisted Cross*, 187.
80. Bergen, *Twisted Cross*, 183.
81. Bergen, *Twisted Cross*, 189.
82. Quoted in Bergen, *Twisted Cross*, 187.
83. Stanley Grenz, *Theology for the Community of God* (Grand Rapids, MI: Eerdmans, 2000), 133.
84. "Guiding Principles," in Cochrane, *Church's Confession under Hitler*, 222–23.
85. Grenz, *Theology for the Community of God*, 133.
86. Grenz, *Theology for the Community of God*, 392.
87. See Ferguson, et. al., *New Dictionary of Theology*, 585; and Grenz, *Theology for the Community of God*, 134–37.
88. See Thomas Aquinas, *The Summa Theologica*, in *Great Works of the Western World*, Volume 17, translated by Fr. Laurence Shapcote, and revised by Daniel J. Sullivan (New York: Encyclopaedia Britannica, 1993), 12–14. For useful works of these arguments and Aquinas' methods, see Anthony Kenny's *The Five Ways: St. Thomas Aquinas' Proofs of God's Existence* (London: Routledge & Kegan Paul, 1969); and John Goyette, Mark S. Latkovic, and Richard Myers, eds., *St. Thomas Aquinas and the Natural Law Tradition: Contemporary Perspectives* (Washington, DC: The Catholic University of America, 2004).
89. Grenz, *Theology and the Community of God*, 134.
90. Grenz, *Theology and the Community of God*, 134–35.
91. Grenz, *Theology and the Community of God*, 135.
92. John Calvin, *Institutes of the Christian Religion*, translated by Henry Beveridge (Peabody, MA: Hendrickson, 2008), 25.
93. See S. Paul Schilling, *Contemporary Continental Theologians* (New York: Abingdon Press, 1966), 24–25. This is an argument prevalent among Confessing theologians and pastors, including Barth and Brunner. See Heinz Zahrnt, *The Question of God: Protestant Theology in the 20th Century* (New York: Harcourt, Brace 7 World, 1969), 62.
94. Grenz, *Theology for the Community of God*, 135.
95. Paul Tillich, *A History of Christian Thought: From Its Judaic and Hellenistic Origins to Existentialism*, edited by Carl Braaten (New York: Harper and Row, 1968),

244; see also Paul Scott Wilson, *A Concise History of Preaching* (Nashville: Abingdon, 1992), 89.

96. Grenz, *Theology for the Community of God*, 136.

97. Grenz, *Theology for the Community of God*, 136. See also Arthur Cushman McGiffert, *Protestant Thought Before Kant* (London: Duckworth, 1911), 195–210.

98. Millard Erickson, *Christian Theology*, Second Edition (Grand Rapids, MI: Baker, 1998), 180.

99. Koppel Pinson, *Pietism as a Factor in the Rise of German Nationalism* (New York: Octagon Books, Inc., 1968), 15.

100. See Pinson, *Pietism*, 15–17; and Liah Greenfeld, *Nationalism, Five Roads to Modernity* (Cambridge, MA: Harvard University Press, 1992), 314–15.

101. See Kenneth Scott Latourette, *A History of Christianity, Vol. 2, Reformation to the Present* (Peabody, MA: Prince Press, 1997), 894–95.

102. This discussion is largely reliant upon David Blackbourn's, *History of Germany 1780–1918: The Long Nineteenth Century, Second Edition* (Malden, MA: Blackwell, 2003), 28; and also Greenfeld's *Nationalism*, 322–30.

103. Greenfeld, *Nationalism*, 328–30.

104. Jerry Dawson, *Friedrich Schleiermacher: The Evolution of a Nationalist* (Austin: University of Texas Press, 1966), 29–30.

105. Excellent treatments of Schleiermacher's life and work include Richard Brandt, *The Philosophy of Schleiermacher* (New York: Harper and Brothers, 1941); Jerry Dawson, *Friedrich Schleiermacher: The Evolution of a Nationalist* (Austin: University of Texas Press, 1966); Wilhelm Dilthey, *Das Leben Schleiermachers*, ed. H. Mulert, Second Edition (Berlin: W. de Gruyter and Company, 1922); Richard Niebuhr, *Schleiermacher on Christ and Religion* (New York: Scribner, 1964); and Martin Redeker, *Schleiermacher: Life and Thought*, translated by John Wallhausser (Philadelphia: Fortress Press, 1973).

106. Dawson, *Friedrich Schleiermacher*, 29–30. Schleiermacher, in his systematic theology, *The Christian Faith*, argues that "The common element in all howsoever diverse expressions of piety, by which these are conjointly distinguished from all other feelings, or in other words, the self-identical essence of piety, is this: the consciousness of being absolutely dependent, or, which is the same thing, of being in relation with God." Schleiermacher, *The Christian Faith*, translated and edited by H.R. Mackintosh and J.S. Stewart (Edinburgh: T&T Clark, 1989), 12.

107. Friedrich Schleiermacher, *On Religion: Speeches to Its Cultured Despisers* (Louisville, KY: Westminster/John Knox Press, 1994), 36–40; see also John E. Wilson, *Introduction to Modern Theology: Trajectories in the German Tradition* (Louisville, KY: Westminster//John Knox Press, 2007), 47.

108. Schleiermacher, *On Religion*, 101.

109. Schilling, *Contemporary Continental Theologians*, 19; and Zahrnt, *The Question of God*, 66.

110. Eberhard Busch, *Karl Barth: His Life from Letters and Autobiographical Texts* (Philadelphia, PA: Fortress Press, 1976), 223–6; and Will Herberg, "The Social Philosophy of Karl Barth," in *Community, State and Church*, by Karl Barth (New York: Anchor Books, 1960), 38.

111. Erickson, *Christian Theology*, 187–8.

112. The sociologist Peter Berger writes that this event marked the beginning of Barth's theology, which "was, at its very core, a thunderous *no* to all the assumptions and achievements of Protestant theological liberalism." See Berger, *Heretical Imperative*, 71.

113. Schilling, *Contemporary Continental Theologians*, 19.

114. Karl Barth, *Evangelische Theologie im 19. Jahrhundert* (Zurich: Zollikon, 1957), 6. The translation is from Alister McGrath, *The Making of Modern German Christology, 1750–1990* (Grand Rapids, MI: Zondervan, 1994), 124.

115. Berger, *Heretical Imperative*, 72.

116. Mark Linday, *Covenanted Solidarity: The Theological Basis of Karl Barth's Opposition to Nazi Antisemitism and the Holocaust* (Issues in Systematic Theology) (New York: Peter Lang, 2001), 15–16; Wilson, *Introduction to Modern Theology*, 176; also see McGrath, *Making of Modern German Christology*, 124.

117. Karl Barth, *The Epistle to the Romans*, translated from the sixth edition by Edwyn Hoskyns (New York: Oxford University Press, 1968), 126; Berger, *Heretical Imperative*, 75; and Grenz, *Theology for the Community of God*, 137.

118. Philip Melanchthon, *The Loci Communes of Philip Melanchthon*, translated by Charles Leander Hill (Eugene, OR: Wipf & Stock, 2007), 68.

119. Erickson, *Christian Theology*, 189–90.

120. Erickson, *Christian Theology*, 189.

121. It may be helpful to note that the translation of the German adjective *"evangelisch,"* is properly rendered in English as "Protestant," not "evangelical," which in the United States has historical and political connotations. Thus, in the United States the Lutheran and Reformed churches are mainline churches (not evangelical) while in Germany they are *"evangelisch"* churches (those that began in the Protestant Reformation). See Bergen, *Twisted Cross*, 5. Yet, for the sake of simplicity and common usage, I will render the Deutsche evangelische Kirche (DEK) as the German Evangelical Church.

122. Even before the formation of the PEL, pastors had formed loose associations against candidates of the German Christian movement in the church elections. One example is the *Jungreformatorische Bewegung* (Young Reformation Movement), led by Walter Künneth, Hanns Lilje, and Gerhard Jacobi. They rejected the German Christian movement's antisemitism and they sought a return to Lutheran reformation principles. See Helmreich, *German Churches under Hitler*, 142, 146.

123. Helmreich, *German Churches under Hitler*, 147.

124. Helmreich, *German Churches under Hitler*, 147.

125. Helmreich, *German Churches under Hitler*, 147.

126. Helmreich, *German Churches under Hitler*, 156; Barnett, *For the Soul of the People*, 63. See also Gerlach, who reports that 6,000 joined by the end of 1933. Gerlach, *And the Witnesses Were Silent*, 33.

127. Cochrane, *Church's Confession under Hitler*, 102.

128. Karl Barth, *Theological Existence To-Day!: (A Plea for Theological Freedom)*, translated by R. Birch Hoyle (Eugene, OR: Wipf and Stock Publishers, 2011), 114–15.

129. Cochrane, *Church's Confession under Hitler*, 103.
130. Helmreich, *German Churches under Hitler*, 149–50; Solberg, ed., *A Church Undone*, 249.
131. Helmreich, *German Churches under Hitler*, 149–50.
132. Solberg, ed., *A Church Divided*, 256–58.
133. Bergen, *Twisted Cross*, 17.
134. Helmreich, *German Churches under Hitler*, 151; and Gerlach, *And the Witnesses Were Silent*, 46.
135. Bergen, *Twisted Cross*, 17.
136. Bergen, *Twisted Cross*, 17.
137. Susannah Heschel, *The Aryan Jesus: Christian Theologians and the Bible in Nazi Germany* (Princeton, NJ: Princeton University Press, 2008).
138. Heschel, *The Aryan Jesus*, 69.
139. Heschel, *The Aryan Jesus*, 69.
140. Scholder, *The Churches and the Third Reich*, vol. 1, 553.
141. See Rolf Ahlers, *The Barmen Declaration of 1934: The Archeology of a Confessional Text* (Toronto Studies in Theology) (Lewiston, NY: Edwin Mellon Press, 1996); Barnett, *For the Soul of the People*, 53–56; Gerhard Besier and Gerhard Ringhausen, *Bekenntnis, Widerstand, Martyrium: Vom Barmen 1934 bis Plötzensee 1944* (Göttingen: Vandenhoeck & Ruprecht, 1986); Cochrane, *Church's Confession under Hitler*, 140–75; Helmreich, *German Churches Under Hitler*, 162–163; Jan Rohls and John Hoffmeyer, *Reformed Confessions: Theology from Zurich to Barmen* (Louisville, KY: Westminster John Knox Press, 1998); Scholder, *The Churches and the Third Reich*, Vol. 2, 122–71.
142. See Helmreich, *German Churches under Hitler*, 161–163; and Bergen, *Twisted Cross*, 12.
143. Helmreich, *German Churches Under Hitler*, 162; Barnett, *For the Soul of the People*, 4; and Schilling, *Contemporary Continental Theologians*, 22.
144. Eberhard Busch, *The Barmen Theses Then and Now*: The 2004 Warfield Lectures at Princeton Theological Seminary (Grand Rapids, MI: Eerdmans, 2010), 2.
145. Kurt Dietrich Schmidt, *Die Bekenntnisse und grundsätzlichen Äusserungen zur Kirchenfrage des Jahres 1933* (Göttingen: Vandenhoeck & Ruprecht, 1934).
146. Busch, *The Barmen Theses Then and Now*, 3–4.
147. Eberhard Busch, *The Barmen Theses Then and Now*, 5.
148. Barnett, *For the Soul of the People*, 55.
149. "The Declarations, Resolutions, and Motions Adopted by the Synod of Barmen," on May 29–31, 1934, in Cochrane, *Church's Confession under Hitler*, 239.
150. Klaus Scholder, *The Churches and the Third Reich*, 149.
151. Scholder, *The German Churches and the Third Reich*, 149.
152. Busch, *Barmen Thesis Then and Now*, 22.
153. Busch, *Barmen Thesis Then and Now*, 22.
154. Busch, *Barmen Thesis Then and Now*, 10–11.
155. Busch, *Barmen Thesis Then and Now*, 10–11.
156. Busch, *Barmen Thesis Then and Now*, 26.

157. "Barmen Declaration," in Cochrane, *Church's Confession under Hitler*, 242; see also Matheson, *The Third Reich and the Christian Churches*, 45–47.

158. Cochrane, *Church's Confession under Hitler*, 192–193, 206.

159. See Barnett, *For the Soul of the People*, 11; Green, *Lutherans against Hitler*, 181–83.

160. "Barmen Declaration," in Cochrane, *Church's Confession under Hitler*, 241. See also Schilling, *Contemporary Continental Theologians*, 22.

161. "Barmen Declaration," in Cochrane, *Church's Confession under Hitler*, 241.

162. Cochrane, *Church's Confession under Hitler*, 180–185.

163. "Barmen Declaration," in Cochrane's *Church's Confession under Hitler*, 242.

164. Bergen, *Twisted Cross*, 29–30.

165. Solberg, *A Church Undone*, 407–408.

166. See Doris Bergen's *Twisted Cross*, 1.

167. Schilling, *Contemporary Continental Theologians*, 22.

168. "Barmen Declaration," in Cochrane's *Church's Confession under Hitler*, 244.

169. Jantzen, *Faith and Fatherland*, 146.

170. Jantzen, *Faith and Fatherland*, 146.

171. Jantzen, *Faith and Fatherland*, 146.

172. Helmreich, *German Churches under Hitler*, 163.

173. Barnett, *For the Soul of the People*, 69; and Helmreich, *German Churches under Hitler*, 163.

174. Barnett, *For the Soul of the People*, 69; Conchrane, *Church's Confession under Hitler*, 140–145; and Helmreich, *German Churches under Hitler*, 161.

175. Barnett, *For the Soul of the People*, 69; and Helmreich, *German Churches under Hitler*, 161.

176. Helmreich, *German Churches under Hitler*, 161–62.

177. Helmreich, *German Churches under Hitler*, 161.

178. Helmreich, *German Churches under Hitler*, 161.

179. Helmreich, *German Churches under Hitler*, 164.

180. Helmreich, *German Churches under Hitler*, 165.

181. Robertson, *Christians against Hitler*, 10, 65. Unfortunately, reliable statistics on Confessing Church membership in all the German regions are not available, and so estimates of a cumulative total are not available.

182. Helmreich, *German Churches under Hitler*, 166–67; and Robertson, *Christians against Hitler*, 48.

183. Robertson, *Christians against Hitler*, 35.

184. Helmreich, *German Churches under Hitler*, 162; and Robertson, *Christians against Hitler*, 35. Robertson also notes that many congregations openly supported their pastors if they were disciplined or lost state sanction, and so they did not need to petition their regional brotherhood council for financial assistance.

185. Helmreich, *German Churches Under Hitler*, 175–88.

186. Helmreich, *German Churches under Hitler*, 167.

Chapter 3

A Fettered Gospel

On a boat out on the Wannsee on September 24, 1933, Martin Niemöller and pastor Fritz Müller, his colleague in Berlin-Dahlem, drafted a statement on behalf of the Pastors' Emergency League to prepare for the first national synod in Wittenberg just a few days later. They printed the statement and had it distributed and displayed on trees and bulletin boards for untold numbers of people in Wittenberg to see.[1] The document's fundamental argument was that the church faced a grave threat: the German Christian movement had unmoored the gospel of Jesus Christ from Scripture and instead twisted and bound the gospel to human law. The statement reads in part:

> It must not be that the gospel becomes limited or even inoperative through human law.
> The church office is greatly endangered as a result of pastors and church officials being persecuted because they are unable to follow the group currently ruling in the church. In this way, the office is subject to a lot of human pressure so that the servants of the Word are in danger of becoming servants of men and violating the law, "One must obey God more than men!" We demand from the National Synod that it ensures the full freedom of evangelical proclamation and its bearers through clear resolutions. It must not be that the church proclamation bends to human claims. In this solemn hour, as we must express this protest from a serious need of conscience [*aus schwere Gewissennot*], we vow before God, to apply all strength, that the message of salvation may be proclaimed among us purely and loudly as the revelation of the living God in Christ. We vow, this our commission as servants of the Word alone in the binding to the Holy Scripture, according to the understanding shown in the confessional creeds.[2]

This statement echoed a common sentiment found in PEL and early Confessing Church documents, that the gospel must not be bound to man-made formulas or directives, but that it be bound to Scripture. This term "binding" (*Bindung*) and its derivatives, as it relates to the gospel, appears in the PEL's four-point pledge sent in a general invitation to Protestant pastors throughout Germany on September 21 and here again in the PEL's statement of September 27.[3]

The pastors of the PEL were responding to an historic unmooring of the gospel from Scripture and to a human-made ideology, National Socialism. They recognized a dangerous contradiction in the German churches, that the word of God, which sets men and women free, had become bound or fettered to ideas, customs, and practices that undermined its power and influence. Furthermore, their use of language in this context, of the gospel being bound or fettered, alludes to the apostle Paul's words to his protégé Timothy: "the word of God is not chained" (2 Timothy 2:9). The gospel cannot be chained or fettered to a human source and remain the gospel; yet the German Christians were preaching a nazified gospel as if it were the same ancient message of the church. The PEL pastors claimed that the German Christians were preaching a false gospel, one fettered to blood and soil. At the same time, the PEL reiterated the sentiment of Paul in his second letter to the Thessalonians, in which he asked for prayer in his missionary journeys, that "the word of the Lord may have free course, and be glorified" (3:1). A gospel unfettered from human "chains" can spread freely.

And yet, throughout the history of Christianity, diverse barriers have prevented the "free course" of the gospel, including linguistic, political, cultural, and geographical barriers. Even theological barriers can impede the "free course" of the gospel, as Martin Luther's criticisms of the doctrines and practices of the medieval Roman Catholic Church illustrate. Paul's statement reflects the perennial concern of the church. By the early twentieth century, even before Hitler and the National Socialists came to power in 1933, the gospel had become bound in many German pulpits by the reliance on general revelation (over special revelation) and *völkisch* interpretations of political theology. The PEL pastors demanded a renewed focus on the man-made fetters the church had allowed to hold the gospel down.

While the previous chapter examined the divisions in the German Protestant churches over the question of divine revelation, this chapter and the next will narrow the scope to explore the practices and contours of homiletics in the German Protestant tradition, with special attention given to these man-made fetters. This chapter will begin by discussing various customs and practices in the German Protestant churches that will help provide context for an analysis of preaching. It will then turn to a consideration how elements of German Protestant theology and homiletics contributed to the reliance upon general revelation as the primary standard of authority in preaching by the early twentieth century.

More specifically, this chapter will argue that the pastor became the representative member of the congregation and its unifying agent, giving expression to the religious feelings, experiences, and impulses of the community. The theological doctrines of the orders of creation, the two kingdoms, and the dual revelation of law and gospel fostered nationalism among the clergy, created a new role for pastors as the spiritual caretakers of the nation, and inhibited criticisms of the state.[4] These theological doctrines presented pastors with sources of general revelation that had the potential to conflict with the special revelation of Scripture. Thus, when National Socialism advanced a racial ideology and vision for Germany that aligned with *völkisch* interpretations of general revelation, pastors either accepted the general revelation as valid or had to acknowledge a conflict and choose between their interpretation of general revelation and the special revelation of Scripture. The result of this fettered gospel was the fracturing of the German Protestant churches and the undermining of Scripture as the Christian authority in preaching.

THE TRADITION OF GERMAN PROTESTANT HOMILETICS

A discussion of modern preaching must begin with the towering figure of the Reformed church pastor and theologian Friedrich Schleiermacher.[5] As discussed in the previous chapter, Schleiermacher was influenced by Pietism and romanticism to reinvigorate the Christian faith after a century of the Enlightenment. This aim is evident in his approach to homiletics. Preaching, according to Schleiermacher, was the common expression of feeling in a faith community. The preacher is a representative member of the congregation, given no higher status or pride of place, who must seek to give voice to its harmony and unity. In one of his 1799 speeches to Christianity's "cultured despisers," Schleiermacher wrote,

> When one stands out before the others he is neither justified by office nor by compact; nor is it pride or ignorance that inspires him with assurance. It is the free impulse of his spirit, the feeling of heart-felt unanimity and completest equality, the common abolition of all first and last, of all earthly order. He comes forward to present to the sympathetic contemplation of others his own heart as stirred by God, and, by leading them into the region of religion where he is at home, he would infect them with his own feeling. He utters divine things and in solemn silence the congregation follows his inspired speech. If he unveils a hidden wonder, or links with prophetic assurance the future to the present, or by new examples confirms old truths, or if his fiery imagination enchants him in visions into another part of the world and into another order of things, the trained sense of the congregation accompanies him throughout.[6]

For Schleiermacher, preaching was a means to explore and intensify religious feeling in a community of faith. But more than this the pastor has the responsibility of leading his congregation in the experience of religious feeling, in navigating the direction the church is to take. Barth commented on this sensibility: "In his capacity as a living personality, with the common impulses as his starting point, he has to steer the bark of the congregation as it floats down the stream of feeling."[7] The pastor, then, exercises great influence in giving voice to the impulse of religious feeling and experience of his congregation.

Schleiermacher's influence in the German church and its theology was immense. For the next century his view of religion as feeling would dominate theological discussion and inspire pastors, theologians, historians, and philosophers to examine the means by which one may come to the knowledge of God. The German liberal theological tradition emerged from this context. In the German Protestant churches of the nineteenth century, religious authority was challenged; it no longer rested secure on the biblical texts. Pastors and theologians could read a variety of sources from which to cull religious authority, including reason, feeling, experience, history, and the biblical texts themselves.[8] The pastor had the difficult job of mediating all these sources of knowledge to his community of faith in a consistent and coherent manner.

Schleiermacher significantly impacted the field of homiletics. He elevated homiletics as field of study in practical theology, apart from the classical discipline of rhetoric, to which it had previously been relegated.[9] As a field within practical theology, homiletics "[sought] to identify methods for effective mediation of the essence of Christianity through preaching," drawing on philosophical and theological insights, and developing principles and practices specific to preaching.[10] Moreover, he argued that the state should support the discipline of theology (and by extension the sub-field of homiletics) in public universities because the state needed well-educated clergy in the churches as institutions that contribute to an enduring and peaceful society.[11] Schleiermacher's distinctive theological approach and his work in developing homiletics as a subdiscipline of practical theology considerably impacted German universities and Protestant churches over the next century.

For example, at the turn of the twentieth century, the theologian Jonhannes Bauer emphasized the centrality of the preacher in the pulpit, leading and edifying the congregation through his personal confession of faith.[12] In the 1912 edition of the encyclopedia *Die Religion in Geschichte und Gegenwart*, Bauer wrote the article "*Homiletik*," in which he asserted that the sermon is the "free, individual, living confession of faith and personal proclamation of saving faith."[13] While the biblical text provides the guidance for the sermon, the pastor has the freedom to ensure the text speaks to the situation of the congregation.[14] One can readily see traces of Schleiermacher's emphasis on the pastor's experience and personal dependence upon God in preaching.

The biblical text is preached and the text is key, but Bauer argues that the preacher's life experience in faith is the confirmation of the gospel's veracity. Bauer wrote,

> The sermon is speech, and it follows a single specific purpose, namely, to determine the will of the listener so as to decide for a religious-moral idea, feeling, or act ... The effect is not an externally manageable action, but rather the production of the attitude, the feelings, that is, the edification. It is based, by the way, in every speech that seeks moral purposes with moral means, on the preacher's personal conviction of the truth of the matter he represents, the gospel.[15]

The idea is an old one, that living faith is best exemplified in a blessed Christian life. The pastor's confession is a testimony to God's benevolence and faithfulness, and as such, must be shared with the community of faith for the benefit of all. Thus, as one of the most trusted and authoritative members of the faith community, the preacher had considerable influence in applying his personal views and convictions to the life of the congregation. A potential problem, as Barth commented in his own treatment of homiletics, was that this reliance upon a personal confession of faith in the pulpit is a poor and potentially dangerous substitute for biblical exegesis and a coherent theology.[16]

The stress on religious feeling and experience was to encourage an act of the will, a decision of spiritual significance. Eugen Sachsse's book, *Evangelische Homiletik: Ein Leitfaden für Studierende und Kandidaten* (1913), a homiletic textbook for seminarians, charged pastors to edify congregations by appealing to feeling and will. The aim of the sermon is not simply to arouse religious feeling, but to direct the feeling to significant action:

> Also, the sermon has a practical purpose, but it does not want to bring about an isolated decision, but to promote the Christian life, i.e., to edify. The essence of Christianity is renunciation from sin and faith in the grace of God in Christ. "Believe and turn unto the gospel." That was the goal of all the preaching of Christ (Mark 1:15). This decision should be caused by recognition and feeling, set into motion through the message: the kingdom of God is at hand! All spiritual life exists in recognition, feeling, will; these three functions can never be separated. In particular, the religious life takes place in all three functions; it seizes the entire person in all its power ... This is the edification of Christians; it is the aim of every sermon. The sermon is to promote the recognition, intensify the feeling, and determine the will.[17]

The sermon is to serve as the spark to ignite religious feeling that compels the individual's will to action—to repentance and the cultivation of the Christian life. Sachsse argued that the resourceful preacher will appeal not only to reason in expounding the scriptural text, but to "the entire person," including feeling and the will, to encourage men and women to repent of their sins and believe in the work of God in Christ. He offered advice about how to best communicate and appeal to the whole person in the context of a community of faith, where the language, symbolism, and imagery of the sermon and sanctuary appeal not simply to reason or Scripture, but to feeling and the will.

While Protestant pastors appealed to the whole human person in emphasizing feeling, experience, and will, they by and large did not appeal with equal measure to both testaments in the Christian Scripture. There was an assumption that preaching was necessarily based primarily upon the New Testament. The prevailing belief was that the Hebrew Bible was an inadequate and inferior portion of Scripture that lacked the clear gospel message proclaimed in the New Testament.[18] Its value for the church relied upon a Christological interpretation. Scott Gibson offers several reasons why these assumptions were prominent in the early twentieth century, not only in Germany but in Christian churches in the West more generally: first, biblical Hebrew is perceived to be a more difficult language to master than biblical Greek; second, the culture of the Hebrew Bible is perceived to be more foreign than that of the New Testament; third, pastors had not appreciated how dependent the New Testament is upon the Hebrew Bible; and fourth, pastors assumed that the advent of Christ precluded the need for the Hebrew Bible.[19]

The neglect of the Hebrew Bible in Christian preaching reflects a failure to appreciate the Hebrew Bible on its own terms. Moreover, it reflects a judgment of the perceived inadequacy of the Hebrew Bible, not only in content, as it presents "only" the Old Testament, but also for the edification and sanctification of the Christian community of faith. Given the perceived inadequacies, it prevented engagement with Jewish scholars, past and present, on Jewish interpretations of the Hebrew Bible, because of the perception that Christians do not have anything to learn from Jewish interpretations (as they are presumably working with an inferior source).

If preaching meant proclaiming the gospel of Jesus Christ, then pastors were left wondering what to make of the Hebrew Bible. If a preacher neglected the preaching of the Hebrew Bible from a conviction of its lesser or even insignificant status in the canon, then how could the Church make sense of its sacred history? Very few of the homiletic texts reviewed in the present discussion specifically treat the Hebrew Bible as a source base for sermons. This in itself is telling. It may indicate a lack of appreciation of the Hebrew Bible texts and an unwillingness to engage in a period of sacred history common to Jews and Christians.

This is not to suggest that pastors did not preach from the Hebrew Bible—they certainly did. But as will be discussed in the next chapter, Confessing

Church pastors recognized among their fellow pastors a lack of use and appreciation for Hebrew Bible, which they sought to correct.

One rare example of a theologian specifically treating the preacher's use of the Hebrew Bible at length is Christian Palmer in his classic work *Evangelische Homiletik*, a 500-page magnum opus on homiletics. After briefly serving as a pastor, Palmer became a professor of practical theology at the University of Tübingen. The book was published in 1842, and went through six editions by 1887; it was used as a standard text in seminaries throughout the second half of the nineteenth century.[20] Palmer reiterates the common theme in Christian homiletics that the Hebrew Bible is not sufficient to present the gospel in a sermon, but that the Christian preacher must depend upon the preaching of the New Testament. If the pastor does preach from the Hebrew Bible, he must find Christ in the text to demonstrate the continuity of God's blessing from the time of Adam to the advent of Jesus in Bethlehem.[21]

> But it is the nature of all God's actions among human beings that he gradually goes to work, and so also is the appearance of Christ not like a sudden meteor illuminated in the history of the world, but it is like the starting point of a new series . . . This preliminary revelation [i.e., the Hebrew Bible] is itself, in turn, the Word of God, but not independently, for its sufficiency has its focus outside itself, in the New Testament.[22]

According to Palmer, the Hebrew Bible is not to be understood in its own terms. The Hebrew Bible is to be interpreted according to the Christian understanding. Again, this is not new to homiletics, only a clear example of this style of interpretation presented in a standard mid-nineteenth century textbook on preaching for seminarians.

Despite this view of the Hebrew Bible as incomplete and only useful in relation to the New Testament, Palmer emphasizes that this sacred text is God's revelation to humanity, and as such, it ought to be cherished. He writes, "We give [sermons] with a special love, as we very much wish that every opportunity in our churches should be used to better exploit the treasure of the Hebrew Bible to the benefit of the community."[23] Christian pastors are to commonly use the text, treasure its riches, and profit from its lessons. The problem is that Palmer seems to present mixed messages here: the Hebrew Bible is valuable, but it is inferior to the New Testament. The preacher is left to wonder why he should rely on the Hebrew Bible at all.

Thus, at the turn of the twentieth century the German Protestant pastor faced considerable challenges to the authority of the Christian Scripture in preaching, not the least of which was the low valuation of the Hebrew Bible. The preacher had at his disposal various other sources upon which to base any given sermon, including feeling, experience, reason, and a religious reading of history.

Stepping back for perspective, as Mark Correll argues, one may distinguish two broad groups of pastors and theologians in the German Protestant churches in the late-nineteenth and early twentieth century in terms of their primary source of religious authority.[24] "Believing" pastors and theologians were religiously conservative (though not necessarily politically conservative) and relied upon Scripture as the authoritative source for life and faith. This group was clearly on the defensive in nineteenth-century Germany as biblical criticism made considerable historical and literary contributions to the study of Scripture as a collection of ancient religious documents. In contrast, "critical" theologians and pastors occupied the liberal side of the religious spectrum, "[perceiving] human reason as the ultimate arbiter of the Bible's enduring value for Christians."[25] "Critical" Christians made tremendous inroads into theology school faculties and the pastorate in the nineteenth century. Given the deep roots of the Protestant tradition in the German Empire, this conflict over religious authority had tremendous implications. Correll asserts, "The Christians of Germany, the land of Luther, faced a crisis of modernity that threatened Germany's whole structure from the universities and the political establishment all the way to the parish congregation."[26]

THE BIBLICAL TEXT AND PRACTICAL APPROACHES TO PREACHING

Before examining the theological fetters that bound the gospel as the Nazi Party gained influence in Germany, a few words are in order about pastors' practical approaches to preaching by the early twentieth century. Pastors had some latitude in regard to selecting the sermon's biblical text. Their decisions about which text to preach on were informed by various factors, including the needs and expectations of their congregation, the goals of the church's leadership or elder board, the customs of the church, and the inclinations of the pastor himself. The pastor could choose which text to preach from or he could rely on the church's lectionary to provide the passage for the week's sermons. Provincial churches developed their own liturgies to help guide their pastors and congregations through the Scripture, such as the Old Prussian liturgy and the Bavarian liturgy. The lectionary would guide the congregation through the Bible in an ordered and thoughtful manner based on the season in the liturgical calendar. But a pastor could also select the biblical text himself. For example, he could preach a series on a given theme he considered important for his congregation, such as the Kingdom of God or the principle of Christian love.

But invariably the biblical text would be chosen from the Luther Bible (which was revised in 1912). The Luther Bible was the standard translation and had been for centuries. From the moment Luther's translation hit the presses in the sixteenth century, it made a profound impact on the daily lives of Germans, as Philip Schaff memorably stated:

> The Bible ceased to be a foreign book in a foreign tongue, and became naturalized, and hence far more clear and dear to the common people. Hereafter the Reformation depended no longer on the works of the Reformers, but on the book of God, which everybody could read for himself as his daily guide in spiritual life. This inestimable blessing of an open Bible for all, without the permission or intervention of pope and priest, marks an immense advance in church history, and can never be lost.[27]

Given the widespread popularity and devotional use of Luther's translation, its language and style so familiar to the German people, the German homiletical texts of the nineteenth and twentieth century take for granted that pastors will preach from it.

But there were other translations available. John Nelson Darby, an Irish-Anglo priest in the Church of Ireland who became a leader of the Plymouth Brethren, translated the Bible into German, along with his collaborators. His German translation became the Elberfelder edition of 1871 (revised in 1905 and 1927). Unlike Luther's more dynamic, sense-for-sense translation, Darby's approach was to translate the Hebrew and Greek text word for word, and thus, the Elberfelder text was a more literally accurate but awkward translation. This text would have mostly been used in conservative, free-church groups, such as the Brethren. The third option available to German Protestant pastors was Franz Eugen Schlachter's translation of 1905, published in Bern, Switzerland. Influenced by the holiness movement (within Methodism), Schlachter served as a preacher in the Evangelische Gesellschaft in Bern. While the Elberfelder and Schlachter translations had their advantages, neither could usurp the revised Luther Bible as the standard translation in the German Protestant pulpit. Naturally, as pastors preached, they would themselves translate, exegete, and elucidate key passages to instruct their congregants.

By the 1930s, the length of a typical sermon in German Protestant churches generally lasted between 20–30 minutes, though time limits were also influenced by the liturgical constraints of the worship service.[28] The sermon length also varied between sermon types. For example, a wedding or funeral sermon would typically be shorter than the average Sunday morning sermon. Yet, pastors ultimately decided on how long a sermon should last. Karl Barth, for example, simply advised his theology students that a sermon lasts however long it takes to get the message across.²⁹ However, the pastor must always contend with the varied attention spans of his congregants.

In understanding the popular preaching trends in the three decades immediately before Hitler and the Nazis came to power, the work of Angela Dienhart Hancock is particularly insightful. At the turn of the twentieth century, pastors acknowledge a need to preach to the real needs of the modern Christian.³⁰ The theologian Friedrich Niebergall popularized this kind of preaching by posing the question, "How do we preach to modern people?"³¹ This new trend emphasized the honest application of "lived Christianity" to the reality of the modern world; it meant limiting the exegesis of the biblical text from the pulpit, while instead elaborating on how the text connects to modern life.³² At the same time, preachers responded to demands for "special" sermons on a variety of modern topics, including factory work and housing issues, as well as sermons prepared for specific audiences, such as academics and the working class.³³ Hancock asserts that this approach "was not just the preoccupation of the liberal ('culture Protestant') majority, but of many orthodox Lutheran and pietist pastors as well."³⁴

When the First World War erupted, the German Protestant churches responded to meet the needs of the people in wartime. Some *Landeskirchen* produced lectionaries as a standard format for their preachers to follow, while many pastors argued that they should have a "free text choice" given the special needs of the day.³⁵ In a nation at war, the preacher could give thoughtful expression to the experiences and tribulations of the *Volk*; thus, the subject matter of the sermon was not so much the biblical text but the experience itself.³⁶ The authority of the sermon becomes general revelation as expressed in the life of the *Volk*. The historian Wilhelm Pressel argues that

> The text as God's Word was no longer authoritative. In the war it no longer goes from text to life but from life to the text. It was no longer exegesis of the text but the text serves as a commentary on handling life. Neither the *"Sitz im Leben"* [setting in life] nor the situation nor the theological scope of the text still played a role here. The individual text was nearly opened-endedly adaptable. It was enough if the sermon somehow exhibited the possibility of formal contact to it.³⁷

The pastor would use relevant "individual verses or fragments taken out of context" to support his commentary on how to deal with life's problems.³⁸ Hancock contends that "the practice demonstrates that even when the Bible was included as a 'text' for the sermon, the real 'text' might well be unapologetically elsewhere."³⁹ This development illustrates the acute instability of authority in the pulpit in early twentieth century German Protestant churches.

Mark Correll's examination of wartime sermons of theological candidates in their three- to four-year vicarates after theological study in the university (and thus prior to ordination) reveals the prevalence of preaching based on a nationalist-infused theology. His research indicates that theological candidates widely used Adolph Stoecker's nationalistic preaching model of blessings and curses, and they interpreted the war itself as divine revelation.[40] Victory was inevitable for a faithful Christian nation.[41] Correll asserts, "The preachers told their congregations that the war was part of God's plan for the earth and for the German nation. The war had cosmic, eternal importance; it was fought as much with weapons of faith and prayer as with machine guns and biplanes."[42] Yet German pastors failed to imagine defeat in the First World War, and thus were at a loss to explain the war's outcome.[43] Correll concludes, "the church possessed no valid theology wherein Germany could lose without it being the result of hidden sin or without besmirching the justice of God."[44] This loss of credibility contributed to Germans leaving the church in the Weimar period.[45]

Nevertheless, the war shaped the way many German Protestant preachers understood their work. Their ministry was not only significant as spiritual caretakers of individuals in the church community—pastors' perennial task—but now also for the well-being and healing of the *Volk*.[46] Hancock succinctly formulates their message as follows:

> God gave Germany a tremendous opportunity in 1871 when he sent Bismarck to unify the nation, but Germany had not lived into its destiny. It had been corrupted by the ways of the West: materialism, secularism, individualism, factionalism, selfishness. Deep down, the soul of Germany—the strength of its *Geist*—was still there, but it could achieve its true greatness only if it returned as a Volk to its Christian roots and the moral code that went with it.[47]

Pastors viewed this work as *Völkseelsorge*, the moral caretaking of the *Volk*, broadening the scope of the pastor's care from the individual in the community of faith to the nation.[48] When the war finally ended, when Germans learned of their defeat and began the turbulent transition to Weimar democracy, pastors continued this task of care for the nation, working to ensure the German Protestant churches could be moral guides for national rebuilding.[49]

The practices and customs of early twentieth-century German Protestant homiletics shaped how pastors preached the gospel. The pastors preached according to the grooves or pathways of tradition: the bible translation; the expectations for sermon length, content, and purpose; the reliance on the New Testament over the Old Testament; and the sources of authority the people wanted to (or would) hear. But there were also theological elements that actively restricted or bound the gospel message, to which we now turn.

THEOLOGICAL IMPEDIMENTS TO PREACHING TO NAZI GERMANY

In the aftermath of the First World War, and in the context of the rise of National Socialism, three theological doctrines became the basis for many Protestant pastors' understanding of German nationalism and the meaning of the *Volk*: the distinction between law and gospel, the doctrine of the creation of orders, and the doctrine of the two kingdoms.[50] These doctrines informed the preaching of the pro-Nazi German Christian movement and were a key impetus to Confessing Church pastors' reformation of German Protestant homiletics.

Many Christians sincerely believed that with the rise of Adolf Hitler and the National Socialist movement, "God was now speaking a new message to man through German history."[51] Even many of the foremost theologians of Germany in the 1930s perceived God at work in the National Socialist movement and affirmed the view that God reveals himself in nature and history. Among the most influential of these scholars were Paul Althaus, professor of New Testament and renowned Luther scholar at the University of Erlangen; Werner Elert, a professor of systematic theology at the University of Erlangen; Emanuel Hirsch, a systematic theologian at the University of Göttingen; and Friedrich Gogarten, a systematic theologian at the University of Jena and later Göttingen. They were among the most influential scholars who advocated what historians commonly refer to as "political theology," the idea that obedience to God can be understood in political terms and that God's revelation can be comprehended through interpreting the historical events in a nation.[52] These ideas gained wide currency in early-twentieth-century German Protestantism.

While these theologians accepted general revelation as a valid source of divine knowledge, this does not mean that they jettisoned special revelation. Rather, they attempted to use both sources together to understand the meaning of history and the nature of God, especially in the context of the upheavals of Germany since the First World War.[53] In particular, the doctrines of law and gospel, the creation of orders, and the two kingdoms provided the theological lenses through which pastors could understand the state and *Volk* in terms of general revelation and then convey the derived theological "truths" to their congregations through sermons.

First, the distinction between law and gospel is a core Protestant teaching that German political theologians developed in new ways in the early twentieth century. Luther argued that God spoke two words: the law, which reveals God's commands, and which entail God's punishment for disobedience; and the gospel, which reveals God's promises and blessings, and which offers forgiveness and hope. The Augsburg Confession calls this doctrine a "special brilliant light" that helps to explain and interpret the Scripture. A clear distinction must be made between law and gospel, according to Luther, lest Christians think they can attain salvation through following the law. Luther's key insight is that God speaks his word through the law and the gospel.

In the 1920s and 1930s, German Protestant theologians such as Althaus, Gogarten, and Elert, among others, argued that one may understand God's revelation through the laws of human society. Gogarten, for example, argued that God established the state to ensure stability and peace, staving off chaos; the law of the state is founded upon natural law, which is then formalized according to the particular mores of the *Volk*.[54] Gogarten argued that law as revelation can be known through blood and soil and in God's ongoing providence in the life of a nation.[55] Jantzen elucidates the logic as follows: "If God was the sole guide of history and the unique force behind any existing political power, then political history and contemporary politics were simply ongoing revelations of God's law."[56]

According to this form of political theology, obedience to God entails political obedience. If God governs the history of the nation, then one can know the character of God and also God's will for the nation. Political theology is thus antidemocratic in the sense that the individual does not elect the leader, but rather the leader is chosen by God.[57] Scholder contends that "One cannot understand how Christians were ready to accept the flood of hate and vulgarity which *völkisch* antisemitism spewed forth without realizing that the beginnings of political theology had made the right of the *Volk* the embodiment of the divine will in creation."[58] The individual is called to serve and sacrifice for the *Volk*—devotion to the *Volk* is an expression of obedience to God. As Hancock argues, "The survival of the German *Volk* was a matter of obedience to the God who brought it into being for a special, holy reason."[59]

Second, and related to the distinction between law and gospel, the Lutheran doctrine of the orders of creation clarifies how one can understand general revelation in the God-given structures of human society. Luther argued that everyone belongs to and participates in the universal orders of creation through which the laws and commandments of God may be revealed. Each person lives in a variety of structures as a natural part of life; these structures include family, nation, government, and economic system, among many others. The doctrine of the orders of creation asserts that because God created the earth, "it stood to reason that traces of the Maker could be found in his creation" as well as in human history.[60] Furthermore, it stresses that God is still active in the world through these orders. For example, in marriage and the family, God ensures procreation; in civil government, God exercises his rule; and in the Church, God is "working salvation through human instrumentality."[61] Thus, one can know God's nature and will through participation in these orders of creation. As the theologian Carl Braaten argues, the orders of creation "means there is a double revelation of God. This duality permeates the whole system of theological categories and lies at the base of the familiar distinctions made, for example, between God hidden and revealed (*Deus absconditus et Deus revelatus*), creation and redemption, law and gospel, the two kingdoms."[62]

German theologians in the 1920s and 1930s contributed significantly to the doctrine of the creation of orders, notably, the Lutheran theologians Paul Althaus, Friedrich Gogarten, and Werner Elert, as well as the Reformed theologian Emil Brunner. Althaus, for example, argued that the state is created by God to unify and stabilize society, and thus, it must be obeyed; while natural orders are imperfect, participating in them allows one to contribute to God's ongoing care and providence in the world.[63] One can support the state, despite its excesses or imperfections, knowing that God instituted the state as a means to accomplish God's will in the world. Advocates argued that this position aligns with the apostle Paul's admonition in his letter to the Christians in Rome, a key text supporting obedience to the state:[64]

> Let every person be subject to the governing authorities; for there is no authority except from God, and those authorities that exist have been instituted by God. Therefore whoever resists authority resists what God has appointed, and those who resist will incur judgment. For rulers are not a terror to good conduct, but to bad . . . It is the servant of God to execute wrath on the wrongdoer. Therefore one must be subject, not only because of wrath but also because of conscience (Romans 13:1–5).

Through God's creation of the order of the state, society is blessed with peace, unity, and stability. By this line of reasoning, resistance to the state is, by definition, at cross-purposes with God's will for society. Thus, obedience to the state is the Christian's proper response. Jantzen convincingly argues that one of the key reasons for pastors, specifically in the areas of Nauen (Brandenberg), Pirna (Saxony), and Ravensburg (Württemberg), to support the "National Socialist political revolution" was "their theological predispositions toward obedience to the state and the importance of created orders such as blood, soil, and authority."[65]

One of the strongest fetters that bound the gospel in the German Protestant churches in the 1920s and 1930s was the understanding of *Volk* (people) and *Rasse* (race) as orders of creation. Althaus' *Leitsätze zur Ethik*, published in 1929, includes both alongside the state, the family, and the legal system.[66] Althaus argued that God created each *Volk* with its own biological and cultural characteristics, and that each should remain distinct and separate.[67] In the second edition of his pamphlet *Theologen der Ordnungen* (1935), Althaus wrote that one can see not only God's majestic creativity in the distinctions among the world's peoples, but also the need for ethnic segregation: "There is an antipathy that separates the races and peoples, and this intuition cannot be eradicated by consciously repressing it in the name of philanthropy or the brotherhood of humanity."[68] For Althaus, *Volk* is an order of creation that cannot be altered or undermined by political or ecclesiastical interference.

Indeed, the church's task of preaching has a critical role to play in the stability of the orders of creation. Luther argued that preaching serves the interests of the government by bringing the people of God together, thereby maintaining peace and order.[69] The sermon's unifying effect serves a political and social function, not simply a spiritual function.[70]

In practice, the doctrine of the orders of creation placed constrictions on the church's preaching. If the doctrine is valid, then presumably the pastor would be in no position to challenge or condemn a specific order, given that all orders are holy, despite their imperfections. For example, if the state is an order created by God, and one in which God's laws and commandments may be known, then how can the pastor condemn the state in a sermon? To do so would place special revelation (Scripture) in authority over and above the general revelation expressed in the natural order. In doing so, one would give ultimate authority to special revelation, a notion at odds with Protestant liberalism, as previously discussed. However, this conflict presupposes that one would perceive the two sources of revelation at odds in the first place.

Moreover, if one perceived a conflict in the orders of creation and Scripture, the Christian could only judge based on subjective reasoning.[71] Althaus' argument for resistance to the state is a case in point. In *Theologen der Ordnungen*, Althaus allows for opposition to the state if, first, God calls one to opposition (as Jesus instructed his disciples to leave their families to follow him), or second, if one's "implicit sense" judges an order.[72] As Ericksen points out, both are subjective bases to oppose an order: "If Althaus did not oppose the *Ordungen* as they developed in the Third Reich, it was because he did not believe they contradicted his 'implicit sense' of what the *Ordnungen* should be. Another person might oppose these *Ordnungen* on the same basis."[73] In short, the doctrine presented pastors in Nazi Germany with the complex task of evaluating orders such as the state, *Volk*, and race as presumed sources of general revelation. Before a pastor could express dissent or opposition to these orders in Nazi Germany, he must first acknowledge a conflict with Scripture, then decide Scripture must be the standard to judge the order, and finally evaluate the order using Scripture as the standard.

The third theological sense through which pastors perceived the state and *Volk* was the doctrine of the two kingdoms. Romans 13, mentioned earlier, was the basis for Luther's doctrine of the two governances (or regiments) under God, that of earthly rulers and that of the church, whereby the Christian owes political obedience to the earthly ruler and spiritual obedience to God and the church.[74] According to this doctrine, to be a good Christian meant to also be an obedient citizen. This doctrine became deeply rooted in the German states during the Reformation when Protestant churches left the Catholic fold and sought the protection of provincial rulers, who became their patrons and titular heads.[75] Thus, by the twentieth century, "Institutionally and ideologically . . . the German Evangelical Church was aligned with the state, a situation formalized over the centuries by law."[76] Even the Barmen Declaration of 1934, accepted by Confessing Church pastors of both Lutheran and Reformed backgrounds, did not explicitly challenge the two kingdoms doctrine, though it did remind the Nazi regime that God sanctioned the state's duty to serve the public, to keep the peace, and to stay out of church affairs.[77]

It is critical to keep in mind that Luther and subsequent Lutheran theologians did not argue that the two kingdoms are totally separate, as if the political realm had total autonomy from the rule of God.[78] The central idea of the doctrine is that God is sovereign over both realms, and that God has divided the rule of the world into these two realms, giving the leaders of each responsibilities of service for the well-being of human society. The church leader is called by God and commissioned with caring for the souls in his community of faith, to provide spiritual nourishment and guidance, and to train the new generation to live lives of faith. The political ruler is called by God to rule benevolently, to maintain stability and peace, and to bless the good and punish the wicked. Both the clergy and the rulers are called to serve, to be the hands of God's providence in the world.

But the doctrine of the two kingdoms presented challenges to the preacher who may have felt compelled to oppose the National Socialist government from the pulpit. According to the doctrine, a preacher who criticized a political ruler or government would transgress the boundaries of the two realms. The preacher would assert for himself the duties of service and guidance that God commissioned for the ruler. The preacher would then have no moral authority to challenge the ruler from doing the same thing to him by telling the church how to do its job of caring for the souls of the nation. At the same time, for a clergyman or ruler to interfere in the other's realm would be an offense against God for taking more authority than God had given. The doctrine of the two kingdoms placed a wall, as it were, between the church and the state in which the servants of each minded their own affairs.

These doctrines of political theology are evident in the sermons of the German Christian movement, revealing a fettered gospel in service of the state. For example, in one anonymous but obviously pro-Nazi sermon delivered at Christmas in 1936, in the town of Solingen, the preacher recalled the German winters of ancient days when families would gather on the winter solstice, attach torches to a tree in the woods, and take joy that daylight would last a bit longer every day.[79] The pastor compared the post-First World War years with the days before the solstice, when Germany was in its deepest, darkest days—then finally light broke and a leader appeared. The pastor proclaimed, "The Sun is rising ever higher, with our ancient German symbol, the Swastika, and its warmth surrounds the whole German people, melts our hearts together into one great German community."[80] True to the Nazi reading of history, the preacher affirmed that God had not "forgotten or forsaken" the German people.[81] God has clearly blessed the nation in appointing Adolf Hitler to lead Germany into its day in the sun. "Adolf Hitler," he preached, "is our benefactor," the one who has overcome "the winter night" to lead us to a new and brighter day.[82] Remarkably, there is no mention of the manger, Jesus Christ, or the Christian meaning of Christmas. The "good news" is the advent of Hitler as the leader of the German nation.

To give another example, Pastor Hans Baumgärtner from Nürnberg wrote one of six sermons and addresses by various church leaders included in a 20-Pfennig pamphlet called *Deutches Christentum*, published by a Nürnberg press in 1937. Among the titles of sermons and addresses are the following: "What Do We Owe Our Fallen?," "We Want to Be German Christians, Not Jewish Christians!," and "Jewish-Christian—German Christian?" Baumgärtner's sermon was entitled "Adolf Hitler—A Man of God," likely delivered shortly after Hitler's speech on January 30, 1937, commemorating four years of the Nazi state. The pastor argued that God has given Hitler as a gift to Germany and indeed the whole world, "for the fight of light against the darkness." Hitler, Baumgärtner asserted, is a "man of God" sent to uplift Germans out of the muck of "extorted guilt-lies [Schuldlüge], . . . impotent anger and mute despair," following German defeat in the First World War.[83] He called Hitler a "figure of light" (*Lichtgestalt*), and he called God the "Father of light" (*Vater des Lichts*).[84] One can infer a close relationship, then, between Hitler and God, as if Hitler is a son of God. This German Christian reading of history since 1918 infers specific knowledge of God: God sent Hitler as a gift to rehabilitate a devastated German nation; God is working in and through Hitler to bless the German people. But Baumgärtner transgressed the bounds of orthodoxy in stating that the German people place their faith in Hitler himself. Quoting Göring, Baumgärtner stated: "Our trust, our love, our faith in you [Hitler] is unlimited!"[85] He even attributed to Hitler characteristics properly belonging to God: "Happy Germany! Blessed people, who can call this man their own! How do you see in the scriptures? '[God] gives grace to the humble!'"[86] The evidence of sermons like these indicates that at least some pro-Nazi German Christians interpreted their nation's recovery after the First World War as a form of divine revelation about role and nature of Adolf Hitler as Führer.

CONCLUSION

Since the inception of the Christian form of the sermon in the first century, the church has used it to inspire the soul, educate the mind, and convert the heart. As Martin Luther once said, the task of preaching is "to feed the soul, make it righteous, set it free, and save it."[87] Despite the many different forms and occasions of the sermon and in all the Christian pulpits around the world, these are the elemental aims of the sermon. Looking to Jesus Christ as the model, the preacher seeks to convey the revelation of God to his or her congregation, confident that God will do a good work in the life of the believer. By definition, the sermon is an instrument to convey God's Word to humankind.

Yet, as the apostle Paul's Second Letter to the Thessalonians illustrates, the "free course" of the gospel is never assured; rather, most often the gospel is preached despite obstacles of diverse kinds that impede its path, including theological barriers. By the early twentieth century, the German Protestant churches had developed several customs and practices that, when Hitler and the Nazis gained popularity in 1920s and came to power in 1933, proved deeply problematic for their unity and identity. The reliance on general revelation—especially the reliance on reason, religious feeling, and the doctrines of the distinction between law and gospel, the orders of creation, and the two kingdoms—became a prism through which German Protestant pastors interpreted Hitler's rise to power. Yet as pastors and theologians attempted to formulate and preach nature's "speech," they could not agree on its parameters and boundaries as a form of divine revelation. The church had not developed consistent or agreed-upon rules to determine how nature's "speech" could be rightly interpreted, distilled, and conveyed to the Christian faithful. And thus, the standard of what is or is not general revelation is the pastor's subjective judgment.

Enter Karl Barth and the "new school" theologians, who attempted to reinstate a standard means of preaching God's revelation to the churches.[88] The next chapter will analyze the emergence of this "new school" of homiletics in response to the state of German Protestant preaching in the late-nineteenth and early twentieth century. Their approach sought to maintain autonomy in the churches, build a stable foundation upon which to preach the gospel, and stand in non-conformity and opposition to the Nazi regime and its racial ideology.

NOTES

1. Helmreich, *German Churches under Hitler*, 147 and 492.
2. Joachim Gauger, ed., *Chronik der Kirchenwirren*, Vol. 1 (Elberfeld: J. Gauger, 1934), 105.
3. Helmreich, *German Churches under Hitler*, 146–147.
4. Jantzen, *Faith and Fatherland*, 31; Hans Tiefel, "The German Lutheran Church and the Rise of National Socialism," *Church History*, Vol. 41 (3), 1972, 326–336; and Hancock, *Barth's Emergency Homiletic*, 162.
5. See Robert Ericksen, *Theologians under Hitler*, 11.
6. Schleiermacher, *On Religion*, 151.
7. Barth, *Homiletics*, 22.
8. John Wilson, *Introduction to Modern Theology: Trajectories in the German Tradition* (Louisville, KY: Westminster John Knox, 2007), 84–87.
9. Hancock, *Karl Barth's Emergency Homiletics*, 140.
10. Hancock, *Karl Barth's Emergency Homiletics*, 140.
11. Hancock, *Karl Barth's Emergency Homiletics*, 140.
12. Johannes Bauer, in his article, "Homiletik," in *Die Religion in Geschichte und Gegenwart; Handwörterbuch in gemeinverstänlicher Darstellung*, edited by Friedrich Schiele and Leopold Zscharnack (Tübingen: Verlag von J.C.B Mohr, 1912), 126; Bauer writes: "*die Predigt ist immer auch personliches Glaubensbekenntnis.*"
13. Bauer, "Homiletik," 126.
14. Friedrich Wintzer, *Die Homiletik seit Schleiermacher bis in die Anfänge der 'dialetischen Theologie' in Grundzügen* (Göttingen: Vandenhoeck & Ruprecht, 1969), 143.
15. Bauer, "Homiletik," 125–126.
16. Barth, *Homiletics*, 34–37.
17. D. Eugen Sachsse, *Evangelische Homiletik. Ein Leitfaden für Studierende und Kandidaten* (Leipzig: A. Deichert'sche Verlagsbuchhandlung Nachf., 1913), 138.
18. Scott Gibson, "Challenges to Preaching the Old Testament," in *Preaching the Old Testament*, Scott Gibson, ed. (Grand Rapids, MI: Baker Books, 2006), Kindle edition, location 176.
19. Gibson, "Challenges to Preaching the Old Testament," Kindle edition, location 176.
20. Wintzer, *Die Homiletik seit Schleiermacher*, 93–94.
21. Finding Christ in the Hebrew Bible would often be demonstrated through selective metaphors (e.g., the rose of Sharon in the Psalms), prefigurations (e.g., Jacob's wrestling partner in Genesis), and prophecies of the messiah in the prophetic books.
22. Christian Palmer, *Evangelische Homiletik* (Stuttgart, 1845), 238.
23. Palmer, *Evangelische Homiletik*, 248.
24. Mark Correll, *Shepherds of the Empire: Germany's Conservative Protestant Leadership, 1888–1919* (Minneapolis, MN: Fortress Press, 2014), 6–10.
25. Correll, *Shepherds of the Empire*, 7.
26. Correll, *Shepherds of the Empire*, 22.

27. Philip Schaff, *History of the Christian Church, Volume 7, The German Reformation* (Peabody, MA: Hendrickson, 2011), 341.

28. This range is based on my own reading aloud of sermon manuscripts. Wilifried Lempp criticizes the common rule of 30 minutes as arbitrary in his work *Zwanzig Thesen über zeitgemässe Predigt* (Stuttgart: Verlag der Ev. Gesellschaft), 1937, 25.

29. Barth, *Homiletics*, 122.

30. Hancock, *Barth's Emergency Homiletic*, 154.

31. See Hancock, *Barth's Emergency Homiletic*, 154. The question forms the title of Niebergall's book, *Wie predigen wir dem modernen Menschen?* (Tübingen: J.C.B. Mohr, 1909).

32. Hancock, *Barth's Emergency Homiletic*, 154–155. See also Wintzer, *Die Homiletik seit Schleiermacher*, 123.

33. Hancock, *Barth's Emergency Homiletic*, 156. See Bernhard Dörries, *Die Welt Gottes: Ein neuer Jahrgang Predigten* (Gottingen: Vandenhoeck & Ruprecht, 1911).

34. Hancock, *Barth's Emergency Homiletic*, 157.

35. Hancock, *Barth's Emergency Homiletic*, 159.

36. Hancock, *Barth's Emergency Homiletic*, 159.

37. Quoted and translated by Hancock in *Barth's Emergency Homiletic*, 159. See Wilhelm Pressel, *Die Kriegspredigt 1914–1918 in der evangelische Kirche Deutschlands* (Göttingen: Vandenhoeck & Ruprecht, 1967).

38. Pressel, *Die Kriegspredigt*, 36.

39. Hancock, *Barth's Emergency Homiletic*, 159.

40. Correll, *Shepherds of the Emipre*, 224–225.

41. Correll, *Shepherds of the Empire*, 227.

42. Correll, *Shepherds of the Empire*, 224.

43. Correll, *Shepherds of the Empire*, 238.

44. Correll, *Shepherds of the Empire*, 238.

45. Correll, *Shepherds of the Empire*, 239.

46. Hancock, *Barth's Emergency Homiletic*, 160–161.

47. Hancock, *Barth's Emergency Homiletic*, 161–162.

48. Hancock, *Barth's Emergency Homiletic*, 162.

49. Hancock, *Barth's Emergency Homiletic*, 163.

50. Jantzen, *Faith and Fatherland*, 31; and Tiefel, "The German Lutheran Church," 332–334.

51. Robert Ericksen, *Theologians under Hitler: Gerhard Kittel, Paul Althaus, Emanuel Hirsch* (New Haven, CT: Yale University Press), 86.

52. Hancock, *Karl Barth's Emergency Homiletic*, 69–70.

53. Ericksen, *Theologians under Hitler*, 25. As Ericksen argues, the acceptance of special revelation and the exclusion of general revelation did not necessarily prevent one from joining the Nazi Party. Some theologians who sided with Barth and the Confessing Church did initially support Hitler, such as the dialectical theologian Friedrich Gogarten; and others who accepted the view that one can interpret history as a means of knowing God were oppositional to Hitler from the start, such as the existentialist philosopher and theologian Paul Tillich.

54. Wilson, *Introduction to Modern Theology*, 21.

55. Jantzen, *Faith and Fatherland*, 28.
56. Jantzen, *Faith and Fatherland*, 28.
57. Scholder, *Churches and the Third Reich*, vol. 1, 105. See also Hancock, *Barth's Emergency Homiletic*, 70.
58. Scholder, *Churches and the Third Reich*, vol. 1, 107. See also Hancock, *Barth's Emergency Homiletic*, 70.
59. Hancock, *Barth's Emergency Homiletic*, 70.
60. Green, *Lutherans against Hitler*, 199.
61. Green, *Lutherans against Hitler*, 199–202.
62. Carl Braaten, *No Other Gospel! Christianity Among the World's Religions* (Eugene, OR: Wipf and Stock, 2000), 120.
63. Paul Althaus, *Theologie der Ordnungen, Zweite, erweiterete Auflage* (Gütersloh: Verlag C. Bertelsmann, 1935), 9–16; Ericksen, *Theologians under Hitler*, 100–101.
64. Niemöller, *Here Stand I*, 118. See Barnett, *For the Soul of the People*, 47–48; and also Matthew Hockenos, *A Church Divided: German Protestants Confront the Nazi Past* (Bloomington: Indiana University Press, 2004), 23 and 27.
65. Jantzen, *Faith and Fatherland*, 42.
66. Ryan Tafilowski, "A Reappraisal of the Orders of Creation," in *Lutheran Quarterly* 31, no. 3 (Autumn 2017): 291.
67. Tafilowski, "Reappraisal of the Orders of Creation," 291.
68. Translated by Tafilowski in "Reappraisal of the Orders of Creation," 293. See Althaus, *Theologie der Ordnungen*, 53.
69. Carl Braaten, "God in Public Life: Rehabilitating the 'Orders of Creation,'" in *First Things*, December 1990, accessed on April 8, 2022, retrieved from https://www.firstthings.com/article/1990/12/god-in-public-life-rehabilitating-the-orders-of-creation.
70. Braaten, "God in Public Life."
71. Ericksen, *Theologians under Hitler*, 101.
72. Althaus, *Theologen der Ordnungen*, 15–17. See Ericksen, *Theologians under Hitler*, 101.
73. Ericksen, *Theologians under Hitler*, 101.
74. Probst, *Demonizing the Jews*, 11–12.
75. Barnett, *For the Soul of the People*, 11.
76. Barnett, *For the Soul of the People*, 11; see also 47–48.
77. Hockenos, *A Church Divided*, 23 and 27.
78. This discussion is based on Lowell Green's analysis of the doctrine of the two kingdoms in *Lutherans against Hitler*, 200.
79. The sermon is reproduced in Conway, *Nazi Persecution of the Churches*, 364–365.
80. Conway, *Nazi Persecution of the Churches*, 365.
81. Conway, *Nazi Persecution of the Churches*, 364.
82. Conway, *Nazi Persecution of the Churches*, 365.
83. Baumgärtner, *Deutsches Christentum*, 11.
84. Baumgärtner, *Deutsches Christentum*, 12 and 14.

85. Baumgärtner, *Deutsches Christentum*, 12.

86. Baumgärtner, *Deutsches Christentum*, 12. The language ("Dem Demütigen gibt er Gnade!") is directly from 1 Peter 5:5.

87. Martin Luther, "The Freedom of a Christian," in *Three Treatises*, translated by W. A. Lambert and revised by Harold Grimm (Philadelphia: Fortress Press, 1970), 280. My aim here is to paint a picture of the theological world of the preacher in the Nazi period, to highlight some of the key theological terms, concepts, and movements that have critical importance for the Confessing Church. It is important to note that Christianity has a wide variety of expressions and emphases, and that this presentation is meant as a general introduction to the period, not as a conclusive statement of Christianity.

88. Old, *Reading and Preaching of the Scriptures*, 763.

Chapter 4

The Confessing Church and the "New School" of Homiletics

While the fault line between the Confessing Church and the German Christian movement rested on the question of divine revelation, their differences became publicly manifested in their preaching to Nazi Germany. Confessing pastors and theologians re-evaluated the demands of the gospel in this time of great social and political upheaval, and developed a new approach to homiletics.[1] Church historian Hughes Oliphant Old argues that a "new school of preaching began to spring up over the whole of German-speaking Protestantism," one that "[reaffirmed] biblical preaching."[2] He asserts that Confessing Church pastors "recast Protestant preaching in the course of their resistance," and that "[this] was probably the most important event in the history of twentieth-century preaching."[3] Though I would argue Old overstates their "resistance" in the churches (given Kershaw's categories used in this study), he correctly identifies a "new school" of homiletics, an unmistakable shift in preaching. I aim to contribute to Old's claim by distinguishing the key elements that set this new school of homiletics apart.

Even before 1933, the theologian Karl Barth recognized a shift in Protestant homiletical theory away from the dominant liberal theology of the nineteenth and early twentieth centuries and toward neo-orthodoxy. This was a move "that rejected the notion that historical investigation could provide absolute certainty as to the events recorded in scripture, upon which scholars had hoped to build secure theology . . . [and] it renounced the attempt to make man's experience of God a starting-place for theology."[4] I will examine the precise nature of these changes in homiletics that enabled the Confessing Church to utilize the sermon as a means of non-conformity and opposition.[5]

Given the Confessing Church's focus on the biblical texts as the single most important source of divine revelation, Confessing pastors considered preaching the fundamental means by which divine revelation is publicly shared with the community of faith. Furthermore, they took preaching seriously as the primary method for the institution of the church to influence German society under Nazi rule. The sermon for the Confessing Church became the most basic and common method of publicly expressing dissent and opposition to the German Christian movement and the Nazi regime, though regrettably an under-utilized method. Moreover, the sermon became a means for the Confessing Church to assert its identity as the "true" German Protestant Church, faithful to the Scriptures and the Reformation confessions.

This chapter will focus on the contributions of leading Confessing Church figures in developing a revitalized approach to homiletics in the 1930s, specifically treating the work of the Swiss Reformed theologian from the University of Bonn, Karl Barth; the Lutheran pastor and lecturer (*Privatdozent*) in theology at the University of Berlin, Dietrich Bonhoeffer; the Lutheran professor of practical theology from the University of Erlangen, Wolfgang Trillhaas; and the Lutheran pastor of the Leonhardkirche in Stuttgart, Friedrich Wilhelm (Wilfried) Lempp. In creating this "new school" of homiletics, these pastors and theologians underscored a few critical points that differentiated the Confessing Church approach to preaching. First, they stressed adherence to the biblical texts as the sole authority of the church in the ministry of preaching, as opposed to the centrality of the pastor as the mediator between the people and the biblical texts. Second, they emphasized that preaching is a means of sanctification in the world, a "weapon" to fight the spiritual battles of the time. Third, they argued that the sermon must be specially placed in the liturgy in direct relation to the sacraments of baptism (when possible) and communion because preaching must interpret and be interpreted by the sacraments. And fourth, they asserted that the church must affirm the value and common use of the Hebrew Bible in Christian preaching. Each of these elements contributed to a distinct approach to homiletics that set Confessing Church sermons apart from those of the German Christian movement. These characteristics gave Confessing pastors a foothold to express non-conformity and opposition to the German Christian movement and the Nazi regime.

THE "NEW SCHOOL" OF HOMILETICS

As previously discussed, Confessing Church leaders believed that the German liberal Protestant tradition became unmoored from the orthodox bedrock of the church, the biblical texts themselves. If one can sidestep the authority of the biblical texts by preaching from one's own experience, feeling, or social or political philosophy, then what happens when one's experience differs from another's? Many pastors grew increasingly concerned that the German liberal Protestant tradition left an open door, particularly to the German

Christian movement, to the preaching of unchristian and even anti-Christian claims in the service of the Nazi regime.

This "new school" of homiletics, often associated with neo-orthodox circles, asserted the reliability of the biblical texts for religious and moral truth as preserved by the church. This meant a return to an orthodox Reformation approach that emphasized the biblical texts as the ultimate source of authority for the knowledge of God. However, the neo-orthodox approach did not assert the authority of Scripture for empirical historical or scientific truth; it still made use of the advantages of biblical and historical criticism. Old argues that preachers of this "new school" believed that "Only this strongly biblical sort of preaching had the authority to denounce the apostasy of the day."[6] They became increasingly critical of the type of preaching that relied upon the preacher and his religious experience, feeling, and philosophies, and instead they elevated the importance of the biblical texts as the sole basis of authority in preaching.

Indeed, the phrase "new school" should be placed in quotation marks as Confessing pastors did not wish to provide a wholly new approach to homiletics, but to return to biblical preaching as affirmed by the reformers. Trillhaas argued that "People have believed in new and recent times that they can master emerging crises by going 'new ways,' to which the much-called preaching emergency belongs. But the ways of the church are indicated. It's not about going new and different ways, but to go the right way with new fidelity and new conscientiousness."[7] According to the "new school" theologians, the German Protestant churches had gotten into poor habits that have weakened their ability to meet the crisis posed by the National Socialist interventions in the churches. These theologians hoped to clean house and set the preacher's task in order.

The four distinguished Confessing Church leaders—Barth, Bonhoeffer, Trillhaas, and Lempp—re-evaluated the preacher's task of proclaiming the gospel in the context of Nazi Germany, and each disseminated his views in the classroom or in published form. These texts provide an excellent indication not only of how they taught and encouraged pastors to preach, but also how they wished to preach differently from their liberal Protestant predecessors. Barth, Bonhoeffer, and Trillhaas were all pastors and theologians who taught the subject of homiletics in Germany in the 1930s to young adults interested in pursuing a career in the ministry. At the University of Bonn, Barth taught two seminars on homiletics in 1932 and 1933, and his text, *Homiletics*, is a compilation of students' notes that he approved for publication in 1966. Bonhoeffer taught homiletics from 1935–1937, as the leader of the Confessing Church seminary in Finkenwalde. He was executed in a Nazi prison at the end of the war on April 9, 1945, and thus did not have the opportunity to revise or otherwise approve these lectures for publication.

Unlike Barth and Bonhoeffer, their colleagues Trillhaas and Lempp are virtually unknown in the English-speaking world. Trillhaas was born in 1903, and in his late 20s became a gifted professor of pastoral theology at the University of Erlangen. But he was also an early and ardent supporter of the PEL, and later the Confessing Church. As a result, he was held back in his career, along with several of his fellow Confessing Church colleagues, because of his opposition to the Nazis and National Socialism.[8] Trillhaas was not only a professor of pastoral theology at the University of Erlangen, but he was also a pastor at Trinity Lutheran Church in Erlangen.[9] As professor and pastor, Trillhaas published a homiletics textbook to meet the new pastoral challenges of his day. The book was entitled *Evangelische Predigtlehre*, and it was published in 1935 with the reputable Christian-Kaiser Publishing House.

Lempp was born in 1889 and began his work in pastoral ministry in Stanislau in 1919. In 1935 he began ministry as the pastor of the Leonhardkirche in Stuttgart, where he also served as the city dean.[10] His primer on preaching in Nazi Germany, *Zwanzig Thesen über zeitgemaeße Predigt*, was published in 1937 by the Evangelischen Gesellschaft in Stuttgart. The work methodically but concisely moves through twenty foundational theses for contemporary preaching, ranging in topics from the pastor's humble approach and the sermon's grounding in Scripture to the sermon's purpose of transforming the lives of the Christian faithful in godliness. Of the four homiletic texts I have found that were composed between the years 1933 and 1945, only Lempp's and Trillhaas' texts were actually published and made available to active pastors and seminary students in the Nazi dictatorship. Like Barth and Bonhoeffer, Lempp's and Trillhaas' works of homiletics demonstrate academic rigor as well as a deep engagement with the practical concerns of pastors who were tasked to preach weekly to their congregations.

It is important to keep in mind that three of the four—Bonhoeffer, Trillhaas, and Lempp—introduced their lectures or text after the Reich Bishop Ludwig Müller issued the so-called "muzzling decree" (*Maulkorbgesetz*). Inundated with criticism in the German churches over a variety of missteps, including his treatment of the respected Bodelschwingh as his rival to the office of Reich Bishop in the summer of 1933, the debacle at the Berlin Sportspalast on November 14, 1933, as well as the incorporation of church youth groups into the Hitler Youth in December 1933, Müller attempted to silence critical voices in the Protestant churches by issuing the "Ordinance for the Restoration of Orderly Conditions in the German Evangelical Church" on January 4, 1934.[11] This "muzzling decree," as it became known, sought to restore peace and order within the German Evangelical Church—and also between the church and the Nazi regime. It stated that anyone who stirred up controversy in the church in violation of the decree would be "automatically suspended from office and a formal disciplinary process [would] be initiated immediately with the aim of removing him from office."[12] The decree "forbad pastors from discussing current controversies during church services, specifying that church services were to be used only for preaching the Gospel, not for discussing church-political matters."[13] In this light, one can see Bonhoeffer and Trillhaas advising students to focus their sermons on the Scriptures not simply to emphasize the gospel message to bring spiritual renewal to Germans, but perhaps also to help seminarians abide by the law. This may account in part for why one does not see more common and forceful subversions of the Nazi regime and its ideology, as will be discussed in the following chapters. Even so, the theologians believed the gospel to be a powerful weapon against Nazi ideology, but it had to be wielded with care.

These homiletics lectures present four Confessing Church leaders' views on the preacher's task. Though one cannot argue they are representative of the views of all pastors in the Confessing Church, they are immensely important because they indicate how the leadership adapted its methods of ministry to confront the German Christian movement and a regime that appeared intent on "coordinating" the German churches or limiting their influence in Nazi Germany.

SCRIPTURE AS THE BASIS AND STANDARD OF PREACHING

The first main theme emphasized in the "new school" of homiletics is the authority of Scripture for preaching. No other pastor or theologian had more of an impact in this regard than Karl Barth. He began his homiletics lectures with an evaluation of the history of German preaching. He concluded that nineteenth and early twentieth-century homiletics can be characterized by an emphasis on the preacher as subject, as the mediating representative of the Christian community of faith. As previously mentioned, this was a problem that he believed contributed to the lack of precision of much liberal theology.[14] Christian pastors did not just have one source of revelation to choose from—the biblical text—but they had a variety in the arsenal of general revelation that they had to prioritize and employ in the pulpit. These sources could complement, challenge, or undermine the traditional authority of the biblical texts. For Barth, it was obvious to see how the pastor's theology could become less precise, perhaps muddled, and in some cases contribute to the loss of conviction amid the differing voices about the knowledge of the nature and work of God.[15] Barth argued that because of this problem, liberal theology consistently failed to proclaim Christian theology with scholarly rigor. For example, in a criticism of one of the leading liberal German theologians of the period, Johannes Bauer of the University of Heidelberg, Barth condemned the liberal Protestant approach that emphasized ethics at the expense of the clarity of theology: "We have here a theology that is totally superficial, verbose, ill-defined, and in the final analysis obscure."[16] Barth argues that German liberal Protestantism lacked the necessary precision to sustain Germany after the devastation of the First World War. A new approach was needed. He argued that the Scripture must be the sole authority in preaching the gospel because it alone had the spiritual power to redeem, to work in, and to sanctify those who received it.[17]

But even in the early twentieth century, Barth noticed a slight shift in homiletics away from this emphasis on the preacher as a mediator of divine knowledge. One example in this shift, he contends, is Leonhard Fendt's argument for a return to evangelical preaching in the tradition of the reformers. A pastor in Magdeburg and then a professor of practical theology at the University of Berlin, Fendt defined preaching as an act of worship in which an academically trained and religiously ordained Christian proclaims the gospel of salvation, the Christian *kerygma*:

> [The *kerygma* is given] to the people of [Jesus'] own day in their own terms, but without impairing or supplementing the substance of the *kerygma*, and to do this, not for pedagogic, aesthetic, or other important human reasons, but because the Christian *kerygma* is the Word to which the promise is annexed, that by this Word the Holy Spirit will awaken faith wherever and whenever God pleases.[18]

The preacher is not to add to the Scripture, alter its meaning, or change it in any way, but to proclaim it and let it do its work among the people. In stark contrast to the homiletics of Schleiermacher and subsequent German liberal Protestants, Fendt argued for a return to the Reformation dictum of *sola scriptura*, that the authoritative revelation of God necessary for salvation is found in the biblical text alone.[19]

Barth posited that a new dawn of homiletics had arrived, and he hoped to provide an impetus to reform the preaching ministry for the twentieth century. Preaching is the fundamental act of the church.[20] For Barth, "Preaching is simply the form in which the church's existence comes most clearly to expression"; it is through preaching that the church relives the words and actions of Jesus of Nazareth, inspiring its mission to the world.[21] And thus the church and its pastors must preach with conviction and understanding.

Barth argued that preaching is constituted of several fundamental elements, which if absent, undermine the efficacy of the sermon.[22] This model would become the standard of the Confessing Church. First, preaching conforms to God's revelation as contained in the biblical texts, and thus the preacher's religious experience, feelings, or philosophies are an irrelevance and distraction. Second, preaching occurs in the context of the church, and its mission is to bring the gospel to all nations, including Jews. This is its place and purpose. Third, God commands the proclamation of the gospel. Therefore, preaching is obedience to this commission. Fourth, individuals who sense God's "calling" will step forward to preach the gospel. Fifth, preaching is a heralding of the coming of God. Sixth, it is an exposition of the biblical texts, a carefully and conscientiously prepared statement of God's Word. Seventh, it is the expression of "free human words" spoken by one living by God's grace and the forgiveness of sins. Eighth, it is for those whom God has already acted in Christ. And ninth, the Holy Spirit is "the starting point, center, and conclusion" of preaching.[23] Taking all of this into consideration, Barth offered a clear and concise definition of preaching:

> Preaching is the Word of God which he himself speaks, claiming for the purpose the exposition of a biblical text in free human words that are relevant to contemporaries by those who are called to do this in the church that is obedient to its commission.
>
> Preaching is the attempt enjoined upon the church to serve God's own Word, through one who is called thereto, by expounding a biblical text in human words and making it relevant to contemporaries in intimation of what they have to hear from God himself.[24]

This is not a new definition of preaching, but a clear distillation of what preaching is and does according to the scriptural mandate.[25] As Peter Berger writes, Barth's view of the Word of God, "originally spoken to the prophets and witnesses of the past, is contained in the Holy Scriptures and is ever again made alive in the preaching of the church."[26]

The fundamental characteristic of this new shift in homiletics is a return to the Reformation idea that Scripture is the primary basis of the knowledge of God, and thus the foundational authority for the preacher. In fact, Luther's reformation movement in Germany took the name *Evangelische Kirche* to emphasize the belief that the gospel (*euangelion*) was the primary source of authority in the Christian life. In the Protestant tradition the sermon has served as the centerpiece of the worship service, and this is due to Christians' understanding of the gospel as constitutive of the church itself. The sermon, as a reading and exposition of the biblical texts to the community of faith, unifies the various elements of the worship service—it gives meaning to them: the liturgy, hymns, baptism, communion, and prayers.

Echoing Fendt, Barth was adamant that the biblical texts alone dictated the content of the sermon, not the ambitions of the preacher or the perceived needs of the congregation.[27] He categorically disagreed with Schleiermacher's view that the preacher must preach the gospel in accordance with the common religious impulse of the congregation.[28] For Barth, the preacher must allow his agenda and interests to fade into the background and let God speak through him. The preacher merely repeats the gospel; he does not create it or add to it. God speaks, and God reveals; the preacher is simply the messenger.[29] Barth argued that the task of preaching is fundamentally to "[preach] the past and future revelation of God, the epiphany and *parousia* of Jesus [his advent and return]."[30] It is through preaching that the biblical texts become God's Word, they are experienced as God's Word, and thus the church becomes the place where Christians can hear the voice of God. Thus, the preacher must be humble and sober, utterly dependent upon God to hear the needs of God's people.[31] The task of preaching, then, becomes a sort of prayer.[32]

Barth's homiletics reflects his position in the Barmen Declaration that the Scripture is the basis of the knowledge of God, thus rejecting general (or natural) revelation. While this position was accepted at the Barmen Synod by the Confessing Church, it concerned (and even alienated) many German Lutherans who believed that the doctrine of the orders of creation was essential to a Lutheran identity.[33] Barth conceived of God as "wholly other," that there existed an "infinite qualitative distinction" between man and God, and thus, that history and nature are not reliable sources for knowledge of God.[34] He believed that the German Christian movement and Nazis exploited this doctrine of creation to support their own racial and fascist ideologies.[35] The fact that many Lutherans joined the Confessing Church—Niemöller, Bonhoeffer, Trillhaas, and Lempp among them—indicates their acknowledgment of the problem of interpreting (and preaching) the orders of creation and their awareness that the German churches' response to the Nazi regime and the German Christian movement rested on a strong view of Scripture as the one unassailable and foundational source of the knowledge of God.

Barth's work of re-orienting German Protestant homiletics at the dawn of the Third Reich can hardly be overstated. Recently, the theologian Angela Dienhart Hancock has persuasively argued that Barth's new approach constituted an "emergency homiletic" in that he "began to imagine a theology free enough to call into question every ideology, every hegemony, and every claim to ultimacy that arose from the human sphere, even if it arose from the church."[36] Hancock goes so far as to argue that Barth's new approach made the classroom in which he taught "a place of resistance in Germany."[37] She contends that Barth's "insistence that preaching can only happen in the event 'church' [the preaching of God's revelation in a particular situation] must be read in contrast to the claims of the Political Theologians, i.e., that preaching should be directed to the *Volk* and *Volksgemeinschaft*, not the 'church' per se, especially not the 'church' defined in actualistic terms."[38] While I would argue that Hancock overstates the nature of this resistance in the classroom, given our distinctions between dissent, opposition, and resistance, Barth's homiletical approach certainly gave Confessing pastors sure footing from which to offer criticism of the Nazi regime and the German Christian movement. In effect, he taught future pastors how to carve out room in the sanctuary from which to challenge the regime and the German Protestant churches. The following chapters will reveal the extent to which Confessing pastors utilized this "emergency homiletic."

While Barth was the pathfinder of this "new school" of homiletics, Bonhoeffer also offered incisive instruction in the context of Nazi Germany. Bonhoeffer's homiletics lectures at the Confessing Church seminary in Finkenwalde from 1935 to 1937 emphasized the same central point as Barth, that Scripture is the basis of our knowledge of God, and thus the sure foundation of Christian preaching. Bonhoeffer's lectures offer insights into how a persecuted church trained the next generation of pastors to address the challenges of preaching under the Nazi regime. But before proceeding to Bonhoeffer's agreement with Barth that preaching must be grounded in the authority of the biblical text above all else, it will be helpful to provide the context of his lectures.

At the urging of seminarians, clergy, and presbyteries, the Confessing Church leadership in Prussia, known as the Old Prussian Council of Brethren, established five seminaries under the direction of five well-respected and trusted leaders of the Confessing Church: Pastor Herman Sasse in Elberfeld in 1934; Professor Otto Schmitz in Bielefeld-Sieker in 1934; Professor Hans Iwand in Bloestau, Prussia in 1935; Pastor Gerhard Gloege in Naumburg, Silesia in 1935; and lastly, Pastor Dietrich Bonhoeffer in Zingst, Pomerania in 1935 (the seminary later moved to Finkenwalde).[39] Bonhoeffer received a stipend of 360 marks a month and was named the director of the institution, a status that protected him against the requirement to swear an oath of loyalty to Hitler.[40] He was charged with directing the seminary and teaching twenty-three ordination candidates, mostly from Berlin-Brandenburg.[41] Unlike an academic setting, this preachers' seminary offered a communal atmosphere in which a variety of spiritual practices regularly took place, such as prayer, meditation, confession, communion, and even exercise, in addition, of course, to Bonhoeffer's academic lectures. This was an intimate environment in which Bonoheffer trained and mentored young men to go out and do God's work in the world.

In his homiletics lectures, Bonhoeffer agreed with Barth's argument that preaching is grounded in the authority of the biblical texts above all else.[42] He emphasized that the sermon is the activity of God speaking to the congregation the Word of life. The preacher then must step into the background as God communicates through the Word.[43]

> Our [the preachers'] speaking must become clearly independent of our own personal aims because God must speak through it. This inherent life of the Word

itself must be audible every time the Word is spoken. In the proper sense, God is the one who speaks, not us. We must make room in every speech for the inherent purpose of the Word itself.[44]

Of course, this is not to say that God is actually delivering the sermon, as if God is behind the pulpit. Rather, the idea is that the preacher speaks not his own word, but God's Word as revealed in Scripture.[45] The discernable distance between the preacher and the Word is crucial. Like Barth, Bonhoeffer argued that the Word is not the preacher's, but God's; the preacher is merely the messenger of the good news.[46] The purpose of the sermon, then, is for the congregation to learn this Word and remember it as they go out into the world.

Bonhoeffer forcefully argued that the sermon must be based on the one true source of all knowledge of God, that is, the biblical text.[47] The sermon is distinguished from all other forms of speech because it is an "exposition of a biblical text."[48] He argued, "Since the sermon is the proclamation of the Word of God, its whole promise rests upon the assumption that it remains *bound* to the scripture and the text [emphasis added]."[49] Note this language of being bound, or fettered. In the last chapter, one can see clearly that God's Word had become bound to political theology in the early twentieth century in a way that undermined its effectiveness and impeded its "free course" in Germany. Pastors in the Confessing Church commonly spoke of themselves as being "bound" to Scripture in their sermons. The preacher is bound to the gospel in what he speaks. As such, Bonhoeffer advised that the sermon should be based on a particular biblical text, a specific pericope (a unified segment of biblical verses) in most instances.[50] But when it is not, such as in occasional or holiday sermons, then it must still be based in accordance with the biblical texts. In sum, the preacher can rely upon no other authority than the special revelation in preaching to the community of faith, and therefore, the various other sources of liberal Protestant preaching—religious experience, feeling, historical interpretation, or political ideologies—retain no special authority.

Reiterating the same themes of Barth and Bonhoeffer, Trillhaas contends in his homiletics text *Evangelische Predigtlehre* that the pastor must preach based on the biblical texts, subjecting his own will to the demands of the gospel. He writes, "The Church of Jesus Christ lives from the Word and sacrament as the gifts of their Lord. It is never the church of free speech. As it is *bound* to the written word, so is their sermon *bound* to Scripture, explained and confirmed through the sacrament [emphasis added]."[51] Again, like Bonhoeffer, Trillhaas reminds the pastor that they and the church are bound to Scripture. He seeks to reorient the pastor to trust in the immovable anchor of Christian truth—the Scripture. Only in this way, he argues, can the the pastor faithfully preach the Scripture for a specific time and place to the Christian community of faith. "The commissioned human preacher is therefore only the secondary and indirect subject of Christian preaching."[52]

This reliance upon the gospel accounts for the relative stability of the Christian message through the centuries. As Trillhass argues, "The Christianity of preaching is thus decided in its content, not on the good will of the preacher . . . What a fate would have long ago overtaken the church if Christianity depended upon the sermon of the preacher's 'Christianity.'"[53] When Trillhaas published this work in 1935, he knew that the only way for the Church to serve as an unwavering and dependable institution upon which to rebuild Germany would be to acknowledge the gospel as its sure foundation and foremost authority.

Lempp reiterated the arguments of Barth, Bonhoeffer, and Trillhaas, stating that "God should come in the preached Word."[54] He continued, "Now, God does not stand in the pulpit, but the little man."[55] The pastor preaches the Word of God in humility and submission. Lempp memorably phrased the pastor's approach this way: "[The preacher] gives out what he has received. Our sermon does not go to the melody: In my view, one can say something like this . . . ' but according to the melody: 'Thus, says the Lord.'"[56] Singing to the right melody is one reason Lempp admonished pastors not to preach politics from the pulpit: "Let us leave the political speeches to the politicians!"[57] To drive the point home, Lempp also used the metaphor of the pastor as ambassador, not conveying his own message, but the Lord's message. The ambassador's success depends on getting his ruler's message to the people.

This theme of Scripture as the basis and standard of preaching was further expressed and developed in Fendt's three-volume textbook on practical theology, *Grundriss der Praktischen Theologie für Studenten und Kandidaten* (1938). Though not specifically a homiletics text, Fendt agrees with much that Barth, Bonhoeffer, Trillhaas, and Lempp argued. He stated,

> The content of preaching is thus the Bible. But the reason why the Bible provides the sermon content lies in God's kingdom efficacy, which began in Jesus from God, and will be accomplished in Jesus Christ from God; but even now is done, in "the between-times of faith," from God in Christ and in the Holy Spirit . . . Thus the sermon is not just a lecture about religious matters and religious people, not some instruction about the Bible, but service in God's kingdom efficacy; so the sermon must preach the content of the Bible (or in other words: Jesus Christ as the content of the Bible).[58]

Readily apparent is a distancing from any reliance upon feeling or religious experience in establishing the authority of the preacher or his message. The proclamation of the life, ministry, death, resurrection, and ascension of Jesus Christ has the greatest power to awaken faith in the despairing individual.

Furthermore, Fendt connects his homiletic with the necessity to live a right and just life according to the values and principles of the kingdom of God. The sermon is a message designed to instruct the Christian of the content of the biblical texts, that her or she may know and apply them in daily life. The moment a preacher departs from reading the biblical texts he compromises his service as a preacher of the kingdom of God.

The reliance on the biblical texts as the foremost authority in preaching is a crucial development in the history of twentieth-century homiletics because it significantly limits debates among Christians about the validity, relevance, or authority of a preacher's religious experience, feeling, views of natural theology, and providential interpretations of history. Confessing Church homileticians called for conformity, simplicity, and clarity in preaching so that Christians sitting in the pews Sunday after Sunday did not have the opportunity to question or challenge a preacher's conclusions that are based on mere feeling or opinion. This approach was particularly important in a period of political and ecclesiastical struggle. The approach effectively united Christians on the basic and authoritative source that all Christians, of whatever stripe, agree is revelation—though of course, they may still argue about its interpretation.

THE SERMON AS INSTRUMENT OF SANCTIFICATION

The second key theme in the "new school" of homiletics is that the sermon must be understood as an instrument of sanctification—in short, God works through the sermon to make people holy.[59] This theme intensifies in its expression from 1933 to 1937, the dates of our sources, possibly indicating increasing concern in the context of Nazi Germany and the persecution of the churches. In Barth's 1932–1933 lectures, he argued that preaching is an act of God that brings light into the world and that transforms people. The sermon is an instrument of change. He put it like this:

> A human being becomes a hearer of the Word of God: This is our sanctification. The human being, the preacher, the listener—they are not left to themselves. They still are what they were before. But they are not left in peace . . . Anything that we might say here about the power of God's Word to create anew is much too weak in view of the rest and unrest that are present when in faith a human being may grasp the calling of Jesus Christ.[60]

This idea that God acts in the sermon to sanctify Christians is not new in the history of the Christian tradition.[61] The emphasis is that God alone is the subject—again, the preacher fades into the background. God is the one who sanctifies the human being. The hearer must, in turn, make a decision to step out in faith. Preaching, then, becomes an activity that seeks to change people for the better, to change systems and institutions for the better.[62] As Barth puts it, "[Preaching] must stand under the insight that all things must change."[63] For Confessing Church pastors, preaching is an act of hope in a world that desperately needs it.

In *Theological Existence To-day*, published in 1933, concurrently with his homiletics lectures, Barth elaborates on the power of the preached Word to disrupt and transform the world. He writes, "[T]he Word of God clears out of the way everything that might oppose, so that it will triumph over us and all other opponents, for the reason that it has triumphed already, once for all, over us and on our behalf, and over all its other opponents."[64] Remarkably, Barth acknowledges the power of this Word to "triumph" not only over opponents—such as members of the German Christian movement—but also over "us." Thus, the pastor can expect the mere preaching of the gospel, pure and true, to positively impact the world around him—and even himself.

Barth's insight underscores the problem of the binding Scripture. If the Scripture is bound to the ideologies or politics of the day, or to the thoughts, feelings, and experiences of the pastor, then it loses its power of sanctification—as it becomes an adulterated gospel. Furthermore, if the pastor were to bind the Scripture in this way, he would claim power over it, to use it as an instrument of his will in the world, rather than acknowledge its power over him, to transform him and his congregation into Christlikeness. This insight reveals a conflict over power dynamics at work in the German churches, in terms of the pastor's relationship to Scripture: while the German Christians wished to use the gospel to advance the National Socialist ideology for national and spiritual renewal, Confessing Christians wished to unleash the gospel as a power *unto itself* to achieve spiritual regeneration.

The purpose of the sermon was not to express the values of the *Volk*; it was not to unify the *Volk*; and it was not to preserve, maintain, or reinforce the identity of the *Volksgemeinschaft*. These are the aims of the German Christian movement. Rather, the purpose of the sermon was to educate, inspire, and convert Christians to become more like Christ, to become better disciples.[65] In working toward the sanctification of the Christian, the Word must, as Barth said, "clear out of the way everything that might oppose," including national, racial, or personal interests.[66] In contrast to the efforts of the German Christian movement, the work of the Word was to align hearts to the Kingdom of God and its values, not the Third Reich and its ideology.

Trillhaas elaborated on the same point. He asserted that "the sermon is a power over hearts."[67] It has the power to challenge people where they stand in the world, to change the way that people think and behave. Significantly, Trillhaas pointed out that the sermon is thus not only for the continuing sanctification of Christians but also for non-Christians as well. "The word from the pulpit, supported in the mouth of an eloquent preacher by manifold influences on the mind in the form of music and ceremonies, can also influence irreligious people . . . The sermon is a public power. This power is placed in the hands of the pastor."[68] The image Trillhaas painted is that of a pastor in a spiritual struggle, confronted by Christians and non-Christians alike who must undergo a change of heart—a process of renewal in a time of crisis. The pastor must understand the power of the sermon if he is to use it effectively in this struggle.

Likewise, Bonhoeffer argued that the preacher must rely upon the biblical text to act, to sanctify the lives of those who hear, and to battle the forces of evil in the world. The pastor cannot rely on his own experiences or wisdom, but must engage in "the proclamation of the Word and the warning of the godless."[69] He writes, "Beyond that we cannot say anything, and we cannot force anything to happen either. We must leave everything up to the Word."[70] The preacher steps into the background to allow the freedom of the Word to emerge as the agent of change. Bonhoeffer argued that the work of this Word should be understood in terms of spiritual warfare, as if the preacher himself is engaged in combating evil from behind the pulpit: "As a witness to Christ, the sermon is a struggle with demons. Every sermon must overcome Satan. Every sermon fights a battle."[71] Thus, the sermon becomes a weapon against evil, apathy, ignorance, and aggression.

It is important to remember that Confessing Church pastors preached these sermons in a context in which all social and cultural institutions had been coordinated to the Nazi regime. Nazi-approved messages saturated German society through the radio, cinema, newspapers, and books. Richard Evans argues that by 1937–1938, "virtually all the organs of opinion-formation in German society had been taken over by Goebbels and his Propaganda Ministry, co-ordinated, purged of real and potential dissenters, Aryanized and brought under ideological, financial and administrative control."[72] That is, all except for the Confessing Church, which maintained its institutional and theological autonomy, thus becoming one of the very few places in Nazi Germany where public opinion could be debated and shaped. In this context Bonhoeffer and other like-minded pastors used sermons as a way to confront or oppose the Nazi propaganda machine, to "fight a battle" using the resources of the Christian tradition against National Socialist ideology.

Lempp also strongly asserted the importance of the sermon as a weapon in an age of spiritual warfare. In fact, this is one reason the preacher must rely on Scripture as the basis and standard for the sermon: the power of the sermon is based on God's Word. The preacher ought to preach with a seriousness of manner and intent, cognizant that his message is the most important message that his audience will hear in the hubbub of daily life. But perhaps most important, Lempp asserted that the pastor does not simply preach against worldly terminology or a church political party, but against an "anti-god power" (*gottfeindliche Macht*) in the atmosphere.[73] "Every sermon," he wrote, "means a battle against the present 'Prince of the power in the air,' who must be defeated."[74] This statement is evidence that Lempp believed spiritual warfare was taking place in Nazi Germany at this time, and that the sermon was an instrument or weapon to engage the spiritual powers. Lempp's use of the epithet, "Prince of the power in the air," is a direct quotation from the apostle Paul's letter to the Ephesians: "You were dead through the trespasses and sins in which you once lived, following the course of this world, following the [prince] of the power of the air, the spirit that is now at work among those who are disobedient" (2:1–2). Though the name Satan is not mentioned, this is the usual interpretation. Lempp believed evil forces were at work in the world and that the preacher is uniquely equipped to combat evil by the authority of the biblical texts through the practice of preaching.

But Lempp does not simply name the enemy. He also calls the pastor to fight. "The eschatological horizon of the Bible is again apparent . . . And in the middle of this decision-making struggle, we stand in every sermon . . . We are only small soldiers in this great struggle of supernatural powers. But every time we enter the pulpit, we stand directly on the front, indeed, we leave the protective trench, and on the orders of our great commander we go into the storm."[75] The pastor has a duty, and what is more, he has a powerful weapon with which to fight. While the sermon is the offensive weapon, pastors also have defensive tools at their disposal. Lempp advised pastors to use the "whole armor of God" that St. Paul mentions in his letter to the Ephesians, "For our struggle is not against enemies of blood and flesh, but against the cosmic powers of this present darkness, against the spiritual forces of evil in the heavenly places." Pastors must arm themselves with the "belt of truth," the "breastplate of righteousness," the "shield of faith," the "helmet of salvation," and the "sword of the spirit" (Ephesians 6:10–17). In periods of conflict throughout the history of the church, this language is not unusual or unique, but it reflects a mentality that the biblical texts and its gospel message are the greatest weapons of offense and defense that the Christian can utilize. Finally, Lempp argued that the pastor must be "fearless, upright, and manly," a leader whom all can look upon for clarity, direction, and an example of a faithful and righteous life.[76]

It is no coincidence that this notion of the sermon as a sanctifying practice becomes conceived in more aggressive terms in the early years of the Nazi regime. The intra-church struggle and the Nazi regime's intrusions into ecclesiastical affairs revealed significant differences in how German Protestants understood divine revelation. Pastors and theologians such as Barth, Bonhoeffer, Trillhaas, and Lempp perceived a great spiritual danger for Christians in Nazi Germany, and they wanted pastors to understand the pulpit as a stage from which to wage spiritual warfare, a platform from which to shine a light.

THE WORD AND THE SACRAMENTS

The "new school" of homiletics addressed not only the content of the sermons, but also the organization of the Sunday liturgy. In early twentieth-century Germany, it was commonplace in the Protestant churches not to celebrate communion regularly in Sunday services.[77] Barth considered the lack of consistent celebration of the sacrament a significant problem in the Protestantism of his day. Barth stated, "The weakness today is that we do not administer the sacrament at Sunday worship. In practice baptism ought to come at the beginning of the service—in the presence of the congregation—and communion at the end. The sermon would then have its meaningful place in the middle between the two."[78] Bonhoeffer, too, lamented that "this Supper continues to be the exception in the services of our churches."[79]

The roots of this issue go back to the Protestant Reformation. The reformers sought to counter the Roman Catholic stress on the Eucharist as the focal point of the worship service by emphasizing the sermon. For example, Luther argued for the balance between the preached Word and sacrament in the divine service, one spoken to the congregation and the other given the individual.[80] Indeed, the historian Roland Bainton argues that in the early phase of the Reformation "the sermon was given a prominence place" in the service.[81] Thus began a shift of emphasis among Protestants from the Eucharist to the sermon in worship services. Kenneth Wieting argues that the principal reason for the diminishment of communion in Sunday services from the time of the Reformation was simply the limited number of congregants coming forward to receive the Eucharistic elements, especially in the countryside. He writes, "the opportunity to receive was adjusted downward to reflect the lack of communicants to receive."[82] One reason fewer congregants came forward to receive the elements is the renewed attention to their spiritual fitness, heeding the apostle Paul's admonition that "Whoever, therefore, eats the bread or drinks the cup of the Lord in an unworthy manner will be answerable for the body and blood of the Lord" (1 Corinthians 11:27). Thus, Luther argued in his treatise *Form of the Mass and Communion for the Church at Wittenberg* (1523) that communicants should receive communion frequently, but he also encouraged them to announce their desire to receive the Lord's supper and submit to private confession beforehand and catechetical examination once a year to prevent them from receiving the elements unworthily.[83] These recommended (not commanded) practices may have discouraged communicants from going forward to receive the elements on a regular basis. Moreover, Frank Senn has argued that the Protestants' most significant reform "in the mass [i.e., communion] was the insistence that when it was celebrated, it was to be received by the faithful. If there were no communicants to receive the sacrament, the mass was not celebrated."[84] By the early twentieth century the practice of celebrating communion on Sunday mornings was infrequent in German Protestant churches. The "new school" theologians in Nazi Germany perceived this issue as a significant problem for the church and argued for the consistent celebration of the sacraments in direct relationship to the preaching of Scripture. The sermon and the sacraments belong together. In fact, Barth called the Protestant over-emphasis on preaching at the expense of the sacraments "a disruption, a distortion, and even a destruction of the church."[85] For the "new school" theologians, the sermon—the preached Word—must be delivered in the light of the sacraments.

The question is *why*. In short, they argued that the sermon interprets and is interpreted by the sacraments.[86] Barth argued that the sermon is the "central act" of the Protestant worship service, and that it is directly related to the sacraments.[87] "There is preaching in the full sense only where it is accompanied and explained by the sacraments."[88] Preaching is a commentary on the sacraments, proclaimed after baptism (a sign of dying to self and rising to new life) and before communion (a sign of membership in the body of Christ).[89] As an interpretation of the sacraments, the sermon gives meaning to the church's identity. Trillhaas elaborated, "The Church of Jesus Christ lives from the Word and sacrament as the gifts of her Lord. As her Word is *bound* to Scripture, so is her scriptural sermon *bound*, explained, and confirmed through the sacrament. The sacraments without the Word is silent. The Word without the sacrament lacks the seal."[90] Once again, note the emphasis on the binding of the church's proclamation, the pastor's sermon, to Scripture. The sacrament, together with the Word, not only "explains" the sermon but "confirms" it as well. Without the celebration of the sacrament, the sermon stands alone, without comment, without correction, and without confirmation.

Lempp, too, emphasized the connection between the sermon and the sacrament. Lempp invokes a musical metaphor to make his point. The gospel should be joyfully preached to the "melody" of "Comfort, comfort my people," and thus, he argued, "the gospel preaching culminates in baptism and the Lord's Supper."[91] Baptism reminds the Christian, "Do you know how rich you are?"[92] And the Lord's Supper reminds the congregant, "You can get everything you need: forgiveness of sins, life, and salvation."[93] The sacraments are not incidental to the liturgy or the sermon, but they provide a dynamic opportunity to draw the Christian into deeper fellowship with God. Thus, the preacher should preach in a manner that reflects the grace and abundance of the sacraments as gifts of God for the people of God.

The binding of the Word to the sacraments entails the submission of the pastor's message to the truths encapsulated and preserved in the sacraments. Baptism reminds the Christian of dying to self and rising to new life "in the name of the Father, Son, and Holy Spirit" (Matthew 28:19). Communion celebrates the body and blood of Christ, given "for the forgiveness of sins" (Matthew 26:28). To receive the sacraments requires that one submit to the Word. The pastor may not go beyond or contradict these words of commission and institution in the sermon or he would risk dissonance that could become apparent to the congregation. Thus, if a pastor were to contend in a sermon, for example, that God sent Adolf Hitler as a savior for Germany, or that God has especially blessed the "Aryan" race, then the celebration of the sacraments could—though not necessarily or in every case—reveal the incongruity of the preached message.[94]

The regular celebration of the sacraments is a way to keep the sermon aligned with the Word. This is not to suggest that pastors never preached without celebrating the sacraments—the celebration of the sacraments may not always be possible or practical. But the "new school" theologians understood this functional aspect of the sacraments and argued for the consistent celebration of the sacraments—bound to the preached Word—for a healthy and vibrant church.

THE USE OF THE HEBREW BIBLE

Along with a renewed reliance on the authority of the biblical texts for preaching, an emphasis on the sermon as an instrument of sanctification amid spiritual warfare, and the proper placement of the sermon in the context of the sacraments, the last important emphasis in the post–First World War shift in homiletics is a defense of preaching from the Hebrew Bible. Although one can detect a degree of ambivalence about the significance of the Hebrew Bible in its own right apart from the New Testament, it is clear that Barth, Bonhoeffer, Trillhaas, and Lempp, desired that the Church regain an apparently lost appreciation for the Hebrew Bible as a foundational component of the Christian biblical texts, to rely upon it as an authoritative source for preaching.[95]

Barth encouraged his students to preach from the Hebrew Bible, but his advice is more in keeping with the traditional views expressed by Christian Palmer, as discussed in the previous chapter. Barth argued that preachers must preach from the Hebrew Bible and that they should not neglect any part of the biblical texts. However, he writes,

[The Old Testament] is valid only in relation to the New. If the church has declared itself to be the lawful successor of the synagogue, this means that the Old Testament is witness to Christ, before Christ but not without Christ. Each sentence in the Old Testament must be seen in this context . . . As a wholly Jewish book, the Old Testament is a pointer to Christ . . . The Old Testament points forward, the New Testament points backward, and both point to Christ.[96]

Thus, while Barth encourages preachers to use the Hebrew Bible, he taught them how to use it appropriately in service of the gospel message. Barth is careful here not to encourage giving the text a "second sense" and not to "oppose historical and Christian exposition to one another," but rather he promoted an interpretation of the text that "points beyond itself" to Christ.[97] One can detect the anti-Judaic notion that the Hebrew Bible is only valid in relation to the New Testament.

Bonhoeffer took a step further and reminded his students that Christians cannot obediently preach the gospel while at the same time neglecting much more than half of the Christian biblical texts. The Hebrew Bible is the sacred history of God's work in the world, and therefore, Christians must esteem, study, and preach from the text as they do with the New Testament. He argued,

The Old Testament must once again be preached much more often. For Luther it was a relevant part of the Holy Scripture, although he saw the New Testament as the glad tidings of the fulfillment of the Scripture. Schleiermacher, on the other hand, refused to preach from the Old Testament.[98]

This admonition indicates that in the early twentieth century many in the Protestant churches considered the Hebrew Bible to be obsolete, incomplete, or inferior to the New Testament and its testimony of Jesus Christ. Additional research is needed to gain a greater understanding of the frequency of Christian preaching generally from the Hebrew Bible prior to 1933, but based on Bonhoeffer's comments it appears in the early twentieth century that its use paled in comparison to that of the New Testament. Bonhoeffer tried to recalibrate the church's view and use of the Hebrew Bible. Bonhoeffer would follow his own advice: of the 56 sermon manuscripts in the historical record dating from 1933 to 1945, 17 (or 30%) of them were based on the Hebrew Bible.

In contrast to Barth's and Bonhoeffer's minimal but incisive treatment on preaching from the Hebrew Bible text, Trillhaas offered his readers a full chapter on how to integrate the Hebrew Bible in the preacher's task. He argued that this is a "special difficulty" for the Christian pastor because the Hebrew Bible presents an "indirect witness to Christ" as opposed to the direct witness of the New Testament. He stated without equivocation that "any rejection of an Old Testament text, however it may be justified, betrays a misunderstanding of the New Testament revelation on decisive points. This is already the case where one suspects in the Old Testament a document of Judaism."[99] Trillhaas took direct aim at the German Christian movement, which sought to undermine the credibility of the Hebrew Bible and to remove it from the Christian canon.[100] The biblical texts, he argued, are not the work of man—or of one particular people—but a work of God. It is God's Word. The preacher must acknowledge two profoundly important truths, that "the God of the Old Testament is the God and Father of Jesus Christ" and that "the Old Testament was the Bible of Jesus."[101] The Christian cannot tolerate any qualitative division between the Old and New Testaments, or the identity of the God portrayed in each. Trillhaas' treatment of the Hebrew Bible encouraged Christians to identify with the Jews as spiritual kin, as a people of faith with the same God and, in part, the same biblical texts.

In contrast to Barth, Bonhoeffer, and especially Trillhaas, Lempp did not emphasize that preachers should preach from the Hebrew Bible more often. Rather, it appears that he *assumed* pastors should. He called the Old Testament "the framework" in which to understand "the great deeds of God" and "the great history of the salvation of God."[102] The Hebrew Bible is not only an essential part of the Christian canon, but it's the framework that gives it meaning.

The pulpit became a battleground over the validity and value of the Hebrew Bible in the Christian community of faith in Nazi Germany. Furthermore, to acknowledge the value and place of the Hebrew Bible as a foundational text in the church and to fight for its use in preaching was to undermine Hitler's claim that the Jews are the corruptors of culture while the "Aryans" are the only "founders" of human culture.[103] The very use of the Hebrew Bible in preaching—whether appealing to the moral injunctions of the Mosaic law, exploring the depth of insight and feeling in the psalms or deriving inspiration from the life-affirming stories of faith and courage of Israel's heroes—gives lie to Hitler's well-worn assertions about Jews and Jewish culture.

THE SERMON MANUSCRIPT

Barth, Bonhoeffer, Trillhaas, and Lempp each emphasized the sermon as the proclamation of the gospel based on the authority of the biblical texts, and thus, they underscored dignity and sacred nature of the preacher's task. It is no surprise that each strongly encouraged pastors to consider their words carefully. Moreover, three of the four urged future pastors to write a manuscript of each sermon to ensure they stay on message. Throughout the history of the Church, countless preachers have used manuscripts from which to preach. But it is significant in the context of Nazi Germany, that Barth,

Bonhoeffer, and Trillhaas—each a well-respected theologian associated with the Confessing Church—encouraged future preachers to write down their sermons in manuscript form. Each argued that the preacher must undertake the preaching task seriously, to express the gospel in measured words, and to articulate theology carefully to his or her congregation.[104] Preaching *ex tempore* or by a mere outline would not suit the seriousness of the task.

Barth argued that preaching is a sacred commission unique to the office of the pastor. As such, preaching is a blessed endeavor that demands commitment, preparation, humility, and focus. For these reasons Barth heartily recommends that pastors write their sermons in manuscript form.[105] The sermon is not just another speech, but it is understood to be God's revelation to the world, to the Christian community of faith. Thus, it must be undertaken very seriously and soberly. He wrote,

> A sermon is a speech which we have prepared word for word and written down. This alone accords with its dignity. If it is true in general that we must give an account of every idle word, we must do so especially in our preaching. For preaching is not an art that some can master because they are good speakers and others only by working out the sermon in writing . . . It is the central act of Protestant worship . . . Only a sermon in which each word is carefully accounted for is a sacramental act.[106]

Every word must be weighed and measured. There could be no room for mistakes, ambiguity, inappropriate levity, or distraction. The sermon was not an occasion for speaking impromptu or "off script," because the very words of the sermon by definition necessitated reflection and prayer as a sacred element of the liturgy.[107]

One should note, however, that just because a pastor composed a sermon manuscript does not mean that he actually read it directly word for word—though one might surmise this for a great number of extant sermons. Furthermore, this is not to say that pastors from other churches (e.g., Roman Catholic) did not share the same practice of composing a manuscript.

Bonhoeffer reiterates the considerable preparation entailed in composing a sermon. One cannot just walk up to the pulpit and deliver a quality sermon that does justice to the gospel message. Each sermon requires careful thought, prayer, and contemplation on a biblical text.[108] Invoking the name of a giant in German Protestantism and a personal and family friend, Bonhoeffer offers this tidbit of practical advice: "The preacher should not avoid writing out his sermon. Adolf von Harnack said, 'My pen is much wiser than my head.'"[109] He also presents a number of practical suggestions to the seminarian on the writing of sermon manuscripts: begin with prayer, develop an outline, write in the light of day, ask specific exegetical questions of a text, take plenty of time to write and reflect on the sermon, begin on Tuesday and finish on Friday (at the latest), and memorize the "thoughts," not words, of the sermon manuscript to internalize the message.[110] But he added,

> The congregation does not want to be shown a child which was born in the study. The work of sermon preparation should set free the hour in the pulpit and not hinder it or lead to fear. The quality of this preparation will determine how much concentration the preacher can develop in the pulpit.[111]

The preparation in the study, the writing of the manuscript, is all only prologue. The preacher relies upon the Holy Spirit to be present when he steps into the pulpit and to work in his heart and in the hearts of the congregants. For this reason, the preacher is to pray before and after delivering the sermon.

Trillhaas also recommends writing out the sermon in manuscript form in keeping with the dignity and gravity of the preacher's task. Again, like Barth and Bonhoeffer, the advice is to write out the sermon and to preach from it to prevent verbose extemporizing. "The pastor must have a plan and may in no case yield in the pulpit to such a present tendency to have ideas and suddenly 'come to talk about something else' . . . The manuscript is the indispensable and most reliable weapon against the chatter in the pulpit."[112] The concern is to keep the preacher on message and to maintain focus on the prepared material, which is based on an extensive study of the biblical text. And again, the issue at stake is the foundation upon which the sermon is based: upon the biblical texts and not on the impulse of the pastor.

The consistent admonition among Confessing Church theologians to write out the sermon in manuscript form is significant because it highlights their emphasis on the authority of the biblical texts in preaching, taking us full circle to the first main theme emphasized by the "new school" of homiletics. The manuscript anchors the pastor in the gospel message as elucidated and explored in hours of study, prayer, and contemplation. The pastor should not rely on charisma, the ability to "read" the congregation while preaching or draw inspiration on the dynamic in the sanctuary. In fact, Bonhoeffer even argued that the pastors should not gesticulate or employ superlatives or exclamations (the Word is the exclamation); preaching is a service, not a performance.[113] This is the polar opposite image of Hitler as charismatic leader, energized by the crowd, responding to its cues, while relying on his own ideology.[114]

CONCLUSION

Each of the fundamental elements of the "new school" of homiletics directly addressed significant problems of the Confessing Church in Nazi Germany. First, the conviction that the Scripture is the sole basis of divine knowledge and, thus, for preaching, directly challenged Nazi racial ideology and interpretations of history. Second, the conception of the sermon as an instrument of sanctification became a significant method for preachers to serve Christians by preparing them to face the challenges of the Nazi regime. Third, the liturgical placement of the sermon in the context of baptism and communion provided context to interpret and understand the meaning of the sermon, and thereby to preserve and maintain the church's identity amid persecution and Nazi interventions in church affairs. Lastly, the argument to value and use the Hebrew Bible introduced an opportunity for Germans in the Third Reich to recognize the Jewish foundations of Christianity and to see the Jews in a new light as the people entrusted with God's revelation.

The influence of this "new school" of homiletics on the history of preaching and theology in Germany is immense, especially considering the leadership and work of Barth. One historian has argued that Barth, as the leading representative, has offered a theology of preaching that is a double-edged sword. "On the one hand, without it present-day preaching would not be so pure, so biblical, and so concerned with central issues, but on the other hand, it would also not be so alarmingly correct, boringly precise, and remote from the world."[115] In other words, while he advances preaching that is biblical and meticulous, his approach may dismiss the human elements that make the sermon relevant to politics, society, and culture. In focusing on the Scripture as the basis for the sermon, the pastor might lose sight of contemporary problems that demand a biblical response.

Yet Barth and these Confessing Church homileticians seek to unfetter the Scripture from the political theology of German Protestantism so that it may have "free course" to impact lives in Nazi Germany. Their aim was to free the gospel to do God's work in the world. But they had another aim as well. While they unfettered the Scripture, they fettered themselves to it. To use another metaphor, they were seeking to use Scripture as an anchor to steady the ship of the church amid a tempest.[116] They recognized the inability of general revelation—in its myriad permutations—to provide stability and harmony in the church, but more importantly, to ensure that Christians honored God by the integrity of their faith.

The sermons of Confessing pastors reflect their theology and convictions about divine knowledge unlike any other primary source of the Nazi period. An examination of these sermons offers a rich and detailed record of the messages they sought to convey to the German faithful week after week. If one listens carefully, one can hear the pastor's passion and perspectives through the page and place him- or herself in the church amid the men and women of the congregation. But one can also hear Confessing pastors distinguish themselves from their German Christian colleagues in how they treat Scripture in their sermons as the standard of truth, as opposed to merely one measure alongside, for example, Nazi racial ideology. Thus, the Confessing Church sermons are tremendously valuable as a source to understand how the conflict within the German Protestant churches played out in the public square. It is to the sermons we now turn.

NOTES

1. Hughes Oliphant Old, *The Reading and Preaching of the Scriptures in the Worship of the Christian Church, volume 6, the Modern Age* (Grand Rapids, MI: Eerdmans, 2007), 763.

2. Old, *Reading and Preaching of the Scriptures*, 763. At the same time, Heinz Zahrnt has argued that "the renewal of Protestant theology in the twentieth century arose from the central task of the Church, that of preaching, or more precisely from the 'specific problem of the pastor, the sermon.'" As Barth pointed out, the pastor must speak to the tremendous problems of modern life using the Scripture. "He wants to speak to *men*, to the fabulous contradiction in their lives, but he has to do so as a pastor by means of the no less fabulous message of the Bible." Thus, developments in preaching and theology in the early twentieth century went hand in hand. See Zahrnt, *The Question of God*, 17.

3. Old, *The Reading and Preaching of the Scriptures*, 759.

4. Ferguson, et. al., *New Dictionary of Theology*, 456; see also Karl Barth, *Homiletics*, 42–43. Peter Berger's concise definition of "neo-orthodoxy" is useful: "Neo-orthodoxy is the reaffirmation of the objective authority of a religious tradition after a period during which that authority had been relativized and weakened." See Peter Berger, *The Heretical Imperative: Contemporary Possibilities of Religious Affirmation* (New York: Anchor Press, 1979), 79. Also, as a matter of clarification, the meaning of "Scripture" in this context and throughout this dissertation refers to the Christian scripture, which includes the Old (or First) Testament and the New (or Second) Testament.

5. Peter Berger argues that "Insofar as there was resistance to Nazism in German Protestantism, neo-orthodox . . . was the ideology of that resistance." See Berger, *The Heretical Imperative*, 73.

6. Old, *Reading and Preaching of the Scriptures*, 763.

7. Wolfgang Trillhaas, *Evanglische Predigtlehre* (München: Chr. Kaiser Verlag, 1935), 9.

8. Green, *Lutherans against Hitler*, 328.

9. Green, *Lutherans against Hitler*, 328.

10. Kurt Meier, *Der Evangelische Kirchenkampf, Band 1, Der Kampf um die "Reichskirche"* (Göttingen: Vandenhoeck & Ruprecht, 1976), 250.

11. See Cochrane, *Church's Confession under Hitler*, 129; Helmreich, *German Churches under Hitler*, 153–54; and Bethge, *Dietrich Bonhoeffer*, 341.

12. "The Muzzling Decree, 4 January 1934," in Matheson, *The Third Reich and the Christian Churches: Documents*, 41–42.

13. Green, *Lutherans against Hitler*, 92.

14. See Barth, *Homiletics*, 38

15. Barth, *Homiletics*, 34.

16. Barth, *Homiletics*, 34.

17. Barth, *Homiletics*, 75–81. See also, Berger, *Heretical Imperative*, 74.

18. Quoted in Barth, *Homiletics*, 42.

19. See Edwin Charles Dargan, *A History of Preaching, Vol. 1, From the Apostolic Fathers to the Great Reformers, A.D. 70–1572* (New York: Burt Franklin, 1968), 376–80; and O. C. Edwards Jr., *A History of Preaching* (Nashville: Abingdon Press, 2004), 304.

20. See John Stott, *Between Two Worlds: The Art of Preaching in the Twentieth Century* (Grand Rapids, MI: Eerdmans, 1982), 16; and Dargan, *History of Preaching I*, 12 and 552.

21. Smart, *The Divided Mind of Modern Theology*, 20.

22. Barth, *Homiletics*, 43. Barth is not reinterpreting the nature and meaning of preaching; rather he is summarizing historical characteristics of preaching in the Christian tradition. This list of characteristics is often repeated in standard texts on homiletics and the history of preaching. See David Buttrick, *Homiletic: Moves and Structures* (Minneapolis, MN: Fortress Press, 1987), 29–44; Thomas Oden, *Pastoral Theology: Essentials of Ministry* (New York: HarperCollins, 1983), 127–39; Stott, *Between Two Worlds*, 50–91; and Paul Scott Wilson, *A Concise History of Preaching* (Nashville, TN: Abington Press, 1992), 11–20.

23. See Stott, *Between Two Worlds*, 15.

24. Barth, *Homiletics*, 44.

25. Barth's definition of preaching is consonant with the earliest Christian traditions. Guerric DeBona concisely summarizes the elements of preaching as liturgical, exegetical, and prophetic; that is, preaching occurs in a religious context for a religious purpose, it is grounded in the Scriptures, and it speaks God's word to a living community of faith. See Guerric DeBona, *Fulfilled in Our Hearing: History and Method of Christian Preaching* (New York: Paulist Press, 2005), 9; and also Yngve Brilioth, *A Brief History of Preaching*, translated by K.E. Mattson (Philadelphia: Fortress Press, 1965), 8–10.

26. Berger, *Heretical Imperative*, 74.

27. In this sense, Barth "placed the theologian in his proper place, 'beneath' holy scripture." See Zahrnt, *The Question of God*, 20.

28. See DeBona, *Fulfilled in Our Hearing*, 16–17.

29. See Berger, *Heretical Imperative*, 74; Schilling, *Contemporary Continental Theologians*, 20; and also Zahrnt, *The Question of God*, 118.

30. Barth, *Homiletics*, 86.

31. See Stott, *Between Two Worlds*, 320–22.
32. Barth, *Homiletics*, 90.
33. Green, *Lutherans against Hitler*, 177–78.
34. Barth, *The Epistle to the Romans*, 10.
35. Green, *Lutherans against Hitler*, 199.
36. Angela Dienhart Hancock, *Karl Barth's Emergency Homiletic*, 18.
37. Hancock, *Karl Barth's Emergency Homiletic*, xiv.
38. Hancock, *Barth's Emergency Homiletic*, 216–17.
39. Bethge, *Dietrich Bonhoeffer*, 422.
40. Bethge, *Dietrich Bonhoeffer*, 424.
41. Bethge, *Dietrich Bonhoeffer*, 424.
42. Dietrich Bonhoeffer, *Bonhoeffer: Worldly Preaching*, edited by Clyde Fant (Nashville, TN: Thomas Nelson, 1975), 156.
43. This understanding of the preaching of Scripture as giving expression to God's voice is evident even in earliest Christian preaching. See Wilson, *A Concise History of Preaching*, 19.
44. Bonhoeffer, *Worldly Preaching*, 170.
45. Schilling, *Contemporary Continental Theologians*, 20.
46. As John Stott argues, preachers do not invent the gospel message, but "it has been entrusted to them." Stott, *Between Two Worlds*, 136.
47. Bonhoeffer, *Worldly Preaching*, 170. The historian O. C. Edwards notes that sermons are not always based on a particular biblical text, though they usually are. Here Bonhoeffer takes a strong stand to ensure the sermon is based on the biblical text. See Edwards, *A History of Preaching*, 4.
48. Bonhoeffer, *Worldly Preaching*, 156.
49. Bonhoeffer, *Worldly Preaching*, 156.
50. Bonhoeffer, *Worldly Preaching*, 156. The theologian David Buttrick comments on the reliance on the authority of Scripture in sermons in the Christian tradition, and notes that the authority connotes the "power to command and wisdom to consult." Thus, basing the sermon on a biblical text provides congregants with authority that the preacher alone does not have. See David Buttrick, *Homiletic: Moves and Structures* (Philadelphia: Fortress Press, 1987), 239–40.
51. Trillhaas, *Evangelische Predigtlehre*, 24.
52. Trillhaas, *Evangelische Predigtlehre*, 33.
53. Trillhaas, *Evangelische Predigtlehre*, 35.
54. W. Lempp, *Zwanzig Thesen über zeitgemässe Predigt* (Stuttgart: Verlag der Ev. Gesellschaft) 1937, thirteenth thesis, 6.
55. Lempp, *Zwanzig Thesen*, 6.
56. Lempp, *Zwanzig Thesen*, 7.
57. Lempp, *Zwanzig Thesen*, 16.
58. Leonhard Fendt, *Grundriss der Praktischen Theologie für Studenten und Kandidaten; Abteilung 1. Grundlegung, Lehre von d. Kirche, vom Amt und von d. Predigt* (Tübingen: Mohr, 1949), 76–77.
59. See DeBona, *Fulfilled in Our Hearing*, 5; and also Stott, *Between Two Worlds*, 105–107.

60. Barth, *Homiletics*, 74.

61. See Stott, *Between Two Worlds*, 100–101; Edmund P. Clowney, *Preaching and Biblical Theology* (London: Tyndale Press, 1961), 24; P.T. Forsyth, *Positive Preaching and the Modern Mind* (New York: A.C. Armstrong and Son, 1907), 6.

62. David Buttrick writes, "Preaching is the 'Word of God' in that it participates in God's purpose, is initiated by Christ, and is supported by the Spirit with community in the world." The idea here is that preaching is an activity that actively seeks the reconciliation of the world to God, to align the values of our lives and institutions to God's values as revealed in the Christian Scriptures. See Buttrick, *Homiletic*, 456.

63. Barth, *Homiletics*, 55.

64. Karl Barth, *Theological Existence To-day!* (A Plea for Theological Freedom), translated by R. Birch Hoyle (Eugene, OR: Wipf & Stock, 2015), 11–12.

65. Bonhoeffer, *Worldly Preaching*, 161.

66. Barth, *Theological Existence To-Day!* 11.

67. Trillhaas, *Evangelische Predigtlehre*, 59.

68. Trillhaas, *Evangelische Predigtlehre*, 59–60.

69. Bonhoeffer, *Worldly Preaching*, 165.

70. Bonhoeffer, *Worldly Preaching*, 165.

71. Bonhoeffer, *Worldly Preaching*, 133.

72. Richard Evans, *The Third Reich in Power* (New York: Penguin, 2005), 213.

73. Lempp, *Zwanzig Thesen*, 32.

74. Lempp, *Zwanzig Thesen*, 32.

75. Lempp, *Zwanzig Thesen*, 33.

76. Lempp, *Zwanzig Thesen*, 36–37.

77. Hancock, *Karl Barth's Emergency Homiletic*, 216.

78. Barth, *Homiletics*, 60.

79. Bonhoeffer, *Worldly Preaching*, 176.

80. See Martin Luther, *Luther's Works, Volume 36, Word and Sacrament II* (Augsburg Fortress, 1959), 348f.

81. Roland Bainton, *The Reformation of the Sixteenth Century, Enlarged Edition* (Boston: Beacon, 1985), 72.

82. Kenneth Wieting, *The Blessings of Weekly Communion* (St. Louis, MO: Concordia, 2006), 115. Wieting shows through statistical evidence that the Lutheran Church-Missouri Synod faced the same issue that Barth and the other "new school" theologians pointed out. In this denomination in 1930, a communicant would receive the elements an average of 2.10 times per year, and the numbers would slowly increase to 3.22 times a year by 1950. See Wieting, *The Blessings of Weekly Communion*, 147.

83. Martin Luther, "An Order of Mass and Communion for the Church at Wittenberg," in *Martin Luther's Basic Theological Writings, Third Edition*, edited by Timothy F. Lull and William R. Russell (Minneapolis, MN: Fortress Press, 2012), 311–21. See Frank Senn, "The Reform of the Mass: Evangelical, but Still Catholic," in *The Catholicity of the Reformation*, edited by Carl E. Braaten and Robert W. Jenson (Grand Rapids, MI: Eerdmans, 1996), 39–40.

84. Senn, "The Reform of the Mass," 39.

85. Barth, *Homiletics*, 59.
86. Barth, *Homiletics*, 59.
87. Barth, *Homiletics*, 119.
88. Barth, *Homiletics*, 58.
89. Barth, *Homiletics*, 58.
90. Trillhaas, *Evangelische Predictlehre*, 24.
91. Lempp, *Zwanzig Thesen*, 42–43.
92. Lempp, *Zwanzig Thesen*, 43.
93. Lempp, *Zwanzig Thesen*, 43.
94. Certainly, pro-Nazi German Christians celebrated baptism and communion in their own services and apparently saw no incongruity. But the sacraments presented obstacles to those who would divide the Church or present the Nazis' version of the gospel, their own "good news," given that the sacraments are embodiments of the gospel, that is, ritual practices that retell the "good news" of Jesus Christ.
95. This neglect of the Hebrew Bible is evident in the work of the influential early-nineteenth century Friedrich Schleiermacher. The historian David Larson notes that in the ten-volume collection of Schleiermacher's sermons, there are only 20 sermons based on Hebrew Bible texts. See Larson, *The Company of Preachers*, 353.
96. Barth, *Homiletics*, 80–81.
97. Barth, *Homiletics*, 80–81.
98. Bonhoeffer, *Worldly Preaching*, 160–61.
99. Trillhaas, *Evangelische Predigtlehre*, 99.
100. See Susannah Heschel's superb history, *The Aryan Jesus*, which tells the story of Protestant Christians, many of whom were members of the German Christian movement, who formed the Institute for the Study and Eradication of Jewish Influence on German Religious Life. As the title implies, this group not only sought the dismissal of the Hebrew Bible and a revision of the New Testament, but also advanced the argument that Jesus was not Jewish but "Aryan," thus preserving the possibility for antisemites to continue to worship Jesus as the Son of God. See Heschel, *Aryan Jesus*, 1–2, 13, and 26.
101. Trillhaas, *Evangelische Predigtlehre*, 100.
102. Lempp, *Zwanzig Thesen*, 17.
103. Adolf Hitler, *Mein Kampf*, translated by Ralph Manheim (Boston: Houghton Mifflin, 1971), 290.
104. The American theologian and pastor Jonathan Edwards is a notable case in point; see Stott, *Between Two Worlds*, 255. Also, the historian O.C. Edwards specifically mentions the American pastor Harry Emerson Fosdick and Anglican Archbishop John Tillotson as clergymen who habitually read sermons from manuscripts, yet he also makes the sweeping generalization that, "with rare exceptions, the most effective preachers have not preached from manuscripts." Though his meaning of "effective" is not entirely clear, my research suggests that if he is correct, one can see a more careful and conscientious approach to sermon construction and delivery in the Nazi period than is evident in much of church history. See Edwards, *A History of Preaching*, 836.
105. Barth, *Homiletics*, 119. See also Hancock, *Karl Barth's Emergency Homiletic*, 300.

106. Barth, *Homiletics*, 119.
107. See Stott, *Between Two Worlds*, 255–57. For example, one of the chief leaders of the Confessing Church, Martin Niemöller, transcribed every word of his sermons, with great attention to detail. See Robertson, *Christians against Hitler*, 59–60.
108. Bonhoeffer, *Worldly Preaching*, 145–46.
109. Bonhoeffer, *Worldly Preaching*, 149.
110. Bonhoeffer, *Worldly Preaching*, 148
111. Bonhoeffer, *Worldy Preaching*, 149.
112. Trillhaas, *Evangelische Predigtlehre*, 165–66.
113. Bonhoeffer, *Worldly Preaching*, 172
114. Ian Kershaw, *Hitler, 1889-1936, Hubris* (New York: Norton, 1998), xix–xxx.
115. Zahrnt, *The Question of God*, 118.
116. The metaphor of the church as a "little boat" was used by Pastor Paul Schneider in a sermon on January 28, 1934. See Schneider's sermon in Dean Shroud's *Preaching in Hitler's Shadow: Sermons of Resistance in the Third Reich* (Grand Rapids, MI: Eerdmans, 2013), 91.

Chapter 5

Challenging Nazi Ideology

The Sunday following Dr. Reinhold Krause's controversial Sports Palace speech on November 13, 1933, a Lutheran pastor named Heinrich Vogel (1902–1989) countered with vigor from his pulpit in the village church (Dorfkirche) of Dobbrikow-Nettgendorf, south of Potsdam.[1] The future Barmen Synod member preached a provocative sermon based on 1 Kings 18:17–40.[2] The text tells the story of the prophet Elijah's dramatic confrontation with King Ahab of Israel and the 850 prophets of Baal and Asherah, a god and goddess of the peoples of the Levant. King Ahab introduced Baal worship into Israel, and his wife, the notorious Queen Jezebel, actively persecuted the prophets of Yahweh (1 Kings 16–17). Israel had wandered from the worship of the one true God, and Elijah was commissioned to help bring them back.

In the story Elijah posed a question Israel needed to answer: "How long will you go limping with two different opinions? If the Lord is God, follow him; but if Baal, then follow him" (1 Kings 18:21). What follows is a dramatic confrontation between God and Baal, with the Israelites looking on, waiting to see which deity would reveal the greatest power. As Baal's prophets called upon him to light the fire of his own sacrifice, there was only silence. Yet, according to the narrative, God demonstrated his power spectacularly with fire from heaven, consuming the water-logged sacrifice Elijah prepared. The Israelite witnesses, eyes open in awe and wonder, acknowledged the obvious truth and said, "The Lord indeed is God; the Lord indeed is God" (1 Kings 18:39b). Elijah then commanded the Israelites to slay the prophets of Baal.

Vogel explicitly parallels the people of God in Israel and Nazi Germany. The people of God are being led astray by false prophets serving wicked leaders. Vogel infers that Hitler's attempted nazification of the German Protestant churches was akin to Ahab's institution of Baal worship in Israel, complete with a cadre of false prophets and newfangled religious thought and rituals. Vogel presented Elijah as a Jewish champion who stood up to the wicked king and the false prophets. Taking on the mantle of Elijah before the German Christian false prophets, Vogel proclaimed to his congregation,

> You have heard what was said at the Sports Palace: abolishing of the Old Testament, trimming [*Beschneidung*] of the New Testament, etc. And the worst of what was said in this Sports Palace rally is not even that. It is that the Old Testament has been spoken of as a book full of Jewish cattle-drivers and mafia stories. So then, the cross of Christ has been rejected . . . Ask yourself, what would Luther say? What would Luther have done in this Sports Palace rally? I say to you, he would not have been silent like the church leaders, but he would have climbed on a chair and shouted: that is damage to our faith; that is blasphemy.[3]

With clarity and insight, Vogel condemned Krause's assertion that the German Christians sought to reform German Protestantism along the lines of Luther. Vogel offered two reasons why their movement represented not a reformation but a revolution: first, they introduced a "violent spirit" (*Gewaltgeist*), and second, they espoused "heresy." Reformation, Vogel argued, is always the work of the Holy Spirit, not a "violent spirit." It is carried out by a "broken person whom God has chosen."[4] He argued that like the prophets of Baal and Asherah, the clergy of the German Christian movement had chosen to overturn worship of the true God among the people of God to replace it with a sacrilegious system.

Invoking Elijah as a Jewish hero and Luther as a German hero, Vogel clarified what their response must be as a congregation to the German Christian revolution: to stand up and declare "blasphemy." To the Christians of his congregation at the Dorfkirche, Vogel reiterated God's "either/or" call of allegiance as in the days of Elijah.[5] A decision must be made, he argued. Remarkably, he used an Israelite prophet, the Hebrew Scripture, and the history of the Jews to call back the German people to the true faith in God.

Scholars have long known about Vogel's opposition to the Nazi regime in his work in the leadership of the Confessing Church and in his teaching in an underground seminary in Berlin, yet sermons like this demonstrate that he also opposed the Nazi regime from within the walls of the sanctuary and behind the pulpit.[6] Not surprisingly, throughout the Nazi period Vogel was harassed, arrested, and imprisoned multiple times by the Nazi regime, but he was consistently supported by his congregation.[7]

Vogel's sermon illustrates the possibilities of expressing criticism of the Nazis and pro-Nazi Christians from the pulpit in the Third Reich. This chapter will explore the varieties of ways that Confessing Church pastors expressed dissent and opposition (as defined in chapter 1) to National Socialism as a perceived false belief system that has wreaked havoc in the

German Protestant churches. Expressions of dissent range from the use of deliberate word choices to protecting the traditions and identity of German Protestantism. Expressions of opposition range from criticisms of the German people for worshiping false gods, such as Hitler and the "Aryan" race, to the condemnation of Nazi policies. While the expression of dissent indicates dissatisfaction with specific elements of Nazi ideology or governance, expressions of opposition clearly attempted to challenge the dominance of the Nazi state, at least in regard to Nazis' and pro-Nazi supporters' infringements in church theology and practice.[8] Sermons may be understood as oppositional to the Nazi regime when pastors presented mutually exclusive tenets of Christianity and National Socialism and when they condemned the various "false idols" of Nazism, such as race, the German nation, fallen heroes, and Hitler as Führer.

My aim in this chapter is to examine the wide range of possibilities for pastors to express dissent and opposition to perceived Nazi false beliefs from the pulpit in an effort to better understand the nature of their expressions and what they tell us about conflict within the German Protestant churches and between the churches and the state. The Barmen Confession's assertion that Scripture is the primary source of knowledge of God placed Confessing Church pastors in a position to directly and indirectly challenge Nazi and pro-Nazi Christian assertions about the priority of history and race as sources of knowledge of God. The pulpit was the primary battleground Confessing Church pastors used to confront the perceived Nazi "blasphemy," as Vogel put it in the example above. These sermons reveal the intensity of religious conflict between the German Protestant churches and between the church and the Nazi state, particularly over the questions of orthodoxy and the sources of divine knowledge, and they demonstrate that pastors were willing to engage in public debate from the authority of the pulpit.[9] Further, as will become apparent in this chapter and subsequent chapters, pastors could repeatedly offer criticisms from the pulpit before the Nazi state would permanently silence them through imprisonment in a concentration camp (yet with harassments and arrests in the meantime). Indeed, pastors' religiously based criticisms against National Socialist intrusion in church affairs took on political meaning in the context of the Nazi state.[10] Confessing Church pastors had a platform and ready audience to criticize the Nazi regime, its leaders, ideology, policies, persecutions, and supporters in the German Christian movement. This research confirms the historiography that contends that the German churches were among the only institutions in Nazi Germany where Germans could voice public criticism against the regime and its ideology.[11] However, it must be stated at the outset that the relative infrequency and at times implicit nature of the criticisms support the conclusions of historians such as Gerlach and Barnett who assert that the majority of Confessing

Church pastors did not speak out effectively in opposition against the Nazi dictatorship, its ideology, or policies.[12]

As will be demonstrated in this chapter and the following chapter, the criticisms of National Socialism, the Nazi state, and leaders are presented explicitly and implicitly, and they are always framed by the biblical text so that the meaning is often multi-layered and dynamic, extending from the contemporary political and social situation in Nazi Germany to the sacred history recounted in Scripture. Furthermore, their expressions, like Vogel's in the previous example, frequently draw on two thousand years of church history, often from the Reformation, thereby contributing historical meaning to the weight of their criticisms. Vogel's question, "What would Luther have done in this Sports Palace rally?" compels his Lutheran congregation to reflect biblically and historically on Krause's astounding assertions about the nature of Christianity and to simultaneously consider the reasons for Luther's stand against the Roman Catholic Church, notably his conceptions of *sola fide* (faith alone) and *sola scriptura* (Scripture alone)—convictions at odds with German Christian teaching—as foundational elements of their Protestant faith.

This chapter will begin by clarifying the pastors' posture of obedience as Christians "subject to their governing authority" (Romans 13). Obedience to the state was the default position from which they expressed criticism. The chapter will then explore the history of Confessing Church preaching against the perceived Nazi false belief and neo-paganism, espoused specifically within the German Christian movement and more generally in the society and culture of the Third Reich. Unlike previous chapters, this one will not follow a chronological organization; rather, it will take a thematic approach to explore the myriad ways pastors offered dissent and opposition to Nazism as a perceived worldview in competition with Christianity. The chapter will focus on the early years of the Nazi regime, the high point of conflict between the Confessing Church and the German Christian movement. I will follow this thematic approach in the subsequent chapters as well.

A POSTURE OF OBEDIENCE

At the outset it is necessary to state that criticisms of the Nazi state, its leadership, and its ideology from the pulpit were by and large presented from a posture of obedience to the state. As previously discussed, various factors informed German Protestant pastors' sense of duty to the state, notably the apostle Paul's injunction in Romans 13 that every person be "subject to the governing authorities." Luther's doctrine of the two kingdoms further elucidates the realms of responsibility between the church and the state; as

Christians are blessed by both, so also, they have duties to both. Likewise, as previously discussed, political theology in early twentieth-century German Protestantism advanced an understanding of obedience to God in political terms and the idea that one can know God as revealed through a nation's development.[13] If a nation's laws, government, and history are revelations of God, then obedience to the state is in line with obedience to God. In short, obedience to the state was a duty that German Protestants widely acknowledged.[14] The question for pastors who felt the need to criticize the regime was, How does one voice criticism from a posture of obedience and thereby remain a dutiful subject of the state?

To see how pastors may have understood this issue and threaded the needle, it will be helpful to start with the Barmen Confession of May 1934, specifically the fifth of the six theses, which focused on the relation of the church to the state. Instead of using Romans 13:1 as its grounding text, the fifth thesis uses 1 Peter 2:17, "Fear God. Honor the Emperor." The confession acknowledged that the state uses the threat and exercise of force to ensure justice and peace and affirmed "the responsibility of the rulers and of the ruled," though it did not spell out what these responsibilities were. Specifically, the statement did not state explicitly that Christians owe the duty of obedience, though this may certainly be inferred as one responsibility of the ruled to the rulers. Rather, the fifth thesis explicitly states that the Church "trusts and *obeys* the power of the Word by which God upholds all things [emphasis added]."[15] As discussed previously, the confession established the Word of God as the standard, the authority, by which Christians live in community and relate to the state. The theologian Paul Althaus of the University of Erlangen criticized this fifth thesis because it advanced the "political concept of the liberal state under the rule of law" and not an authoritarian system derived from the divine order of the German nation.[16] Eberhard Busch argues that the fifth thesis "emerges as a supportive argument for the democratic state under the law," allowing for the ruled to criticize the rulers for not honoring their God-given responsibilities according to Scripture.[17] While the Barmen Confession provided room to criticize the state when it did not live up to its responsibilities outlined in Scripture, Confessing Church pastors had to learn what opposing the regime meant in practical terms.

One illuminating example of this struggle is found in a sermon Martin Niemöller preached in February 1935, a full two years after Hitler's rise to power. The sermon was based on Romans 13:1, a key biblical text on obedience to the state. In the sermon Niemöller reflected over the past couple years and expressed deep sadness that the great expectations of the Nazi rise to power had turned to a nightmare and that the regime had "shattered" the hopes of Christians because of its anti-Christian worldview and persecution of the German churches. He proclaimed:

> We see more and more clearly how there is being propagated a new paganism which wishes to have nothing to do with the Saviour who was crucified for us, while the church which acknowledges that Saviour as its only Lord is reproached with being an enemy of the state and has difficulty in obtaining a hearing for its most earnest assurances to the contrary.
>
> And it is hard, bitter hard, for us to bear this ignomy. Our good conscience rebels violently when in one breath people call us criminals and traitors to our nation.[18]

Niemöller and his Confessing Church colleagues occasionally spoke in the passive voice to avoid naming the persecutors or offenders, but his audience could certainly connect the dots to identify the Nazis and pro-Nazi supporters in the churches as perpetrators.

This sermon reveals evidence of a battered and bruised Confessing Church that is trying to figure out how to respond to Nazi "blasphemy" and persecution. At that point in 1935, the Nazi regime had attempted the subjugation of the German Protestant churches with the establishment of the *Reichskirche*, leveraging the support of church leaders from the German Christian movement in the church elections of July 1933. Pro-Nazi members of the German Christian movement passed the Aryan Paragraph in regional churches to rid Nazi Germany of non-Aryan clergy, and they were in some cases successful, such as in the Evangelical Church of the Old Prussian Union. In addition, the German Protestant churches witnessed their youth movements dissolve into the Hitler Youth in December 1933.[19] Niemöller and other like-minded pastors founded the Pastors' Emergency League, which later became the Confessing Church, to stop Nazi intrusions in church affairs. As a result of these conflicts and the Confessing Church's demand for ecclesiastical autonomy, the Nazi persecutions of Confessing Church pastors increased. Confessing Church records indicate that the Nazi regime disciplined 1,043 Confessing Church pastors by October 1934, including interrogations and arrests.[20]

Yet, even in this tenuous situation, Pastor Niemöller followed the advice of the apostle Paul and counseled his congregation to seek guidance from scripture, to "bow to the dispassionate objectivity of the Word of God," and to submit to the Nazi regime and acknowledge its mandate to administer the law, to protect citizens, and to "resist the actions of the evildoer."[21]

Even so, Niemöller argued, Christians have a right to disobey, "but this right may be exercised only when we are asked to do wrong, and then it is a duty, for 'one must obey God rather than men.'"[22] For Niemöller, one of the preeminent leaders of the Confessing Church, this was the criteria for disobedience: when and only when the state asked Christians to do wrong, that is, something against the Word of God. He does not provide examples or specifics on this rule of Christian opposition. He leaves it for the individual

Christian to reflect upon. But it is a remarkable example of a pastor explaining to his congregation the possibility of opposition to the Nazi regime. Niemöller's sermon presents an ambiguous approach to the Nazi regime: it is, on the one hand, critical of elements of National Socialist ideology, but on the other hand, the criticisms are offered from a posture of obedience to the state.

While the Barmen Confession and Niemöller may have cracked the door open to the possibility of opposition, other Confessing Church pastors seemed more inclined to keep it shut. The German Social Democratic Party in exile (Sopade) received a transcript of an anonymous Confessing Church sermon on Romans 13 (once again), delivered on October 11, 1937, in which the pastor emphasized obedience to the Nazi state.[23] The pastor declared, "Every one of us, without exception, must be in subjection to the Nazi Führer-state as the authority which actually has power over us . . . So for us the National Socialist authority is ordained of God, that we should be in subjection to her."[24] The pastor preached at a time when the Nazi persecution of the churches continued unabated. Just that year, the Gestapo closed down Confessing Church seminaries, driving them underground, and arrested hundreds of pastors, including the Confessing Church leader Otto Dibelius of Berlin, who was put on trial for conspiracy against the state for an open letter he sent to the Minister of Church Affairs, Hans Kerrl, critical of Nazi ideology.[25]

Yet this anonymous pastor argued that regardless of whether the authority respects the teachings and ministry of Jesus, Christians should remain obedient to it. He continued, "Authority remains authority, even if it does injustice, just as father remains father and mother, mother, even if their children do injustice."[26] The pastor seemed to acknowledge that the Nazi regime had committed injustice (thus the comparison to an unjust parent), and yet this reality did not obviate the Christian's duty of obedience to the state. Unlike Niemöller, this pastor did not entertain the possibility that the state could demand the citizen to commit evil—nor did he consider what to do in such an instance. No doubt this sermon came as unwelcome intelligence to the Sopade, as it looked for evidence that opposition might emerge from a united Confessing Church. Sermons such as these demonstrate that pastors modeled obedience to the Nazi state for their congregants, placing themselves under the authority of Scripture in doing so. The continued adherence to the Christian duty of obedience to the state is one key element in understanding why Confessing Church pastors did not speak out more explicitly and forcefully against the Nazi state.

DRAWING THE BOUNDARIES

Confessing pastors at times used the pulpit to clarify and differentiate their position from National Socialists and their supporters, often reframing concepts or words that the Nazis appropriated. These expressions reveal dissent among the pastors. As discussed in chapter 1, dissent is not meant to undermine the Nazi regime, work toward its downfall, or limit its dominance in any way, but merely to express dissatisfaction. One clear example of a contested concept is the Hitler greeting (*Hitlergruß*), "Heil Hitler," said in conjunction with the upraised right arm. The Nazi regime made the Hitler greeting a "general civic duty and . . . mandatory in all party and state buildings and commemorative sites" on July 13, 1933.[27] But the use of *Heil* (salvation) as a wish and greeting in Germany goes back centuries.[28] Cornelia Schmitz-Berning notes a biblical basis in passages such as Revelation 7:10, in which the multitude of God's people say in unison, "Salvation belongs to our God who is seated on the throne" (*Heil sei dem, der auf dem Stuhl sitzt, unserm Gott*).[29] By the later eighteenth century, *Heil* was widely used as an "emphatic expression of wishes and greetings," meaning that the speaker wished salvation and health to the person he or she greeted.[30] Into the twentieth century, one might hear "Heil Kaiser and Reich," "Heil my fatherland," and into the 1920s, "Heil Ludendorf" and "Heil Hitler."[31] The greeting "Heil Hitler" not only expresses hope for the health of Hitler, but it also implies that he is the one through whom blessings and healing come.[32] This biblical wish and greeting, *Heil*, coupled with the Hitler salute confuses the basis for hope in the desired "salvation." What was once a short-form greeting that implied salvation comes from God became greeting that implied salvation comes from Hitler.

Thus, when Confessing pastors commented in their sermons on the use of *Heil* in the Third Reich, their aim was often to reorient the Christian's perception of the source of salvation. One pastor who took issue with the Nazi use of *Heil* was Pastor Julius Sammentreuther. A mere ten days after the Nazi regime decreed the use of the *Hitlergruß* on July 13, 1933, Sammentreuther reflected in a Sunday sermon on Isaiah 62:11 and the prophet's proclamation to the people of Israel, "See, your salvation comes." Sammentreuther argued that this announcement of salvation is "a profound Word" (*ein tiefes Wort*) at the core of the gospel message. He did not explicitly criticize the Nazi greeting, Hitler, or the National Socialist government for using the *Hitlergruß*, but he tried to put the greeting *Heil* in a biblical context, to reassert the Christian claim on this word, that salvation only comes from God.[33]

Confessing pastors also pushed back on German Christians' appropriation of Protestant history. Martin Luther's legacy became a key point of contention. German Christians used his memory to validate their nazification of the Christian faith. Recalling the sermon that opened this chapter, Vogel asked the rhetorical question, "What would Luther do?" If Luther were to sit before a German Christian like Reinhold Krause or Ludwig Müller and listen to their assaults on the content of the Christian faith, it is clear, Vogel argued, that he would courageously stand for the gospel truth. Vogel's sermon reveals the concern that German Christians ignored Luther's message while celebrating his spirit; they focused on his style but not his substance.

A good case in point is Martin Niemöller's sermon on the day of the Reformation Festival, October 31, 1933, two weeks before Krause's speech. Niemöller preached at his Dahlem church on Romans 3:28, a passage central to the Lutheran tradition: "For we hold that a person is justified by faith apart from works prescribed by the law." In this All Hallows' Eve sermon, Niemöller reminded his church that it must choose its own path to travel: the neo-pagan or the Christian. Without explicitly naming the German Christian movement, Niemöller criticizes those who praise the "Luther spirit" (*Luthergeist*) to extol the courage and tenacity of the man and yet at the same time neglect the content of his message:

> Certainly I do not wish to dissuade anyone from taking the man Luther as a pattern; but I must certainly dissuade anyone from thinking—nay, I must seriously warn anyone against thinking—that the struggle for existence between the Protestant church and Rome and the neo-pagans of today could possibly be waged and won with this Luther spirit.[34]

This term "Luther spirit" had been used by Nazis and pro-Nazi supporters to link Nazism and Protestantism. For example, it appeared in the German Christian movement's ten-point program to advance their candidates in the 1932 church elections.[35] A few months after Hitler and the Nazis came to power, during celebrations of Luther's 450th birthday, the Königsberg Gauleiter (Nazi district leader) and future Reich Commissioner of Ukraine Erich Koch explicitly stated that the Nazis cultivated Luther's spirit.[36] As Ericksen argues, this term "illustrates the German Christian desire to be tied into German history and the 'German spirit,' and Martin Luther had simply the largest shoulders on which to rest such an idea."[37] German Christians wanted to claim Luther's "Germanness" and heroism but downplay his doctrine.[38] Remarkably, this desire to preserve Luther's doctrinal legacy was a bond of unity connecting pastors who may have supported Nazism but refused to compromise traditional Protestantism together with pastors who criticized Nazism as a false ideology.

It is one thing for Niemöller to dissent over the use of Luther's memory within the German Protestant churches, but it is quite another for him to publicly point out "the struggle for existence" between the Church and "neo-pagans" of Nazi Germany. He warned his congregants not to be swayed by the loud voices and bold proclamations of the "neo-pagans" commandeering the legacy of Luther in an attempt to advance a new reformation in Germany. Instead, he exhorted them to remain steadfast in the traditional faith. For Niemöller, Luther's great contribution to Christianity was his emphasis on faith alone, not his forceful, heroic personality. Niemöller criticized those in German society who say: "'If you are as much of a nationalist and as much of a socialist as your Führer desires, you are a Christian though you may not know it.'"[39] He continued, "It is even said that our whole nation would be doing the will of God if only it has purified its species and race. Deeds of the law on which to base a claim to God's favor! Of course Christ is to remain and faith is to remain—they are also to remain."[40] For the Christian, he argued, there exists one path to salvation, and that is through Christ as testified in the Scripture; thus, all other "gods or demigods" can only distract and lead one astray.[41] This sermon is a clear example of how dissent over the perceived German Christian abuse of Luther's memory within the Protestant churches led a pastor into direct opposition to Nazi ideology.

These sermons reveal a controversy in the German Protestant churches about how to interpret and use the legacy of Martin Luther to address current issues in the German Protestant churches. Luther as a German hero played a significant role in drawing boundaries and establishing identities between the German Christian movement and the Pastors' Emergency League (and later the Confessing Church). In a later chapter we will turn to explore the use of Luther's legacy to address antisemitism in the Nazi regime.

Dissent may also be discerned in pastors' specific word choices that advanced the autonomy of the German churches vis-à-vis the Nazi state. Klemperer once asked what one may do "if the cultivated language is made up of poisonous elements or has been made the bearer of poisons?"[42] His answer: the individual has a choice not to use the "poisoned" language. For example, a pastor may prefer to say *das Vaterland* ("fatherland") rather than *der Führerstaat* ("the Führer state") or variations of the term.[43] For example, Helmut Gollwitzer briefly commented in a sermon on the Lord's Prayer published in 1941 that Catholics who have been "very concerned about life and the Fatherland" often pray the rosary and the Lord's Prayer together.[44] His meaning would have been subtly different had he said *"der Führerstaat"* instead, which would infer a desire for the preservation of Hitler's Germany. Using the term *Vaterland* draws on the long history of the German people, transcending any one political state or time frame, whereas using the term *Führerstaat* not only infers the legitimacy of the particular political system but also limits the reference to a specific time and place.

One may also discern a pastor's dissent when using the term *der Bürger* ("the citizen") and its various forms to refer to German citizens rather than *der Volksgenosse* ("people's comrade," which carries racial and ethnic connotations).[45] While the former simply refers to a fellow subject of the state with specific rights under the law, the latter adds to this meaning the Nazi conception of a racially pure member of the state.[46] For example, Alfred de Quervain, in a sermon series on the Ten Commandments, argued that the preached word has the power to change lives: "Anyone who has heard the word has awakened from his dreams as a citizen (*Bürger*), as a statemen, as a judge, as a soldier and his political thinking and actions have found a new focus."[47] By using *Bürger* instead of *Volksgenosse*, Quervain serves his main point that the preached word orients the publicly active individual to the things of God, as opposed to other loyalties. Indeed, pastors had to consciously decide whether to use words imbued with Nazi ideology or not, words such as *Volksgemeinschaft*, *Arier*, and *Gleichschaltung*. The meaning of non-conformist word choices is significant because language contributes to the shaping of our perspectives and beliefs—and even our actions.[48] Klemperer argued that to use Nazi language would be to "abandon oneself" to it, so that it "increasingly dictates [one's] feelings and governs [one's] entire spiritual being."[49] A pastor simply using expressions of dissent—without even commenting or elaborating on why he made the word choice—demonstrated a degree of independence from Nazi ideology, and even dissent from specific elements of it.

This is not to say that pastors aligned with the Confessing Church only or always used non-conformist language, but simply that they oftentimes did. It should also be stated that pastors who used non-conformist expressions may not have been motivated by dissent against Nazi ideology; rather, they could have used these expressions merely from force of habit or a desire to appeal to their specific audience (among other motivations). Thus, the use of these non-conforming expressions may best be understood as a potential sign of a pastor's dissent.

In considering expressions of dissent and opposition from the pulpit, it is worthwhile to consider the obvious. Could one argue that the simple act of preaching the gospel message clearly and persuasively constitutes an act of opposition? Dean Stroud has made the insightful argument that "when a preacher exegetes the biblical text faithfully and in obedience to the biblical text, he may find himself challenged to say dangerous words that will demand from him 'civic courage' (*Zivilcourage*)."[50] This assertion accounts well for the assumption embedded in the Protestant tradition that the preached Word is an agent of sanctification—an instrument of positive change—in the world (see discussion on this in chapter 4). Stroud continues, "Without the preacher intending to be controversial or political, the Holy Spirit may make him so in the faithful hearing and proclaiming of Scripture."[51] In the context of Nazi Germany, he argues, the passionate and eloquent proclamation of the gospel is "daring" and a form of resistance.[52] Stroud makes a provocative point that the faithful preaching of Scripture itself constitutes resistance in the context of Nazi Germany.[53]

Although I would disagree with Stroud's assertion that a passionate preaching of the gospel is sufficient to qualify the sermon as a form of resistance (as defined in chapter 1), he makes an important point that Scripture itself, and Scripture clearly elucidated in a sermon, can potentially undermine the prevailing political and social systems and their values. For example, in a confirmation sermon on April 9, 1938, in Kieckow, Bonhoeffer preached on the story of the father in Mark 9 who asked Jesus to heal his sick child, "if he were able." Jesus responds to the father, "If you are able! All things can be done for the one who believes." Then follows the verse upon which Bonhoeffer bases his sermon, the father's response, "I believe; help my unbelief!" (Mark 9:14). Bonhoeffer argued that our "Yes" to God demands our "No" to all that opposes God, "to all injustice, to all evil, to all lies, to all oppression and violation of the weak and the poor, to all godlessness and mocking of the Holy."[54] Bonhoeffer's clear reading of the Scriptural text and powerful preaching could be understood as dissent that blurs into opposition from the pulpit. Indeed, it is hard to believe that his hearers would not have thought of Hitler, the Nazis, and National Socialism in this context.

Even a somewhat obscure text could provide a basis for inspiration to deny Nazism and its values. For example, Pastor Wilhelm Busch of Essen preached a sermon on February 22, 1944, on Matthew 27:42, which reads, "If he be the King of Israel, let him come down from the cross, and we will believe him." True faith, Busch argued, is based on Scripture, not wishes; and it does not say "climb down from the cross," but rather "I will go with you to the cross, so that I might live with you, who have risen from the dead."[55] True faith, he argued, is living in the way of the cross, not in the world, and not in the way of National Socialism; one must deny oneself, take up one's cross, and follow Christ, not Hitler.

Likewise, the attentive congregant may contemplate the Christian concept of sacrificial love as preached in a sermon and relate to his Jewish neighbors in brave ways that undermine Nazi policies of exclusion. Or a congregant may reflect on a pastor's sermon on how "the whole world lies under the power of the evil one" in his or her time and place, thereby calling into question the ideology and policies of the Nazi state. In fact, the list of verses that can inspire the heart to critique contemporary political systems and ideologies is virtually innumerable. Indeed, a pastor may purposefully select a text to encourage their congregants to critique aspects of the Nazi state, or a pastor may even be drawn to preach on a particularly impactful passage by the given lectionary.

However, Stroud's assertion that a faithfully preached sermon may be understood as a form of resistance is a theological claim, not a historical claim. It cannot be demonstrated using extant primary sources. First, one cannot definitively conclude that a pastor *intended* to offer dissent or opposition by selecting a particular passage if he did not connect the biblical text to the contemporary situation (either directly or indirectly). After all, the German Christians preached on many of these same texts, and yet they supported Nazi ideology. Second, if Stroud is correct that sermons that faithfully proclaimed the gospel constituted a form of resistance, then one would expect the churches to be hotbeds of resistance. But the fact of the matter is that they were not (as discussed in chapter 1). The churches had the potential to become sites of significant opposition to the Nazi regime, given the failure of *Gleichschaltung* (coordination) in the churches, and yet unified opposition did not materialize. Third, as will be argued in depth in chapter 9, the Nazi secret police did not concern themselves with passionate preaching of the gospel, indicating they did not consider it a threat to the regime; they did not perceive passionate preaching of the gospel, in itself, as opposition or resistance. Their reports indicate concern over direct or indirect expressions that sought to undermine the Nazi regime and its leadership and ideology. Fourth, even though a pastor may have intended to express opposition by preaching a particular passage, we would still need evidence from the congregant to confirm that it was understood as such. After all, most congregants do not take the time to record their thoughts about sermons after they are preached (though evidence may indeed surface in the future). Lastly, I am not aware of any evidence to suggest that resisters to the Nazi regime, such as members of the White Rose group or the conspirators of the 20 July bomb plot, were inspired to resist because of the passionate preaching of the gospel. Their individual lives of faith may certainly have formed their decisions to resist, but there is no evidence as far as I am aware to suggest that specific sermons in which the pastor faithfully preached the gospel had a direct impact on their decisions to actively resist.

In sum, expressions of opposition comprise a wide range of words and phrases that indicate dissatisfaction in some sense with the Nazi regime. While a pastor's intent, specific meaning, or desired outcome may not always be clear when using these expressions, they provide the historian with nuanced evidence of pastors' responses to inter-church debates and the rise of the Nazi regime. Let us now turn our attention to pastors' statements of opposition that clearly undermined Nazi ideology and the state.

AGAINST NAZI FALSE BELIEFS

At times pastors challenged, criticized, or condemned elements of National Socialism, the Nazi regime, and even specific leaders, thereby undermining them publicly from the authority of the pulpit. As pastors formulated their sermons, they occasionally commented on the unwarranted Nazi elevation of race, ethnicity, and nationalism that denies the universality of Christianity. Of the over 900 sermons analyzed, 60 of them contain statements that unequivocally criticize National Socialism (though, again, these sermons cannot be understood to be representative of all Confessing Church sermons). These statements of opposition more clearly indicate the intent and motivation of the pastor to directly undermine Nazi ideology compared to expressions of dissent. In the pastors' efforts to make their congregants aware of the perceived contradictions between Christianity and National Socialism, they spoke of contemporary threats to Christianity and the German churches. This section will explore how some pastors used sermons to challenge their congregations and realign Christian allegiance from the state or Hitler back to God.

To begin, merely pointing out apparent contradictions between National Socialism and Christianity could subvert the Nazi state's totalitarian claim on the individual.[56] For example, Pastor Rudolf Eberhard from Spremberg preached a sermon on an unspecified national holiday in 1933, that expressed the need for Christians to evaluate how consistently National Socialism and Christianity relate to one another. He stated unequivocally, "We must decisively reject all attempts to come to a *völkish* religion. One can't make religions. Religion occurs solely through the revelation of God himself." He continued in a more diplomatic vein,

> I need only recall the question of the nationality and the purity of the race, and the effort to eradicate all foreign influence from national and state life. These thoughts call for a balance and for reconciliation with the thoughts of the old gospel of the Father in Heaven and his crucified Christ. They want to be purified, deepened and clarified. It is the thoughts that today have found the swastika as their symbol.
> But to us it is about the vital nerve of the poignant question of our nation: Will the swastika as a sign of nationalist idealism [*völkischen Idealismus*] encounter and see the cross of Golgotha, the sign of biblical Christianity?[57]

Eberhard advised his congregation to use Christianity as the standard by which to judge National Socialism. While he diplomatically acknowledged the possibility of striking a "balance" or "reconciliation" between the two worldviews—the Christian and the Nazi—he clearly stated that Christians cannot lose sight of what makes them Christian, that is, believing in the "old gospel," the "good news" of God's revelation, that God rules and saves through the work of Jesus on the cross. Thus, Christianity is the standard through which Nazi ideas must be interpreted. Nazism must "see the cross," meaning, it must give way when apparent contradictions to Christianity emerge. The task, as Eberhard argued, is to work to adapt National Socialism to biblical principles, not the other way around. Herein is his criticism: the German churches cannot let Nazi ideology and its symbol, the swastika, silence the gospel message available to all people, regardless of race or nationality. This sermon of 1933 is a window into the debate within the German Protestant churches about how to come to terms with the success of National Socialism and the establishment of the Nazi state. Clarifying the apparent contradictions gave pastors the opportunity to affirm which belief system they believed must have pride of place in the Christian heart.

The problem some pastors had with National Socialism was that it presented false idols to the German faithful as objects of worship. These false idols could include Hitler, the "Aryan" race, the German nation, and the "fallen heroes" of the past. Just a month after Hitler's rise to power, Dietrich Bonhoeffer preached a sermon in Berlin on the first Sunday of Lent, February 26, 1933, on Gideon's great faith in trusting God to defeat his enemies on the battlefield (Judges 6:15–16; 7:2; 8:23). Bonhoeffer argued that all people put their faith in something, and he asks his audience to reflect upon what this is for them. He affirmed that Christians can trust in only one lord, and they must then offer worship to God alone. He criticized those Christians who attempted to place another savior on the altar. Bonhoeffer declared,

> In the church we have only *one* altar—the altar of the Most High, the One and only, the Almighty, the Lord, to whom alone be honor and praise, the Creator before whom all creation bows down, before whom even the most powerful are but dust [emphasis in original]. We don't have any side altars at which to worship human beings.[58]

It has been suggested that Bonhoeffer was referring to the adoration of Hitler as the savior of Germany by some in the German Christian movement.[59] Indeed, given the context, it seems this interpretation is the correct one. But Bonhoeffer does not explicitly mention Hitler by name in this sermon. His focus is on issuing a warning to all those who put their ultimate faith and hope in themselves or others as opposed to God. He contended, "all the altars of gods and idols fall down, all worship of human beings and human self-idolization. They are all judged, condemned, cancelled out, crucified, and toppled into the dust before the One who alone is Lord."[60]

Just as a warning about the exaltation of false idols can help Christians spiritually reorient themselves in the church, so also can a reminder of the

Church's core identity as the body of Christ. After all, the nature of the Church's identity lies in its confession that Jesus is the Christ. The success of the German Christian movement and the disunity of the German Protestant churches raised a question that cut to the quick: In whom or what does the Church ultimately confess faith for salvation? This is a question pastors used to clarify what was at stake in the inter-church debates between the German Christians and the Confessing Church.

For example, just a few months after Bonhoeffer's remarkable Lenten sermon, he preached another oppositional sermon in Berlin on July 23, 1933, on the challenges facing the German Protestant churches. This was the very day of the previously mentioned church elections.[61] Hitler even weighed in on the elections, broadcasting a fifteen-minute speech on the radio supporting the German Christian movement's candidates in an attempt to align the churches with National Socialist ideology.[62] Bonhoeffer used the famous passage in Matthew 16:13–18, in which Peter declared Jesus the Christ. Jesus responds to his confession, "on this rock I will build my church." It is a passage that speaks to the very nature and identity of the Church: simply, the Church confesses Jesus as "the Christ, the Son of the living God." Bonhoeffer urges his listeners to maintain and protect the Church that "confesses Christ, the Confessing Church—not the church of opinions and ideas."[63] Nazi ideas have no place in the Church, Bonhoeffer argued, and Christians should vote accordingly.

Bonhoeffer argued that the task of Christians was not to build the Church themselves, to form it into something new, but to continue to confess Christ. Bonhoeffer perceived in the German Christian movement a desire to adapt the church, to revise its teachings, to rebuild it for a new era. He responded, "Whoever thinks he can build the church is already destroying it. For what he is building is a temple for idols, without knowing or wishing it."[64] This sermon presents an election-day debate about the nature and identity of the German Protestant churches. Bonhoeffer supported a traditional understanding of the Church as one that fundamentally confesses Christ and argued against the German Christian movement, which sought to change it to suit the times.

Likewise, pastors challenged the practice of hero worship or of giving the living or dead undue reverence, thereby reorienting Christians to right worship of God. In a sermon on July 23, 1933, Robert Frick of Bethel warned Christians about figures and symbols that can lead one astray from the gospel message. Frick argued that, yes, Germans ought rightly to celebrate the lives and sacrifices of national heroes and leaders, such as Martin Luther, as well as the kings and prophets of Scripture, such as Solomon and Jonah. But this appreciation must have its limits or one risks worshiping idols in the place of God. In a bold, succinct style, he summarized the rule Christians always ought to follow. "No other symbol than the symbol of the cross—no other leader [*Führer*] than the living Christ . . . Only one symbol: the cross! Only one leader [*Führer*]: Christ! And only in the knowledge of our powerlessness is given the assurance of his power!"[65] Frick asserted that Christians in Germany must remember that their allegiance, their source of unity and strength, lies in God, not worldly Führers—clearly a reference to Hitler. The concern is that Christians in Nazi Germany are being distracted or, at worst, duped into worshiping unworthy symbols and leaders, such as the swastika and Hitler, respectively. Confessing pastors such as Bonhoeffer and Frick explicitly named the sin of idol worship in an attempt to reorient Germans to a true faith in God alone.

Remarkably, the distress evident in these sermons of opposition is not predominantly about Hitler's policies or the Nazi regime's manner of governing; rather, the concern is focused on the elevation of Hitler, the swastika (as a symbol of National Socialism), and the Nazi state as idols of worship or undue reverence. Pastor Wilhelm Hertzberg of Caldern (near Marburg) speaks specifically to this point in a sermon on Ephesians 2:19–22, delivered in July 1933. He preached on God's miraculous work of building the Church on the "foundation of the apostles and prophets," and he affirmed that no political leader or state can save the Christian people. He argued,

> Christ is the cornerstone of our lives. Our soul needs him. We need him for our guilt and for our death. We must have him as our savior and bringer of peace (*Friedebringer*). No one, no state, no political leader (*Führer*) can give us peace and happiness. Only he can do that, in whose hands is time and eternity, who is set to judge the living and the dead.[66]

We see this same theme in another sermon by Pastor Hans Schnieber of St. Johannes in Leipzig. At the evening service of the people's Day of Mourning (*Volkstrauertag*) 1933, also the Second Sunday of Lent, he warned his congregants against making idols of leaders. He closed his sermon with prayer and thanks to "the highest Leader [*Führer*], Jesus Christ."[67] Neither Herzberg nor Schnieber explicitly named Hitler or criticized his work as the Chancellor of Germany. Their concern in these sermons does not appear to be what Hitler has done in office or his plans for the future of Germany but rather the hero worship they perceive other Christians giving to him. Furthermore, these sermons can be read as criticisms of Hitler's own self-promotion as *der Führer*, as the savior for the German people.[68] While they directly criticize Germans who set up Hitler as a savior-figure, they indirectly condemn Hitler for setting himself up as a leader to be revered.

Pastors who chose to criticize National Socialist ideology faced significant risks. The preaching ministry of Pastor Paul Schneider (1897–1939) illustrates the immanent dangers involved in publicly criticizing National Socialism as a false ideology.⁶⁹ Schneider was a pastor from a small rural parish in Hochelheim, not far from where he grew up. At the age of 17, Schneider enlisted in the German army to serve in the Second World War, earning the Iron Cross, Second Class. After the war he matriculated at the university in Giessen. As part of his theological education, he served a year-long practicum with a coal mining community so that he could personally engage with laborers to better understand their struggles and needs, and in his own words, to see "into what little corner of their hearts religion had hidden itself."⁷⁰ Schneider continued his ministry with the working classes in a Berlin suburb on the east side until 1926, when his father died. This gave him the opportunity to return to Hochelheim and become pastor in his stead.

Schneider's appointment lasted eight years, from 1926 to 1934, when his reputation among the community suffered because of his vociferous criticisms of the German Christian movement and, in particular, against Nazi leaders, such as Goebbels.⁷¹ In one of his last sermons, delivered on January 28, 1934, just one month before the community and his church compelled him to resign, Schneider offered a scathing critique of the German Christian movement and Nazism. He based his sermon on two texts: first, the story of Jesus calming the stormy sea in Luke 8:22–25; and the second, from Matthew 14:22–32, the story of Jesus' walking on the water in a stormy sea, asking Peter to have the faith to step out of the boat and walk. Schneider opened with the obvious: the German Evangelical Church is in the midst of a terrible storm caused by the ambitions of German Christian members to adapt Christianity to the racial ideology of Nazism. He continued,

> Insofar as they place "blood and race" alongside the will of God as authentic sources of revelation, alongside the will of God revealed alone in the words of Scripture, alongside Jesus as the only mediator between God and men, they, in all truth, fall away from the living God and his living Christ. In our church a blazing fire has broken out over these matters, and there can be no peace until those who have betrayed the pure teaching and those wolves who have come into the sheepfold in sheep's clothing have vacated their bishops' chairs and their seats as our representatives.⁷²

Schneider did not mince words. He refused to allow pro-Nazi Christians to place "blood and race" alongside scripture as an authoritative source of divine revelation. He even took aim at one figure he considered responsible for the confusion in the church, Alfred Rosenberg. He condemned the "naked paganism" of Rosenberg's book, *The Myth of the Twentieth Century* (*Der Mythus des zwanzigsten Jahrhunderts*), published in 1930.

But what is perhaps most interesting about this passage is Schneider's condemnation of "wolves" who have come into the German Evangelical Church and taken up the seats of authority, as bishops and representatives of the provincial churches. He preached this sermon just six months after the July 1933 church elections and after Hitler hand-picked Ludwig Müller as bishop of the *Reichskirche*. The church cannot be at peace with wolves "protecting" the sheepfold. Schneider warned his congregants to wake up in the midst of a tempest, to batten down the hatches, and to fight for the survival of the "little boat of the church . . . traveling on stormy seas."[73]

This sermon was the last straw for Schneider's congregation, who pressured him to resign. Schneider found friendlier congregations in the Confessing churches and began working as a pastor simultaneously in the Rhineland towns of Dickenshied and nearby Womrath. Schneider continued to preach against the German Christian movement and Nazism, and had been arrested three times, at which point, on July 24, 1937, the Nazi regime banished him from his congregations and the area, a punishment known as "internal exile."[74] While Schneider initially refused to leave his congregations at Dickenshied and Womrath, his wife and friends compelled him to flee to Baden-Baden, which he finally did. However, the ruling elders at his church in Womrath urged him to return because the people had no pastor to serve their spiritual and pastoral needs. He returned on October 3, 1937, to preach once again. Schneider delivered his last sermon, first in Dickenshied, and then made his way to Womrath to preach—though he would never make it. The Gestapo pulled him over, arrested him, and took him to jail in Koblenz.[75] On November 27, 1937, Schneider was brought to the concentration camp at Buchenwald. Relentless, he continued to preach in the camp. He even criticized Nazi atrocities in the camp. After beatings and torture did not silence him, the camp infirmary staff gave him a lethal injection of strophanthin on July 18, 1939. He was the first Protestant clergyman murdered in the concentration camps of Nazi Germany.[76]

Schneider's story, like that of Niemöller's, reveals that pastors had a degree of freedom in the pulpit to frequently criticize the Nazi regime and its ideology. While Schneider was harassed and arrested, and while he lost his pastorate and had to find new work, he was not sent to a concentration camp until after four years of voicing criticisms from the pulpit—again, like Niemöller. One critical sermon was generally not enough to send a pastor to a concentration camp, though, as will be discussed in chapter 9, it was enough to draw the attention of the Gestapo. We will see this dynamic play out in the subsequent chapters.

Like Schneider, some Confessing Church pastors occasionally took aim from the pulpit at specific Nazi leaders as purveyors of the perceived Nazi blasphemy. What is most remarkable is that these pastors did not target

Hitler as the preacher *par excellence* of Nazi ideology—the key formulator and popularizer of National Socialism. To target Hitler directly as the most influential proponent of Nazism would transgress the line of obedience to governing authorities. Instead, pastors focused attention on less predominant but still influential proponents of Nazi ideology and *völkish* religion. The two most common targets of criticism were Alfred Rosenberg and Arthur Dinter.

Rosenberg, as previously noted, was the author of *The Myth of the Twentieth Century* and a prominent ideologue of Nazi Germany. He became the head of the Office of Foreign Affairs in 1933 and remained its leader until the fall of Nazi Germany. In 1941 he became the Reich Minister for the Occupied Eastern Territories. But it was Rosenberg's approach to Christianity—as outlined in *Der Mythus*—that drew the ire of Confessing Church pastors. He advanced the notion that Christianity was an antiquated, obsolete, and life-denying superstition that was destined for the rubbish heap of history. But more than this, he argued that Germans faced two enemies from within, yet both of which had international ties: the Jews and Christians (especially Catholics).[77] Barnett encapsulates Rosenberg's position succinctly: "Germany's churches compromised the ideals of Volk and Fatherland by their 'shameful' worship of the cross, which . . . had no place in the spiritual life of a proud people."[78] The *Mythus* did not simply deny the truth claims of Christianity, but it designated the faith a detriment to the German *Volk* and Christian worship as tantamount to treason. This is why Rosenberg in particular attracted the criticism of pastors. Hitler, at least, in the Nazi Party Platform, committed to the support of "positive Christianity," as nebulous as this phrase was.

Arthur Dinter was a First World War veteran who propagated a brand of German *völkisch* religion in his bestselling novel *Die Sünde wider das Blut* ("The Sin Against the Blood") of 1919 and subsequent novels, and via the *Geistchristliche Religionsgemeinschaft* ("Spiritual Christian Religious Community"), founded in 1927, later renamed the *Deutsche Volkskirche* ("German People's Church").[79] Dinter also served as the National Socialist Gauleiter of Thuringia from 1925 to 1927, at which point Hitler removed him for fostering religious dissension.[80] Yet he remained an extraordinarily popular *völkisch* religious leader who sought the "de-judaization" of Christianity, including the removal of the Old Testament from the Christian canon as it was, he claimed, "based upon lies and betrayal, business and profit."[81] Moreover, George Kren and Rodler Morris have argued that Dinter "was decisive in defining the Nazi image of the Jew" as demonic force.[82] He advanced the notion that Jesus was an "Aryan" and that Christianity had been corrupted by the Jewish faith.[83]

Confessing Church pastors directly criticized Rosenberg and Dinter for the perceived damage they had done to the German churches. Martin Niemöller was a particularly outspoken critic. For example, in a sermon entitled "Mary and Martha," delivered on Septuagesima Sunday (ninth Sunday before Easter) in 1935, he reflected on the status of the German churches in Nazi Germany. He asked, "What shall we in the Confessional Church do, that our nation may be saved for the Lord Jesus Christ and led back to the Christian faith? Can this result be achieved by a united church, by bishops and synods, or by discussions with the German Christians, with Dinter and Rosenberg?"[84] The health of the German churches is not dependent upon organization, Niemöller argued, or the installation of new leadership and governance, or especially compromises with individuals or groups that want to adapt it or transform it to suit the new challenges of the day. Niemöller asserted that the approach of the Nazis and their supporters is wrong-headed and can only lead to the decline of the German churches. Only one thing needed to be done, he argued, and that was to confess Christ before God and humanity. Confession defines the Church and it is the only action that can renew it. In other sermons Niemöller called Dinter's perspective an "antichrist worldview" (*christusfeindliche Weltanschauung*) and Rosenberg's ideology a source of "utter confusion" in the church, leading to a "semi-darkness where we cannot see the way."[85]

Likewise, Pastor Paul Hinz of Kolberg tackled Rosenberg's claims about Christianity head-on in a sermon on September 1, 1935. From the pulpit of St. Marien Cathedral he preached on Romans 8:33–39, in which the apostle Paul proclaims triumphantly that Christians "are more than conquerors through him who loves [them]." Hinz criticized those in his own day, such as Rosenberg, who rejected the Jewish and Christian concepts of sin and grace. He says, "Rosenberg and many speakers who follow him claim that sin and grace are terms that the Jewish Rabbi Paul introduced from Jewish thought into Christianity and with which he had falsified the original message of Jesus."[86] Hinz directly challenged the notion that Christian concepts such as grace and sin make for a "weak-minded" and "submissive" people. Christians are "more than conquerors," able to confront the worst of humanity and, with God's help, to change for the better. Hinz's sermon not only criticized pro-Nazi Christian attempts to "aryanize" Christianity by diminishing Judaism as its foundation—and will be discussed later at length—but it also publicly challenged Rosenberg for his false and damaging characterization of Christianity.[87] In sum, when criticizing specific figures, Confessing Church pastors predominantly targeted those who were perceived to be most dangerous to the unity and orthodoxy of the German churches.

As can be gleaned from the examples already given, pastors used the demands of the biblical text to challenge their congregants to re-evaluate their priorities in faith and to take a stand with Christ. They occasionally selected biblical texts that referred in some sense to making a choice in the present moment, and then applied the action verbs of the biblical text as admonitions to their congregations in the present. An illustrative example is a sermon Paul Hinz preached at a military service on August 25, 1935, in which he encouraged the bold confession of Christ before God and men.[88] He used two texts as the basis for his sermon. One was Matthew 10:32–33, in which Jesus says to his disciples, "Everyone therefore who acknowledges me before others, I also will acknowledge before my Father in heaven; but whoever denies me before others, I also will deny before my Father in heaven." Relaying Jesus' admonition, Hinz argued that Christians must confess Christ before men.

The other text he used, Ephesians 6:10–17, includes numerous action verbs. I will quote the text in full and emphasize the calls to action.

> Finally, *be strong* in the Lord and in his mighty power. *Put on* the full armor of God, so that you can *take your stand* against the devil's schemes. For our struggle is not against flesh and blood, but against the rulers, against the authorities, against the powers of this dark world and against the spiritual forces of evil in the heavenly realms. Therefore *put on* the full armor of God, so that when the day of evil comes, you may *be able to stand your ground*, and after you have done everything, to stand. *Stand firm* then, with the belt of truth buckled around your waist, with the breastplate of righteousness in place, and with your feet fitted with the readiness that comes from the gospel of peace. In addition to all this, *take up* the shield of faith, with which you can extinguish all the flaming arrows of the evil one. *Take* the helmet of salvation and the sword of the Spirit, which is the word of God (Ephesians 6:10–17, emphasis added).

The Apostle Paul's admonitions to the Christians in Ephesus become Hinz's admonitions to Christians in Kolberg. Hinz acknowledged the difficult times in which Christians lived, and argued that the way forward for Christians was to make a decision and confess Christ. In confession, the Christian "fight[s] anti-Christian beliefs."[89] Remember, he said,

> Christ himself, our eternal Lord, our highest commander, is given all power in heaven and on earth . . . And his order of mobilization is summarized in one word, from the previously-selected text: Confess! Confess him before men! That is what we are called to do. And no one can be a Christian without confessing.[90]

The military tenor of the sermon suits not only the immediate context of a military worship service but the context of the Church Struggle as well. The instruction to "confess" is not simply about differentiating within the German churches "true" believers from those seeking to adapt Christianity to National Socialist principles, but more importantly, it acknowledges the Christian belief that there is power of salvation in the proclamation of the gospel. For pastors like Hinz, the gospel is a force that changes lives and, as Barth says, casts out demons. In this sermon Hinz readied his congregation for battle.

In addition to pastors criticizing specific elements of Nazi ideology, they could also use the Christian faith to identify and condemn Nazi policies that are based on National Socialist ideology. A sermon by Gerhard Ebeling delivered on July 17, 1940, in Berlin-Hermsdorf provides an illustrative example.[91] Ebeling was at one time a student of Dietrich Bonhoeffer at the seminary at Finkenwalde.[92] After graduating with a degree in theology from the University of Basel in 1938, he first began preaching to a congregation in Berlin that split during the Church Struggle, with some Confessing Church members in the congregation along with some German Christian members. A Thuringian German Christian pastor preached from the pulpit.[93] Ebeling preached in the only place he could within the church walls, a small space set apart in the sanctuary designated for Confessing Church members or supporters. This status essentially made him an illegal Confessing Church pastor. As one writer comments, "he was not the legal pastor of the Confessing group nor had the recognized church ordained him, but rather the 'illegal' Confessing Synod of Berlin-Brandenburg."[94] However, this situation was short-lived as Ebeling was drafted as a medic upon the outbreak of the Second World War just one year later.

Yet remarkably, he found time to preach when he came home from the front. One such opportunity presented itself in the summer of 1940 when a couple approached Ebeling to conduct a memorial service for their son. They told him that their son had mysteriously died of an unknown illness at an institution for the mentally ill.[95] The parents believed that their son had been killed as part of a Nazi regime policy to "euthanize" men and women with mental illnesses or disabilities. By the summer of 1939, Hitler and the Nazi regime began planning a "euthanasia" program, known as Action T4, a mundane codename for a chilling program, which was run from the Chancellery in Berlin, on Tiergartenstrasse 4.[96] The "euthanasia" program targeted men and women in asylums for the mentally ill, who were deemed "unworthy" of life, and thus "burdens" to society.[97] The program initially employed numerous functionaries, including doctors, nurses, lawyers, and professors to administer the program. By the summer of 1940, rumors spread among the populace about Nazi efforts to murder the mentally ill and disabled, even sparking protests by leading churchmen such as Cardinal Adolf Bertram of Breslau and, most famously, Bishop Clemens August von Galen of Münster, whose sermons galvanized public opposition to the Nazi policy and forced Hitler to close the T4 killing centers and decentralize the program.[98] Approximately 70,000 Germans were killed in the open phase of the program, from January 1940 to August 1941, while around 130,000 were killed afterward.[99] This figure does not include tens of thousands murdered in the program throughout Nazi-occupied Europe.[100]

Ebeling heard this family's story and agreed to conduct the memorial service on July 17, 1940. The sermon focused on Matthew 18:10, which states, "Take care that you do not despise one of these little ones; for, I tell you, in heaven their angels continually see the face of my Father in heaven." On the one hand, Ebeling warned the mourners not to speculate about what happened to this man, and yet, on the other hand, he identified the "little ones" as those "the world pushes aside, from whom people walk away, about whom no one inquires."[101] They are "the ones whom the world despises for the sake of its own belief"; and they are "those with no rights and the sick."[102] This sermon is a condemnation of the false belief system in Nazi Germany that has denigrated lives of the "little ones" as, in Nazi parlance, lives "unworthy of life." Ebeling encouraged the mourners at this man's memorial service to model their behavior after Jesus, who "called 'injustice' 'injustice,' 'wrong' 'wrong,' and 'sin' 'sin.'"[103] And even more, he admonished them not to "not abandon those Christ has accepted and for whom he died."[104] Christians of Nazi Germany, according to Ebeling, must "stand with the sick and the weak and those without rights to the end."[105]

This sermon is remarkable because it implicitly acknowledges what the family suspected, that this man had been murdered because he was ill, and that the reason he was murdered was because he was despised according to worldly "belief." Ebeling does not name Hitler, the National Socialist regime, or its ideology, yet the sermon condemns a society and a mental health system under Nazi control that denied dignity and life to the "little ones," those who could not care for themselves. In this way, it is a direct criticism of National Socialism. This sermon is a call to reconsider values in Germany and to stand up for those the Nazis have swept aside as "worthless." The following chapters will explore the myriad ways pastors criticized other Nazi policies, such as the persecutions of the churches and Jews.

CONCLUSION

Confessing Church pastors challenged Nazi ideology in a variety of ways from the pulpit. The pulpit became a primary location for pastors to publicly offer dissent or opposition to the perceived Nazi blasphemy. Indeed, one can consider the pulpit as the front line in the Confessing Church's struggle to retain autonomy, preserve orthodoxy, and protect tradition.

These sermons contributed to a public conversation about the nature and values of National Socialism. Expressions of dissent ranged from conscientious word choices to assertions about the nature of the Protestant

Reformation, each reflecting dissatisfaction with elements of National Socialism or the ecclesiastical reforms of pro-Nazi supporters. They help to reveal the general contours of pastors' perspectives of the Nazi state. They do not reflect a pastor's intention to undermine the Nazi regime or limit its dominance, but simply to express discontent. Yet expressions of opposition went further to criticize Hitler, the Nazi leadership, or the notion of the superiority of the "Aryan" race or the German nation, thereby undermining them as not worthy of worship or undue reverence. Statements of opposition clarified points of conflict between National Socialism and Christianity as belief systems. While the distinctions between dissent and opposition may become blurred at times—as can be seen in this chapter—the categories can be useful in distinguishing the meaning of critical expressions, as well as the pastors' intent in voicing them.

Statements of opposition served to delegitimize the Nazi totalitarian claim to the individual.[106] The sermon provided a means to preserve the church's identity, theology, and practice. They redirected the allegiance, obedience, and even worship of Christians away from the world and toward God. Furthermore, these sermons of opposition undermined the priorities and policies of the Nazi regime, providing an alternate vision for German society.

But Confessing Church pastors took to the pulpits to condemn more than just Nazi ideology. As hinted in some of the examples in this chapter, pastors also at times explicitly criticized the Nazi regime for its persecution of the German churches and pastors, to which we will now turn.

NOTES

1. See chapter 2 for a detailed discussion of Krause's speech.

2. Heinrich Vogel, Sermon manuscript: Reformationsgedächtnistag, I Könige 18:17–40, 19 November 1933, Papers of Heinrich Vogel, EZA 665/75.

3. Vogel, *Sermon on I Kings 18:17–40*, EZA 665/75.

4. Vogel, *Sermon on I Kings 18:17–40*, EZA 665/75.

5. Vogel, *Sermon on I Kings 18:17–40*, EZA 665/75.

6. Barnett, *For the Soul of the People*, 80.

7. "Heinrich Vogel." *The Canterbury Dictionary of Hymnology*. Canterbury Press, 2021, http://www.hymnology.co.uk/h/heinrich-vogel, accessed on May 19, 2021.

8. Thus, these sermons may be considered oppositional according to Kershaw's distinctions between resistance, opposition, and dissent; see Kershaw, *The Nazi Dictatorship*, 170–171.

9. The pastors and the number of incidents are the following: Dietrich Bonhoeffer (7), Helmut Gollwitzer (2), Franz Hildebrandt (6), Paul Hinz (8), Heinz Pflugk (1), Rudolf Eberhard (1), Friedrich Frick (1), Hans Iwand (1), Günther Harder (2), Hans Hertzberg (1), Hanns Lilje (1), Martin Niemöller (19), Rudolf Bultmann (1), Julius

Sammentreuther (1), Paul Schneider (2), Hans Schnieber (1), George Schulz (1), Karl von Schwartz (1), Wilhelm Staehlin (1), Heinrich Vogel (2).

10. Barnett, *For the Soul of the People*, 92.

11. Barnett, *For the Soul of the People*, 55; and Klaus Scholder, *The Churches and the Third Reich, Vol. 2, The Year of Disillusionment 1935, Barmen and Rome* (Philadelphia: Fortress Press, 1988), 169. See also Kirk, *Nazi Germany*, 108.

12. Gerlach, *And the Witnesses were Silent*, vii–viii; and Victoria Barnett, *For the Soul of the People: Protestant Protest Against Hitler* (New York: Oxford University Press, 1992), 198–199.

13. Hancock, *Karl Barth's Emergency Homiletic*, 69–70; and Jantzen, *Faith and Fatherland*, 28.

14. See Barnett, *For the Soul of the People*, 11; Uriel Tal, *Christians and Jews in Germany: Religion, Politics and Ideology in the Second Reich, 1870–1914* (Ithaca, NY: Cornell University Press, 1975), 292.

15. Cochrane, *The Church's Confession under Hitler*, 241.

16. Busch, *Barmen Then and Now*, location 1642. See also C. Nicolaisen, *Der Weg nach Barmen. Die Entstehungsgeschichte der theologischen Erklaerung von 1934* (Neukirchen-Vluyn: Neukirchener Verlag, 1985), 88.

17. Busch, *Barmen Then and Now*, location 1642.

18. Martin Niemöller, *Here Stand I*, translated by Jane Lymburn (New York: Willett, Clark & Co., 1937), 118.

19. Conway, *Nazi Persecution of the Churches*, 57, 72; Helmreich, *German Churches under Hitler*, 153, 263.

20. Barnett, *For the Soul of the People*, 83.

21. Niemöller, *Here Stand I*, 119–121.

22. Niemöller, *Here Stand I*, 122

23. *Deutschland-Berichte der Sozialdemokratischen Partei Deutschlands (Sopade), Vierter Jahrgang 1937* (Salzhausen: Verlag Petra Nettelbeck, 1980), 237–239.

24. *Sopade 1937*, 237.

25. This law banning the seminaries was officially known as the Himmler Decree of August 1937. See Barnett, *For the Soul of the People*, 87; and Conway, *The Nazi Persecution of the Churches*, 208–211.

26. *Sopade 1937*, 287.

27. Tilman Allert, *The Hitler Salute: On the Meaning of a Gesture* (New York: Metropolitan Books, 2008), 30.

28. Cornelia Schmitz-Berning, *Vocabular des Nationalsozialismus, ed. 2. durchgesehene und überarbeitete* (Aufl. Berlin: De Gruyter. 2007), 299.

29. Schmitz-Berning, *Vocabular des Nationalsozialismus*, 299. All German translations of the Bible are from the Luther 1912 edition, unless otherwise indicated.

30. Schmitz-Berning, *Vocabular des Nationalsozialismus*, 299.

31. Schmitz-Berning, *Vocabular des Nationalsozialismus*, 299.

32. Tilman Allert, *The Hitler Salute*, 39–40.

33. *Dein Wort ist deiner Kirche Schutz*, 124–126.

34. Niemöller, *Here Stand I*, 61.

35. Robert Ericksen, "Luther, Lutherans and the German Church Struggle," in *Kirchenliche Zeitgeschichte* 12 (1) (1999), 300.
36. Richard Steigmann-Gall, "'Furor Protestanticus': Nazi Conceptions of Luther, 1919–1933," in *Kirchliche Zeitgeschichte* 12 (1), 274.
37. Ericksen, "Luther, Lutherans and the German Church Struggle," 300.
38. Ericksen, "Luther, Lutherans and the German Church Struggle," 300, 306.
39. Niemöller, *Here Stand I*, 64.
40. Niemöller, *Here Stand I*, 64.
41. Niemöller, *Here Stand I*, 64–65.
42. Klemperer, *Language of the Third Reich*, 14.
43. For example, see Friedrich von Bodelschwingh, *Lebendig und Frei: Predigten, 2. Folge* (Bielefeld: Verlagshandlung der Anstalt Bethel, 1947),136; and Josef Rüling, *In der Nachfolge Jesu Predigten nach dem Gang des Kirchesjahres* (Leipzig: Heinsius, 1936), 20, 152.
44. Helmut Gollwitzer, *"Wir dürfen hören..." Predigten* (München: Chr. Kaiser Verlag, 1941), 61.
45. For example, see Paulus Hinz, Sermon manuscript on Mark 1:14–15, entitled "Von der rechten Büsse," 20 November 1935, Kolberg Dom, Papers of Paulus Hinz, EZA 766/5.
46. Schmitz-Berning, *Vocabular des Nationalsozialismus*, 662–664.
47. Alfred de Quervain, *Das Gesetz Gottes: Die zweite Tafel* (München: Chr. Kaiser Verlag, 1936), 18.
48. Klemperer, *Language of the Third Reich*, 14.
49. Klemperer, *Language of the Third Reich*, 14.
50. Stroud, *Preaching in Hitler's Shadow*, 44.
51. Stroud, *Preaching in Hitler's Shadow*, 44.
52. Stroud, *Preaching in Hitler's Shadow*, 184.
53. Stroud, *Preaching in Hitler's Shadow*, 54–55, 184.
54. Bonhoeffer, *Theological Education Underground*, Kindle location 14025.
55. Stroud, *Preaching in Hitler's Shadow*, 176.
56. See Michael Burleigh, *The Third Reich: A New History* (New York: Hill and Wang, 2000), 252–255.
57. Anton, *Nationale Feiertagspredigten und Ansprachen*, 45.
58. Bonhoeffer, *Berlin*, 462.
59. Bonhoeffer, *Berlin*, 462; see editor's notes on this sermon. Scholder's *The Churches and the Third Reich, Vol. 1*, also mentions the practice of a Nazi man in 1933, condemned to death for the murder of a communist in Upper Silesia, who fashioned for himself a little altar in his cell with Hitler's picture before which to pray (page 180).
60. Bonhoeffer, *Berlin*, 467.
61. See chapter 3 for a discussion of the church elections of July 23, 1933.
62. "Radio Broadcast by Hitler on the Church Elections, 22 July 1933," in Matheson, *The Third Reich and the Christian Churches: Documents*, 28; see also Helmreich, *German Churches under Hitler*, 142.
63. Robertson, ed., *Dietrich Bonhoeffer's Christmas Sermons*, 78.

64. Robertson, ed., *Dietrich Bonhoeffer's Christmas Sermons*, 80.
65. Kampffmeyer, ed., *Dein Wort ist deiner Kirche Schutz*, 47–48.
66. Kampffmeyer, ed., *Dein Wort ist deiner Kirche Schutz*, 55.
67. Anton, ed., *Nationale Feiertagspredigten und Ansprachen*, 203.
68. See Ian Kershaw, *Hitler: 1889–1936, Hubris* (New York: W.W. Norton, 1998), 483–486.
69. This biographical sketch is in large part based the excellent profile of Schneider by Dean Stroud in *Preaching in Hitler's Shadow*. He also provides the context in which this sermon of January 28, 1934, occurred. See also Albrecht Aichelin, *Paul Schneider: Ein radikales Glaubenszeugnis gegen die Gewaltherrschaft des Nationalsozialismus* (Gütersloh: Chr. Kaiser/ Gütersloher Verlagshaus, 1994); Rudolf Wentorf, *Der Fall des Pfarrers Paul Schneider: Eine biographische Dokumentation* (Neukirchen-Vluyn: Neukirchener Verlag, 1989); and *Paul Schneider, Der Prediger von Buchenwald*, ed. Margarete Schneider (Neuhausen/ Stuttgart: Hänssler, 1995).
70. Quoted in Stroud, *Preaching in Hitler's Shadow*, 87.
71. Stroud, *Preaching in Hitler's Shadow*, 88.
72. Stroud, *Preaching in Hitler's Shadow*, 90–91.
73. Stroud, *Preaching in Hitler's Shadow*, 90–91.
74. Stroud, *Preaching in Hitler's Shadow*, 106.
75. See Rudolf Wentorf, *Der Fall des Pfarrers Paul Schneider: Eine biographische Dokumentation* (Neukirchen-Vluyn: Neukirchener Verlag, 1989), 98.
76. See Stroud, *Preaching in Hitler's Shadow*, 106; Trence Prittie, *Germans against Hitler* (Boston: Little, Brown, 1964), 117–19; Conway, *Nazi Persecution of the Churches*, 209; and Claude Foster Jr., *Paul Schneider: The Buchenwald Apostle: A Christian Martyr in Nazi Germany. A Sourcebook on the German Church Struggle* (West Chester, PA: West Chester University, 1995).
77. Barnett, *For the Soul of the People*, 26.
78. Barnett, *For the Soul of the People*, 26.
79. See Steigmann-Gall, *The Holy Reich*, 30–31; and Conway, *Nazi Persecution of the Churches*, 13.
80. Steigmann-Gall, *The Holy Reich*, 59.
81. Quoted in George M. Kren and Rodler F. Morris, "Race and Spirituality: Arthur Dinter's Theosophical Antisemitism," in *Holocaust and Genocide Studies*, 6 (3), 1991, 242.
82. Kren and Morris, "Race and Spirituality," 246.
83. Kren and Morris, "Race and Spirituality," 239.
84. Niemöller, *Here Stand I*, 136.
85. Michael Heymel, *Martin Niemöller: Dahlemer Predigten, Kritische Ausgabe* (Gütersloher Verlagshaus, 2011), 266, 443.
86. Paul Hinz, Sermon manuscript on Romans 8:33–39, 1 September 1935, Collected Sermons of Paul Hinz, EZA 766/38.
87. In fact, Rosenberg was one of the most often criticized Nazi officials for voicing anti-Christian beliefs. His book, *The Myth of the Twentieth Century*, published in 1930, made him a leading and popular proponent of the Nazi "false ideology"

frequently condemned by Confessing Church pastors. See Barnett, *For the Soul of the People*, 26; and Helmreich, *German Churches under Hitler*, 154–155.

88. Paul Hinz, Sermon manuscript: "Durch die Wahrheit zur Freiheit," Pentecost 1943, Collected Sermons of Paul Hinz, EZA 766/5.

89. Hinz, "Durch die Wahrheit zur Freiheit," EZA 766/5.

90. Paul Hinz, Sermon manuscript: "Durch die Wahrheit zur Freiheit," Pentecost 1943, Collected Sermons of Paul Hinz, EZA 766/5.

91. Stroud, *Preaching in Hitler's Shadow*, 150.

92. This biographical sketch is largely based on the information provided in Dean Stroud's *Preaching in Hitler's Shadow* (Grand Rapids, MI: Eerdmans, 2013), 147–149. Stroud examines the context in which this sermon of July 17, 1940, occurred.

93. Stroud, *Preaching in Hitler's Shadow*, 147.

94. Stroud, *Preaching in Hitler's Shadow*, 147.

95. Stroud, *Preaching in Hitler's Shadow*, 147.

96. See Richard Evans, *Third Reich at War* (New York: Penguin, 2009), 82–101; Burleigh and Wippermann, *The Racial State: Germany 1933–1945* (New York: Cambridge University Press, 1991), 101–104, 141–149. The Nazi T4 program of murdering the mentally and chronically ill by gas in vans or killing centers was a precursor to the Nazi mass murder of Jews by lethal gas. See Debórah Dwork and Robert Jan van Pelt, *Holocaust: A History* (New York: W.W. Norton, 2002), 260–265; Christopher Browning, *The Origins of the Final Solution: The Evolution of Nazi Jewish Policy, September 1939—March 1942* (Lincoln, NE: University of Nebraska Press, 2004), 183–193; Leni Yahil, *The Holocaust: The Fate of European Jewry*, translated by Ina Friedman and Haya Galai (New York: Oxford University Press, 1987), 308–311.

97. Conway, *Nazi Persecutions of the German Churches*, 268–269.

98. Conway, *Nazi Persecutions of the German Churches*, 271–272; Michael Phayer, *The Catholic Church and the Holocaust, 1930–1965* (Bloomington, IN; Indiana University Press, 2000), 68–69.

99. For a discussion of the T4 "euthanasia" program and the figures of people murdered, see Browning, *The Origins of the Final Solution*, 189–192; Richard Evans, *The Third Reich at War* (New York: Penguin, 2009), 524–530; and Peter Longerich, *Holocaust: The Nazi Persecution and Murder of the Jews* (New York: Oxford, 2012), 277–280.

100. Browning, *The Origins of the Final Solution*, 189–192; Evans, *The Third Reich at War*, 524–530; and Longerich, *Holocaust*, 277–280.

101. Stroud, *Preaching in Hitler's Shadow*, 151–152.

102. Stroud, *Preaching in Hitler's Shadow*, 151–152.

103. Stroud, *Preaching in Hitler's Shadow*, 151–152.

104. Stroud, *Preaching in Hitler's Shadow*, 152.

105. Stroud, *Preaching in Hitler's Shadow*, 152. Helmut Thielicke, in his autobiography, *Notes of a Wayfarer*, describes a similar approach to a funeral service he led for a judge who "remained true to his faith" while serving the Nazi government. Thielicke provided a meditation on "the infinite worth of the individual before God," for the family of this man and the individuals present, many of whom he assumed were members of the Nazi Party and the SA. See Helmut Thielicke, *Notes of a*

Wayfarer (New York: Paragon House, 1995), 140. Special thanks to Kyle Jantzen for this reference.

106. Michael Burleigh, *The Third Reich: A New History* (New York: Hill and Wang, 2000), 252–255.

Chapter 6

Against the Nazi Persecution of the Churches

On the first Sunday after Pentecost, May 23, 1937, Confessing Church pastor Hans Ehrenberg publicly spoke out against the Nazi persecution of the German churches. His comments were not based simply on what he heard and witnessed, but on personal experiences as a man classified in Nazi Germany as *Volljude* (or full Jew). By the spring of 1937, Nazis in Bochum forced Ehrenberg out of his pastorate and into an unknown future. This Pentecost sermon would be one of his very last to the congregation he served for 12 years.

He chose as his text Romans 11:32–36, in which the Apostle Paul expressed wonder at God's "unsearchable" ways and judgments and encouraged Christians to rest in God's mercy. While Ehrenberg admitted that the end of his ministry in Bochum felt like a kind of death, he maintained faith that this exclusion from his community of faith was not the end. He reminded his audience that at the bleakest moment of Christ's crucifixion, after death on the cross and entombment, Christ resurrected from the grave. Ehrenberg proclaimed to his congregation, as much as to himself, "My office shall die. Very well, it dies, but it rises up again if we humble ourselves before he who is the Victor over death."[1] He then expanded the scope of his hope beyond the future of his own office and into the future of the churches in Germany, churches persecuted by the Nazi regime. He preached,

> Therefore, know: It is not our real difficulty [*echte Not*] that large masses leave the church, but that the Church still does not believe that in its impotence it is stronger than the world . . .
> Let us suffer together and continue to resist together!
> Let us be sad together, repent together [*gemeinsam Buße tun*], and experience the victory of grace together.[2]

Remarkably, he explicitly connected his own racial persecution as a man of Jewish ancestry with the religious persecution of the German churches. Ehrenberg lamented the disunity of the church, its despondency in terrible times, and its subsequent lack of vigor and dominance. But he took this opportunity, at the end of his tenure as pastor to his congregation, to call the church to repentance, particularly for weakness of faith. He encouraged his congregation to lean upon each other and rely upon the strength that only God can provide in faith. Just as the church came together by the power of the Holy Spirit at Pentecost, so now must the church unify in the grace and mercy of God in the midst of persecution.

Furthermore, he argued that this unity, this standing together, required a standing "against" as well: "Let us suffer together and continue to resist together!"[3] While his call to suffer and resist together may sound vague, its meaning in the context of the sermon indicates that the church ought to stand together against those who seek its division and loss of influence. He spoke as an oppressed man forced to leave an oppressed institution, and his parting remarks serves to encourage Christians to persevere amid suffering and resist together. After delivering the sermon and then leaving the church, Ehrenberg remained in Nazi Germany until the pogrom of November 9–10, 1938, commonly known as *Kristallnacht* (Night of Broken Glass), when he was rounded up along with approximately 30,000 Jews across Germany and sent to a concentration camp.[4] Immediately upon his release in 1939, he went into exile in England, where he continued to serve in the Church..

Ehrenberg's sermon reveals a common theme among sermons in the Confessing Church that criticized the regime. Pastors occasionally condemned the Nazi persecution of the German churches. Of over 900 sermons examined in this study, 36 clearly condemned the Nazi persecution of Christians.[5] But the pastors did not simply condemn the Nazi regime for persecution to publicly air grievances. In keeping with the purpose of the sermon to draw one closer to God, they used their concerns about the persecution for two specific spiritual purposes. First, the sermons criticizing the Nazi regime for persecution directed the eyes of the congregant (and the Christian who suffers) to the consolation of God's love, and they affirmed unwavering trust in God's eternal justice, reminding the Christian that evil will not go unpunished. God's love and justice are intertwined in these sermons, the former a consolation to the persecuted and the latter a warning to the persecutors. And second, they remembered the persecuted faithful, drawing the Church as the community of God together. Just as the sermons that condemned Nazism as a false belief sought to realign Christians to right worship of God, so these sermons that criticized Nazi persecution sought a spiritual purpose, to console the Christian community and draw them close to God.

As illustrated in Ehrenberg's Pentecost sermon, expressions that condemn persecution are dynamic and multi-faceted. They not only draw Christians closer to God and one another, but they serve to alienate the Christian from the Nazi regime, at least to a degree. This chapter will argue that these expressions signify opposition to the Nazi regime by explicitly naming or clearly implying the identity of wrongdoers (those who have broken good faith and accepted moral norms); by spreading information publicly about the identity of the wrongdoer and the specific injustices committed; and, in the context of a worship service, by invoking God as Judge against the wrongdoer and Consoler for the persecuted. In these three ways the pastors actively worked toward ending the Nazi persecution of the German churches.

THE NAZI PERSECUTION OF THE CHURCHES

The Nazi persecution of the German churches has been well researched and thoroughly documented.[6] As previously discussed, from the early days of the Nazi regime, clergymen who did not toe the line were harassed and arrested, such as occurred in the dispute between the German Christian faction and supporters of Friedrich von Bodelschwingh over leadership of the *Reichskirche* in May 1933.[7] While von Bodelschwingh won the church election in a landslide victory of 91 to 8, the Nazi regime countered the opposition to ensure a German Christian victory.[8] Barnett writes, "A number of pastors were fired, suspended, or arrested, and the 'German Christians' and Nazi party mounted a vicious campaign against von Bodelschwingh," thereby compelling him to resign.[9] As tensions between the church and state intensified due to continued Nazi interference in church affairs, the regime harassed and initiated mass arrests of Confessing Church pastors for minor infractions such as pastors taking "illegal" collections of funds and supporting colleagues by reading *Fürbittenliste* (intercessory lists) from the pulpit.[10] The arrests were meant to intimidate and harass clergymen, to manipulate them into a posture of obedience to the state.[11]

The regime took action when Confessing Church pastors acted in unison against National Socialist ideology. In March 1935, for example, Pastor Heinrich Vogel, along with two other pastors, composed a statement condemning Nazi "heathenism" and the totalitarian state as a response to the Nazi recommendation to teachers and students to use Alfred Rosenberg's "ideological handbook of the Nazi movement," *The Myth of the Twentieth Century*, in classrooms.[12] They wrote the statement for Confessing Church pastors to read, each from their own pulpits. Years later, Vogel recounted writing the statement in a hotel room, cognizant of the "immense responsibility" of representing the church that "dared to speak in God's name."[13] He recalled,

Now, I sat there in my hotel room with my paper and wrote ... Afterward, I returned to my friends, read it to them, and I can still hear how one of them laconically said, "So, we'll all end up in jail." And that's what happened. The totalitarian state noticed indeed that it wasn't just the *Myth of the 20th Century* being attacked, but its totalitarian demands, and it reacted by arresting 700 at once, namely, all those who read the statement.[14]

These pastors took a unified and forceful stand against Rosenberg's summation of Nazi ideology, and the regime responded with mass arrests, intending to intimidate and silence dissenting pastors.

Moreover, the Nazi state attempted to limit the financial autonomy of the Confessing Church by forbidding the collection of funds not approved by the Ministry of Church Affairs (the law passed on March 11, 1935) and confiscating property. Pastors could be arrested for collecting funds for colleagues who ran afoul of the regime. For example, in 1937, Pastor Franz Hildebrandt was arrested and briefly imprisoned for forwarding collections from Confessing churches to the Council of Brethren (instead of the regional church consistory).[15] Conway asserts that by November 1937, over 700 pastors were arrested for the illegal collection of funds.[16] In August 1937, Heinrich Himmler, the head of the Gestapo, designed and began the implementation of plans to seize church lands and property, thereby significantly limiting the German churches' ability to function and minister to their communities of faith.[17] The regime seized church hospitals, orphanages, monasteries, and schools, terminating ministries and putting teachers, caretakers, and ministers out of work.[18]

The Nazi regime and pro-Nazi supporters also attempted to limit the unity and effectiveness of the Confessing Church by targeting its pastors through a variety of measures. Even if the Nazis did not arrest or harass a Confessing pastor, they designed various means of silencing dissenters, such as terminating employment in their church, prohibiting a pastor from lecturing or preaching, and denying stipends or funding.[19] As previously mentioned, the Gestapo closed Bonhoeffer's seminary at Finkenwalde, compelling him and his colleagues to establish the seminary underground, where the state could not interfere. By November 1937, 27 of the Finkenwalde seminarians had been sent to prison, and by January 1938 the regime prohibited Bonhoeffer from traveling to Berlin and the Brandenburg province.[20] Moreover, in summer 1938, as Conway writes, "all pastors were forbidden to teach religious instruction in State schools. Orders were issued banning the Confessing Church's private seminaries ... All theological students were obliged to become members of one or other of the Nazi affiliated associations."[21] It is no surprise that sermon criticisms about Nazi persecutions of the German churches increased in 1934 in the wake the Nazi institution of the Reich Church and spiked 1937 amid the intensified Nazi oppression Conway describes.[22]

Beyond harassing, arresting, or imprisoning dissenting clergymen, the regime surveilled them. It kept a watchful eye on their pulpits and ministries. While a whole chapter of this study is devoted to the Nazi regime's spying activities on clergymen, suffice it to say at this point that the regime utilized Nazi spies and informants through the Gestapo and the SD to report on dissenting pastors. If a pastor was perceived to express opposition to the Nazi regime (whether they intended to express criticism or not), they could be reported to the Nazi secret police. Surveillance is an oppressive form of persecution, intimidating the subject by displaying the pervasiveness of state power, within and beyond the walls of the sanctuary. Thus, surveillance is a method of social control that instills fear and silences the subject, whether or not the subject is in fact being surveilled. The subject only needs to be aware that the state is watching out for dissent. This form of persecution aimed to prevent pastors from preaching the gospel in a manner that would undermine the Nazi regime and its ideology.

While historians have thoroughly researched how the Nazi regime persecuted the German churches, there is still debate about the purpose and aims of the persecution. Conway has argued in his classic work *The Nazi Persecution of the Churches, 1933–1945* that the regime intended the total eradication of the churches from Germany. He points to the regime's violent persecution of the clergy in the Warthegau in the Second World War, as well as statements by top Nazi leaders such as Martin Bormann, to demonstrate Nazi long-term plans against the churches.[23] Conway concludes that Hitler and the Nazi regime "sought to prevent the Churches from exercising any influence over national affairs, and . . . [attempted] to drive [the churches] into obscurity to die out as unlamented relics of the past." In contrast, Steigmann-Gall has more recently argued that the regime aimed to align the Protestant churches to Nazi ideology, "to serve Volk and Führer in the new Germany."[24] The complete synchronization of the churches with National Socialism would mark the end of the German Christian "Reformation" in Germany. Thus, the Nazi persecution of the churches was not meant to eliminate the churches but to serve the process of synchronizing them to Nazi ideology. He contends that "[t]he creation of a unified Reich Church would have meant a stronger church organization," but one subservient to the state.[25] Weikart has challenged Steigmann-Gall's interpretation, noting that Hitler himself regretted creating the Reich Church because it was easier to dominate a divided church.[26] Moreover, Weikart argues that the Nazi leadership indeed intended to eradicate Christianity in Germany, but through "an incremental, not cataclysmic, approach."[27] Hitler's intention of slowly but methodically destroying Christianity in Germany can be seen in numerous policies, such as seizing control of the education of youth from the churches, planning not to rebuild bombed out churches after the war (except in the cases of churches with exceptional artistic value), and developing plans for new city expansions without churches.[28] Regardless of the differences between these interpretations, they agree that the Nazi intent was effectively the end of traditional Christianity in Nazi Germany.

Yet, despite the persecutions, some Confessing Church pastors refused to be intimidated or silenced, and they spoke out against the Nazi oppression of the Protestant churches. Of the over 900 sermons analyzed, 37 contain statements that unequivocally condemn the persecution of the churches. These sermons were delivered by 12 of the 95 total pastors included in this study. Again, as with the sermons that criticized National Socialism as a false belief system, these public but infrequent expressions of criticism against Nazi persecution were most prevalent in the early years of the regime, before the outbreak of the Second World War. Though I do not claim that this sample of over 900 sermons is representative of all Confessing Church (or other Christian) sermons from January 1933 to May 1945, one can clearly see criticisms raised in key periods of persecution, notably during the creation of the Confessing Church in 1934 and the mass arrests of pastors in 1937. As Johnson argues in his work *Nazi Terror*, an analysis of Gestapo investigations of clergymen (Catholic and Protestant) from the Cologne Special Court files indicates a spike that culminates in 1937, "the crescendo of the Nazis' campaign against the church," and which tapers off considerably in 1938.[29] Likewise, the criticisms of Nazi persecution declined considerably in this sample of 900 sermons. Only 5 of the 36 occurred in wartime, and of these only one was delivered in Germany. This was a sermon written by Bonhoeffer but delivered by an unknown lector at an unknown location for the first Sunday after the New Year 1940.[30] The German pastor of Jewish descent Franz Hildebrandt delivered three over the British Broadcasting Corporation (BBC) into Germany.[31] And Karl Barth preached one on September 24, 1939, in Zurich. Thus, 31 of the 36 sermons with oppositional content took place before the war.

However, it should be noted that the total number of wartime sermons (278) is a fraction of the over 900 total sermons included in this study. Though Hitler's regime waged war for six of its dozen years, the wartime Confessing sermons in this collection comprise a minority. This may simply be an anomaly of the sample. But if not, the most obvious reason for this is that there were simply fewer pastors to preach. Of the 18,000 Protestant pastors in Nazi Germany in 1941, 6,800 were mobilized in the army or navy.[32] Not only pastors, but non-ordained vicars and theological candidates were called up as well. This is the reason why Bonhoeffer's underground seminary finally folded: the remaining students were mobilized for war.[33] By October

1944, 45% of all pastors and 98% of non-ordained vicars and candidates were mobilized.[34] This left a much smaller contingent of pastors at home to preach.[35] Also, given that the wartime need to ration paper supplies meant a reduction in newspapers printed across Germany (approximately 1,450 newspapers shut down by 1943), we can surmise that publishing houses sharply decreased the publication and distribution of sermons.[36] Thus, the historical record for wartime sermons is limited but still useful in understanding Confessing Church pastors' preaching during the Second World War.

THE CONSOLATION OF GOD'S LOVE AND JUSTICE

As pastors are the spiritual guides of their faith communities, it is not surprising that they offered encouragement to their communities of faith. Predominantly, messages of encouragement emphasized the love and justice of God and the hope that the persecution of the German churches will one day end. For example, on January 21, 1934, Bonhoeffer preached to his German congregation in London on Jeremiah 20:7, a passage about God's overwhelming presence and the calling of His messengers. In the wider context of the biblical passage, the corrupt priest Pashhur struck the prophet Jeremiah and put him in the stocks, persecuting him for prophesying against the idolatry endemic in Judah. In short, the passage presents an inter-Jewish struggle for the true faith in Judah. Using this Scripture passage as the basis for his sermon, Bonhoeffer directly linked the inter-Jewish struggle in ancient Judah with the Church struggle in Nazi Germany. Christians in the Third Reich are being treated like Jeremiah of old—struck down and put in the stocks. Midway through the sermon Bonhoeffer reflected on the perils Christians encounter in Nazi Germany simply for standing for the truth of the gospel:

> Today in our home church, thousands of parishioners and pastors are facing the danger of oppression and persecution because of their witness for the truth. They have not chosen this path out of arbitrary defiance, but because they were led to it; they simply had to follow it—often against their own wills and against their own flesh and blood . . . How often they must have wished that peace and calm and quietness would finally return; how often they must have wished that they did not have to keep on threatening, warning, protesting, and bearing witness to the truth![37]

Bonhoeffer's sermon reflects the fragmentation of the German churches and the hostile combativeness of the Church Struggle. He did not explicitly say who oppresses or persecutes, but the context of his time makes it clear who the perpetrators are. Bonhoeffer delivered this sermon just months after the establishment of the PEL, and less than six months since the Nazi establishment of the *Reichskirche* under German Christian leadership. Bonhoeffer implied that the persecutors are the German Christians and, more generally, pro-Nazi supporters within the churches who are compromising the mission of the church and the integrity of the gospel. Furthermore, his linking the prophet Jeremiah to the persecuted pastors bearing witness to the truth implies that the persecutors are those in the Nazi government who have arrested and imprisoned Christians. While Bonhoeffer does not specify the ways in which Christians have been persecuted, he underscores how Christians themselves are "threatening, warning, protesting, and bearing witness to the truth!"

Bonhoeffer is careful not to dwell on the persecutors or the persecuted, but to emphasize God's final victory. These are Bonhoeffer's words of comfort to persecuted Christians in Nazi Germany. Their salvation is not in the might of their own hands, but in Almighty God. Bonhoeffer's use of Jeremiah 20 is remarkable because he is clearly categorizing the German Christians as not only idolaters but persecutors, and he is publicly proclaiming this to his congregation. Moreover, in using this Old Testament passage it is as if he is invoking God as "the dread warrior," as Jeremiah puts in in verse 11, to judge the wicked persecutors of His church. Thus, while Bonhoeffer does not explicitly name the persecutors or state explicitly how they are persecuting the German churches, his sermon is nonetheless a cutting rebuke of the German Christian movement and pro-Nazi supporters who are undermining the church.

Likewise, Pastor Heinz Kloppenburg of Wilhelmshaven offered words of encouragement and perspective in a sermon he preached on April 15, 1934.[38] This sermon was preached just weeks ahead of the Barmen Synod (of which he was a member) and the formation of the Confessing Church. His sermon explored the meaning of Jesus' parable of the Good Shepherd (John 10:12–16) who protects his sheep from the "raging" of a wolf. Kloppenburg spoke of a wolf that attacks and struggles against the kingdom of God, as if this wolf is presently causing mischief in the German churches. He points out that the sheep themselves cannot protect against the wolf, and they cannot rely on hired hands. But they must trust in the true Pastor. In this sense, this sermon is a warning to Christians to beware of the wolf, and it is also an encouragement to trust God.

But in middle of this theological reflection, Kloppenburg pauses to affirm the separation of religious and political affairs. He argues that the state must keep to its domain outside the walls of the church, and the church must focus on its domain inside. He said, "When we gather together in the church, then it is not about political things, but it is about the kingdom of God and his glory."[39] On the one hand, Kloppenburg gives the state the respect and obedience he believes is its due, but on the other hand, he criticizes a "wolf" that seeks to intrude in church affairs to scatter and devour the sheep. Like Bonhoeffer in the previous example, Kloppenburg does not identify the perpetrator, the "wolf" among the sheep. Yet this metaphor is singular, suggesting perhaps Hitler, Müller, or even the devil, though the context does not clarify the identity of the persecutor. Kloppenberg left the identify of this "wolf" conveniently ambiguous. It might be easy for the congregant to focus on the prowling wolf and the havoc he creates, but Kloppenburg, like Bonhoeffer, focused on God's steadfast love and justice. While Christians in Nazi Germany may not be able to rid the churches of the "wolf" in their midst, they can trust in Christ as the Good Shepherd. The very act of calling the congregation's attention to the "wolf"—a public proclamation of the "wolf's" guilt and sin for causing disunity in the churches—allows them to appreciate more fully the steadfast love of the Good Shepherd.

There was perhaps no more vocal critic of the Nazi persecution of the German churches than Martin Niemöller, who often used strong and colorful language to make his point. He too focused on trusting God's love and justice in times of persecution. For example, on Passion Sunday in 1934, Niemöller preached on Psalm 43, which reads in part: "Vindicate me, O God, and defend my cause against an ungodly people; from those who are deceitful and unjust deliver me!" He explicitly and publicly detailed the persecutions and clearly implicated the perpetrators, thereby condemning the Nazi regime for its persecution of the Protestant churches. He declared,

> Today all the bells of the German Protestant churches are silent, and in every divine service a prayer of intercession is being said for the five Protestant pastors from Hesse and Saxony who have been taken away from their congregations and put into the concentration camp in spite of the remonstrances made by the interim church management to the authorities. And so the only course left open to us is to act according to the words, "Whether one member suffers, all the members suffer with it," and we turn, seeking justice and help, to the supreme and highest court.[40]

Niemöller continued his condemnation by mentioning a "dear young colleague" in Frankfurt who was arrested nearly three weeks prior because he refused the order of an "unlawful bishop" to leave his church—and his congregation refused to leave him as well.[41] This sermon is one of the few examples in the sample of over 900 sermons in which a pastor clearly identified the perpetrator as the Nazi regime. Only the Nazi government can arrest and imprison pastors in a concentration camp.

Niemöller counseled his congregation to turn to God's "justice and help, to the supreme and highest court." Like the previous examples, the public proclamation of persecution is not simply to give voice to grievances, or to openly detail the persecutions, but to invoke God as righteous Judge against the perpetrators. He is publicly naming the Nazi regime as an opponent of the people of God, and thus of God Himself. Yet, Niemöller acknowledged that he and his congregation are bitter and may have a hard time forgiving their persecutors. But he asked for mercy and grace to be able to do so. He did not advocate any course of action except to trust in "the light and the truth of God, which are present in Jesus Christ, [and which] have a compelling force," that will bring lasting change.[42]

Likewise, Niemöller also explicitly spoke out against the German Christian movement's persecution of Christians, with the state's support. In a sermon in October 1934, he responded to a series of events that began a few months earlier in March, when the Reich Bishop Müller and the newly appointed legal administrator of the *Reichskirche*, August Jäger, attempted to dissolve the leadership of the provincial churches that resisted coordination into the *Reichskirche*, including that of the popular bishops of Württemberg and Bavaria, Theophil Wurm and Hans Meiser respectively.[43] And so Müller decided to make a public stand and single out Wurm as an example.[44] On April 16, 1934, Müller issued a radio announcement stating that the *Reichskirche* determined that Wurm was unacceptable as a church leader and public figure. Yet the people of Württemberg roundly supported their bishop, and just a couple days later, on April 22, Wurm held his own conference at the Ulm Cathedral to plan the founding of a new and independent church government.[45] A few other provincial churches followed suit and resisted the subjugation of the *Reichskirche*, including Bavaria, Westphalia, and Brandenburg. Only a month later, like-minded Protestants would gather at the National Synod in Barmen, where they would approve the Barmen Declaration in defiance of the *Reichskirche*.

Yet the conflict continued into autumn when Müller and Jäger used coercive measures to interfere in the leadership of the provincial churches. In the months of September and October, they manufactured trumped up charges and placed Wurm and Meiser under house arrest, searching their offices and taking legal control of the provincial leadership, under the direction of the *Reichskirche*. The arrests and usurpation of church leadership led to considerable popular condemnation of both Müller and Jäger. Christians throughout Württemberg and Bavaria demonstrated in support of their bishops, and pastors condemned the unjust treatment of their leadership in church services.[46]

And this leads us to Niemöller's confrontational sermon based on Matthew 21, delivered on October 14, 1934.[47] The passage describes the growing animosity of the chief priests and religious elites against Jesus. The sermon is entitled, "The Father's Will," and the first words he spoke are a condemnation of the German Christian movement:

> The lawful bishop of the province [Theophil Wurm] has been deposed by an unlawful and unchristian synod. He and his fellow workers have been deprived, with the aid of secular authority, of their personal liberty and have been forbidden to act in an official capacity . . . We are already receiving new reports of the violent attack of the anti-Christian forces on the church in Bavaria; there, too, a reign of terror is being set up, while the public is being misled by lies and half-truths. The bishop of Bavaria [Hans Meiser] also has been deposed and robbed of his personal freedom, and that so-called "union" which is destroying a church already united in creed and constitution has been carried out with the assistance of temporal power against the unanimous will of the Protestant community.[48]

Niemöller does not name the bishop of Württemberg, Theophil Wurm, the Bishop of Bavaria, Hans Meiser, nor the Nazi officials who removed them from office, Reich Bishop Ludwig Müller and the leader of Reich Church Affairs, August Jäger. Yet he names their titles so that the identities of the persecutors and persecuted cannot be mistaken. This exclusive use of titles also underscores the fact that the church hierarchy (and thus the church) is under attack, not simply individual Christians. Niemöller refers to this attack upon the church as a "reign of terror" facilitated by "lies and half-truths." But what is most remarkable about this sermon is the specificity of the persecutions mentioned. The lawful bishops have been deposed and robbed of freedom; the church is being destroyed; and violent attacks are made against the church. Perhaps most significant, Niemöller names not only the German Christians as the perpetrators, but the secular state as well. In fact, in this one short paragraph, he mentions the Nazi regime's support of the German Christian persecutors twice, lest any should forget under whose authority the German Christians act, thereby explicitly naming the state as a persecutor of the churches.

Niemöller spoke of this time as an "hour of darkness" akin to Jesus' trial in the Garden of Gethsemane—Christians must prepare themselves for betrayal and temptation.[49] He asked his congregants to reflect on their obligation to remain obedient to the will of God, to reevaluate where their allegiances lie and upon whom they place their trust. This reflection should be accompanied by repentance, he argued, which should strengthen obedience and trust. He continued,

> Repentance: heart searching and conversion. However strange it may sound, that is the Lord's call to us in this conflict, so that we may not carry on the struggle as our own cause in lighthearted self-confidence, while talking of professing and confessing our faith in him. Now amid the satanic temptations of this period of persecution, we can less than at any time dispense with going quietly apart and mercilessly submitting our own will and our own passion to

the will, the jurisdiction of the Lord Jesus Christ, and then, under his guidance, making a new beginning in faith, in obedience to his word and in the confidence that he himself will carry on his cause.[50]

This paragraph provides insight into the source of the conflict in the churches. Niemöller appears to indicate that the Nazi regime and the German Christian movement are inspired by a demonic force, asserting that "satanic temptations" are at the heart of the Church Struggle. Ultimately, this is a battle of the spiritual realm, not the temporal realm, and thus the battle must be fought with spiritual means. Thus, Niemöller advises his congregants to repent and trust in God. These actions in turn will inspire renewed obedience to God. Yet this introspection and soul-searching do not in themselves lead to active and public acts of opposition or resistance in the service of the persecuted—like those in Württemberg. This call to action is spiritual in nature, intending to create a spiritual impact, yet which, in time, will directly improve the social and political spheres. As it turned out, Hitler, facing considerable popular opposition, compromised to manage dissent and reinstated Wurm and Meiser to their bishoprics.[51]

Niemöller knew that speaking out against the regime in this manner could lead to his arrest and incarceration. He knew ever since his meeting at the Reich chancellery with Hitler, Göring, Müller, and Wilhelm Frick, the Minister of the Interior on January 25, 1934. Hitler had Göring, the chief of the Prussian secret police, read a transcript of a private phone call between Niemöller and the theologian Walter Künneth, in which the former made a joke at Hitler's expense. Niemöller attempted to explain, stating that the church opposition desired the well-being of the church, the German people, and the state, to which Hitler curtly replied, "Leave the care of the Third Reich to me. You take care of the church."[52] Niemöller said his response was just as firm: "You said leave the care of the German people to me. To that I must say that neither you nor any power in the world is in a position to take away the responsibility God entrusted in us to care for our people."[53] He knew at that point that his days were numbered. After the war, Niemöller recalled this period of preaching, "In every sermon I have prepared since then, I have done so with the feeling that today is the last sermon—What do I have to say now to my congregation?—before I am taken down."[54]

As the establishment of the *Reichskirche* failed to unify the German Protestant churches, the Nazi regime turned to the creation of the Ministry of Church Affairs in 1935 under the leadership of Hanns Kerrl. While the Nazi strategy shifted, their goal remained the same. As Conway concludes, the Nazis continued to wage an ideological struggle "to capture the heart and mind of the whole German nation and to establish a new cult to replace the two-thousand-year-old influence of Christianity."[55] At the same time, the

Nazi regime instigated a "campaign of terrorism and intimidation" carried out by the Gestapo to demoralize and silence opposition within the German churches.[56] Matters intensified in 1937 when Himmler, the head of the Gestapo, began the implementation of plans to seize church lands and property, severely undermining dissenting pastors' financial security.

Likewise, during the persecutions of 1937, pastors spoke out against the regime's persecution of the churches. For example, Heinrich Vogel preached a sermon on November 11, 1937, based on Psalm 94:12–19, a hymn which deserves to be quoted at length:

> Happy are those whom you discipline, O Lord,
>   And whom you teach out of your law,
> Giving them respite from days of trouble,
> Until a pit is dug for the wicked.
> For the Lord will not forsake his people;
>   He will not abandon his heritage;
> For justice will return to the righteous,
> And all the upright in heart will follow it.

The hymn provides hope and encouragement in times of persecution, reminding the faithful that God is near and God is Judge of the wicked. Vogel referred in this sermon to the persecution of the German churches, though he did not explicitly name Hitler or the Nazi government or the German Christian movement as the perpetrators. But he specifically spoke of the "wave of over 700 arrests" in the church.[57] By mentioning the arrests it becomes clear that the perpetrator is the Nazi regime itself, for who else has such authority? This is another example of a Confessing Church pastors publicly spreading news of Nazi persecutions, effectively naming the perpetrator and clarifying the nature of the persecution. Moreover, he calls on God as Comforter of His people. Vogel affirmed that the Church's mission

> is the message of the victory of the grace of God all over the world to align in the certainty that God himself creates and gathers the pious hearts, whom God will judge . . . It says to the world, which does not know, that everything that lives, that people and states in truth are held together through nothing other than the victory of the law of God's grace.[58]

This intercessory sermon called upon God to comfort Christians in this time of persecution. Vogel reminded his congregants that the message of the church stands in stark contrast to the Nazi message of power and domination. He encouraged them by asserting that God's grace conquers all.

Vogel's sermon, as well as the previous examples, demonstrate how pastors connected the sacred past as revealed in Scripture to their present moment.

The passages the pastors chose to speak about the persecution of the churches illuminate their thinking about the motives of their persecutors. For example, in Vogel's sermon, the psalm speaks of the "wicked" as the persecutor of God's chosen. They are those who disobey God's law and act contrary to his purposes. Among the examples we have already seen, the persecutors in Scripture are identified as deceitful and ungodly people; as wolves among the sheep; and as the chief priests and Jewish religious elites who persecuted Jesus. Scripture provides the pastors with ways of understanding the motives of their persecutors. The German Christian and Nazi persecutors are not portrayed as simply at cross-purposes with the churches, but they are malevolent actors purposefully causing harm to pastors and the churches.

Moreover, the pastors publicly and unequivocally compared their persecutors with these biblical figures, thereby helping their congregations understand how dangerous they are. In connecting the "wicked" or "ungodly" of the biblical past with the German Christian movement and the Nazi regime, the pastors are not simply commenting on their moral failure in relation to the churches, but proclaiming to their congregations that despite pretenses to the contrary, their persecutors are acting as enemies of God—they are actively working against God's purposes. The picture that emerges from these sermons on persecution is that the German Christians and the Nazi regime are not understood as means or tools of God's judgment on Germany or the churches (such as using biblical texts about the Assyrian or Babylonian persecutions might imply), but that they are in fact enemies of God. This perspective means that the difference between the Confessing Church and their persecutors is not simply about theology or church policy—as if the better argument or stronger organization can win the day—but it reaches down to the oppressors' "wicked" hearts, a problem requiring a spiritual solution. In mistreating God's people, persecutors reveal their hostility against God. At the same time, the label "persecutor" does not imply benign passivity, as if the Confessing Church could easily dismiss their opponents as harmless, but rather it means continual and active harm to the German churches that must be opposed.

The outbreak of the Second World War marked a turning point in the persecutions and Nazi church policy.[59] Hitler acknowledged that he needed a unified nation to wage war, and so he called a truce in the Church Struggle.[60] He gave up trying to unify the German Evangelical Church. Yet still, in the early months of the war, the Nazi regime initiated measures to diminish the German churches further, and among them was the closure of various Catholic churches that were "too far" from air-raid shelters; the melting of church bells, many historic and valuable; and restrictions on religious journals to advertise among military personnel.[61] By late-1940, other measures were added, including restrictions of Catholic priests to substitute teach in the schools; the closure of various theological organizations and universities; the banning of religious orders to accept novices; and the requirement for churches to bury anyone on church property regardless of their confession or lack of belief.[62] Thus, while Hitler and the Nazi regime gave up on forcing the unity and harmony of the German churches along National Socialist lines, they still meddled in church affairs and persecuted the churches in a variety of ways.

Yet again, these persecutions did not keep all pastors silent. In a sermon delivered in January 1940, in a Confessing Church underground seminary, Bonhoeffer affirmed a common theme found throughout Church history, that though the people of God are persecuted, God is not silent and will deliver them. The sermon was based on Matthew 2:13–23, reflecting on the story of Herod's slaughter of the innocents at the time of Jesus' birth. Bonhoeffer observes that the people of God—Israel and the Church—have been persecuted throughout history, and will continue to be persecuted. But there is hope. He proclaimed, "The mighty Herod is dead without having attained his goal, but Jesus lives."[63] Throughout the Church, the persecutors have come and gone. "Nero is dead, Diocletian is dead, the enemies of Luther and the Reformation are dead, but Jesus lives, and with him lives those who are his."[64] This is a sermon of hope and encouragement for the seminarians, to stay faithful in a difficult time. Though Bonhoeffer did not name Hitler and the Nazis here, it is clear that they belong with Herod, Nero, and Diocletian as persecutors of God's people. These are after all Christians driven underground to study and worship by a regime that finds their faith dangerous.[65] In the context of worship and spiritual formation, Bonhoeffer publicly implied the identity the church's persecutors and invoked God to bless the persecuted. Moreover, he named the persecutors as among the defeated and future dead—separated from new life found in Christ.

In all these sermons that condemn the persecution of the churches, Confessing Church pastors rarely mentioned the name of Hitler. One of the very few examples is found in a sermon given by Karl Barth on September 24, 1939, in Horgen, Switzerland—well beyond the reach of Nazi authorities. He preached on Ephesians 3:14–21, which speaks of God's great love of the Christian family, which also includes the noteworthy doxology: "Now to him who is able to do immeasurably more than all we ask or imagine . . . " Barth considered what he described as the great love of God for his people, and then he said, "What then could Hitler, Stalin and Mussolini and their ilk [*ihresgleichen*] ever do to those who believed?"[66] This statement places Hitler alongside the leader of the "godless" communist power in Europe, Stalin, who was known in Germany as an infamous persecutor of Christians.[67] The fact that this one statement explicitly naming Hitler's persecution of Christians is virtually all we have in over 900 Confessing Church sermons in this sample indicates that pastors in Germany preferred to speak of persecution of the churches as the action of groups or institutions—the German Christian movement and the Nazi state. It would be speculation to suggest that the pastors blamed Hitler but feared to publicly criticize him specifically.

Barth's sermon is one of 89 sermons delivered outside Nazi Germany in lands of exile, refuge, and mission. Confessing Church pastors who had to flee Nazi Germany for whatever reason often found themselves before welcoming (and often German) congregations abroad, particularly in England, Switzerland, and the United States. Though a Confessing pastor may give voice to an oppositional statement, the fact that such a statement occurred in a safe and perhaps even friendly environment limits the impact such a statement can have—at least on those who have the power to cause political or social change in Germany. In this way, sermons in exile are quite distinct among this collection of sermons of Confessing Church pastors. Unfortunately, we do not know the contexts in which most of these sermons were delivered, nor the identities of the individuals who heard them. Thus, we cannot know if congregants heard these sermons and contributed in some way towards the effort to undermine the Nazi regime—through the giving of resources or participating in the war effort in some way.[68] At the very least these sermons reveal what Confessing pastors believed were the most important messages for Christians to know, giving us unique insights into what Christians abroad knew about what was happening in Nazi Germany.

REMEMBERING THE PERSECUTED

In addition to sermons that encouraged congregants to trust in the love and justice of God, Confessing Church pastors also preached sermons that explicitly remembered the persecuted and spread the news about their persecution. Pastors not only condemned the persecutions but took the time to consider the meaning and impact of the persecutions. Within the context of a worship service, Confessing pastors portrayed Christians as a minority persecuted by unjust government.

Pastors sought to make sense of their persecution in light of Scripture, perceiving the oppression as a sign of a deep spiritual struggle. One Lutheran named Peter Brunner, pastor of the Protestant Church in Ranstadt and Effolderbach, opened a sermon on Reformation Sunday in 1934 by turning to the writings of the apostle Paul. Specifically, he used a key passage from Paul's writings when he was imprisoned, 2 Timothy 2:9, which says, "the word of God is not chained." Brunner argued that Paul's persecution was not meant simply to silence him but rather to bind God's Word. He said, "The people [*Die Menschen*] thought to bind the Word of God by binding the apostle. But the people were mistaken. They could bind the apostle, but they could not bind the Word of God. Thus it has always been in the history of the Church."[69] Brunner then recounted in specific terms the nature of the "violent suppression of the Word of God in our presence," publicly condemning the Nazi regime and spreading the word about the "police violence [used] against confessionally faithful [*bekenntnistreue*] Protestant regional churches" in the preceding weeks.[70] He condemned the arrest and detention of two Protestant bishops in their homes (meaning Theophil Wurm of Württemberg and Hans Meiser of Bavaria) and the dismissal of pastors who publicly proclaimed the Word of God. Brunner himself lost his position as a professor of theology at the University of Giessen the year prior because of his activities against the German Christian movement in the area.[71] He asserted that the persecutors' actions are foolish because they bind men in an attempt to bind the Word of God. They will know soon enough, he said, that the gospel is power, "dynamite"—it is an "explosive force that again and again breaks apart all attempts to hold it down by force and thus frees itself from all ties."[72]

Brunner's sermon is remarkable for its fiery language against the German churches' persecutors, but even more for its insights into how the German churches themselves sought to fetter God's Word. The Nazis were not the only ones who sought to bind the Word of God. In the last 100 years, Brunner argued, the German churches had employed reason to restrict the freedom of God's Word. Moreover, they had "bound God's word to nature and history." The "modern man" says, "No, I hear God's voice also in nature, also in history I listen to his speech, and the voice in my blood—it is God's voice." Brunner offered a succinct and damning summation:

> See my friends, that is the heresy of modern man, that he wants to take captive God's Word, God's revelation, through other false, so-called "revelations" in nature and history, in blood and soil. In our time we have had to reap the ominous fruits of these heresies in our church. One could report for hours about how one has wanted to fetter and bind God's Word for a year and a half, that one has delivered the gospel of Jesus Christ to the powers of this world. Race, blood, soil, Nordic soul, folkish primal forces and the like are given out as revelations and set next to God's Word. But where I place such world forces next to God's Word, where I place Christ and the Nordic soul, Christ and the folkish forces, Christ and racial blood side by side as revelations of God, then Christ is actually bound to the powers of this world and as in the garden of Gethsemane captured and led away from our midst."[73]

The binding of the Word is the binding of Christ. This evocative metaphor underscores the stakes of the spiritual struggle in which Christians find themselves. Christians must not only support persecuted pastors, but they must actively break the chains that bind the Word of God. Brunner called his congregation to "stand up like one man for the freedom of the gospel, for the freedom of God's Word, for the freedom of the Christ-established Church."[74] He proclaimed, "Just as Luther in his time freed God's word from the fetters of the papacy, then it applies to today [that we must] free God's Word from the fetters of an ethnic religion [*völkischen Religion*]."[75] If the Nazis persecuted the churches in an attempt to bind the Word of God, then Christians should do everything they can to fight for its freedom. Again, according to Brunner, the Word of God is an "explosive" force capable of breaking through all attempts to hold it down. This is Brunner's strategy to ending the persecution. Their obligation as Christians is to stand together and bind themselves to the Word of God. Only in this way can they reform their churches as Luther had done.

Brunner offered an extended discussion of the persecuted churches in this sermon. Virtually the entire sermon is dedicated to understanding the true nature of the persecutions, laying bare for his congregation to see the sins of the Nazi persecutors. It reveals the true nature of the persecutors as enemies of God, directly working at cross-purposes to God's will. In the months following this sermon, the German Christian movement attempted to takeover Brunner's church, which he fought, and he was subsequently branded an anti-Nazi, arrested, and sent to Dachau concentration camp for four months.[76]

Likewise, Niemöller often remembered the persecuted in his sermons to his congregants in Dahlem. On the fifth Sunday after Epiphany 1935, in a sermon entitled, "Fellowship in the Gospel," Niemöller spoke of the church conflict as a time of life and death for the German Protestant churches. It was a time of "freedom or more bitter slavery, peace or renewed struggle."[77] He spoke of pastors who had been driven out of the church without pay, and how Christians had been there to serve them and their families. Confessing churches took up offerings to support pastors who had fallen afoul of the Nazi regime or the German Christian authorities and lost their jobs. In fact, this was one of the first tasks of the Confessing Church's Council of Brethren, to care for pastors and their families.[78] Niemöller spoke of the German Evangelical Church as divided and lukewarm, referring to one of the seven churches in the Book of Revelation.

In the sermon, Niemöller celebrated the promise of Christian unity, even despite the Church Struggle. He spoke of Christians taking care of one another, particularly pastors who have lost their jobs because of their confession of faith:

> The fact that not one of the many hundreds of our brethren who have been driven from office has had to suffer want with his family, the fact that helping hands have been stretched out from all sides—and that not only once, but again and again during many months—is surely reason for joy and gratitude. For who

would have thought that there was still so much sympathy and unity of spirit in our poor church, which has been so split up and has grown so lukewarm?"[79]

From the pulpit Niemöller spread the news that "hundreds" of men lost their jobs due to the Church conflict—not a handful or even scores, but hundreds. This sermon clearly and publicly demonstrated sympathy and support for these men and their shared cause. Moreover, Niemöller encouraged his congregants by reminding them of the history of ancient Israel, "'the more [Israel's enemies] afflicted them, the more they multiplied and grew.'"[80]

The Confessing Church actively informed its congregants of Nazi persecutions of pastors and even laymen through the readings of intercessory lists.[81] These documents enumerated church "members who had been arrested, banished, or forbidden by the Gestapo to preach or to travel," and they were read during services to encourage their congregants to pray for them.[82] They were made a part of the liturgy to inform the congregation of the persecution and to invoke God as Comforter, sometimes linked directly to the prayers and other times to the sermon itself. The lists bonded and galvanized the Confessing Church movement amid unprecedented conflict and disunity in German Protestantism.[83] Some pastors argued that the lists should not be used, in the words of Bishop August Marahrens, "as pressure from the church public upon state organs," and so they left off the list those arrested for political reasons.[84] Yet the Nazi regime itself viewed the lists as political provocation. In fact, the intercessory lists are extraordinary primary sources in the historical record that enable one to understand the scope and depth of the Nazi persecution of the German churches.[85]

Pastors often viewed persecution as a context for spiritual growth. In a sermon delivered on September 3, 1938, in the town of Groß-Schlönwitz, Bonhoeffer preached on Romans 5:1–5, a text that speaks of character forged through suffering and perseverance. In the sermon Bonhoeffer said, "Our church has suffered great affliction during the last few years: destruction of its order, the incursion of false proclamation, much enmity, evil words and slander, imprisonment and distress of all kinds, up to this very hour."[86] Bonhoeffer did not explicitly name the persecutors, those who are afflicting, destroying, imprisoning, or speaking falsely, but one may infer he is talking about the German Christians and the Nazi regime (as no one else can "imprison"). He publicly listed the forms of persecution for his congregation and, moreover, emphasized that the persecution continues unabated. Yet he counseled his listeners to take heart in their sufferings and to look to Christ as an example of bearing them.

It is significant in the context of the Christian tradition for pastors to cast themselves and the churches as "the persecuted." This language places the Confessing Church in the role as righteous victims, who through merely living their lives faithfully are targeted and attacked unjustly. Confessing Church pastors thus placed themselves in the same category as the persecuted early churches during the Roman Empire, as well as the stories of the Christian martyrs throughout the past two thousand years. By setting themselves within this narrative of a persecuted church, these pastors affirmed the Christian belief that the outcome of this persecution is certain—that God will defeat the persecutors and liberate the oppressed. This is why the sermons reveal a hopeful tone.

In remembering the persecuted the pastors informed their congregations of the material needs of the persecuted—the pastors who have lost their positions and need help supporting their families. By spreading the word of the persecutions the pastors shed light on the true nature of the Nazi regime and the ideology that drives it. Moreover, each recounting of the trials of the German churches reveals how congregants can "love one another," uniting them more profoundly as the body of Christ. In these ways, the sermons that address the Nazi persecution of the churches are not so much meant to spread news of Nazi evils but to help the church process the persecutions and survive stronger and more united than before.

This theme of Christian unity is demonstrated in a sermon delivered over the BBC airwaves from England into Nazi Germany on May 24, 1942, by the German pastor of Jewish descent Franz Hildebrandt. The day was Pentecost Sunday, a day celebrating the descent of the Holy Spirit on the early Christians, unifying them as the Church. Not surprisingly, sermons against Nazi persecution took place in lands of exile as well, spreading the word abroad about the suffering of the German churches. Hildebrandt fled Nazi persecution in 1937, and became a pastor to a German congregation in London during the Second World War. The sermon is a reflection on the Pentecost story in Acts 2:1–13, in which the Spirit of God, through a rush of wind and tongues of fire, unified men and women into the Church. This great moment in the early Church represents a reversal of the Tower of Babel, a reunification of humanity after an era of division, misunderstanding, and struggle. Yet Hitler and the Nazis plunged Europe into the Second World War, pitting Christians against each other on the battlefield. Hildebrandt asked Christians under Nazi domination to consider their unity in faith rather than disunity in war:

> We think of our brothers in the persecuted churches in Germany, Holland and Norway that are not silent, but have opened their mouths, and we know how serious it is that they began to preach as the Spirit gave them utterance. It is the exact counterpart to the scene of Babel: what the human spirit has divided in its arrogance, God's Spirit, which descended upon us, has united and reconciled.[87]

The German listener of this sermon was confronted with a reality contrary to that propagated by the Nazi regime: the bond between a people is not based upon race, ethnicity, class, or geography, but upon God the Creator. At Pentecost Christians around the world sing in one voice, united as the Church.

This sermon is one of at least 13 that Hildebrandt preached over the radio from the BBC in Great Britain to audiences in Nazi Germany. Religious broadcasts were restricted during wartime in Nazi Germany, and thus BBC programs such as Hildebrandt's may have been among the few religious services available on the radio.[88] Most remarkable about Hildebrandt's BBC sermons is that he actually hoped and counted on Germans to break the law just to listen over the radio. Germans listened to foreign radio programming at great risk to themselves and their families; punishments could include imprisonment or execution.[89] In the case of Hildebrandt's work, the content of his broadcasts was not news or updates on the war's progress, but a word of peace and assurance to Germans weary of war. More importantly, it gave Germans a new perspective with which to judge Hitler and the Nazi regime. His sermons took courage in that his critical comments of Hitler and the Nazi regime could have been construed by his fellow Germans as treasonous and as serving the enemies of the nation (particularly Great Britain). Thus, he risked ostracism at home and among his German colleagues. However, unlike pastors who preached openly in German society, he did not face the possibility of arrest by the Gestapo or imprisonment as an agitator. Simply stated, he preached from the safety of a microphone across the English Channel, far out of the Nazis' reach. Nevertheless, these sermons are immensely significant because they demonstrate the concerns a Confessing pastor would express to his fellow Christians in Germany if given the freedom and the chance.

It goes without saying that sermons delivered out in the open in German society are the most important in our discussion of Confessing sermons as expressions of opposition to the Nazi regime. These sermons were delivered in churches across Germany, where Germans freely sat in their pews to listen to the gospel message. Pastors preached these sermons at regular Sunday services, holidays, confirmation celebrations, and weddings and funerals. This act of preaching in public may have required a degree of courage, depending on how oppositional the content of the sermon was and on whether the pastor believed he had a sympathetic congregation or not. A pastor cognizant that his congregation judged every word he preached might pause before expressing any sentiments of opposition or dissent out of fear of punishment. In contrast to sermons delivered in exile, an underground seminary, a concentration camp, or over the radio, Confessing pastors freely preached these sermons out in the open in German society and contributed to the on-going discussions of religion and politics in Nazi Germany.

Using the Christian scripture as a source base, the pastors drew on Christian traditions to oppose unjust persecution, to criticize National Socialism as a false ideology, and as we will see, to support Jews and Judaism. Thus, the Christian scripture and traditions were the platform from which the pastors formulated and launched opposition, in contrast to the acts of opposition and resistance from other groups in German society, such as the conspirators of the July 20, 1944, plot or the White Rose student group in Munich. Rather than use bombs or broadsides, Confessing Church pastors used sermons to undermine the dominance of the Nazi regime.

In voicing public criticism, pastors undermined the fabricated image of Hitler and the regime as respectful of the churches' right to carry out its religious functions in society. Nazi persecution of Christians amounts to a betrayal of Christians by those purporting to be Christians themselves (or at least those supposedly respectful of Christianity in German society).[90] The pastors' acts of opposition in this collection of sermons meant to re-define Hitler and the Nazis (or pro-Nazi supporters) as enemies of God, Christians, and the gospel. In this way, they sought to challenge the legitimacy of the Nazi regime, at least in its actions and policies towards the German churches.

CONCLUSION

Confessing Church pastors occasionally took to the pulpits to condemn Nazi persecution of Christians and the German churches. As with sermons that criticized Nazi ideology as a false belief system, so also sermons that stood up to Nazi persecution reveal that pastors had freedom in the sanctuary to undermine the Nazi regime. The sermons examined in this chapter demonstrate that opposition to persecution was dynamic and multi-faceted. In the simple act of proclaiming persecution in a worship service, the pastor identified the persecutor, publicized the offense in a community with the aim of spreading the news, and invoked God as Comforter of the persecuted and Judge of the persecuted.

The pastors who delivered these sermons against Nazi persecution appear to have been clearly influenced by the new school of homiletics, as described in chapter 4. For the most part, the sermons do not name persecutors individually or dwell on the persecution per se. Rather, Confessing Church pastors ensured that the sermon was composed to serve the interests of the gospel message, not a political agenda or a pastor's personal inclinations. Confessing Church pastors conscientiously made the biblical texts the basis of their preaching and submitted their political and social views to its authority.[91] In other words, the sermons that reported persecution did not deviate from the purpose of a sermon, to draw the congregant nearer to God in a spirit of worship. The sermons demonstrate that that Confessing Church pastors did not rely on their own abilities or efforts to extricate themselves from the oppression of the Nazi state, but they relied upon God's love and justice.

However, one should not over-emphasize the oppositional nature of these sermons. In very few of these sermons do we find a sustained attack on Hitler or the regime's policies. We do not find sermons that call for organized and united action against the state in response to persecution. With the possible exception of Niemöller's sermons, the Confessing Church pastors' critical comments examined in this chapter are not part of a sustained attack on the regime, its leadership, or specific policies. Instead, they are isolated comments in the context of a sermon's theological reflections.

Nevertheless, these sermons, like the sermons that challenged Nazi ideology, served to delegitimize the Nazi regime—at least to a degree—by implying that persecutors of the churches have taken actions that make them opponents of God, and thereby have incurred God's judgment. By invoking God as Comforter of the persecuted and Judge of the persecutors, the pastors served to undermine the Nazi claim that the regime is the right and just ruler of Germany. They do not go so far as to advocate or act in disobedience to the state, but this reasoning can provide the groundwork that may justify disobedience.

Confessing Church pastors who spoke out against the Nazi regime and the German Christian movement for persecuting the German churches risked persecution themselves. In identifying the persecutors and publicly revealing the nature of their persecutions, and in invoking God as Comforter and Judge, pastors undermined the regime and its leaders as unjust rulers, and thus destabilized their legitimacy as the God-instituted rulers of the state. This criticism asserts not only that the Nazi state is unjust in its treatment of its citizens, but that the leadership is in some sense anti-Christian and at odds with the tradition of the German Reformation. Furthermore, the persecutions call into question Hitler's and many Nazi leader's claims to be Christians themselves or at least respectful of the Christian tradition.[92] The public protests demonstrate the freedom pastors had in the pulpit to push back against Nazi actions and policies.

NOTES

1. Hans Ehrenberg, Sermon on May 23, 1937, in *Drei Predigten* (Bochum: F.W. Fretlöw, 1937), 16.
2. Ehrenberg, *Drei Predigten*, 16.
3. Ehrenberg, *Drei Predigten*, 16.
4. Evans, *Third Reich in Power*, 581.

5. One must keep in mind that this sample is not representative of all sermons delivered in Nazi Germany.

6. For example, see Barnett, *For the Soul of the People*; Conway, *The Persecution of the Churches*; Helmreich, *German Churches under Hitler*; Kurt Meier, *Der evangelische Kirchenkampf*; and Scholder, *The Churches and the Third Reich*, 2 vols; and Kevin Spicer, *Resisting the Third Reich: The Catholic Clergy in Hitler's Berlin* (DeKalb, IL: Northern Illinois University Press, 2004).

7. Barnett, *For the Soul of the People*, 34.

8. Barnett, *For the Soul of the People*, 34.

9. Barnett, *For the Soul of the People*, 34.

10. Helmreich, *German Churches under Hitler*, 162; Robertson, *Christians against Hitler*, 35. Robertson notes that many congregations openly supported their pastors if they were disciplined or lost state sanction, and so they did not need to petition their regional brotherhood council for financial assistance.

11. See Barnett, *For the Soul of the People*, 83; Conway, *The Nazi Persecution of the Churches*, 208–211.

12. Barnett, *For the Soul of the People*, 80; Gerlach, *And the Witnesses Were Silent*, 80; and Conway, *The Nazi Persecution of the Churches*, 56.

13. Barnett, *For the Soul of the People*, 80.

14. Barnett, *For the Soul of the People*, 80.

15. The Council of Brethren was the leadership body of the Confessing Church, whereas the regional church consistory was the leadership body of the *Reichskirche*. See Bonhoeffer, *Theological Education Underground*, Kindle edition, location 1329. Upon his release Hildebrandt immigrated to England and found work as a minister.

16. Conway, *The Nazi Persecution of the Churches*, 209.

17. Conway, *The Nazi Persecution of the Churches*, 245.

18. Conway, *The Nazi Persecution of the Churches*, 245.

19. Conway, *The Nazi Persecution of the Churches*, 210.

20. Bonhoeffer, *Theological Education Underground*, Kindle edition, 825.

21. Conway, *The Nazi Persecution of the Churches*, 210.

22. Of the 36 sermons that express explicit criticism of the Nazi persecution of the German churches, four were delivered in 1934 (with none in 1933) and 13 in 1937. The caveat, however, is that this sample of over 900 sermons cannot be understood as representative of all Confessing Church sermons, and thus the apparent increases during these years could be anomalies of the sample.

23. Conway, *Nazi Persecution of the Churches*, 311–314. See also Ericksen and Heschel, *The German Churches Face Hitler*, 434.

24. Steigmann-Gall, *The Holy Reich*, 216.

25. Steigmann-Gall, *The Holy Reich*, 188.

26. Weikart, *Hitler's Religion*, 121.

27. Weikart, *Hitler's Religion*, 143.

28. Weikart, *Hitler's Religion*, 107–146.

29. Johnson, *Nazi Terror*, 225.

30. Bonhoeffer, *Theological Education Underground*, Kindle edition, 14339–14435; see also Barnett, *For the Soul of the People*, 159–72.

31. For a full treatment of Hildebrandt's sermons in over the BBC, see Skiles, "Franz Hildebrandt on the BBC: Wartime Broadcasting to Nazi Germany," *Journal of Eccesiastical History* 74, Issue 1, January 2023, pp. 90–115.

32. For a discussion of the mobilization of German pastors, see Helmreich, *German Churches under Hitler*, 306–308.

33. Robinson, *Dietrich Bonhoeffer's Christmas Sermons*, 126.

34. Helmreich, *German Churches under Hitler*, 306.

35. Incidentally, this situation led to many women, often the wives of pastors, filling in and leading congregations; see Helmreich, *German Churches under Hitler*, 308.

36. Evans, *The Third Reich at War*, 565.

37. Bonhoeffer, *London*, 352.

38. Heinz Kloppenburg, Sermon manuscript on John 10:12–16, 15 April 1934, Papers of Heinz Kloppenburg. EZA 613/65.

39. Heinz Kloppenburg, Sermon manuscript on John 10:12–16, EZA 613/65.

40. Niemöller, *Here Stand I*, 139.

41. See Helmreich, *German Churches under Hitler*, 170–172; and Barnett, *For the Soul of the People*, 63–65.

42. Niemöller, *Here Stand I*, 142.

43. See Conway, *Nazi Persecution of the Churches*, 81–83; Green, *Lutherans against Hitler*, 95–96; Helmreich, *German Churches under Hitler*, 171–172; and Meier, *Der evangelische Kirchenkampf*, 174–175.

44. Conway, *Nazi Persecution of the Churches*, 82.

45. Conway, *Nazi Persecution of the Churches*, 82–83.

46. Conway, *Nazi Persecution of the Churches*, 98–99. See also Nathan Stoltzfus, *Hitler's Compromises: Coercion and Consensus in Nazi Germany* (New Haven, CT: Yale University Press, 2016), 52–79.

47. Niemöller, *Dahlemer Predigten*, 238–243.

48. Niemöller, *Here Stand I*, 104. For the historical background, see Helmreich, *German Churches under Hitler*, 170–172; and Barnett, *For the Soul of the People*, 63–65.

49. Niemöller, *Here Stand I*, 106.

50. Niemöller, *Here Stand I*, 109.

51. Stoltzfus, *Hitler's Compromises*, 76.

52. Hockenos, *Then They Came for Me*, 106.

53. Hockenos, *Then They Came for Me*, 107.

54. Quoted in Michael Heymel, *Martin Niemöller: vom Marineoffizier zum Friedenskämpfer* (Darmstadt: Der Lambert Schnieder, 2017), 73.

55. Conway, *Nazi Persecution of the German Churches*, 95–96.

56. Conway, *Nazi Persecution of the German Churches*, 96.

57. Heinrich Vogel, Sermon manuscript on 11 November 1937, Papers of Heinrich Vogel, EZA 665/76.

58. Vogel, Sermon manuscript on 11 November 1937, EZA 665/76.

59. Conway, *Nazi Persecution of the German Churches*, 232.

60. Conway, *Nazi Persecution of the German Churches*, 232.

61. Conway, *Nazi Persecution of the German Churches*, 237.

62. Conway, *Nazi Persecution of the German Churches*, 238.

63. Bonhoeffer, *Theological Education Underground*, Kindle edition, location 14397.

64. Bonhoeffer, *Theological Education Underground*, Kindle edition, location 14406.

65. See Bonhoeffer, *Theological Education Underground*, Kindle edition, location 809–828. The editor of this volume writes, "At the end of August 1937, Heinrich Himmler, the head of the secret police, banned Confessing seminaries, as well as related activities such as the taking up of church collections."

Bonhoeffer's sermon is one of 16 sermons of the over 900 examined in this study that was delivered in the Finkenwalde seminary. Sixty-seven seminarians graduated between 1937 and 1939 (when the seminary was underground) and moved on to church apprenticeships in local parishes (Bonhoeffer, *Theological Education Underground*, Kindle edition, location 825). These sermons had a limited impact on the German population and, for the most part, did not take place "out in the open" in German society. Nonetheless, they did harden the resolve of confessing seminarians to withstand Nazi propaganda and the coordination of the Protestant churches, and thus, helped them to preserve their own faith tradition.

66. Karl Barth, *Fürchte Dich Nicht! Predigten aus den Jahren 1934 bis 1948* (Chr. Kaiser Verlag München, 1949), 200.

67. See for example Kenneth Scott Latourette's *A History of Christianity, Vol. II* (New York: Prince Press, 1997), 1396–1399.

68. In a few cases we know that pastors even petitioned to congregations abroad for assistance for the German churches, such as Bonhoeffer's work in winning the support of German congregations in Britain for the Confessing Church, and Friedrich Forell's preaching to New Yorkers for assistance to the German churches. See Eberhard Bethge, *Dietrich Bonhoeffer: A Biography* (Minneapolis: Fortress Press, 2000), 402–404. See also Forell's speech, "Church Life and Church Work in Germany and America," delivered sometime in 1944. Friedrich Forell Collection, Papers of the Newcomers Christian Fellowship, University of Iowa Libraries, Special Collections, Iowa City.

69. Peter Brunner, "Reformationsfestpredigt 1934," undated, Papers of Peter Brunner, Archiv der Evangelischen Kirche im Rheinland (AEKR), Bestand 7NL 006.

70. Brunner, "Reformationsfestpredigt 1934," AEKR, 7NL 006.

71. See Stefanie Huesmann, *Mut zum Bekenntnis: Peter Brunners Widerstand im aufkommenden Nationalsozialismus* (Freimund Verlag, 2011); see also *Dietrich Bonhoeffer Works, Volume 17, Indexes and Supplementary Materials*, edited by Victoria J. Barnett and Barbara Wojhoski (Minneapolis, MN: Fortress Press, 2014), 287.

72. Brunner, "Reformationsfestpredigt 1934," AEKR, 7NL 006.

73. Brunner, "Reformationsfestpredigt 1934," AEKR, 7NL 006.

74. Brunner, "Reformationsfestpredigt 1934," AEKR, 7NL 006.

75. Brunner, "Reformationsfestpredigt 1934," AEKR, 7NL 006.

76. See Huesmann, *Mut zum Bekenntnis*, 92–123; see also *Dietrich Bonhoeffer Works, Volume 17*, 287.

77. Niemöller, *Here Stand I*, 124.

78. Robertson, *Christians against Hitler*, 35.
79. Niemöller, *Here Stand I*, 126.
80. Niemöller, *Dachau Sermons*, 128.
81. Barnett, *For the Soul of the People*, 81.
82. Barnett, *For the Soul of the People*, 90; See also Conway, *Nazi Persecutions of the Churches*, 209; and Helmreich, *German Churches under Hitler*, 215.
83. Barnett, *For the Soul of the People*, 91.
84. Quoted in Barnett, *For the Soul of the People*, 90–91.
85. Helmreich, *German Churches under Hitler*, 215.
86. Bonhoeffer, *Theological Education Underground*, Kindle edition, location 13914.
87. Franz Hildebrandt, Sermon on Acts 2:1–13, 24 May 1942, Papers of Franz Hildebrandt. For an in-depth examination of Hildebrandt's radio ministry with the BBC, see my article, "Franz Hildebrandt on the BBC: Wartime Broadcasting to Nazi Germany," *Journal of Ecclesiastical History* 74, no. 1 (January 2023), pp. 90–115. This discussion reprinted with permission by Cambridge University Press.
88. Helmreich notes that "In the first years of the regime, religious broadcasts were encouraged and a morning religious hour was a regular part of all network programs. From 1935 on, restrictions were gradually imposed—sometimes speakers were censored, funds were not available, or the program was dropped entirely. Over the protests of church leaders, both Protestant and Catholic hours were ended on April 7, 1939. During the war, even the customary morning orchestral playing of church chorales at the spas was stopped" (*German Churches under Hitler*, 222).
89. Richard Evans writes, "The moment the war broke out, tuning in to foreign stations was made a criminal offence punishable by death. It was all too easy, in apartment blocks poorly insulated for sound, for listeners to face denunciation to the authorities by fanatical or ill-intentioned neighbors who overheard the sonorous tones of BBC newsreaders coming through the walls. Some 4,000 people were arrested and prosecuted for 'radio crime' in the first year of the law's operation, and the first execution of an offender came in 1941" (*The Third Reich at War* [New York: Penguin Press, 2009], 576–77).
90. See Steigmann-Gall, *The Holy Reich*, 3. He advances the provocative argument that "leading Nazis in fact considered themselves Christian (among other things) or understood their movement (among other ways) within a Christian frame of reference."
91. See Old, *The Reading and Preaching of the Scriptures in the Worship of the Christian Church*, 759, 763.
92. Steigmann-Gall, *The Holy Reich*, 3.

Chapter 7

"The Bearers of Unholy Potential"

On June 30, 1935, in the Pomeranian town of Kolberg (Kołbrzegu), near the Polish Corridor, Pastor Paulus Hinz stepped into the pulpit at the red brick St. Marien-Dom to preach on Romans 10:1–5.[1] The towering and spacious Gothic cathedral, situated at the center of town since its construction in the early fourteenth century, seated hundreds. By this time, Hinz's career was on the rise. He was 36, a veteran of the Great War, and a leader in the Confessing Church movement, even serving on the Pomeranian Provincial Council of Brethren (*Bruderrat*, or governing council). A well-respected and popular pastor, Hinz later developed a reputation for praying for pastors persecuted by the Nazi regime.[2]

On this early summer day in 1935, Hinz took to the pulpit and preached on the topic of the Jews. This sermon was delivered after the Nazi regime had already begun its persecutions against German Jews, including the Nazi-sponsored boycott of all Jewish shops on April 1, 1933, and the passage of the Civil Service Law of April 7, 1933. The latter effectively barred Jews and Socialists from national, state, and local civil service employment, prohibiting them from careers as school teachers, professors, and government officials and employees.[3]

In his sermon Hinz took as his starting point the words of the apostle Paul in the Epistle to the Romans about the Jews after the death and resurrection of Christ. Paul wrote,

> Brothers and sisters, my heart's desire and prayer to God for them [Jews] is that they may be saved. I can testify that they have a zeal for God, but it is not enlightened. For, being ignorant of the righteousness that comes from God, and seeking to establish their own, they have not submitted to God's righteousness. For Christ is the end of the law so that there may be righteousness for everyone who believes. Moses writes concerning the righteousness that comes from the law, that "the person who does these things will live by them." (10:1–5)

Paul's emphasis was on the hope of salvation for the Jews, noting Jewish "ignorance of the righteousness that comes from God," and their need of that righteousness through Christ.

Hinz connected the ancient biblical text with the context of the church in his day. In his sermon he emphasized Paul's criticisms of the Jews. Hinz argued that because Israel rejected Christ in "stubborn blindness" to God, Israel was no longer God's chosen people, but instead "under the judgment of God's wrath."[4] Moreover, in a veiled condemnation of Nazi racism, Hinz criticized the Jews for trusting in their own descent, in blood and race, and in their own mistaken sense of chosen-ness. He reminded his congregation of the anti-Judaic theme of the Jews' curse in Matthew 27:25. According to the gospel writer, the Jews demanded that Pilate crucify Jesus and free Barabbas: "[Jesus'] blood be on us and on our children!" This curse, Hinz contended, had "uncannily" been accomplished throughout history and even to their day. In this sermon he clearly conflated ancient and contemporary Jews, portraying them as the same throughout history. The sermon takes a biblical text that appears, without historical context, to be critical of the Jews and adds traditional Christian anti-Judaic theology, ending with a "proof" for all to see and verify: the punishment of Jews in history.

While the historical record does not reveal the congregation's response to this sermon, it was by no means unusual or out of the ordinary in the Christian pulpits of Nazi Germany. Hinz's sermon reveals several key elements of anti-Judaic theology that arise from time to time in Confessing Church sermons, and which I will explore in this chapter.

Hinz's sermon exposes a close connection between anti-Judaic beliefs expressed and the biblical text examined. He used Paul's criticism of Jews to launch into his own criticisms. Though this is not always the case, it underscores the necessity of reading Confessing Church sermons together with the biblical text and noting the correspondence and divergence of the two. How are pastors using Scripture to lend authority to anti-Judaic beliefs? Moreover, as Hinz's sermon demonstrates, Confessing Church pastors perceived their Jewish contemporaries through a thick lens of millennia of history and tradition. Thus, any interaction with their increasingly singled-out and persecuted Jewish neighbors resulted not simply from a sense of human connection but also from the troubled history of Christian anti-Jewish beliefs.

This example also highlights a significant problem in interpreting Confessing Church sermons: understanding the nature of the prejudice expressed. It is critical to acknowledge that the lines that distinguish anti-Judaism and antisemitism have been blurred for centuries, even as far back as Emperor Constantine's rule. As Raul Hilberg has shown, anti-Judaic theology had been reinforced in canonical law with legal restrictions, pogroms, and discrimination throughout Church history since the fourth century, indicating ethnic and social prejudice as well as religious animosity.[5] The Nazi regime instituted many of these same measures against the Jewish people, such as the prohibition of intermarriage, restrictions on occupations, and marking clothing with identifiers.[6] As will be demonstrated in this chapter, Confessing Church sermons at times reveal racial prejudice embedded in religious prejudice.

Yet one cannot necessarily assume that beliefs directed against the Jews in the context of a sermon delivered in Nazi Germany are the same as racial prejudice found in the newspapers and propaganda of the Nazi regime. Likewise, one cannot necessarily assume that holding beliefs critical of Judaism necessarily infers that one approaches Jews with animosity or hatred. After all, Paul himself disagreed with other Jews who argued that Jesus was not the Son of God, and yet he advocated a respectful and loving approach to engaging with them so as to facilitate their conversion (cf. Romans 9–10).[7] This is simply to say that it is not always possible to clearly discern a pastor's intention in expressing anti-Judaic beliefs or how their words would have been interpreted by their congregation. Thus, this chapter focuses on the anti-Judaic messages themselves in the context of antisemitism in Nazi Germany.

Nonetheless, historians have demonstrated the pervasiveness of anti-Jewish prejudice in all segments of the German population, including pastors affiliated with the German Christian movement, the Confessing Church, and those who remained "neutral" regarding the Nazi state.[8] Wolfgang Gerlach has convincingly argued that "Most Christians [in Nazi Germany] saw the Jews as objects of either damnation or evangelization," a position that drastically limited their concern for and actions in support of non-Christian Jews in Germany.[9] Historians have demonstrated the virtual silence of the German Churches, and the Confessing Church as well, in coming to the aid of European Jewry caught in Nazi persecutions—a silence resulting from ingrained anti-Jewish prejudice.[10] Furthermore, Victoria Barnett has examined the great complexity and heterogeneity among Confessing Church members; the movement included moderates and radicals, nationalists and antisemites, and even Nazi Party members. The only thing they had in common "was their opposition to the absolute demands of Nazi ideology on their religious faith."[11]

If we widen the scope of those who opposed Nazism to resisters of the Nazi regime and rescuers of Jews, again, anti-Jewish prejudice was widespread.[12] Historians have shown the pervasiveness of antisemitism among the officer's corps in the German military, even among those in the resistance who would conspire against the Nazi regime to end the war and Nazi policies of Jewish persecution.[13] Among Christians who actively resisted the Nazis and rescued Jews, we find the same prejudice prevalent.[14] Yet for rescuers and resisters, their sense of honor, duty, and concern and care for their country and the oppressed outweighed traditions of anti-Jewish prejudice, compelling them to act and speak out against the Nazi regime. I will demonstrate that Confessing Church pastors, as citizens who wanted to limit Nazi infringements in the German Protestant churches, also expressed anti-Judaic beliefs, even in criticizing the Nazi regime at the same time.

Thus, the central question of this chapter is: If an ordinary citizen were to step inside a church, sit in the pew, and listen attentively to a Confessing Church pastor, what messages might they hear about the Jews and Judaism in this period of extraordinary exclusion and persecution? Throughout the more than 900 sermons examined in this research, I have located 35 sermons that expressed anti-Judaic beliefs and 44 that expressed pro-Jewish sentiments.[15] I must reiterate that these sermons should not be understood as representative of all Confessing Church sermons. This chapter will explore how Confessing Church pastors made anti-Judaic statements that corroborated the Nazi antisemitic narrative that the Jews and their religion are in some sense pernicious or destructive. The next chapter will examine how pastors expressed support for the Jewish people, honored Judaism as a foundation of the Christian religion, and even spoke out against the Nazi persecution of the Jews.

These sermons taken together, as analyzed in this chapter and the next, reveal not only ambivalence among Confessing Church pastors about Judaism and the Jewish people but millennia-long ingrained prejudices that often came to the surface. As some of these sermons demonstrate, even when a pastor supported the Jewish people or affirmed the value of Judaism as a basis of Christianity, anti-Judaic comments may have undermined these messages.

This research is significant, first, because it is the only study to extensively treat expressions of support for Jews as well as the nature of anti-Jewish prejudice expressed from the Christian pulpits in Nazi Germany. In short, my analysis treats seriously sermons as a source base for understanding Christians' perceptions of Jews and Judaism in Nazi Germany. To underscore how unique this approach is, I have found only one monograph to treat the topic of antisemitism in the sermons of German churches, the Israeli historian Walter Zvi Bacharach's *Anti-Jewish Prejudices in German-Catholic Sermons* (2000).[16] While Bacharach examines Catholic sermons of the nineteenth century and not Protestant sermons from 1933–1945, he concludes that Catholic theology as expressed and disseminated in sermons throughout Germany greatly contributed to the prevailing view that Jews were inferior, criminal, spiritually corrupt, and thus deserving of divine punishment.[17]

Second, this research is significant because it clarifies the nature of anti-Jewish prejudice in Confessing Church pulpits and demonstrates that it was predominantly religious in expression (though at times racial prejudice comes to the surface as well), in stark contrast to the virulent racial antisemitism espoused by pastors in the German Christian movement or by members of the Nazi regime and its propaganda machine. Third, this research reveals that Confessing Church pastors often employed anti-Judaic beliefs not simply to denigrate the Jews or assert the superiority of Christianity, themes common throughout the history of the Church and in twentieth century German Protestantism more specifically,[18] but intentionally to challenge the Nazi regime and its racial policies and ideology. They used anti-Judaic tropes to compare Jews to Nazis, thereby condemning the Nazi obsession with race and claims of racial superiority and "chosen-ness." And fourth, this research nuances the common argument that pastors of the German churches remained silent as their Jewish neighbors faced unprecedented persecution by the Nazi regime. While the support of the Confessing Church pastors for Jews was admittedly meager, this research provides a greater understanding of what they actually said from the pulpit in support of the Jews and Judaism in Nazi Germany.

In this chapter I wish to critically engage Confessing Church pastors' theological perspectives of Jews and Judaism and their significance in the historical context of Nazi persecution. My aim here is to examine the anti-Judaic messages congregants may have heard on any given Sunday from within the walls of Confessing churches, cognizant that these same beliefs were expressed for two thousand years in Christian pulpits.

VARIETIES OF ANTI-JEWISH PREJUDICE

Anti-Judaism has roots in the early Christian movements of the first century, as Jews and Christians, who were predominantly of Jewish origin, clashed over the interpretation of the identity and meaning of Jesus of Nazareth and the emerging Christian theology. The disagreements naturally contributed to animosity on both sides. As the Christian faith spread throughout the Roman Empire, the number of non-Jewish Christians began to outnumber Jewish Christians, and religiously based animosity against the Jewish people became more firmly ingrained in the theology of the early Christian churches. Various charges against the Jews became popular and entrenched in Christian theology for the next two millennia.

The term "anti-Judaism" is fraught and controversial. In using this term I am not referring merely to disagreement with or opposition to specific principles or tenets of the Jewish faith. One could likewise be anti-fascist, anti-atheist, or anti-Buddhist, but not feel hostility toward fascists, atheists, or Buddhists. Disagreement does not necessarily entail enmity. A Christian may disagree with Jews about the person of Jesus Christ and his work based on reason and a sound reading of Scripture, and yet still respond to Jews in love and respect. I am using the term "anti-Judaism" in its traditional sense to indicate an aversion or hostility to Judaism and Jews based on religious, non-rational grounds, that is, based on religious convictions or interpretations of Scripture and history.[19] Hannah Arendt succinctly writes that anti-Judaism is "religious Jew-hatred, inspired by the mutually hostile antagonism of two conflicting creeds."[20] Enmity toward Jews as a people group is an elemental component of anti-Judaism as commonly understood. In this sense, anti-Judaism may be understood as prejudice against the Jews, and these biases have become prevalent Western culture as standard antisemitic tropes.

Anti-Judaic prejudice asserts the following claims: first, that the Jews as a people are stubborn or wayward; second, that the Jews as a people rejected Jesus, or that they hated him and put him to death (and thus, the charge of deicide); third, that God has cursed the Jews for rejecting Jesus; fourth, that God has punished the Jews ever since for rejecting Jesus; and fifth, that upon the rejection of Jesus and the establishment of the Church, God has broken his covenant with the Jews, and that they have thus ceased to be the people of God.[21] Based on these anti-Judaic beliefs, Christians in the middle ages even accused the Jews of the blood libel, that the Jews kidnapped and killed Gentile children to use their blood in the preparation and cooking of their Passover and Sabbath meals.[22] Anti-Judaism, or as some call it, religious antisemitism, has existed throughout the centuries and continues even to the present day. Each of these elements reflects not simply disagreement with the Jews over theological matters or the interpretation of the life of Jesus but hostility to the Jews as an essentialized people group.

While one may believe in the superiority of the Christian faith as a religious system over Judaism and not be hostile to Jews, it is hard to argue that one can express any one of these five anti-Judaic tropes without either being hostile to Jews or being perceived as hostile to Jews.[23] For example, if one believes that God has cursed the Jews for the crime of deicide, and one is a follower of God, then it would appear that one would affirm God's curse, and in essence, take on God's posture of hostility toward the Jews as his or her own stance. If one believes that God has punished the Jews as a wayward people ever since the crucifixion of Jesus, then it would appear that one would see in the Jew as a Jew an enemy of God and thus one's own enemy—again, if one follows God. If one believes that God has forsaken the Jews as his chosen people and broken his covenant with them because of their "waywardness," and that the Christian church has replaced the Jews as the chosen people, then it seems one would necessarily view the Jew as a Jew as morally and spiritually corrupted, and thus deserving of contempt. The five tropes listed above are particularly important in the context of Nazi Germany as they can appear to directly support Nazi assertions that the Jews as a people group are pernicious, by nature inferior, and the cause of social corruption.

But one must allow for pastors to hold apparently contradictory beliefs concerning the Jews in Nazi Germany. For example, one could believe that God cursed and punished the Jews for the crime of deicide and yet to also assert that Christians should not feel contempt toward them, as incongruous as this may seem.[24] A case in point is a sermon that Peter Brunner preached on August 8, 1942, based on the apostle Paul's famous text on the Jews in Romans 11:1–22. Brunner argued that "since the destruction of Jerusalem [in AD 70], the Jews have stood as a strange enigma, as a terrible monument" of God's judgment, clearly indicating the traditional view that God has cursed and punished the Jews as a perpetual witness to his judgment. Later in the sermon he said, "Now Israel as a national association [*Israel als Volksverband*] is excluded from salvation."[25] Yet Brunner argued that this punishment cannot be understood as final, for "God has not rejected his people."[26] While Christians must not be arrogant or hold Jews in contempt, he argued, they must carefully consider the history of the Jews lest they experience the same punishment for a lack of faith and obedience.[27] This sermon indicates that one could hold to the curse and punishment of the Jews and yet not explicitly assert contempt toward them. But the question is whether one can essentially argue for the truth of the legend of the Wandering Jew and yet not harbor contempt for the Jews (at least subconsciously). Moreover, the preaching of this trope, regardless of warnings to the contrary, could encourage a congregation's contempt for the Jews as a "cursed" people.

The hostility inherent in these anti-Judaic tropes prepared the way for Nazi persecution of the Jews.[28] As Hitler became Chancellor and the Nazis came to power, the Jews were already labelled by many Christians as wayward and errant. The Jews were already condemned as haters of Christ and deicides. The Jews were already considered cursed and marked. The Jews were already believed to be providentially punished. The Jews were already understood as God-forsaken and outcast.

But one cannot conflate religious anti-Judaism with modern racial antisemitism, which argues the racial inferiority or perniciousness of the Jewish people, often advanced through eugenics and scientific racism.[29] Antisemitism posits that Jews are fundamentally different in race and blood, and therefore, they cannot be "converted" into the superior group, however defined. In fact, the term "antisemitism" itself was coined as recently as the 1870s by Wilhelm Marr, a German journalist who aimed to distinguish traditional religious anti-Judaic beliefs from a supposedly more modern and scientific bias against the Jews.[30] Antisemitism simply refers to hatred toward the Jews as a distinct race or people group.[31]

The ambivalence of many German pastors toward the Jews in the Nazi dictatorship must be understood in the context of a long history of anti-Judaic and antisemitic prejudice against the Jews in Europe. By the early twentieth century, various strands of anti-Jewish prejudice can be distinguished, though they can blend together. In addition to the religious form, social, economic, and political prejudices emerged, going centuries back to the Middle Ages, each interacting with and feeding off the others. Although all prejudice is destructive and dangerous, it can take shape and manifest in a variety of ways. As such, it is important to emphasize that Confessing Church pastors' biases and theological understandings of Jews and Judaism varied.

In the late nineteenth and early twentieth centuries, many Europeans demonstrated social prejudice by viewing the Jews contemptuously as peddlers, robbers, and shirkers. Yet at the same time, Jews were overrepresented in professions with high visibility, such as journalism, medicine, and the law (and they were under-represented in others).[32] Many Europeans viewed apparent social and economic divisions in society with suspicion and resented Jews for their level of achievement and influence. This social or economic prejudice is perhaps best understood as a form of class conflict, for example, when a German peasant resented his Jewish landlord for what he perceived as high rents, and then connected all Jews to exploitation.[33]

Political antisemitism emerged in the later nineteenth century, and it is opportunist in nature, often used as a propaganda tool by politicians to stir up animosity against the Jews in the hopes of unifying an electoral base.[34] Two very important figures in the German-speaking lands were Adolf Stoecker, a leader in the Christian Social Party in the 1870s, and Karl Lueger, the mayor of Vienna at the end of the 1890s and into the early twentieth century. Political antisemitism targeted the Jews as the alien "other" and associated them with all the negative qualities in one's society, whether that is capitalist exploitation, or the rise of socialism, communism, modernity, or atheism. In the late nineteenth and early twentieth centuries in Germany and Austria, political organizations adopted antisemitism simply because it appealed to the broad masses of the people; antisemitism made sense of the problems and challenges that people faced in the emerging liberal European society.[35] Politicians singled out Jews and blamed all evils on them, and in this way they consolidated political support. One-dimensional antisemitic political parties and organizations declined in Germany after 1900, and yet antisemitism as an ideology became more respectable and ended up being absorbed into many political organizations as one element among many on their platforms.[36]

The most virulent and uncompromising of the various types of prejudice is racial antisemitism. This ideology emerged in the eighteenth century and became increasingly popular as Europeans applied social Darwinist theories to the human race and society in the nineteenth century.[37] At this point, racism was common in Europe, spreading through the influence of philosophy, science, and even art criticism. As the distinguished historian George Mosse has argued, "Racism was not really the product of one particular national or

Christian development, but a worldview which represented a synthesis of the old and the new—a secular religion attempting to annex all that mankind desired."[38] Racial thinkers in this period ranked the races in terms of aesthetics, on how a people's features corresponded to a given ideal, the Greek, Roman, or Germanic. Thus, racism is a "visually centered ideology."[39] For the German racial thinker, the blond-haired, blue-eyed, tall man is superior to the dark-haired, brown-eyed African, because he corresponds to an ideal type. This development made racism completely subjective, whatever its scientific pretensions, and incoherent, given that members of a single "race" exhibit various physical features.

Racial antisemitism allows no "outs" for the oppressed: one cannot convert out, or change economic classes, or switch to a new political party. Race is definitive. Hitler and the Nazis exploited racial antisemitism to define for the German people its reason for catastrophe in the First World War and its aftermath. Hitler argued that the Jews were a race and comprised a boundary-less state; as such, they were a potent threat against the dominance of the "Aryan" race.[40] In fact, European antisemites as early as the 1880s and 1890s demanded various "solutions": immigration, the abolishment of Jewish emancipation, the expulsion of Jews, and even extermination.[41] Hitler understood this racial struggle as a crusade to rid the world of evil, for in his worldview, the Jews were the source of evil. Victory, then, meant the redemption of the world from the clutches of evil.[42] For Hitler, the eradication of the Jews meant the victory of the Aryan spirit, nation, and the fulfillment of Germany's destiny.[43] Thus, *Mein Kampf* and Hitler's speeches are chock-full of the religious language of redemption and apocalypse used to stir up the zeal of the German people, their "righteous" indignation at Jewish misdeeds.[44]

It goes without saying that this conception of race is exceptionally incoherent. In point of fact, there is no monolithic people "the Jews." The Jewish people have lived in many lands, speak many languages, have different physical characteristics, and belong to different ethnicities, such as the Ashkenazim and Sephardim.[45] Racial antisemites and the Nazis in particular created an essentialized, simplified villain, "the Jew."

At this point it is imperative to note that religious prejudice is intricately connected to other forms of prejudice, particularly racial antisemitism. As several scholars of the history of antisemitism have noted, religious anti-Judaism forms the basis of racial antisemitism.[46] Robert Michael argues that "the anti-Jewish aspects of Christian thought and theology, the anti-Jewish Christian mindset and attitudes, and the anti-Jewish precedents provided by the churches' historical relationship to Jews significantly conditioned, and may have determined, the plan, establishment, and prosecution of the Holocaust."[47] The line between anti-Judaism and antisemitism can easily become blurred when one believes the Jewish people, as a people, are stubborn or wayward; that Jews hated and killed Jesus (thus the charge of deicide); that they have been under the punishing curse of God throughout history; and that the Jews have ceased to be the people of God.[48] These views imply a moral or spiritual degeneracy that is passed down genetically from generation to generation; a faith-based anti-Judaism can then easily become a racially based antisemitism.[49]

Having said this, I will use the term anti-Judaism and antisemitism in their traditional senses to preserve their respective religious and racial distinctions. The term "anti-Judaic" is more efficient and less ambiguous than "Christian antisemitism"—"antisemitism" in common usage refers to racial prejudice. But more importantly, the term "anti-Judaic" emphasizes the religious roots of the problem going back through the history of Christianity, through the Middle Ages and the early Christian movements. The term "anti-Judaic" reflects the early Christians' increasingly antagonistic stance toward their former co-religionists, as revealed in Christian condescension towards Jews as the "forsaken" people of God and in accusations of waywardness and deicide—all responses rooted in religious, not racial, prejudice.[50] I will proceed using the term "anti-Judaism" while acknowledging its close relationship to antisemitism.

CONFESSING CHURCH EXPRESSIONS OF ANTI-JUDAISM

After analyzing 900-plus sermons of the Confessing Church, I found 35 that contain expressions of prejudice against the Jewish people or Judaism, voiced by 10 of the 95 Confessing Church pastors examined for this study. These sermons are significant to our understanding of the messages Confessing Church pastors delivered publicly about the Jews and Judaism.

All expressions of prejudice against the Jewish people or Judaism reflect traditional Christian anti-Judaism, a non-rational prejudice based on religious convictions or interpretations of Scripture and history.[51] I have found no evidence of antisemitic expressions that stand alone without mention of religious prejudice. In other words, the primary basis of the anti-Jewish prejudice is religious conviction, which at times implicitly draws on antisemitic tropes.

One must also keep in mind the larger context in which anti-Jewish prejudice was expressed in the German Protestant churches in the Nazi period. From the start, the main concern of the Confessing Church was to oppose the attempts of the German Christian movement to coordinate (or "nazify") the churches by attempting to institutionalize a racial criterion, stipulated in an "Aryan paragraph," to be adopted into church law throughout the German states, thus limiting church leadership, ordination, and even membership to "Aryan" Germans only.⁵² The German Protestant churches vigorously debated the "Aryan paragraph" and they took various positions, which at times reveal anti-Jewish prejudice. Regional churches sought the advice of theological faculty, and two of the more well-known responses were from the theological faculty at the universities of Marburg and Erlangen. The Marburg faculty explicitly and unambiguously opposed the "Aryan paragraph": any person of Jewish descent, who accepts Christianity and is baptized, is a full-fledged member of the Church.⁵³ The Erlangen faculty offered a quite different response, one that acquiesced to racial considerations: historically the church has required biological requirements of faculty (e.g., age, sex, and physical capabilities), so the church could add other biological requirements; at the same time, for a church to prosper, it would help for a pastor to be of the same people as his congregation (a Bavarian leading Bavarians, for example).⁵⁴ They offered a rationale for why separate churches for Jewish Christians might be the best approach.

One of the very few times that the Confessing Church leadership stridently condemned the antisemitism of the Nazi regime was the memorandum of May 28, 1936, issued by the Provisional Church Government and sent directly to Adolf Hitler. Though meant to be a private memorandum for Hitler, the press got its hands on it and published it at home and abroad.⁵⁵ The letter criticized the regime on a range of issues, including the problems of disunity among the Protestant churches, the deification of the Nazi state and Hitler himself, and concerns about de-Christianization in Nazi Germany.⁵⁶ But its condemnation of antisemitism was especially striking, if only because it was so rare a criticism delivered directly to Hitler: "when within the concepts of National Socialist *Weltanschauung* (worldview) an anti-Semitism is forced on Christians which demands hatred of the Jews (*Judenhaas*), there stands opposed to this the Christian command of love your neighbor."⁵⁷ The Nazi regime reacted with vehemence, arresting several pastors and theologians responsible for the letter, including a Jewish man, Friedrich Weissler, an attorney who worked with the Provisional Church Government, and who was sent to Sachsenhausen and murdered. The Nazi reaction reveals the repercussions of speaking out publicly against the Nazi regime, especially against its persecution of the Jews.

Nevertheless, the consensus among historians is that throughout the Third Reich, Confessing Church pastors limited their concerns about Nazi racial policies to their impact on Jewish Christians—to Christians of Jewish descent within the churches—and failed to concern themselves about the persecution of Jews as Jews under the Nazi regime.⁵⁸ In the context of Nazi Germany, one could argue that anti-Jewish expressions from the pulpit indirectly serve to support Nazi racial policies because they are clearly aimed at criticizing or condemning Jews. The following section will focus attention on how

Confessing Church pastors expressed beliefs in the Jews' hatred of Christ, the charge of deicide, and God's subsequent curse, punishment, and forsaking of the Jewish people. Assertions of the waywardness or stubbornness of Jews as Jews are elemental to these assertions.

Perceptions of the Jews' Hatred and the Charge of Deicide

Confessing Church pastors at times used expressions that blamed "the Jews" for rejecting or killing Christ out of hatred, revealing the Jews' spiritual or moral inferiority. These expressions vary widely in judgment and blame. Many of these refer simply and as a matter of fact to the Jews' perverse hatred of Jesus. Some of these retell the trial and crucifixion of Jesus and in so doing argue that "the Jews" hated Jesus and rejected him. For example, in a sermon during the Second World War, Pastor Otto Dibelius, the general superintendent of the Brandenburg Land church, imagined the perspective of the Roman centurion standing beneath the cross of Christ thinking: "Here is something unequaled by all attempts at human hatred which the Jews undertake," and that it was "something superhuman" [*etwas Übermeschliches*].[59] Pastor Bodelschwingh said in 1944 that "Jewish hatred of Christ is a contagious force."[60] Other pastors were more explicit that the Jews actually killed Christ. This point is tremendously significant as the charge of deicide was often used during the Holocaust to justify violence against the Jewish people.[61] The historian Irving Greenberg has noted "literally hundreds" of instances where this kind of statement was made to justify antisemitic violence.[62]

A Passion Sunday service in 1937 by Pastor Martin Niemöller illustrates an historically common perception of the Jews at Jesus' crucifixion. Niemöller preached on Pilate's question to "the masses" at the Passover celebration: would they rather free "Christ or Barabbas?" (Matthew 27:17). He said,

> [W]hen we hear the story of Christ's Passion we have a feeling of sympathy . . . with the figure of this Roman, Pilate, whereas we most emphatically dissociate and separate ourselves from all the others who helped to bring about the death of Jesus. The cold hatred of the Jewish authorities fills us with horror, the groundless and unfathomable treachery of Judas makes us shudder, and *the pusillanimous fanaticism of the multitude* rouses our contempt [emphasis added].[63]

He assumed a common sense of sympathy toward Pilate and a common sense of horror at the Jewish expressions of hatred, treachery, and fanaticism at the crucifixion. He did not discuss his view of the Jews again in this sermon, but this first paragraph alone reveals what was a commonly held view in

Germany that the Jews—its leaders and the masses—were responsible for the execution of Jesus.

While Confessing Church pastors may not have often explicitly linked the Jews at Jesus' crucifixion with the Jews of their own day, these expressions of Jewish hatred and contempt at the crucifixion speak directly to a tradition that the Jews killed Christ and still harbor contempt for him (otherwise, they would be Christians). Ralph Keen writes,

> [Jews] collectively held an image in the Christian imagination that had endured almost as long as the Church itself. Religious anti-Judaism rested in apostolic and patristic portrayals of Christian beginnings, in which the first-century Jewish community willfully rejected the Messianic redemption they had been seeking for so long. Holding the Jewish community accountable for the Crucifixion, although a separate idea with its own context, complemented that reading of the New Testament sources.[64]

Reiterating the charge that "the Jews" killed Christ affirms the anti-Judaic "logic" of God's supposed curse and punishment of the Jewish people, as well as God forsaking them as his covenant people.

Another sermon by Martin Niemöller delivered at the Dachau concentration camp reveals the complexity of asserting this charge of deicide from the biblical text. As mentioned previously, the Gestapo arrested Niemöller in 1937 for vociferously criticizing the Nazi regime. After his subsequent trial, release, and immediate re-arrest as Hitler's personal prisoner, Niemöller found himself among half a dozen other "special prisoners" in the Dachau concentration camp.[65] By Christmastime 1944, the seven men were suddenly allowed—for reasons unknown to them—to worship together as Christians.[66] And they did so despite coming from different Christian traditions.[67] One week later, on December 31, 1944, Niemöller delivered a New Year's Eve sermon on the story of the man Simeon, the "just and devout" Jew of Jerusalem in Luke 2:29–32. Niemöller stated that Simeon "belonged to the good, pious, humble classes, which were of course numerous."[68] According to Luke's gospel, Simeon faithfully waited for the Lord's Messiah (Luke 2:29–32). Yet, while Niemöller acknowledged the good and pious Jews like Simeon, and praised him for waiting for the Messiah and recognizing him in Jesus, he later in the sermon condemned the Jews of Jesus' day for rejecting him. He made the charged generalization that "The people of Israel could do nothing better with this Saviour than to try him and hand him over to the executioners. 'His own received him not' (John 1:11)."[69] One could argue that the Jews by and large did not "receive" Jesus as the messiah, as the Gospel of John states, yet it is quite another to contend that the Jews "could do nothing better" than have him killed, as if they had no choice or were somehow compelled by their nature. There were of course other options, such as ignoring, competing against, or otherwise sidelining him. Thus, in this one sermon Niemöller presented incongruent messages: he praised the "numerous" "good, pious, [and] humble classes" of Jews, to which Simeon belonged, and he essentialized "the people of Israel" as guilty of deicide. He left the discrepancy for his listeners to reconcile.

The sermons clearly demonstrate the widespread and common theological reading that Jews hated Jesus and were the ones responsible for his crucifixion. A few more examples will suffice. On Good Friday in 1935 Niemöller referred to the Jews as "a whole nation" that "[tried] to get rid of the living God."[70] In December 1936 Hermann Diem stated that the Jews sent Jesus to the cross.[71] Likewise, in late spring 1944 Friedrich von Bodelschwingh said "[the Jews] did not recognize him. That is why they hated and killed him."[72] He adds, "And even today in the assemblies of the Jews, who hold fast to their father's faith, Jesus is called the accursed."[73] In a sermon just a couple weeks later Bodelschwingh referred to the many obstacles that the apostle Paul encountered as he spread the gospel on his missionary journeys, asserting that the "the Jewish hatred of Christ [*Christushaß*] pursued [Paul] at every turn." Bodelschwingh essentialized the Jews based on their hatred of Jesus and inferred the existence of a power that fuels Christian persecution: "the Jewish hatred of Christ."[74] Karl von Schwarz asserted in a sermon that it was not "a gang criminals" that killed Jesus, but "the official Israel [*das offizielle Israel*], the people with the overwhelming religious genius . . . that pronounced the death sentence."[75] Yet Schwarz understands Jesus' execution as a condemnation not of the Jews only but of humanity as a whole.

In expressing the charge of deicide, the pastor contributed to a long-standing tradition of contempt against the Jews for a crime their ancestors supposedly committed. In the context of Nazi Germany such expressions aligned with Nazi ideology about the moral inferiority of the Jews, as well as Nazi policies for Jewish exclusion. Congregants were left to themselves to make sense of these assertions in the context of Nazi Germany, amid the anti-Jewish laws, the "Aryanization" of Jewish businesses, the ghettoization, deportation, and massacres. Moreover, as the Roman Catholic priest Robert Bullock has argued, it does not matter if congregants consciously interpreted statements such as these as a charge of deicide or not, or even whether they were in fact listening. Bullock contends, "When the deicide content is pointed out, most will say it does not mean that or they did not hear it that way or they were not listening. But if prejudices are noncognitive, it is not necessary to be listening in order to learn . . . How can we possibly imagine that this has no effect in sustaining anti-Judaism?"[76] When generalized statements that "the Jews" killed Christ are made without clarification or caveat, the Jews as Jews are denigrated and often perceived as the enemies of God. At the very least,

Christian anti-Judaic theology may have served to "numb" Christians to the suffering and persecution of their Jewish neighbors, becoming a hindrance for them to stand up and protest the Nazi regime.

The Curse and Punishment of the Jews

Another anti-Judaic trope occasionally used by Confessing Church pastors in Nazi Germany was that God has cursed and punished the Jews for the rejection of Jesus. Historically, this trope has been directly related to the deicide charge. Many Christians in Nazi Germany interpreted the persecution of Jews through history and their own day as divine punishment. Martin Niemöller voiced this view three times, more than any other Confessing Church pastor in my sample (twice in 1935 and once in 1936). One example occurred in late summer 1935 (on the tenth Sunday after Trinity). In a sermon entitled, "Ye Would Not!" Niemöller explored Matthew 23:34–39, in which Jesus pronounces "woes" upon the scribes and Pharisees for their unwillingness to accept his gospel message. After criticizing Nazi "positive" Christianity and challenging his congregants to remain faithful to the unsullied gospel message, Niemöller said,

> Today is the tenth Sunday after Trinity, a day which has for centuries been dedicated in the Christian world to the memory of the destruction of Jerusalem and the fate of the Jewish people; and the gospel lessons of this Sunday throw a light upon the dark and sinister history of this people which can neither live nor die because it is under a curse which forbids it to do either.
>
> We speak of the "eternal Jew" and conjure up the picture of a restless wanderer who has no home and who cannot find peace. We see a highly gifted people which produces idea after idea for the benefit of the world, but whatever it takes up becomes poisoned, and all that it ever reaps is contempt and hatred because ever and anon the world notices the deception and avenges itself in its own way. I say "in its own way," for we know full well that there is no charter which would empower us to supplement God's curse with our hatred. Even Cain receives God's mark, that no one may kill him; and Jesus' command, "love your enemies!" leaves no room for exceptions. But we cannot change the fact that until the end of its days the Jewish people must go its way under the burden which Jesus' decree has laid upon it: "Behold, your house is left unto you desolate. For I say unto you, Ye shall not see me henceforth, till ye shall say, Blessed is he that cometh in the name of the Lord!"[77]

Niemöller summed up the reasoning for this nearly two-thousand year "punishment": "the Jews brought the Christ of God to the cross."[78] They did this, he argued, because of their priority of race and nation over faith. The Jews were, as he said, ready to approve of its Messiah just as long and as far as it thought it could gain some advantage for its own plans and aims from him, his words and his deeds. It bears a curse because it rejected him and resisted him to the death when it became clear that Jesus of Nazareth would not cease calling to repentance and faith, despite their insistence that they were free, strong and proud men and belonged to a pure-blooded, race-conscious nation.[79]

Niemöller drew a parallel between the Nazis who advanced "positive" Christianity and the Jews of Jesus' day, and both stand condemned for using religion to claim some advantage for themselves rather than accept the gospel of Christ. He used the anti-Judaic prejudice his congregants would know and understand to condemn the German Christian movement for the same "sins" of ancient Israel: the rejection of Christ, the refusal of repentance and true faith, and the steadfast assertion that they were a "pure-blooded" and "race-conscious nation." Christians and the nation of Germany, he argued, faced the same dilemma about positive Christianity as ancient Israel faced. He ended the sermon with a prayer for God to have mercy on them. This sermon is an example of pastors presenting mixed messages of Jews to their congregations: on the one hand they are criticized as a sinful people and on the other hand they are remembered in prayer as deserving of God's mercy and grace.

Anti-Judaic expressions can convey mixed messages that reveal embedded prejudices. A case in point is a sermon that Pastor Heinrich Grüber preached on Romans 1:16, sometime between October 1941 and June 1943, the dates of his incarceration at Dachau concentration camp. His sermon was entitled "I am not ashamed," echoing the famous line of the apostle Paul, "For I am not ashamed of the gospel; it is the power of God for salvation to everyone who has faith, to the Jew first and also to the Greek" (Romans 1:16). Grüber had been arrested for his leadership of the Grüber Office in Berlin, an organization that supported Christians of Jewish descent by providing legal aid, pastoral care, and welfare aid, as well as facilitating employment abroad and emigration, often by procuring false passports.[80] A conservative estimate indicates that by 1940 the Grüber Office helped 1,100 individuals to emigrate out of Nazi Germany.[81] The Gestapo arrested Grüber in 1941 and sent him to the concentration camp at Dachau, where he delivered this sermon.

In this sermon on Romans 1:16, Grüber too, like Niemoeller, raised the myth of the "eternal Jew," otherwise known as the Wandering Jew. This figure needs reconciliation to God. The myth dates back to medieval Europe and purports to tell the story of a Jew who mocked Jesus as he carried his cross to Golgotha. God cursed and punished the man to wander perpetually until Christ returns in the Second Coming.[82] Grüber argued,

[The] Jews and the Greeks, of whom Paul speaks here [in Romans 1:16], are not so much the members of a people as the bearers of a spiritual attitude that accompanies people through all times. There is not only an eternal Jew [*einen ewigen Juden*], but also an eternal Greek. The Jew is the man for whom everything is ancestry, type, nationality, and tribalism and blood. In his opinion, he is a member of a chosen and gifted people, that is enough for him. The Greeks know about their own self-worth; no matter whether it is through strength or reason, it is one's own being that determines the value and goes its own way.[83]

At first reading, it might appear that Grüber is stating that not all Jews fit the pattern of the "eternal Jew," given that he is focusing on the "spiritual attitude" of not just Jews but any people; and further, he insinuated that not all Jews fit this stereotype. And yet he evoked the stereotype nonetheless, stating the reality of "the eternal Jew," a phase commonly used by Nazi propaganda in his own day to refer to the unchangeable character of the Jews. Schmit-Berning notes that National Socialists often used "ewig" in sense of hereditary biology to refer "to the unity of life in the unbroken chain of hereditary carriers."[84] In fact, the Nazi ministry of Propaganda produced a film on this topic by the same name, *The Eternal Jew*, in 1940, perhaps a year or two prior to Grüber's sermon. Grüber presented the caricature of the Wandering Jew to describe people many Christians of his day would have identified as Jews: those trusting in their own ancestry and blood. At the same time, his comment condemned National Socialists who, like the "eternal Jew," trust in race and blood.

The problem is that Grüber used an ethnic and racial slur to make a point about spiritual flourishing. Despite his caveat of speaking about a "spiritual attitude" that could apply to any people, he still affirmed the reality of "the eternal Jew," evoking a long-standing medieval caricature that would have been familiar to his audience. This notion of a morally corrupted and cursed Jew was consonant with and advanced Nazi racial ideology. Yet his message was that Greeks too (read: contemporary Germans), those who trust in themselves and go their own way, need God's reconciliation and mercy, just like the "eternal Jew." The reconciliation offered to Israel as told in the Hebrew Bible (through a series of covenants between God and Israel) is the same reconciliation available to "Greeks."[85] In other words, the same reconciliation that will give rest to the Wandering Jew is the very same that will give peace to the "eternal Greek." Grüber affirmed that God calls Jews and "Greeks" to reconciliation with God: "To this salvation both Jews and Greeks are called. We do not ask, where you come from and what your father was and who your grandmother was."[86] Again, he condemned National Socialism and Nazi racial policy in Nazi Germany. Thus, Grüber employed a Jewish stereotype to criticize Nazis and to argue that God seeks the reconciliation of all people, including Jews.

Pastors mentioned the supposed curse and punishment of the Jewish people in passing, simply assuming this was common knowledge. Julius Sammentreuther referenced the Jews' rejection of Jesus, and now they have "neither faith nor home."[87] Niemöller referenced "the fate of the people of Israel who made light of the king's invitation" as those in Jesus' parable in Matthew 22:1–14, who refused the king's wedding invitation and were destroyed.[88] Likewise, in another sermon on Luke 19:45–47, he mentioned the destruction of the Temple in 70 AD and spoke of the "peculiar fate of the Jewish people," who refused to "listen to the last and decisive word of God" in Jesus Christ.[89] Brief references such as these indicate that German congregations were well familiar with the view that God punished the Jews for refusing Jesus as the Christ and putting him to death.

Invoking God's punishment of the Jews could also be used to encourage Christians in Nazi Germany to turn from false gods. For example, a sermon by Dietrich Bonhoeffer identified Germans of his day with Israel in rebelling against God, setting up false idols, and then reaping God's punishment as a result. He wrote the sermon to be delivered by his close friend and colleague (and later biographer) Eberhard Bethge at the Mission Festival in Ohlau, Silesia, on October 20, 1941. This was mere months after the start of Operation Barbarossa, Germany's invasion of the Soviet Union in June 1941. But it was also shortly after he began to hear reports within the *Abwehr* resistance of plans for the deportation of Jews to the east.[90] By the fall of 1941, Bonhoeffer had begun his peripheral involvement with *Unternehmen 7* (Operation 7), an intricate plan to smuggle 14 individuals (three of whom were Jews) out of Germany and into Switzerland to report on Nazi treatment of the Jewish population.[91]

Bonhoeffer's sermon used Scripture to compare the ancient Israelites to the Germans of his own day. The sermon was based in part on Jeremiah 16:21, a text that refers to God's teaching the Israelites of his power and might. Bonhoeffer mirrored Jeremiah's admonition against his own people: a time will come when God will cease asking his people to stop idolatry, and he will eventually punish his people to set them right. Reflecting on Jeremiah's text, Bonhoeffer asserted that Israel was a stubborn people who consistently rebelled against God, "worshiping other lords and gods as idols."[92] He appeared to focus in on the Nazis and pro-Nazi supporters in his criticism. He argued, "There is a last resort by which God leads his people (Israel), who have repeatedly misused and resisted God's grace and have toyed with it, to lead them to the recognition of God's authority: namely, the *powerful* angry strike of God's hand [emphasis in the original]."[93] It should be noted that Bonhoeffer had previously asserted that God had rejected and cursed the Jewish people, most notably in his 1933 essay, "The Church and the Jewish Question," and there is no indication that his views changed by this time.[94] Bonhoeffer's sermon appears to follow the same logic of the essay, as Stephen Haynes notes, "Although they remain God's chosen people, Jews suffer under a divine curse for killing their Messiah; scattered and insecure, they will ultimately be welcomed home by God."[95] Like the Jews, Bonhoeffer argued, Christians in Germany have gone astray and have been struck with God's wrath, with "war, crises, imprisonment, distress of all kinds."[96] The meditation is a call for Germans to consider their response to God's "dark revelation": will they return to God or harden their hearts?[97] He said, "In God's anger at you, recognize that God loves you; God wants to be your Lord again! Last chance."[98] Bonhoeffer asserted that God still loves his people—Jews and Christians—even though he punishes them, hoping for their return. After all, a loving father disciplines his children. Bonhoeffer's point is that the German people must humble themselves and turn to God, lest they continue to endure God's wrath.

The Jews as God-forsaken

The fourth anti-Judaic trope that occurred in this collection of over 900 sermons is that God has rejected the Jews as his people and replaced them with the Church. This view is predicated on the belief that the Jews killed Christ and have been cursed and punished by God. In one instance, Paul Hinz preached a sermon entitled "The Church under the Cross" at the Kolberg cathedral on October 10, 1937. His main text was Revelations 2:8–11, and his aim was to encourage his congregants to persevere in a period of church conflict and persecution. The biblical text presents Christ's words for the seven churches, and Hinz focused on Christ's words to the church in Smyrna, a community facing persecution by Jews as the inter-Jewish conflict between Jews and Christians became increasingly hostile in the late first century AD. The biblical texts is as follows:

> I know your affliction and your poverty, even though you are rich. I know the slander on the part of those who say that they are Jews and are not but are a synagogue of Satan. Do not fear what you are about to suffer. Beware, the devil is about to throw some of you into prison so that you may be tested, and for ten days you will have affliction. Be faithful until death, and I will give you the crown of life. Let anyone who has an ear listen to what the Spirit is saying to the churches. Whoever conquers will not be harmed by the second death.

Hinz's addressed a key concern among his congregants in their own time of conflict and persecution, "What will become of the evangelical church?" He looked to this text in Revelation for his answer. He contended that despite the troubles, poverty, and slander, the church must persevere to be what it always has been since its beginning, a "church under the cross." A "church under the cross" cannot be destroyed. Focusing attention on the biblical text, Hinz expressed the anti-Judaic belief that God has rejected the Jews:

> Since Christ came down to earth and was crucified, the Jews as Jews have ceased to be the people of God, the community of God. Since then, these [the people of God] have been the believers in Christ of all countries and times. The promises that were once given to the people of the old covenant have now passed to them. Nevertheless, it was already here in Smyrna and in other early Christian communities that Jews as Jews, trusting in their blood and their race, in the thought: "We do have Abraham for our father," continued to maintain themselves the true community of God. Now, in their hatred against the true community, the church of Jesus Christ, they became a synagogue of Satan.[99]

While Hinz's focus was clearly on the New Testament text, his usage of the phrase, "trusting in their blood and their race" (*im Vertrauen auf ihr Blut und ihre Rasse*) appears to connect the Jews of the ancient world to the Jews of his day. This is an idea he used two years earlier in a sermon on Romans 10, in which he argued that the Jewish people "lost their salvation" because of their waywardness; the Jewish race focused "on its blood and its race" (*auf sein Blut und seine Rasse*).[100] This language of blood and race indicates an eisegetical insertion of modern racialized language into the passage. Nowhere in Revelation or the Scriptures are the Jews referred to as a people who trust "in their blood and their race." While John the Baptist and Jesus certainly criticize certain Jews who trust in their Abrahamic lineage (e.g., Matthew 3:9 and John 8:31–38), their language is not racial. Hinz anachronistically applied modern racial language to characterize first-century Jews' beliefs and used this as the basis for God's rejection of them.

But Hinz's central point is about the nature of the true community of God and protecting it from those who would redefine it based on blood and race, such as those in the pro-Nazi German Christian movement. In discussing the Revelation text, he asserted that "the Jews have ceased to be the people of God" and that they have become a "synagogue of Satan" (*Gemeinde des Satans*), a people that trusts in blood and race and that incites hatred for the "true community" of God. Interestingly, Heinz did not use the word *Schule* to describe this Jewish community as the Luther Bible translates the Revelation text (*des Satans Schule*). Rather he used the word *Gemeinde*, apparently to emphasize that this community is not bound by a building or setting. Hinz used this controversy in the first-century church at Smyrna to argue that the mark of the "true community" of God is trust in God, not trust in one's blood or race. A "synagogue of Satan" can be deluded into thinking it is the "true community" of God. He did not name the pro-Nazi German Christian movement in the sermon, though the context makes his meaning clear. He is apparently drawing parallels between the race-conscious Jews of first-century Palestine and the race-conscious German Christians of twentieth-century Germany, both of whom, he argued, persecuted the true church while claiming to be God's favored people.[101] The church, for its part, must remain "under the cross" and God will ensure its preservation and perseverance. Hinz's primary concern was not to condemn the Jews then or in his own day, but to offer encouragement to a beleaguered Christian community in Germany. But he used an anti-Judaic trope to do so.

Moreover, while some pastors may not have overtly stated that God forsook the Jews, their language clearly indicates that God rejected them and replaced them with the Church. For example, Pastor Köster argued that the time of the Jews came to an end with the advent of Christ, that their history had come to an end, to make way or the Church; but he also asserted that Christianity could become an "overaged and unfruitful people" just like the Jews.[102] In another sermon, Paul Hinz argued that "The promises of the old covenant have now [in the first century] passed to [Christians]"; he said this condemning the race-based conceptions of chosen-ness advanced by "Rosenberg and his followers."[103] And in a later sermon Hinz asserted, "Since Israel ignored the call of God and rejected Christ, Christ's Church has been God's people."[104] The clear message is that God is no longer working through the Jewish people, but rather, God is working to bless the world through the Church.

One may interpret the trope that God forsook the Jews as inherent in the other tropes, that the Jews hated Christ and killed him, and that, as a result, God cursed and punished them. This interpretation requires the assumption that God's punishment of the Jews is perpetual, an assumption that was standard Christian teaching at the time.[105] Only after the Holocaust would theologians exegete Scripture to show that the Hebrew Bible speaks of numerous instances of God relenting in his judgment of a people (e.g., the story of the golden calf and the end of the Babylonian Captivity) and that this trope obviously contradicts the New Testament.[106] For example, the apostle Paul explicitly discussed the state of the Jews in his letter to the Romans: "For the gifts and the calling of God are irrevocable" (11:29). Thus, God's covenant with the Jews stands. But Confessing Church pastors and theologians were not doing this kind of exegesis in Nazi Germany. And thus, as with the other anti-Judaic tropes, this idea that God has rejected the Jews as his people served Nazi assertions that the Jews are a corrupt and pernicious people.

Interestingly, based on this sample, pastors seldom voiced anti-Judaic expressions while preaching from the Hebrew Bible. All but seven of the sermons in this sample that contained anti-Judaic expressions were based on New Testament passages. While it is no surprise that Christian pastors preached predominantly on the New Testament, one must keep in mind that the Hebrew Bible comprises approximately three-quarters of the Christian Bible, with the New Testament forming just one-quarter.

After analyzing the anti-Judaic expressions and the New Testament passages they were based on, it is striking to note that the sources most often used in the gospels were those that discussed the conflicts between Jesus and various Jewish sects (e.g., the Pharisees and Sadducees), as well as the Jewish religious elites who participated in his crucifixion. And in the case of Paul's letters, these texts were most often his attempts to explain the differentiation between Second Temple Judaism and the emergence of the early Christian movements. Not surprisingly, texts that describe conflict more often provided a springboard for pastors to express anti-Judaic sentiments. And yet these same texts were often used intentionally as a basis from which to criticize the Nazi regime and Germans themselves as hard-hearted, obsessed with race and racial purity, and boastful in their chosen-ness by Providence.

General Perceptions of Inferiority

Pastors from time to time also gave expression to a more generalized perception of the Jews as in some sense inferior or corrupted. For example, in an advent sermon pastor Karl von Schwarz opened with the claim that "Israel's perverse nature" (*Israels verkehrte Art*) turned the third commandment to keep the Sabbath holy into "a slave's bondage with which to torment itself."[107] This is an obvious reference to the Jews as legalistic in their religious expression. But the sermon is about God's gift of grace abounding to his people as exemplified in the advent season. One could read this brief mention of "Israel's perverse nature" and reply that it is a simple reference to original sin that could be applied to any group or person. But read in the context of Nazi Germany, and without any clarification or elaboration by the pastor, the message clearly aligns with and supports Nazi assertions of the inferior and corrupted nature of the Jewish people.

Pastor Julius Sammentreuther asserted the "narrow Jewish sense" of the law that focuses on custom, purity, race, and authority, as if all Jews have this inferior, legalistic view of religion.[108] On the surface, statements such as these may appear to simply refer to Christian understandings of the Jewish faith. But, again, in the context of Nazi Germany, sweeping assertions that essentialize a people as embodiments and purveyors of an inferior and corrupting worldview undergird Nazi ideology of the basic inferiority of the Jewish people.

One may ask, didn't Jesus and the apostle Paul, for example, criticize the Jews in their own day? What is the difference between what the New Testament texts have to say about the Jews and Judaism and what Confessing Church pastors said in their sermons? While this is a topic that can easily lead us too far afield, suffice it to say that the New Testament texts are clear that Jesus and the early Christians were engaged in an inter-Jewish conflict, and thus their statements about Jews and Judaism cannot extend to all Jews for all time. For example, when Jesus condemned the Pharisees as sons of the devil in John 8:44 he was clearly not asserting that the Jews as a people are pernicious, but rather denouncing this specific group for its hypocrisy, violence, and refusal to listen to the good news of God's grace.[109] He was making a claim about their spiritual disposition, not their biological origin. He preached to Jewish audiences ready and willing to hear, but also to some, like the Pharisees and Sadducees, who condemned him. Likewise, when the apostle Paul referred to the Jews, "who killed both the Lord Jesus and the prophets," as persecutors of the early churches, he is not referring to all Jews everywhere as deicides (1 Thessalonians 2:14–15). This passage must be understood in the context of this inter-Jewish conflict. By saying "the Jews" he is obviously using a shorthand to refer to the religious elites of the Jewish people; he cannot mean all Jews are deicides as he, the disciples, and the early Christians themselves were Jews. The New Testament offers a complex representation of Jews that must be read in context or serious misunderstandings may result.

But for a pastor in Nazi Germany to essentialize the Jews throughout time as corrupted and legalistic and their faith as obsolete or lifeless is to play into Nazi ideas of Jewish perniciousness and materialism. Without elaboration or clarification, generalized assertions about the Jews or "Jewish" legalism paint all Jews throughout all time as spiritually and even biologically corrupted. Pastors who used anti-Judaic expressions did not use them in the context of an inter-Jewish conflict as in the New Testament, where the distinctions between Jews were understood, but in the context of Nazi Germany where criticisms of Jews and Judaism took on altogether different connotations. Anti-Judaic tropes carry centuries of meaning that could have served to support Nazi views of Jews as essentially inferior and corrupted members of their society.

COMPARING JEWS TO NAZIS

As previously discussed, the sermons reveal that a common purpose in voicing anti-Judaic sentiments was to compare Jews to Nazis as race obsessed and spiritually degenerate, relying on the characteristics of one's own nature for salvation. The historian Uriel Tal has shown—using sources as varied as academic lectures, private letters, and published articles and books—that the leadership of the Confessing Church commonly made comparisons between Jews and Nazis in their conceptions of race and *Volk*, as a means to criticize the Nazi regime, its leadership, and ideology, especially after the mid-1930s.[110] Likewise, Haynes has demonstrated the common usage of anti-Judaic tropes in the anti-Nazi rhetoric among leaders in the German churches, especially in the writings of Dietrich Bonhoeffer.[111] Moreover, the criticism of comparing Jews to Nazis as both creators of a false ethno-nationalist identity implicitly draws on the traditional antisemitic trope of "tribalism," or the belief in the superiority of one's own racial or ethnic group over others.[112] Furthermore, as Haynes argues, this kind of rhetorical strategy among critics of the Nazi regime aimed "to discredit [one's] enemies and in the process exploited and perpetuated an anti-Jewish environment."[113]

Confessing Church pastors not only used anti-Judaic tropes to condemn pro-Nazi supporters outside the German churches but those within the churches, specifically the pro-Nazi German Christian movement. The sermons reflect a significant rift in German Protestantism between the German Christian movement and the Confessing Church. While sermons of the Confessing Church reveal brief expressions of centuries-old religiously based anti-Judaic sentiments, they are a far cry from the sustained attacks found in the sermons of the German Christian movement, which overtly expressed racial prejudice meant to exclude Jews from the church and German society. For example, one sermon by Heinrich Kalb from Wiessenburg, delivered in 1937, entitled *Juden Christ—deutscher Christ?* ("Jewish Christian—German Christian?"), argued for the separation of Jewish Christians from "Aryan" congregations, which he sums up in the phrase, "Germany for Germans, and also in the Church!"[114] He and those in the German Christian movement wished to purify the German churches of all "foreign" elements, particularly church leaders of "foreign" backgrounds.[115] "Only German men may speak to the German people from German pulpits; not Turks, Chinese, or even Jews!"[116] Unlike the anti-Judaic expressions in Confessing Church sermons, the anti-Jewish statements found in German Christian sermons were often racial in nature and explicitly meant to separate Jews from Germans in public life.

As discussed previously, the German Christian wished to "purify" the Christian Scripture of Jewish influence, even cutting out the Hebrew Scripture. The German Christian movement so transformed the theology, practice, and ethics of Christianity through the racial principle of "Aryan" supremacy that it substantively altered the meaning and message of Christianity. To the German Christian, the gospel is not universal, baptism is effective only for "Aryans," and the church must be racially segregated. In other words, the movement engaged in a process of changing the fundamental elements of

Christianity, transforming the religion into a Nazi-based organization. In fact, as Doris Bergen has noted, to many Christians in Nazi Germany the German Christian movement was "barely recognizable as Christian."[117] The German Christian movement celebrated Hitler as a savior of the German people and made efforts to transform Christianity into a *völkisch* religion. The German Christian movement rejected the canonicity of the Hebrew Bible, and made controversial claims about the New Testament, such as the assertion that Jesus was an "Aryan," and that a core element of the gospel message was hatred of the Jews.[118] Susannah Heschel has argued that the German Christian movement spearheaded the formation of an organization in April 1939, the Institute for the Study and Eradication of Jewish Influence on German Religious Life (*Institut zur Erforschung und Beseitigung des jüdisches Einflusses auf das deutsche kirchliche Leben*), a government-sponsored and church-supported institute dedicated to eradicating Jewish influence from Christianity.[119]

Confessing Church pastors responded publicly in the pulpits to what they considered gross heresy in the German Christian position, though at times invoking anti-Judaic tropes. Remarkably, most of the anti-Judaic comments in this sample were not from pastors on the fringe of the Confessing Church, expressing views that would have embarrassed their colleagues. In fact, many of these pastors are widely considered heroes of the Confessing Church. Niemöller courageously spoke out against Nazi intrusions in church administration and theology, and also against persecutions of its pastors. Heinrich Grüber established an office to steadfastly serve German pastors of Jewish descent as they faced persecution by the Nazi regime. They were admired leaders in their movement, and yet they expressed anti-Judaic views that could only have alienated Christians from their Jewish neighbors or confirmed their already-existing antisemitism. If the best and the brightest of Confessing Church pastors, the most courageous and insightful, made such anti-Judaic statements in their sermons, it is logical to conclude along with Baranowski, Gerlach, and Haynes, among others, that these sentiments were deeply ingrained in Christian theology and that they were widespread.[120]

Moreover, anti-Jewish sentiments impacted the relationships between Christians, even fracturing relationships between members of the same congregations. Robert Gellately's study of the attitudes of Germans throughout the Nazi period concerning the regime and its treatment of Jews reveals that many "ordinary" Christians supported Nazi measures, such as the decree of September 15, 1941, forcing Jews aged seven and older to wear the yellow star.[121] Gellately writes of the consternation of many Christians when the yellow star revealed just how many Christians of Jewish descent attended church services: "In some parts of the country, Protestant churchgoers were displeased to note how many (converted) Jews went to church, and demanded of their ministers that they should not be asked to take communion next to these Jews, whom they wanted forbidden to attend common services."[122] Anti-Jewish beliefs resulted in the "shunning" of Christians of Jewish descent, the loss of fellowship and mutual support, and the restriction of rites and sacraments, including communion.[123]

The reception of these anti-Judaic sentiments is tremendously difficult to gauge. I have been unable to find any commentaries or reports from government agencies, such as the Gestapo or SD, or in letters or diaries from colleagues or parishioners. The likely reason is that anti-Judaism had long been an aspect of Christianity and thus no one took note when it was expressed. The post-war reflection of Eberhard Bethge—the friend, colleague, and biographer of Bonhoeffer—illuminates the mindset of German citizens (and not just pastors) under the Nazi regime. In 1989, Bethge gave a talk criticizing the antisemitism of various resistance figures, and he sent a letter to one German critic of his talk. In this letter, Bethge argued that "the 'old tradition' of Christian anti-Judaism had converged with the radical anti-semitism of Nazism."[124] Bethge writes,

> [W]e have simply been long, long blind and—without having been radical anti-Semites—nonetheless we were in our language and consciousness the bearers of unholy potential. I see the problem in that even extraordinary resistance fighters were at the same time still sunk in the kind of language and attitudes whose anti-Jewish content could only be made clear decades after 1945.[125]

Bethge speaks of "we" to argue the pervasiveness of anti-Judaism, even among those who were not "radical anti-Semites," including himself and Bonhoeffer.[126]

The anti-Judaic comments in these sermons indicate that some Confessing Church pastors interpreted the situation of the Jews in Nazi Germany through a theological lens, and yet this opened the door to implicit antisemitic connections. This research supports the assertion that the primary concern of pastors in relation to the Jewish people was "right belief" and conversion, not their material condition as a people group targeted by the Nazi regime for exclusion from German public life.[127]

We can draw several conclusions based on the evidence. The expressions of prejudice revealed in these sermons may overwhelmingly be categorized as non-rational or anti-Judaic, meaning the prejudice is based on religious convictions founded in scripture and a Christian reading of history. In other words, the prejudice expressed is based primarily on explicit religious convictions, not racial convictions. When implicit antisemitic tropes are articulated, they always serve religiously based anti-Judaic assertions. The anti-Jewish prejudice in these sermons contrasts to the explicit antisemitism of the German Christian movement, which utilized irrational antisemitic prejudice, based on fear, paranoia, and envy.[128] Moreover, in the sermons I have studied, I have not found one instance of Confessing Church pastors using Nazi racial terminology—such as *Untermenschen* (sub-humans)—to denigrate the Jewish people, or to blame the Jews for Germany's problems since World War I, again in contrast to the German Christians. Thus, the prejudice against the Jews expressed in these Confessing Church sermons relies upon traditional Christian tropes found throughout the history of the Church.

Yet the sermons reveal just how anti-Judaic views may interact with antisemitic tropes. The expressions of anti-Judaism revealed in these sermons have the potential to overlap with Nazi racial antisemitism in German society, and thereby possibly advance the exclusion of Jews from public life. For example, if a pastor argued that God has punished the Jews as an accursed people since the crucifixion of Christ, then the implications in Nazi Germany are potentially devastating. The congregant may generalize and perceive that the Jews as a people group are evil, pernicious, and immoral; that they conspire to dominate, to destroy Christianity, and thus, that they cannot be trusted.[129] While anti-Judaic tropes may originate in churches, these ideas interact and overlap with other secular ideas outside church doors. For example, scholars have recently contributed much to understanding how religious anti-Judaism blended with antisemitism in academia.[130]

My analysis also reveals that Confessing Church pastors often used anti-Judaic expressions for a purpose and not simply to denigrate the Jewish people. The most common purposes were to advocate for the superiority of Christianity to Judaism and to criticize Nazi ideology regime and its German supporters. Pastors compared the Jews to Nazis as hard-hearted, obsessed with race consciousness and the racial purity of the people, as legalistic, weak, and erroneously convinced of their own "superiority" and "chosen-ness." Again, these comments draw on the antisemitic trope that accuses the Jews of tribalism—taking pride in a false ethno-nationalist identity that denies equality with other groups. Thus, ironically, Confessing Church pastors combated overt Nazi racial ideology by using antisemitic tropes. This demonstrates that anti-Jewish expressions were not often simply extemporaneous comments, or merely meant to denigrate Jews in Germany society, but they were often employed purposefully to challenge the Nazi regime and its racial policies and ideology. Confessing Church pastors had the ability and freedom to criticize the Nazi regime and its ideology by linking them to the Jews and Judaism. Remarkably, the sermons reveal evidence that the churches were sites in Nazi Germany in which Christians could formulate and express limited criticisms of the regime.

Nevertheless, to the attentive congregant sitting in a pew in Nazi Germany, the sermons of the Confessing Church present an ambivalent perspective of the Jews and Judaism. One might have heard an occasional positive word about the Jews, or about the inextricable connections between Judaism and Christianity (as will be discussed in the next chapter). But at the same time, one might have heard a harsh word that reflected centuries of anti-Judaic views that condemn Jews as wayward and deserving of God's punishment. These sermons reveal that anti-Judaic theology in twentieth-century German Protestantism became an impediment to Confessing Church pastors proclaiming clear and unequivocal messages about Jews as the spiritual cousins of Christians and Judaism as a valued and inextricable foundation for Christianity—messages sorely needed in Nazi Germany. It is to sermons with pro-Jewish messages that we now turn.

NOTES

1. This chapter has been previously published in *Studies in Christian-Jewish Relations* (2016). It has been reprinted with permission.

2. See biographical sketch provided by the municipal website Miasto Kołobrzeg: "Pastor Paulus Hinz from Kołobrzeg," April 26, 2014, accessed May 5, 2022, https://www.miastokolobrzeg.pl/historia/8005-pastor-paulus-hinz-z-koobrzegu.html.

3. Kirk, *Nazi Germany*, 41–42.

4. Paulus Hinz, Sermon manuscript on Romans 10:1–15, 30 June 1935, Collected Sermons of Paulus Hinz, EZA 766/38.

5. Raul Hilberg, *The Destruction of the European Jews* (New York: Holmes & Meier, 1985), 10–11.

6. Hilberg, *The Destruction of the European Jews*, 10–11.

7. The apostle Paul, who was himself Jewish, expressed tremendous love for his fellow Jews, writing in Romans 9:3, prior to the previously quoted passage, "For I could wish that I myself were accursed and cut off from Christ for the sake of my brothers, my kinsmen according to the flesh." The New Testament presents his missional approach to the Jews based on love and respect.

8. Alon Confino, *A World Without Jews: The Nazi Imagination from Persecution to Genocide* (New Haven: Yale University Press, 2014); Raul Hillberg, *The Destruction of the European Jews* (New York: Holmes & Meier, 1985); Robert Michael, *Holy Hatred: Christianity, Antisemitism, and the Holocaust* (New York: Palgrave Macmillan, 2006); Christopher Probst, *Demonizing the Jews: Luther and the Protestant Church in Nazi Germany* (Bloomington, IN: Indiana University Press, 2012); and Saul Friedländer, who speaks of the "omnipresence of anti-Semitism in most of the Evangelical Lutheran Church," in *Nazi Germany and the Jews, Vol. 2* (New York: HarperPerennial, 2007), 56.

9. Gerlach, *And the Witnesses Were Silent*, 7.

10. Gerlach, *And the Witnesses Were Silent*; Franklin Hamlin Littell, *The Crucifixion of the Jews* (New York: Harper & Row, 1975); Franklin Hamlin Littell and Hubert Locke, eds., *The German Church Struggle and the Holocaust* (Detroit: Wayne State University Press, 1974); Eberhard Röhm and Jörg Thierfelder,

Juden-Christen-Deutsche 1933–1945, Vols 1 & 2 (Stuttgart, 1990); and Marijke Smid, *Deutscher Protestantismus und Judentum 1932/1933* (Munich, 1990). More recently, Peter Fritzsche has argued that there was "general silence about the fate of the German Jews" in the German churches. See Fritzsche, *Life and Death in the Third Reich* (Cambridge, MA: Belknap, 2008), 119.

11. Barnett, *For the Soul of the People*, 5.

12. See Joachim Fest, *Plotting Hitler's Death: The Story of the German Resistance*, translated by Bruce Little (New York: Metropolitan, 1996), 150; Theodore Hamerow, *On the Road to the Wolf's Lair: German Resistance to Hitler* (Cambridge, MA: Harvard University Press, 1997), 226; Peter Hoffmann, *The History of the German Resistance, 1933–1945, Third Edition* (Montreal and Kingston: McGill-Queen's University Press, 1996), 318; Robert Michael, *Holy Hatred: Christianity, Antisemitism, and the Holocaust* (New York: Palgrave Macmillan, 2006), 165; and Louis Eltscher, *Traitors or Patriots? A Story of the German Anti-Nazi Resistance* (Bloomington, IN: iUniverse: 2013), 64–66.

13. See for example, Eltscher, *Traitors or Patriots?* 64–66; and Hoffman, *History of the German Resistance*, 318.

14. See for example, David Gushee, *Righteous Gentiles of the Holocaust: Genocide and Moral Obligation, 2nd Edition* (St. Paul, MN: Paragon, 2003); and Nechama Tec's two superb books, *When Light Pierced the Darkness: Christian Rescue of Jews in Nazi Occupied Poland* (New York: Oxford University Press, 1986), and *Resistance: Jews and Christians Who Defied the Nazi Terror* (New York: Oxford University Press, 2013).

15. A few sermons expressed both, which will be examined later in this chapter.

16. Bacharach, Walter Zvi. *Anti-Jewish Prejudices in German-Catholic Sermons*, Translated by Chaya Galai. Lewiston: Edwin Mellon Press, 1993.

17. Bacharach, *Anti-Jewish Prejudices in German-Catholic Sermons*, 130–133.

18. My analysis follows the work of historians such as Baranowski, Ericksen, Haynes, among others, that anti-Judaism was a widespread characteristic of early twentieth-century German Protestantism. See Shelley Baranowski, "The Confessing Church and Antisemitism: Protestant Identity, German Nationhood, and the Exclusion of the Jews," in Robert P. Ericksen and Susannah Heschel, eds., *Betrayal: German Churches and the Holocaust* (Minneapolis: Fortress Press, 1999); Kenneth Barnes, *Nazism, Liberalism, and Christianity: Protestant Social Thought in Germany and Great Britain 1925–1937* (Lexington, KY: University Press of Kentucky, 1991), 140–141; Doris Bergen, "Catholics, Protestants, and Antisemitism in Nazi Germany," *Central European History* 27 (1994): 329–348; Wolfgang Gerlach, *And the Witnesses Were Silent: The Confessing Church and the Persecution of the Jews*, translated and edited by Victoria Barnett (Lincoln, NE: University of Nebraska Press, 2000), 236; Stephen R. Haynes, "Who Needs Enemies? Jews and Judaism in Anti-Nazi Religious Discourse," *Church History* 71:2 (June 2002), 341–367; and Uriel Tal, "On Modern Lutheranism and Jews," in *Year Book of the Leo Baeck Institute* (London: Secker & Warburg, 1985), 203–213.

19. See Langmuir, *History, Religion, and Antisemitism*, 152, 252–255; and Michael, *Holy Hatred*, 82–84.

20. Hannah Arendt, *The Origins of Totalitarianism* (New York: Schocken Books, 2004), 3.

21. See James Carroll, *Constantine's Sword: The Church and the Jews* (New York: Houghton Mifflin, 2001); Léon Poliakov, *The History of Anti-Semitism, Vol. 1, From the Time of Christ to the Court of the Jews*, translated by Richard Howard (New York: Vanguard, 1965); Dan Cohn-Sherbok, *The Crucified Jew: Twenty Centuries of Christian Anti-Semitism* (Grand Rapids: Eerdmans, 1997).

22. Michael, *Holy Hatred*, 82–84; and Lindemann and Levy, *Antisemitism*, Kindle edition, location 1640 ff.

23. It is not my contention that any pastors (or Christians) who used these tropes are antisemitic or necessarily bear hostility to the Jews. Rather, my contention is that this language is evidence of anti-Judaic views that indicate hostility—either real or perceived—against the Jewish people as a distinct people group.

24. This interpretation of Scripture is understandably profoundly offensive to Jews and many Christians in a post-Holocaust context.

25. Peter Brunner, Sermon on I Corinthians 12:1–11, 9 August 1942, Papers of Peter Brunner, Archiv der Evangelischen Kirche im Rheinland, AEKR 7NL 006.

26. Brunner, Sermon on I Corinthians 12:1–11, 7NL 006.

27. Brunner, Sermon on I Corinthians 12:1–11, AEKR 7NL 006.

28. Michael, *Holy Hatred*, 5–6; Langmuir, *History, Religion, and Antisemitism*, 252–255.

29. See Michael Burleigh and Wolfgang Wippermann, *The Racial State: Germany 1933–1945* (Cambridge University Press, 1991); and John Weiss, *Ideology of Death: Why the Holocaust Happened in Germany* (Chicago: Ivan R. Dee, 1996).

30. Michael, *Holy Hatred*, 140–141; Lindemann and Levy, *Antisemitism*, 8–9; Carroll, *Constantine's Sword*, 447.

31. The term itself is highly problematic because the word "Semitic" is an adjective that refers to a language group including Hebrew, Arabic, and Phoenician, and the peoples that speak these languages; thus, "antisemitism" should refer to a hatred of all these peoples, but in fact, it has only ever referred to a hatred of the Jews. See Doris Bergen, *War and Genocide: A Concise History of the Holocaust* (New York: Rowman & Littlefield, 2003), 4.

32. Bergen, *War and Genocide*, 6.

33. See for example, Lindemann and Levy, *Antisemitism*, 8, 94–98; and Hillel Levine, *Economic Origins of Antisemitism: Poland and Its Jews in the Early Modern Period* (New Haven, CT: Yale University Press, 1991), 5–10.

34. Peter Pulzer, *The Rise of Political Anti-Semitism in Germany and Austria, Revised Edition* (Cambridge: Harvard University Press, 1988), 25.

35. Pulzer, *The Rise of Political Anti-Semitism*, xxiii, 185, 290–291.

36. Pulzer, *The Rise of Political Anti-Semitism*, ix.

37. George Mosse, *Toward the Final Solution: A History of European Racism* (New York: Howard Fertig, 1985), 72–73.

38. Mosse, *Toward the Final Solution*, xvi.

39. George Mosse, *Nationalism and Sexuality: Respectability and Abnormal Sexuality in Modern Europe* (New York: Howard Fertig, 1985), 134.

40. Hitler, *Mein Kampf*, 232, 302.
41. See Weiss, *Ideology of Death*, 112–127.
42. Thus, Saul Friedländer refers to Hitler's antisemitism as "redemptive antisemitism." See *Nazi Germany and the Jews*, 3; and Bergen, "Antisemitism in the Nazi Era," in Lindemann and Levy, *Antisemitism*, Kindle edition, location 4369.
43. David Redles treats this subject at length in his book, *Hitler's Millennial Reich: Apocalyptic Belief and the Search for Salvation* (New York: New York University Press, 2005), 46–76.
44. Redles, *Hitler's Millennial Reich*, 45
45. See Bergen, *War and Genocide*, 7–8.
46. For example, see Michael, *Holy Hatred*, 5; Carol, *Constantine's Sword*, 382; and Goldhagen, *A Moral Reckoning*, 78–79.
47. Michael, *Holy Hatred*, 5.
48. See Carroll, *Constantine's Sword*; Poliakov, *The History of Anti-Semitism, Vol. 1*; and Cohn-Sherbok, *The Crucified Jew*.
49. Goldhagen argues against making a distinction between the terms anti-Judaism and anti-Semitism because it masks the hatred implicit in anti-Judaism (*A Moral Reckoning*, 78–9). Carroll observes that in the end, "[this] distinction becomes meaningless before the core truth of this history: Because of the hatred of the Jews had been made holy [in the biblical texts], it became lethal" (*Constantine's Sword*, 22).
50. Michael, *Holy Hatred*, 47; and Lindemann and Levy, *Antisemitism*, Kindle location 227 and 4759.
51. See Langmuir, *History, Religion, and Antisemitism*, 152, 252–255; and Michael, *Holy Hatred*, 82–84.
52. See Barnett, *For the Soul of the People*, 128–129; Bergen, *Twisted Cross*, 88–93; Gutteridge, *German Evangelical Church and the Jews*, 91–96; and Helmreich, *German Churches under Hitler*, 144–147.
53. Barnet, *For the Soul of the People*, 129; and Helmreich, *German Churches under Hitler*, 145.
54. Gerlach, *And the Witnesses Were Silent*, 39–41; Green, *Lutherans against Hitler*, 133–142; and *Helmreich, German Churches under Hitler*, 145–146.
55. Helmreich, *German Churches under Hitler*, 200–201.
56. Barnett, *For the Soul of the People*, 83–84; Helmreich, *German Churches under Hitler*, 199.
57. Quoted in Helmreich, *German Churches under Hitler*, 200.
58. See Kenneth C. Barnes, "Dietrich Bonhoeffer and Hitler's Persecution of the Jews," in *Betrayal: German Churches and the Holocaust*, edited by Robert P. Ericksen and Susannah Heschel (Minneapolis: Fortress Press, 1999), 128; Barnett, *For the Soul of the People*, 142; Robert P. Ericksen, *Complicity in the Holocaust: Churches and Universities in Nazi Germany* (New York: Cambridge University Press, 2012), 106; and Gerlach, *And the Witnesses Were Silent*, 7.
59. Otto Dibelius, *Predigten* (Berlin-Dahlem: Verlag die Kirche, 1952), 42.
60. Friedrich von Bodelschwingh, *Lebendig und Frei: Predigten, 2. Folge* (Bielefeld: Verlagshandlung der Anstalt Bethel, 1947), 170.
61. Michael, *Holy Hatred*, 182.

62. Irving Greenberg, "Cloud of Smoke, Pillar of Fire," in *Auschwitz: Beginning of a New Era?* Edited by Eva Fleischner (New York: KTAV, 1997), 308.

63. Martin Niemöller, *God is My Fuehrer: Being the Last Twenty-Eight Sermons*, translated by Jane Lymburn (New York: Philosophical Library, 1941), 169.

64. Ralph Keen, "Antisemitism in Late Medieval and Early Modern Periods," in *Antisemitism: A History*, edited by Albert S. Lindemann and Richard S. Levy (New York: Oxford, 2010), 79.

65. Niemöller describes his fellow inmates as "a Dutch cabinet minister, two Norwegian shippers, a British major from the Indian army, a Yugoslavian diplomat, and a Macedonian journalist." See Martin Niemöller, *Dachau Sermons*, Translated by Robert H. Pfeiffer (New York: Harper & Brothers, 1946), v.

66. For Niemöller this would be the first time in nearly seven years that he could worship together with other Christians. These sermons were thus composed and written in the concentration camp at Dachau by Niemöller himself. See *Dachau Sermons*, vi–vii.

67. Niemöller never understood why his captors suddenly allowed them to worship together—and the indication is that this was a very rare concession and due to their "special" status. He reported that a fellow prisoner, the Dutch Royal minister, simply asked to worship for Christmas service, and that permission was granted. See Niemöller, *Dachau Sermons*, vi–vii.

68. Niemöller, *Dachau Sermons*, 17.

69. Niemöller, *Dachau Sermons*, 25.

70. Niemöller, *Here Stand I*, 146.

71. Diem, *Warum Textpredigt?*, 7.

72. Friedrich von Bodelschwingh, *Lebendig und Frei, 2. Folge* (Bethel: Verlagshandlung der Anstalt Bethel, 1947), 170.

73. Bodelschwingh, *Lebendig und Frei, 2 Folge*, 170.

74. Bodelschwingh, *Lebendig und Frei, 2 Folge*, 179.

75. Schwarz, *Gottes Wort an Gottes Volk*, 127. The sermon is undated.

76. Robert Bullock, "After Auschwitz: Jews, Judaism, and Christian Worship." In *Good News After Auschwitz?* (Macon, GA: Mercer University Press, 2001), 78.

77. Niemöller, *Here Stand I*, 195

78. Niemöller, *Here Stand I*, 195.

79. Niemöller, *Here Stand I*, 196.

80. See Lutherhaus Eisenach. *Wider Das Vergessen: Schicksale judenchristlicher Pfarrer in der Zeit von 1933–1945* (Herausgegeben vom Evangelischen Pfarrhausarchiv, April 1988–April 1989), 18–19; Haim Genizi, *American Apathy: The Plight of Christian Refugees from Nazisim* (Ramat-Gan, Israel: Bar-Ilan University Press, 1983), 29; Helmreich, *German Churches under Hitler*, 329; Probst, *Demonizing the Jews*, 10.

81. Genizi, *American Apathy*, 29.

82. See George Anderson, *The Legend of the Wandering Jew* (Providence, RI: Brown University Press, 1965); and Galit Hasan-Rokem and Alan Dundes, *The Wandering Jew: Essays in the Interpretation of a Christian Legend* (Bloomington, IN:

Indiana University Press, 1986); Michael, *Holy Hatred*, 118, 136; Lindemann and Levy, *Antisemitism*, Kindle location 1021.

83. Martin Niemöller, ed. *Das Aufgebrochene Tor: Predigten und Andachten Gefangener Pfarrer im Konzentrationslager Dachau* (München: Neubau Verlag, 1946), 178–179.

84. Schmidt-Berning, *Vokabular des Nationalsozialismus*, 220.

85. The word "salvation" is used variously in Christian theology to refer, as the *New Dictionary of Theology* indicates, to "any kind of situation in which a person is delivered from some danger, real or potential; as in healing a person from illness, from enemies or from the possibility of death. The noun 'salvation' can refer positively to the resulting state of well-being and is not confined to the negative idea of escape from danger." See *New Dictionary of Theology*, by Sinclair Ferguson, David Wright, et. al., eds. (Downers Grove, IL: InterVarsity Press, 1988), 610.

86. Niemöller, ed., *Das Aufgebrochene Tor*, 180.

87. Sammentreuther, *Predigtmeditationen*, 206.

88. Martin Niemöller, *God Is My Fuehrer*, translated by Jane Lymburn (New York: Philosophical Library and Alliance Book Corporation, 1941), 20. This sermon was delivered on October 25, 1936.

89. Niemöller, *Dein Wort ist deiner Kirche Schutz*, 120–122.

90. Schlingensiepen, *Dietrich Bonhoeffer*, 270.

91. Bethge, *Bonhoeffer*, 747–752; and Elizabeth Sifton and Fritz Stern, *No Ordinary Men: Dietrich Bonhoeffer and Hans Dohnanyi, Resisters against Hitler in Church and State* (New York: New York Review Books, 2013), 96–98.

92. Bonhoeffer, *Conspiracy and Imprisonment*, 625.

93. Dietrich Bonhoeffer, *Conspiracy and Imprisonment, 1940–1945* (Minneapolis: Fortress Press, 2006), 625.

94. Dietrich Bonhoeffer, "The Church and the Jewish Question," in *No Rusty Swords: Letters, Lectures, and Notes, 1928–1936*, edited and introduced by Edwin H. Robertson, and translated by Edwin H. Robertson and John Bowden (London: Collins, 1965), 126–127. On Bonhoeffer's role in the conspiracy against Hitler, Ruth Zerner argues, "While retaining certain traditional Christian images of the cursed Jews, Bonhoeffer refused to allow them to reinforce any fear of action. His thinking on Jews and their Bible may appear to us ambiguous, problematic and tentative in the light of post-holocaust Christian thinking of theology regarding the Jews, but his final actions were unmistakenly heroic." See Ruth Zerner, "Dietrich Bonhoeffer and the Jews: Thoughts and Actions, 1933–1945," in *Jewish Social Studies* 37, no. ¾ (1975), 250. On this topic, see also Stephen Haynes, *The Bonhoeffer Legacy: Post Holocaust Perspectives* (Minneapolis, MN: Fortress Press, 2001), 100–101.

95. Haynes, "Who Needs Enemies?" 361.

96. Bonhoeffer, *Conspiracy and Imprisonment*, 625.

97. Bonhoeffer, *Conspiracy and Imprisonment*, 626.

98. Bonhoeffer, *Conspiracy and Imprisonment*, 626.

99. Paul Hinz, Sermon manuscript on Revelations 2:8–11, 10 October 1937, Collected Sermons of Paul Hinz, EZA 766/6.

100. Hinz, Sermon manuscript on Romans 10:1–15.

101. Haynes, *"Who Needs Enemies?"* 350–367. This research supports Haynes' argument that this usage of anti-Judaic tropes was fairly common in Confessing Church rhetoric.

102. Pastor Köster, Luke 1:39–56, EZA 50/424. The sermon was delivered sometime between 1937 and 1944.

103. Hinz, Sermon on January 9, 1935, EZA 766/38.

104. Hinz, Sermon on September 9, 1937, EZA 766/6. In this remarkable sermon Hinz spends considerable time discussing the Nazi persecutions of the churches, raising issues such as the state controlling church finances and the prohibition on churches from commenting on people leaving the church or even on church elections.

105. Thanks to Victoria Barnett for this insight.

106. For overviews of the developments in Post-Holocaust Theology, see, for example, Carol Rittner and John K. Roth, eds., *"Good News" after Auschwitz? Christian Faith in a Post-Holocaust World* (Macon, GA: Mercer University Press, 2001); and William Skiles, "Reforming the Church's Theology of the Jews," in *The Routledge Handbook of Religion, Mass Atrocity, and Genocide* (New York: Routledge, 2021), 321–330. For a selection of church sources documenting changes in theology of the Jews and Judaism, see, for example, Allan Brockway, Paul van Buren, Rolf Rendtorff, and Simon Schoon, eds., *The Theology of the Churches and the Jewish People: Statement by the World Council of Churches and Its Member Churches* (Geneva: WCC Publications, 1988).

107. Karl von Schwarz, *Gottes Wort an Gottes Volk*, 23.

108. Sammentreuther, *Predigtmeditationen*, 101. See also his comments in another sermon on John 9:24–41, that "the Jews" have "only religion," a "mastered" system, but not God's revelation that illumines the mind and heart; *Predigtmeditationen*, 101

109. The verse reads, "You are from your father the devil, and you choose to do your father's desires. He was a murderer from the beginning and does not stand in the truth because there is no truth in him. When he lies, he speaks according to his own nature, for he is a liar and the father of lies."

110. Uriel Tal, "On Structures of Political Theology and Myth in Germany Prior to the Holocaust," in Yehuda Bauer and Nathan Rotenstreich, eds., *The Holocaust as Historical Experience* (New York, 1981), 122.

111. Haynes, *"Who Needs Enemies?"* 350–367.

112. Haynes, *"Who Needs Enemies?"* 344–347.

113. Haynes, *"Who Needs Enemies?"* 366.

114. Heinrich Kalb, „Judenchrist—deutscher Christ?" in *Deutsches Christentum, dargestellt in Predigt und Vortrag* (Nürnberg: Fr. Städler, 1937), 21.

115. Bergen, *Twisted Cross*, 82–83.

116. Kalb, „Judenchrist—deutscher Christ?" in *Deutsches Christentum*, 19.

117. Bergen, *Twisted Cross*, 2.

118. Bergen, *Twisted Cross*, 142–154.

119. Susannah Heschel, *The Aryan Jesus: Christian Theologians and the Bible in Nazi Germany* (Princeton, NJ: Princeton University Press, 2008), 3, 13.

120. See Baranowski, "The Confessing Church and Antisemitism"; Barnes, *Nazism, Liberalism, and Christianity*, 140–141; Bergen, "Catholics, Protestants, and

Antisemitism in Nazi Germany," 329–348; Gerlach, *And the Witnesses Were Silent*, 236; Haynes, "Who Needs Enemies?" 341–367; and Tal, "On Modern Lutheranism and Jews," 203–213.

121. Robert Gellately, *Backing Hitler: Consent and Coersion in Nazi Germany* (New York: Oxford University Press, 2001), Kindle edition, location 3387.

122. Gellately, *Backing Hitler*, Kindle edition, location 3387. In addition, Helmreich reports that in 1939 "non-Aryan" Christians totaled about 14,000 people—the largest number being Lutheran at 10,461. Add to this number approximately 5,000 "Mischlinge," and the result is a small but significant group. See Helmreich, *German Churches under Hitler*, 329–330.

123. Barnett, *For the Soul of the People*, 132. See also Bankier, *Germans and the Final Solution*, 124–125. Bankier contends that even in 1941, upon the introduction of the yellow star in Germany, many were "surprised how many Jews still lived in Germany, and praised the labeling, which brought them into the open."

124. John W. De Gruchy, *Daring, Trusting Spirit: Bonhoeffer's Friend Eberhard Bethge* (Minneapolis: Fortress Press, 2005), 190.

125. Quoted in De Gruchy, *Daring, Trusting Spirit*, 191.

126. De Gruchy, *Daring, Trusting Spirit*, 191.

127. See Friedländer, *Nazi Germany and the Jews, Vol. 1*, 43–44; and Gerlach, *And the Witnesses Were Silent*, 7.

128. See for example, Bergen, *Twisted Cross*; Robert Ericksen, *Theologians under Hitler: Gerhard Kittel, Paul Althaus, and Emanuel Hirsch* (New Haven, CT: Yale University Press, 1985); and Heschel, *The Aryan Jesus*.

129. Michael, *Holy Hatred*, 12.

130. See for example, Ericksen's *Theologians under Hitler*, and *Complicity in the Holocaust: Gerhard Kittel, Paul Althaus, Emanuel Hirsch* (New Haven: Yale University Press, 1985). See also Heschel's *The Aryan Jesus*.

Chapter 8

In the Defense of Jews and Judaism

On August 2, 1941, the Lutheran pastor and theologian Hans Iwand took to the pulpit of Dortmund's twelfth-century Romanesque Marienkirche and delivered a bold sermon on the theme of Christianity's foundation in Judaism. This sermon came just over a month after the Nazis began Operation Barbarossa, the invasion of Russia, earlier that summer. Up to this time, Hitler and the Nazi regime had not developed a clear and consistent policy concerning European Jewry. Yet the war against the Soviet Union proved a turning point.[1] As the Wehrmacht conquered new territory, the Einsatzgruppen of the SS followed and massacred Jews and Soviet "commissars" on an unprecedented scale.[2] By August 1941, hundreds of thousands of Jews had been massacred by Nazi forces and their allies in Lithuania, the Ukraine, Bialystok, Romania, Belorussia, and the Soviet Union, among other war zones.[3]

While it is possible that Iwand had not heard specific news of the Jewish massacres in the war zones, he was certainly aware of anti-Jewish policies closer to home: the expulsion of Jews from German public and professional life had been long underway; the "Aryanization" of Jewish property and businesses increased since 1937 and 1938; the *Kristallnacht* pogrom of November 9–10, 1938, unleashed coordinated terror on the Jews of Germany; and the ghettoization of Polish Jews began shortly after the start of the Second World War.[4] In conquered lands, Jews under Nazi domination were systematically labeled with a yellow Star of David and thus targeted for persecution (the Nazis applied this policy to Jews in Germany later in September 1941). Iwand himself was particularly sensitive to the problem of Nazi persecution of Christians of Jewish descent. The Nazi regime classified his wife Ilse as *Mischling* ("mixed-breed") first class. She had two grandparents of the Jewish faith.[5]

In the context of the increasing violence, expulsion, and extermination of European Jewry, Iwand preached a sermon that affirmed the central place of

Jews and Judaism in the history of the Church. Commenting on Galatians 1:10–24, a text in which the Apostle Paul discusses the source of his revelation, Iwand asked his congregation,

> Do you think you could perhaps go back on the wide strand of the gospel and you could then see where the source comes from, and you could discover that the source comes from a land that is Jewish, and then you come to God and say, "The source is somewhat dirty there. There is a spirit that we have to bring out [*herausbringen*]"? Oh, how foolish! Have you not realized that this source is from above?[6]

Iwand criticized the perspective of pro-Nazi Christians, such as those in the German Christian movement, who devalued the Hebrew Bible and Judaism because they failed to appreciate the relationship between Christianity and Judaism.[7] They refused to acknowledge the debt that Christianity owes to Judaism. For Confessing Church pastors like Iwand, this is a failure to understand where revelation ultimately comes from, which is, as Paul affirms, "from above."

Iwand's sermon represents one of the fundamental ways that Confessing Church pastors expressed support of Jews and Judaism, through an appeal to a shared religious tradition. In this sermon, Iwand defended the Jewish foundations of Christianity and fought against the nazification of Christianity, which he believed undermined the Christian faith. Like other Confessing Church pastors, Iwand hoped to encourage Christians to gain a fuller and more honest understanding of their own faith, uncompromised by Nazi racial theory. To deny the Jewish origins of Christianity would be to deny the revelation of God in Scripture, a revelation God delivered to the Jewish people first. Therefore, the expressions of pro-Jewish sentiment from Confessing pastors' sermons must be understood not simply as statements in support of Jews or Judaism, but as a defense of the Christian faith by those who would attack its foundations. The support for Jews became inextricably linked with a defense of Christianity and the German Protestant churches.

In this chapter, I will analyze Confessing Church sermons that express support for the Jews and Judaism. The chapter will begin by discussing the significance of preaching from a Jewish sacred text (the Christian Bible) in Nazi Germany, an act that one may argue is a form of dissent in and of itself. Then the chapter will proceed to discuss key themes found in sermons that explicitly support Jews or Judaism in the context of Nazi Germany. The sermons can be grouped according to the following assertions: first, the Jews are the people of God and spiritual cousins of Christians; second, Judaism is the foundation of the Christian faith; and third, the Nazi persecution of the Jews must cease. Regardless of the pastors' motivations or intentions for making these statements, their religiously based pronouncements in support of Jews and Judaism took on political significance as implicit or explicit criticisms of Nazi ideology and racial policy.[8] Thus, positive expressions about Jews could serve as criticisms of the Nazi regime and the German Christian movement.

In consideration of the anti-Judaic tropes examined in the previous chapter, this research reveals the tremendous complexity and even ambivalence that characterized many Confessing Church pastors' thinking about Jews in Nazi Germany. Anti-Judaic theology was prevalent among them, and yet they held the Old Testament in the highest esteem as God's revelation to the Jews and humankind. Moreover, they appealed to the great saints, or "cloud of witnesses," as the writer of the Epistle to the Hebrews states, as heroes of the faith, to include Hebrew figures such as Abraham, Isaac, and Jacob (Hebrews 12:1). This appreciation of the Jewish tradition is evident in the Confessing Church sermons of the Third Reich. Though pastors periodically expressed anti-Jewish sentiments from the pulpit, they also expressed views supportive of Jews and Judaism. While these mixed messages reveal inconsistencies within the Confessing Church, pastors' expressions of support of the Jews and Judaism clearly distinguished them from the explicitly antisemitic perspectives of the pro-Nazi German Christian movement and the regime itself.

THE USE OF THE OLD TESTAMENT AS A FORM OF DISSENT

As we have already seen, pastors could use a biblical story, such as Elijah's confrontation with the priests of the Baals or the Pharisee Gamaliel's sage advice to discern God's work in a social movement, to criticize the Nazi regime and its ideology. By simply using the biblical text to make their case, the pastors in effect undermined the Nazi view of the Jews as corrupters of culture and as racially inferior. By relying on Jewish models, wisdom, tradition, and sacred Scripture, the pastors fundamentally challenge Nazi ideology.

The mere fact that the German churches used Scripture as a basis for their services, liturgy, and worship gives the lie to Hitler's claim that the "Aryan" is the only culture-founder and that the "Jew" is the culture-destroyer.[9] Yet, the Scriptures have been used to build culture ever since their composition. The Jews preserved and passed down Scripture from generation to generation, and it then became the basis of the three monotheistic Abrahamic religions, Judaism, Christianity, and Islam, and thus the basis of each of their cultures. Moreover, one needs only to walk into a German church (of whatever stripe) to readily see the fruit of Jewish culture, from the particulars of the liturgical elements such as the vestments and order of service to the rhythms of prayer and song based on the Psalms. Even the mere evocation of the names of God, from "Almighty God" (El Shaddai) to "Lord of Hosts" (Adonai Tzva'ot), recall Jewish sacred history and derive from Jewish culture.

Yet these elements are not mere relics of the ancient past, but they reveal aspects of who God is, who we are as human, and what is good, true, and beautiful. For example, the mere mention of the proper name of God, Yahweh, the tetragrammaton, means "I am who I am," and it grounds all being, all creation, in God. When Pastor Paul Hinz read Psalm 25:15 aloud to his congregation on March 28, 1943, he directed his congregants' vision to the Hebrew God, Yahweh.[10] The verse reads, "My eyes are ever toward the LORD (dem HERRN), for he will pluck my feet out of the net." The biblical passage explicitly orients one's vision "ever toward" Yahweh as Lord, not Hitler as Germanic savior, or the Aryans as the master race. Without explicitly condemning Hitler or National Socialism, the reliance on the Christian Scriptures in sermons reoriented Germans in the Nazi state to values based on Jewish tradition and culture.

It is worth noting how remarkable it is that Confessing Churches maintained their devotion to the Scriptures in Nazi Germany and read and preached publicly from them in their worship services. Can one imagine any group under the Nazi state gathering together conscientiously on a weekly basis to read any other "Jewish" book and to conform their behaviors, language, rituals, and spiritual lives to its teachings and principles? If that were to happen, surely pro-Nazi agitators would interrupt their meetings, harass participants on the street, and pillory them in Nazi publications such as *Der Stürmer*. And yet the regime dared not prohibit Germans from using the "Jewish" Scriptures, given Christianity's entrenchment in German culture. This fact underscores the remarkable potential for Christians to form and reform their imaginations to see the Jewish people as spiritual cousins, a potential that went sadly unrealized.

Confessing Church pastors drew from the Old Testament in ways that challenged the Nazi image of "the Jew." They preached frequently on the Old Testament, a much-neglected and, among pro-Nazi Christians, much-maligned, source.[11] As discussed in chapter 4, the practice of preaching from the Old Testament among many Confessing Church pastors was consistent with the new shift in homiletics under the leadership of Karl Barth, Dietrich Bonhoeffer, Wilfried Lempp, and Wolfgang Trillhaas. Over 200 of the 900-plus sermons I found were based on the Old Testament, and they were fairly evenly divided between the Pentateuch and histories (62), the Writings (71), and the Prophets (70). Again, it must be said that these figures cannot be understood as representative of all Confessing Church sermons. But this figure suggests that the Confessing Church significantly utilized the Old Testament in its worship services, certainly in contrast to the pro-Nazi German Christian movement. Furthermore, of the 44 sermons that explicitly expressed positive views of Jews and Judaism, 19 of them were based on the Old Testament.

The Book of Psalms was one of the most popular texts of choice in these sermons on the Old Testament. Forty-two of the 900-plus sermons were based on the Psalms alone. One could argue that even when a pastor did not use Scripture to directly or explicitly condemn Nazi ideology in a sermon, the mere use of the Psalms could undermine racial antisemitism. The language is steeped in covenantal language that portrays the Jewish people's desire for God's presence, justice, mercy, help, and forgiveness. Indeed, the Psalms, just to take one book from the Old Testament, is rich in the sacred memory of the Jewish people, recounting the rituals, liturgies, conceptions of the divine, and spiritual disciplines that inform and shape Christian worship.

One could multiply this example numerous times. The Old Testament books are steeped in the language of God's redemptive history, a history that pastors conscientiously kept alive in Nazi Germany as a life-giving source for their communities of faith. Indeed, one could argue that German Protestantism, and Christianity more generally, was so immersed in the Old Testament worldview that it was as the air Christians breathe, and that they were not cognizant of its deeper meaning and significance as a bond with Judaism and Jews in Nazi Germany. While one may argue that the mere use of Old Testament language, concepts, and beliefs in German Protestant churches may comprise a form of dissent to the Nazi racial ideology, Confessing Church pastors at times went a step further to explicitly challenge specific elements of Nazism in their sermons.

THE JEWS AS THE PEOPLE OF GOD

The first major theme in sermons that openly support or defend the Jews and Judaism is the expression that the Jews are the chosen people of God. Confessing Church pastors could use various Old Testament affirmations that God had chosen the Jews specifically to make his name known in all the earth.[12] In the Book of Genesis, for example, in the story of God's covenant with Abraham, God says,

> And I will establish my covenant between me and you and your offspring after you throughout their generations for an everlasting covenant, to be God to you and to your offspring after you. And I will give to you and to your offspring after you the land of your sojournings, all the land of Canaan, for an everlasting possession, and I will be their God (17:7–8).

In the Jewish and Christian traditions, it is through the Jews that God revealed his revelation to humankind. It is an elemental tenet of Christianity that God used Abraham's descendants, the Jewish people, to bless the nations (cf. Genesis 12:1–9).

There was no more common theme among sermons that supported the Jews and Judaism than the assertion that the Jews are the chosen people of God. Eighteen of the sermons explicitly affirm this belief. The expressions would often be concise, straightforward statements affirming that the Jews are the chosen people of God. For example, Karl von Schwartz, the Lutheran cathedral pastor of Braunschweig and the provost of the St. Marienberg monastery, often referred to the Jews as a "chosen" or "special" people of God. I counted five different sermons in which he deliberately pointed out the chosen-ness of the Jewish people, which is more than any other single pastor in this study.[13] Interestingly, these sermons were part of a collection published by Hellmuth Wollermann's Verlagsbuchhandlung in Braunschweig in late 1933 (though some may have been preached earlier). The unusual characteristic of this collection is that all the sermons were based on Old Testament texts. Clearly, Schwartz believed that Christians needed to become more acquainted with the Old Testament.

Furthermore, the Jews are often presented as the beneficiaries of God's grace. In the Christian tradition they are presented as a "fallen" people, chastised by God, yet with a future of redemption and blessing—a picture of Christians in the Church. The common refrain in Scripture is that God will not forever chastise or abandon the people whom he loves and has chosen. He will show them grace and mercy. This theme surely resonated among some Christians in Germany during the Second World War. The war itself was frequently perceived as a judgment of God. For example, one anonymous Confessing Church pastor preached a sermon on July 10, 1942, on the theme of society "falling away" from God.[14] The sermon was delivered a mere seven months after the Japanese attacked Pearl Harbor and after Hitler subsequently declared war on the United States. The sermon was delivered at the start of a period of mass bombing raids by hundreds of British bombers against German cities, Lübeck being the first on the night of March 28–29, 1942, to be followed by Cologne on May 30.[15] Using Deuteronomy 4:25–31 as a base text, the pastor reflected on the story of the Hebrews falling away from God in the wilderness to serve other gods, but he uses this as an analogy for all people, not just Jews. In this regard the Jews are an example for humanity. He argued, "Even before the people of Israel occupies the Promised Land, God already knows that they will fall away and will serve other gods of the land."[16] But God is patient, the pastor affirmed, allowing his children to fall. God comes to them when they cry out and seek his help.

Remarkably, the pastor connected the "fallen-ness" of the Jews and the "fallen-ness" of the German people: both of whom, it is understood, have suffered (or are suffering) for their waywardness. For the pastor, the Jews had suffered as a stateless nation for millennia, and their suffering had reached an apex under the Nazi regime. As will be discussed in detail shortly, massacres and atrocities against Jews during the Second World War was an "open secret" among German adults, especially among those in professions, such as the clergy, that fostered connections between peoples of different backgrounds and professions.[17] It is likely that this pastor knew of the massacres of Jews, just as he most certainly knew of German suffering in the Allied bombing of German cities. According to the pastor, this suffering is a consequence of "falling away" and worshiping other gods.

And yet the pastor spoke of a promise, "the merciful Father . . . will not leave us, nor destroy us, He cannot forget that he has made a covenant with us when we were baptized into his name."[18] This sermon offered a theological criticism of the German people for "falling away." He does not state who specifically has fallen away—all the people, a segment of the people, the regime, or the churches—or how they have fallen away. But he offered hope that God is merciful and faithful to his covenant. It is impossible to tell from the sermon whether the pastor was criticizing the German people for any sin in particular—this vague reference must be interpreted by the congregant.

At the same time, the pastor connected the Germans and Jews together as people who have "fallen away," thus having a similar history. Placing "Jews" and "Germans" in the same category as "fallen away" constitutes a criticism in itself. The Jews and Germans are two peoples whom the pastor believed—at some historical point—had fallen away from God, and in this way, the two are connected in the history of God's redemptive work. The pastor did not comment about whether or not the Jews were still a "fallen" people, but the important point here is that he recognized that "God cannot forget that he has made a covenant with" his people.[19] Like the Jews, Christians in Germany must trust in God's grace and mercy.

This positive assertion of the Jews—that they are the blessed and chosen of God—is oppositional to the Nazi regime because it blatantly undermined Nazi racial ideology. One cannot assert that the Jews are divinely blessed and special and yet at the same time claim that they are, as the Nazis argued, a pernicious and destructive people. Even sermons that speak of the Jews as a "fallen" people still connect them to God's covenant. At the very least this language of the Jews as God's people implies that they are God's favored people, contrary to Nazi claims of Aryan superiority and chosen-ness. Moreover, the assertion that Christians and Jews have the same God closely binds the two together as people of God, and this again contradicts Nazi racial ideology that denigrates Jews as inferior and degenerate human beings.

However, just because a given pastor may assert that the Jews are the people of God did not mean that his sermons were necessarily free of anti-Judaic tropes. One interesting example is from Pastor Köster from Berlin. Sometime between 1937 and 1944, he preached on Luke 1:39–56, the story of Mary's visit to Elizabeth. In this sermon Köster argued that in Christ, God has kept his covenant with his "chosen people." But history changed with the advent of Christ, Köster claimed: with Christ "salvation will go out to all peoples of the earth."[20] His criticisms of the Jewish people start here. Elizabeth is an older, barren wife who represents the "over-aged" and "unfruitful" people of Israel. She carries in her womb the last great prophet of the people, John the Baptist. Köster drew a parallel between the aged and barren Elizabeth and Israel, both of whom are about to give birth to new offspring that will carry the world into a new era. He argued that through Jesus God can breathe new life and the power of salvation into all people.[21] This interpretation of Luke's gospel supports the perception of the Jews as the people of God but presents them as past their prime with an obsolete religion. This perspective may certainly be used to sustain a supersessionist view of Christianity over Judaism. Köster's sermon demonstrates just how ambivalent and confusing some of these sermons may have sounded to congregants sitting in the pews.

Despite the anti-Judaic elements in these sermons, they reveal a common perception among Confessing Church pastors of the Jews as the people of God. And as will be discussed in the next chapter, this positive view of the Jews—that they are blessed and special—aroused the concern of the Nazi regime and its secret police apparatus because it blatantly undermined Nazi racial ideology.

THE JEWISH FOUNDATIONS OF CHRISTIANITY

A second theme in these sermons that support Jews and Judaism is the belief that Judaism is the foundation of Christianity and, as such, Christians should value and appreciate the Old Testament. This assertion directly undermines efforts of the German Christian movement to denigrate the Old Testament and remove it from the Christian canon, as epitomized in the Institute for the Study and Eradication of Jewish Influence on German Religious Life.[22] As discussed previously, Confessing Church pastors stood firm on the conviction that the Old Testament must not be expunged from the Christian scripture, because it is God's Word. The God of the Old Testament is the God of the New Testament, and the Church has no right to change God's Word or to decide what belongs and what does not belong. The Barmen Confession assumes that the entire Scripture, both Old and New Testaments, must be used as the standard from which to judge "the spirits" of the day.[23] To throw out the Old Testament and to diminish God's work among the Jews in the Old Testament would be to deny the totality of God's revelation.

This theme of the foundational nature of Judaism in Christianity occurs nine times in these 44 sermons that support Jews and Judaism. Confessing Church pastors expressed concern that the denial of Christianity's Jewish roots will result in an unstable Church built on a compromised foundation. Pastor Hans Herzberg of Caldern discussed the intimate connection between Christianity's Jewish and Apostolic roots in terms of the common foundation of the Church. He preached a sermon on Ephesians 2:19–20, on June 4, 1933, a mere five months after Hitler's rise to power in Nazi Germany. This early date is important as the Nazi dictatorship was still implementing its oppressive police apparatus, leaving more room for public figures like Herzberg to express opposition to Nazi values.[24] Placing himself in the thick of the Protestant debate about the role of the Old Testament in the Christian tradition, he stated,

> God as the lord of the house [*Hausherr*] has also laid the foundation of the house: "Built on the foundation of the apostles and prophets"; the prophets of the Old Testament, and the apostles of the New . . . The book from which [the Church] hears the Word of God every Sunday, and in your houses has the place of honor, and around which the school children gather: this book is the foundation of the Church . . . There are many people in the Christian Church who want to apply the apostles, but not the prophets, the New but not the Old Testament to the foundation of the Church; and one understands in our day, that it may rather annoy some German countryman to see that the Jewish people were the people of the Bible. And yet we cannot correct the ways of God. His kingdom has not just fallen from heaven. Before there were apostles, prophets have had to pave the way. From both together, from apostles and prophets, from the New and the Old, God has built his Church.[25]

Hertzberg contended that the Bible, of Jewish and Christian origins, has a treasured and foundational place in German society—not only important to churches but in homes and schools. Furthermore, he makes an historical argument about the foundation of the Church, an institution that emerged from the religious and social context of the Jewish people. Hertzberg acknowledged that some may be "annoyed" that Jews and Judaism are intimately connected to the Christian tradition, but he did not cave to this pressure and abandon them. His logic was uncompromising: according to the Old Testament, God entered into a covenant with the Hebrews; the Old Testament is the record of this interaction; and therefore the Old Testament is an integral source for understanding the character and work of God. As such, Christians must maintain its legitimacy in the canon. While the denial of Judaism as a foundation for the Church will result in a compromised "house," even more importantly, it is a sin against God, a denial of his work in history. As Herzberg preached, God is the one who built the foundation, and thus to deny God's work is a grievous sin against God. Moreover, to do away with the Old Testament would be to undermine the very identity of the Church itself.

The concern was not simply addressing the confusion that would result in redefining the Christian scripture or identity. As Caldern and others pointed out, the concern in eliminating the foundation was the destruction of the house. The Erlangen pastor Hermann Sasse touches on this theme in a sermon preached on November 29, 1936, on Hebrews 10:19–25. In his discussion of the biblical text, Sasse commented on the debate between the Confessing Church and the German Christian movement over the value of the Old Testament to the modern German churches. He admitted the Old and New Testament are quite different, but they are united in message. He argued,

> For the difference between the Old and New Testaments is certainly great. It is as great as the difference between the words of the prophets and the proclamation of the apostles, between the promise of the Messiah and the incarnation of the eternal Son of God. But no one can tear apart the two parts of Scripture without destroying them completely. Whoever rejects the Old Testament—as our epistle [Hebrews] shows—also destroys the New Testament.
>
> That is what is announced today in the streets and markets about the Old Testament and of the God of the Old Testament—blasphemy must have the consequences that all blasphemy has.[26]

Sasse offers a message of perseverance as the Confessing Church struggled against Nazi infringements into ecclesiastical affairs and the harassment of pastors. It is a message of diligence to remain faithful to God's revelation as passed down from the Jewish people to the Church. Moreover, it is a warning against blasphemy among Christians. For Sasse, the denial of God's revelation in the Hebrew Bible is blasphemy—a sin against God and the Church. The consequences of this blasphemy, he warns, will be a catastrophe for the Church. One cannot discard God's revelation and expect peace and stability in the churches. If one denies the Old Testament, with its record of God's promises and redemptive activity, then one cannot trust the work of Christ presented in the New Testament, and this lack of faith will inevitably lead to blasphemy. Sasse insightfully argued that the Church cannot be the Church without keeping these two united, in the Old and New Testaments.

Put simply, without the Old Testament the New Testament loses its viability and coherence. Without the Hebrew Bible one could not make sense of Jesus' work, his sense of mission, his religious debates with his interlocutors (such as the Pharisees and Sadducees), how the early Christian movement interpreted his death and resurrection, or how the early churches explained the appeal of the gospel message to the non-Jewish population across the Mediterranean. Sermons like Sasse's represent a stake in the ground for the Confessing Church, that the Hebrew Bible must not be divorced from the New Testament—the two together form the Christian Scripture.[27] This assertion is likewise made in the Barmen Declaration and the theologians and pastors at the forefront of the new school of homiletics, as previously discussed. In this sense, the Confessing Church pastors stand in stark contrast to members of the German Christian movement and Nazi supporters who condemned the Old Testament as immoral, as a thoroughly "Jewish book," as "un-German," and inconsonant with "Aryan" morality.[28]

Sermons such as these in effect forge connections between Christians and Jews based on a common cultural and religious tradition. These statements in support of Jews and Judaism are oppositional to the Nazi state because they imply that Christians who remain true to historic Christianity simply cannot join hands with the Nazis to denigrate Judaism or to de-Judaize the Christian faith. The Protestant churches in Nazi Germany were struggling to maintain their historic Jewish foundations. Furthermore, these sermons are evidence that the German churches became sites in German society where pastors could publicly express anti-Nazi ideas and pro-Jewish sentiment simultaneously. My analysis confirms the research of historians such as Hoffmann, Kershaw, and Kirk, that the German churches were the only institutions in Germany able to withstand Nazi "synchronization" to the regime and its values, thus giving them a modicum of freedom to criticize the Nazi regime and its ideology.[29]

The German churches' public and free struggle to maintain a sense of their Jewish foundations indicates the potential to build community among Jews and Christians in Nazi Germany. While this emphasis on shared traditions will not automatically lead to inter-religious dialogue or community building, the potential is certainly there. David Gushee's research on this topic is particularly insightful. In his inquiry into the motivations among rescuers in the Holocaust, Gushee argues that the most commonly cited religious reason for intervention was "a strong sense of religious kinship with Jews as a people."[30] He provides numerous examples of men and women rescuers who had been taught in their churches that Christians ought to have gratitude for the Jews as the people who gave the world Jesus Christ, his mother Mary, the apostles, and all the prophets of Israel.[31] Thus, the Jewish people are integral to the story of Christianity from its very beginning. In one particular case, Dutch leaders of Protestant denominations protested the dismissal of Jewish civil servants based on the fact that Jesus was born of the Jewish people.[32] In some churches, Jews were not called "Christ-killers"; they were not singled out in this way because the sins of all humanity crucified Christ.[33] At the same time, many Christians gave serious thought to what it meant to be the "chosen" people of God. If God chose them, they could not be "un-chosen"—God's covenant with them must remain intact.[34]

This theme runs particularly strong in the Calvinist tradition, following the Frenchman John Calvin who argued that "God's purpose of election" continues with the Jews, despite the "adoption" of Christians into God's covenant.[35] The autobiography of the Calvinist Corrie ten Boom illustrates this dynamic. She came from a family that participated in rescue efforts during the Second World War in the Netherlands. Based on their readings of the Bible, the family believed the Jews were "the apple of God's eye."[36] Gushee argues that there may be a connection between Calvinists like the ten Boom family and their understanding of Jews as the people of God. He writes, "Calvin found more continuity between the Old and the New Testament than have many other Christian theologians."[37] According to Calvin, the Christian cannot dismiss the Old Testament as irrelevant or antiquated because Christ is revealed in it and cannot properly be understood without it. This is not to say that all Calvinists felt a deep connection with the Jewish people, but that among some Christians, especially Calvinists, this theme proved significant in seeing Jews as spiritual cousins, as part of the same spiritual family. Pro-Jewish statements had the potential to undermine Nazi policies of Jewish exclusion, Aryanization, ghettoization, and extermination.

AGAINST THE NAZI PERSECUTION OF THE JEWS

The third and last main theme expressed in these Confessing Church sermons is the condemnation of Nazi persecution of the Jews. This theme occurs 16 times in this sample of over 900 sermons. In only a couple cases do pastors speak about the persecution of Jews prior to the Second World War. At the heart of these statements is the expression of empathy for a persecuted people, and the argument that love of one's neighbor ought to guide Christian action. The sermons rarely name the perpetrator of the persecution or provide specifics about the form of persecution. But all of them express concern for a suffering people.

Four of these 16 sermons specifically address the equality of Jews and non-Jews, thereby pointing out the injustice of the persecution. One example is a sermon delivered on the second Sunday after Epiphany, likely in early 1934, by Pastor Julius Sammetreuther. He preached on John 1:43–51, a text describing Jesus' selection of Philip as a disciple of Jesus. Philip was a devout Jew who became a follower of Jesus. Sammetreuther used this text to speak out about the Aryan Paragraph, legislation that sought to exclude Jews from the clergy. This law undermined the integrity of the Church as an institution predicated upon the faith of its members. He argued that "God is not bound by a natural characteristic," meaning race or ethnicity, and that the sermon presents an important "opportunity to talk about the Aryan Paragraph and to reject it."[38] Sammetreuther emphasized that God is concerned with the personal characteristics of the individual but not the "natural" characteristics one has no control over.

Likewise, Pastor Paul Hinz preached a sermon that presented the equality of the Jews and Germans as a basis to criticize the Nazi persecution. On September 26, 1943, he preached on the story of the ten men Jesus cleansed of leprosy (Luke 17:11–19).[39] In the months after Germany's defeat at the Battle of Stalingrad, when the outlook on the war began to look terrible indeed for the Germans, Hinz reflected on the divisions that separate human beings from one another. He observed that the astonishing element in Luke's story is that nine of the leprous men were Jews and one was a Samaritan; in the social and religious context of ancient Palestine, these two groups did not inter-relate or commune together in any sense. And yet afflicted with leprosy, the ten men are able to overcome their differences, live together, and, most importantly, find healing together. Hinz argued that the point of this text is that social and spiritual barriers can be overcome, even seemingly insurmountable ones.

The sermons such as these unequivocally undermine the Nazi racial ideology that asserts the Jews are an inferior and pernicious people group. Nazism makes physical or racial characteristics determinative of an individual's worth and moral and spiritual goodness. These sermons explicitly affirm that race and ethnicity should not divide a community or serve as indicators of an individual's value or worth.

Confessing Church pastors could also directly confront the Nazi persecution of the Jews to evoke empathy and understanding. An illuminating example is a sermon Dietrich Bonhoeffer delivered at the funeral of his grandmother, Julie Bonhoeffer, in Berlin on January 15, 1936. This occurred just months after the passage of the Nuremberg Laws in September 1935. While recalling fond memories of his grandmother, Bonhoeffer told of how troubled she was that the principles of her youth—"the inflexibility of law, the free word of free men, the binding quality of the given word, plain and sober speech, honesty and simplicity in personal and public life"—had been betrayed.[40] She could not keep quiet amid this betrayal, he said. Bonhoeffer continued,

> Therefore her last years were deeply troubled by the great sorrow she bore for the suffering and fate of the Jews among our people. She sought to help and suffered with them. She stemmed from a different age, out of a different spiritual world. This world does not sink with her into the grave.[41]

Bonhoeffer emphasized the strangeness of Nazi values to the world in which his grandmother Julie lived. While Bonhoeffer's sermon celebrated this courageous and principled woman, it is even more significant that he presented her as a model for his family to emulate in troubled times. He said that the inheritance that Julie gave his family, her strength of character and great courage, was in the form of an "obligation" to emulate her example as fellow sojourners in Nazi Germany.[42]

Pastors who voiced sympathy for persecuted Jews walked a fine line between referring to the persecution and explicitly condemning the persecutors. To explicitly condemn the Nazi persecutors could mean disastrous consequences for the pastor. A case in point is a sermon by Pastor Julius von Jan of Oberlenningen in response to the nation-wide pogrom on the night of November 9–10, 1938. The pogrom known as *Kristallnacht*, the "Night of Broken Glass," marked a decisive moment in Jan's career.[43] He preached a sermon the next week on November 16, 1938, in which he sought to expose the criminal behavior of his fellow Germans whose passions and hatred had run amok.[44]

The Nazi regime fomented the pogrom in response to an event that occurred on November 7, 1938, when a seventeen-year-old Pole named Herschel Grynszpan shot and fatally wounded a junior official, Ernst vom Rath, of the German embassy in Paris. Grynszpan's grievance concerned another Nazi policy of persecution against the Jews, this time the deportation of foreign-born Jews living in Germany. The Polish government closed its borders to 8,000 of the 12,000 Polish refugees, and Grynszpan's parents were among those stranded at the border.[45] Rath died of his injuries in the afternoon on November 9, 1938, which gave the Nazi regime an opportunity for reprisal against the Jews of Germany. Within twenty-four hours, and at Hitler's instigation, Nazi thugs destroyed over 1000 synagogues and over 7500 Jewish-owned businesses, filling the streets of Germany with broken glass.[46] The number of Jews arrested was approximately 30,000, an astounding number, marking the first time that Jews as Jews were arrested *en masse* and sent to concentration camps.[47] While Nazi records indicate that 91 men died in the pogrom, another 300 Jews, in the depths of despair, committed suicide in its wake.[48]

Most clergymen and church officials were silent about the pogrom the following week, revealing timidity and a concern only for their own.[49] A Confessing Church conference held in Berlin on December 10–12 released a statement on the incident, which read,

> We are bound together as brethren with all the believers in Christ of the Jewish race. We will not separate ourselves from them, and we ask them not to separate themselves from us. We exhort all members of our congregations to concern

themselves with the material and spiritual distress of our Christian brothers and sisters of the Jewish race, and to intercede for them in their prayers to God.⁵⁰

This passage demonstrates a common but problematic theme in Confessing Church opposition, that the church's main focus was limited in practice to the defense of Christian Jews, not to all Jews as such.⁵¹ The Church's main concern seemed to be its autonomy vis-à-vis the Nazi regime, the continuation of its ministries, and the rights of the individual Christians, but not so much on the turmoil occurring outside its own walls. Most pastors simply kept silent about the pogrom.⁵²

Nevertheless, a few Confessing Church pastors did speak out the next week in church services, Jan among them. His sermon was based on Jeremiah 22:2–9, which declares the prophet's role in proclaiming the law of God to his nation, king, and princes who have trampled upon it.⁵³ In the first few lines, Jan accused the Nazi regime of jailing God's prophets and also condemned the German-Christians as liars. A crime has been committed in Paris, he argued,

> Passions have been released, the laws of God jeered at, houses of God that were sacred to others have been burned to the ground, property belonging to the foreigner plundered or destroyed, men who faithfully served our nation (*Volk*) and who fulfilled their duty in good conscience have been thrown into concentration camps simply because they belong to another race . . . Even if the authorities do not admit their hand in this injustice, the healthy sensitivity of the people (*Volk*) feels the truth without any doubt—including where people do not dare speak of this.⁵⁴

Jan preached with boldness and clarity. The German people have lost their way and followed not simply a political religion, but an "organized anti-Christianity," a church established by the state and administered by German-Christians.⁵⁵ Germans have burned "houses of God" to the ground— indeed, he did not say *Synagoge* but *Gotteshäuser* to bridge the distance some might perceive in the houses of worship of the Jewish and Christian traditions. Just as Christians worship in the house of God, so also do Jews.

Jan's condemnation is sweeping: Germans have scoffed at God's laws, burned God's sacred houses, and dishonored courageous veterans—all at the instigation of Nazi "authorities." It is striking that Jan accuses the Nazi regime of orchestrating the pogrom, just days after its occurrence. He even turns a common Nazi phrase against the regime, a phrase often used to describe popular anti-Jewish sentiments: "*the healthy sensitivity of the people (Volk)* feels truth without any doubt [emphasis added]."⁵⁶ Jan echoed the apostle Paul's warning in Galatians 6:7, "God will not be ridiculed. What a person sows, he will reap!"[57] The people must know that God's judgment is coming unless they repent of what they have done.

Word of Jan's sermon spread. Nearly two weeks later, on November 25, at 10:30 pm, a mob of 500 demonstrators found Jan, beat him senseless, and took him to the Town Hall for an hour-long interrogation, which resulted in incarceration at the district prison for four months.[58] One year later, on November 15, 1939, Jan was tried before the Nazi "special court" (*Sondergericht*) and condemned for "misusing the pulpit" and "treachery."[59] His sentence was 16 months. Jan was able to continue preaching after his release in May 1940. In 1943 he was drafted into the Wehrmacht and served on the Russian front, ultimately surviving the war. Jan's story illustrates the danger and costs the Confessing Church pastor faced if he decided to speak out boldly against Nazi persecution and in support of the Jews.

There were other pastors like Jan who spoke out against the Nazi pogrom, such as the Protestant pastor Hermann Seggel of Mistelgau (in the district of Bayreuth). A report from the office of the district governor of Upper and Central Franconia documents an accusation against Pastor Seggel for violating the Reich Criminal Code (130a) and the Law Against Treacherous Attacks Against the Party and the State by preaching a sermon on November 16, 1938.[60] According to the report, Seggel condemned the "acts of rage" of the *Kristallnacht* pogrom the week before, and further, stated that "A Christian did not do such things; these were subhumans." From the authority of the pulpit, Seegel turned the tables on the Nazis by claiming that their supporters, not Jews, were "subhumans," who acted irrationally and against the interests of the nation. The government report does not indicate what, if any, measures were taken against Pastor Seggel.[61]

German pastors were certainly aware of the Nazi persecution of the Jews, though the extent of this knowledge is not certain, particularly regarding the details of the Holocaust. In the 16 sermons that criticize the Nazi persecution of the Jews, the pastors often do not give specifics about massacres of the Jews, the identities of the persecutors, or even the specific nature of the crimes being committed against the Jews. While the language about massacres is often implicit and the perpetrators are never named, the context indicates that the pastors knew of the atrocities. An example is a sermon by Paul Hinz delivered sometime between 1941 and 1943, on the famous passage of 1 John 4:16, which states in part, "God is love, and those who abide in love abide in God, and God abides in them." Hinz observed that if they were to "look out into the world" at war, they would see chaos. "Peoples [*Völker*] are exterminated, races go into the abyss of destruction; a sea of blood and tears, inconsolable sorrow goes over the world."[62] Admittedly, he did not tell his congregation which "peoples" are being exterminated or which "races" are being destroyed, but it seems clear that he was referring to the devastation on the battlefields of Europe among the nations at war. At the same time, it also seems clear that he is referring to the Jewish people, the "race" at the center of Nazi hatred and policies of exclusion and extermination. He uses very strong language here: "exterminated" (*ausgerottet*) and "the abyss of destruction" (*den Abgrund des Unterganges*), both of which indicate the decimation of a population most resembling that of Jews in Germany during this time.

There is even evidence that German pastors of Jewish descent, who had found safety in exile, knew of the atrocities. In a powerful Good Friday sermon delivered on March 30, 1945, just prior to the end of the war in Europe, Friedrich Forell preached a sermon to a German-speaking audience in New York City. The sermon was on the passion narrative in Matthew 27:46.[63] Forell explicitly connected the suffering of Christ with the suffering of many during the Second World War and the persecuted Jews. Furthermore, Forell recalled the image of the Suffering Servant in Isaiah 53 and affirmed that in Christ's suffering humanity is healed. At this point, he connected the ongoing catastrophe in Europe with the passion narrative. He spoke of a woman "whose elderly mother was deported to Poland" where she died, thus indicating he is most likely speaking of the Nazi persecution of the Jews:

> There is so much devilish injustice done, there was so much terrible hatred sown: Only on the cross, on which we find forgiveness, we receive the strength of God to forgive those who have persecuted, expelled, tortured and murdered our loved ones. On the cross Jesus prayed for his murderers, "Father, forgive them." On the cross we learn to pray for our enemies, only on the cross, only on the cross.[64]

True peace, he argued, cannot be attained through political parties or peace conferences, but only by the way of Calvary. This passage does not mention Hitler or the Nazis by name, nor does it refer explicitly to the Jews. But Forell's references could hardly be misunderstood by his audience. The sermon is a condemnation of the war and Nazi atrocities. He spoke of a woman deported to Poland, of the "devilish injustice," the "terrible hatred," and the persecutions and murders. Perhaps it is likely that his audience included Christians of Jewish extraction, given that he spoke of the "murder" of "our loved ones." In any case, his point was that there is a love capable of dealing with the horrors they have experienced and a grace to help them move forward.

CONFRONTING THE PROBLEM OF SILENCE

My research presents a significant problem given the historiography of the German population's knowledge of the Nazi mass murder of European

Jewry, which has been extensively examined.[65] Conservative estimates are that by 1942 and 1943, approximately one-third of the German population had received news in one form or another of the mass murder of the Jews.[66] If one excludes teenagers and children from this equation—those whose parents might have "shielded" them from such knowledge—less conservative estimates indicate that perhaps one-half of the population was aware of the atrocities.[67] This would of course include Confessing Church pastors. Knowledge of Nazi atrocities spread to Germans of all socioeconomic and educational backgrounds through widely listened to BBC broadcasts and also reports of Wehrmacht soldiers returning home from the eastern front.[68] In fact, SD reports and various other sources indicate that Allied broadcasts on Nazi mass murders "were widely listened to and discussed."[69] And yet one does not find overwhelming evidence of pastors speaking out from the pulpit about the atrocities and persecutions. While I cannot claim this batch of over 900 sermons represents all Confessing Church sermons, there were only 16 sermons that specifically addressed the persecutions and the massacres.[70] One should keep in mind that pastors who voiced criticism of the Nazi regime from the pulpit may not have actually written the criticisms in their sermons, or they may have destroyed their sermons after delivering them. Nevertheless, the apparent problem, then, is why did pastors not speak out more often from the pulpit about the massacres and atrocities?

One must consider the impact of the Nazi propaganda machine on Germans throughout the Second World War. Through the constant barrage of propagandistic speeches by Hitler, Joseph Goebbels, and other Nazi leaders, broadcast across Germany, as well as wall posters strategically positioned throughout commuter and pedestrian traffic, the Nazi regime used unambiguous language to express their approach to the "Jewish menace"; they used words such as *Vernichtung* (extermination) and *Ausrottung* (annihilation).[71] The regime reached millions upon millions of Germans who could not help but be exposed to the pervasive propaganda and thereby become informed of the Nazi approach to the Jewish people. It has even been argued that by mid-1942, knowledge of "the mass crimes of the Nazis, and in particular the murder of the Jews, was an open secret in the Reich and among the Allies."[72] There was simply no possibility of keeping crimes so immense a secret hidden from Germans and the peoples of occupied Europe, not with the murders taking place throughout much of Eastern Europe, the millions of victims involved, and the incredible inhumanity of the crimes.[73] Many Confessing Church pastors, who were leaders in their religious communities and ministers to families with sons at war, "who kept their eyes and ears open," would have known about the Nazi mass murder of the Jews.[74]

Given these considerations, a few factors may shed some light on the apparent lack of a robust response to the Nazi persecution of the Jews in the sermons of the Confessing Church. First, one should keep in mind that for most Germans the war and its progress were of utmost concern, not the fate of the Jews.[75] As Ian Kershaw writes, "The Jews were out of sight and literally out of mind for most."[76] Second, one must consider the nature of the knowledge of Nazi atrocities among the German population. While millions of Germans knew of the Nazi massacres of Jews, most failed to put the pieces together to see the full picture of the Holocaust; they simply could not fathom the systematic extermination of all European Jewry.[77]

In fact, none of the sermons mentions any kind of mass, systematic extermination of the Jewish people. The knowledge of the German people was fragmentary and most often based on second-hand information, albeit often from trusted sources (e.g., soldiers returning home). And many simply could not or would not believe the reports or rumors. Nevertheless, some Germans were able to put the pieces together and believed that the worst was true. For example, the White Rose group based in Munich started a leaflet campaign in the summer of 1942, designed to inform the German public of Nazi massacres and lawlessness, even referring to the mass murder of hundreds of thousands of Jews in Poland.[78]

A third reason for the apparent lack of response in sermons was a sense of hopelessness and powerlessness that many must have felt living in a totalitarian society.[79] The news of atrocities would have presented a challenge to pastors: one could ask questions, investigate the stories, speak out against the Nazi regime, and reap the consequences, including possible arrest and imprisonment, or worse. Or one could remain silent, refuse to follow up on the news of atrocities, and continue serving their congregation, hoping to outlive the Nazi regime. In the end, as the historian David Bankier writes, many Germans—and many pastors—"knew enough to know that it was better not to know more."[80] The Confessing Church pastors behaved just like the vast majority of Germans in not speaking out in support of Jews facing Nazi persecution. This reflects several factors: a sense of resignation that there was nothing to be done but wait for the regime to topple; a significant degree of repression under the watchful eyes of the regime's police apparatus, the Gestapo agents and their networks of informers; and also the moral desensitization of nearly a decade witnessing the day-by-day, step-by-step, exclusion of the Jewish people from German public life.[81]

But one must also take into account the anti-Jewish prejudice expressed in the Confessing Church pulpits. The evidence supports the historiography of the churches in Nazi Germany that anti-Jewish prejudice was pervasive among Christians.[82] Sermons that repeated centuries-old tropes that portrayed Jews as wayward, stubborn, as guilty of murdering Christ, and as divinely punished throughout history, could only serve to mitigate any compassion or empathy that a Christian might otherwise feel for their persecuted Jewish neighbors. I would assert that this "unholy potential," as Bethge describes it, prevented pastors from speaking out more often and more forcefully in support of Jews and Judaism.

Moreover, Peter Fritzsche argues that in German society there was a "general silence" about the suffering and fate of the German Jews in Nazi Germany, a silence that filled the sanctuaries of German churches as well.[83] He makes an interesting point that the fate of the Jews lay beyond the Germans' "limits on empathy" because they simply could not imagine being Jewish. While Germans (and Christians) debated the Nazi policy of euthanasia because they could actually imagine this policy causing the suffering of their own families, "they could not imagine being Jewish" and suffering simply for this reason.[84] But as the sermons indicate, Christians had a wealth of religious concepts and principles that could (one might say should) have aided this imagination. Christians share with Jews much of the same sacred history and the same sacred stories that inform and shape moral behavior and spiritual growth. One could argue that this common heritage should have been utilized more often and more explicitly to bond Christians and Jews together in Nazi Germany.

At the same time, as Alon Confino has argued, we must understand not just the impact of Nazi ideology on the German population but the "sentiments" and "sensibilities" that fed the German imagination of "a world without Jews."[85] The Nazis conjured the vision of a new civilization and a new morality fit for a new age, but to achieve this vision, they had to remove the Jews, who represented "evil historical origins."[86] Confino argues, "By persecuting and exterminating the Jews, the Nazis eliminated the shackles of a past tradition and its morality, thus making it possible to liberate their imagination, to open up new emotional, historical, and moral horizons that enabled them to imagine and create their empire of death."[87] Moreover, "Germany's historical origins needed to be purified down to the Jews' shared past with Christianity via the canonical text."[88] This explains why thugs on the pogrom of November 9–10, 1938, not only torched synagogues, but also Torah scrolls, the Hebrew Bible.[89] As Confino contends, the "sentiments" and "sensibilities" evident in Nazi Germany "reveal a Christian culture in German society that identified German nationhood with Christianity and which lent legitimacy that derived from anti-Semitic tradition to anti-Jewish prejudices."[90] One may conclude that in some ways German Protestantism by the Nazi era was a compromised Christianity, weakened by ethnic and racial considerations that were alien to the religion, yet meant to unify and give meaning to the German nation. Thus, German pastors had to contend not only with the continual barrage of Nazi ideology from the Nazi propaganda machine but also with pervasive "sentiments" and "sensibilities" that inspired the Nazi vision of "a world without Jews."

CONCLUSION

The Confessing Church sermons that expressed pro-Jewish sentiments directly opposed specific Nazi beliefs and policies that sought the exclusion of Jews and Judaism from German public life. While some pastors challenged the Nazi view that the Jews were an evil and pernicious people by affirming their status as the chosen of God, others opposed the idea that the Old Testament and Judaism ought to have no part of Christianity by affirming their foundational significance in the Church. A few pastors even condemned the Nazi persecution and massacres of the Jews. While none of these sermons may be categorized as resistance to the Nazi regime in the sense that they aimed for its overthrow, they certainly reveal opposition within the ranks of the Confessing Church in an effort to undermine Nazi racial ideology.

The sermons reveal evidence of a historic dilemma Christians have in relating to Jews and Judaism. On the one hand, Judaism plays a central role in the Christian tradition. From Jesus' ministry in a Jewish context to the inclusion of the Hebrew Bible in the Christian canon, Christianity affirms Jewish religious experience and God's covenant with Israel. On the other hand, elements of the Christian tradition present Jews as "Christ-killers" and as an accursed people.[91] Considering the anti-Judaic expressions examined in the previous chapter and the positive statements in the historical record as explored in this chapter, this research demonstrates ambivalence about the Jews and their persecution in Nazi Germany. The central point is that the pastors defended Jews predominantly as a way to defend the German Protestant churches, to protect the churches' identity, traditions, congregants, and autonomy. By and large, the pastors protected Jews and Judaism insofar as doing so protected the churches.

There is no indication that Confessing Church pastors as a group confronted or came to terms with the ambivalence of their perspectives about the Jews and Judaism. This blindness to the problems of their own theological perspectives certainly played a role in their silence when confronted with Nazi persecution of Jews. In the end, the anti-Jewish theology prevalent in German Protestantism proved a significant barrier to words and actions of neighborly love among Christians in Nazi Germany. Given the pervasiveness of anti-Judaic theology, it is significant that many still spoke out in support of the Jews.

In the following chapter we will examine Gestapo and SD responses to pastors who voiced opposition, such as expressions in support of Jews and Judaism. Secret police reports indicate that the Nazi regime was indeed concerned about Confessing Church pastors voicing opposition from the pulpit.

NOTES

1. See Karl Schleunes, *The Twisted Road to Auschwitz: Nazi Policy toward German Jews 1933–1939* (Chicago: University of Illinois Press, 1990); Christopher Browning, with contributions by Jürgen Matthäus, *The Origins of the Final Solution: The Evolution of Nazi Jewish Policy, September 1939-March 1942* (Lincoln, NE: University of Nebraska, 2004); and Ian Kershaw, *Hitler, the Germans, and the Final Solution* (New Haven: Yale University Press, 2008).

2. See Browning, *Origins of the Final Solution*, 252–63; Lucy Dawidowicz, *The War Against the Jews, 1933–1945* (New York: Holt, Rinehart and Winston, 1975), 125–140; Saul Friedländer, *Nazi Germany and the Jews: The Years of Extermination, 1939–1945* (New York: Harper Perennial, 2008), 207–225; and Timothy Snyder, *Bloodlands: Europe Between Hitler and Stalin* (New York: Basic Books, 2010), 126–127, 182–200.

3. Deborah Dwork and Robert Jan van Pelt, *Holocaust: A History* (New York: W.W. Norton, 2002), 266–278.

4. The earliest rumors of mass killings of Jews are found as early as autumn 1941, though by mid-1942 rumors circulated far and wide and reports were even broadcast by the BBC by autumn 1942. See Kershaw, *Hitler, The Germans, and the Final Solution*, 142; and also Walter Laqueur, *The Terrible Secret: Suppression of the Truth about Hitler's "Final Solution"* (New York: Little Brown & Co., 1981).

5. Dr. F.W. Arnold. *Report of the Kirchliche Hilfsstelle für evangelische Nichtarier* (Büro Pfarrer Grüber). 21 December 1938. Nichtarische Geistliche Kirchengemeindebeamte, Gemeindevertreter usw., von Oktober 1933 bis Dezember 1952. EZA 7/1952.

6. Hans Joachim Iwand, *Nachgelassene Werke, Dritter Band* (München: Chr. Kaiser Verlag, 1963), 92.

7. See Bergen, *Twisted Cross*, 26–27.

8. See Barnett, *For the Soul of the People*, 92.

9. In *Mein Kampf*, for example, Hitler argued, "The destructive effect of the Jew's activity in other national bodies is basically attributable only to his eternal efforts to undermine the position of the personality in the host-peoples and to replace it by the mass. Thus, the organizing principle of Aryan humanity is replaced by the destructive principle of the Jew. He becomes 'a ferment of decomposition' among peoples and races, and in the broader sense a dissolver of human culture." Hitler, *Mein Kampf*, 447.

10. Paul Hinz, "Meine Augen sehen nach dem Herrn," Predigt über Psalm 25:15, am Sonntage Okuli, March, 28, 1943, EZA 766/36.

11. See the previous discussion in chapter 4 on how the "new school" of homiletics addressed the apparent neglect of the Old Testament. See, for example, Bonhoeffer, *Worldly Preaching*.

12. For efficiency of expression I will refer to the descendants of Abraham as "the Jews," while acknowledging that Abraham's descendants were known as "Hebrews" in the time before the settlement of Canaan, "Israelites" with the establishment of the nation of Israel, and "Jews" after the Babylonian conquest of the southern kingdom of Judah.

13. See Karl von Schwarz, *Gottes Wort an Gottes Volk, Ein Jahrgang Predigten* (Braunschweig: Hellmuth WollermannVerlagsbuchhandlung, 1933).

14. Anonymous, Sermon manuscript on Deuteronomy 4:25–31, 28–29 March 1942, EZA 50/424.

15. See Evans, *The Third Reich at War*, 438–441.

16. Anonymous, Sermon manuscript on Deuteronomy 4:25–31, 28–29 March 1942, EZA 50/424.

17. Among the best works on the knowledge of atrocities and massacres against Jews during the Second World War include: Walter Laqueur, *The Terrible Secret*; Hans Mommsen, "What did the Germans Know about the Genocide of the Jews?" in Walter H. Pehle, ed., *November 1938: From 'Kristallnacht' to Genocide* (New York: Berg, 1991), 187–221; David Bankier, *The Germans and the Final Solution: Public Opinion Under Nazism* (London, 1992); Hans Mommsen and Volker Ullrich, ""Wir haben nichts gewusst': Ein deutsches Trauma," 1999 4 (1991): 11–46; Eric A. Johnson and Karl-Heinz Reuband, *What We Knew: Terror, Mass Murder, and Everyday Life in Nazi Germany, An Oral History* (Cambridge, MA: Basic Books, 2005); and Frank Bajohr and Dieter Pohl, *Der Holocaust als offenes Geheimnis: Die Deutschen, die NS-Führung und die Alliierten* (München: C.H. Beck, 2006).

18. Anonymous, Sermon manuscript on Deuteronomy 4:25–31, 28–29 March 1942, EZA 50/424.

19. Anonymous, Sermon manuscript on Deuteronomy 4:25–31, 28–29 March 1942, EZA 50/424.

20. Pastor Köster (first name unknown), Sermon manuscript on Luke 1:39–56, Dated between 1937 and 1944, EZA 50/424.

21. Pastor Köster (first name unknown), Sermon manuscript on Luke 1:39–56, Dated between 1937 and 1944, EZA 50/424.

22. Heschel, *Aryan Jesus*, 3, 13.

23. "The Declarations, Resolutions, and Motions Adopted by the Synod of Barmen," on May 29–31, 1934, in Cochrane, *Church's Confession under Hitler*, 237.

24. Thanks to Frank Biess for this helpful and important insight.

25. *Dein Wort ist deiner Kirch Schutz*, ed, Karl Kampffmeyer (Göttingen: Vandenhoeck & Ruprecht, 1934), 54.

26. Sasse, *Zeugnisse*, 26–27.

27. See Arthur Cochrane, *The Church's Confession under Hitler* (Philadelphia: Westminster Press, 1967), 184–185.

28. Bergen, *Twisted Cross*, 144.

29. See Peter Hoffmann, *The History of German Resistance, 1933–1945, Third Edition*, translated by Richard Barry (Ithaca, NY: McGill-Queen's University Press, 1996), 13; Ian Kershaw, *Hitler, the Germans, and the Final Solution*, 166; and Tim Kirk, *Nazi Germany* (New York: Palgrave, 2007), 108.

30. Gushee, *Righteous Gentiles*, Kindle edition, location 2807. Gushee's analysis relies on rescuer primary sources, such as autobiographies and letters, and also on rescuer research. See Lawrence Baron, "The Holocaust and Human Decency," in *Humbolt Journal of Social Science*, vol. 13, no. 1/2, Humbolt University, 1986; Helen Fein, *Accounting for Genocide* (New York: Free Press, 1979); Donald Dietrich,

Catholic Citizens of the Third Reich (New Brunswick, NJ: Transaction Books, 1988); Samuel Oliner and Pearl Oliner, *The Altruistic Personality: Rescuers of Jews in Nazi Europe* (New York: Free Press, 1988); Peter Hellman, *Avenue of the Righteous*; Michael D. Ryan, ed. *Human Responses to the Holocaust* (New York: Edwin Mellon Press, 1981); Andre Stein, *Quiet Heroes* (New York: New York University Press, 1988); Philip Hallie, *Lest Innocent Blood Be Shed* (New York: Harper & Row, 1979); and Gay Block and Malka Drucker, *Rescuers* (New York: Holmes & Meyer, 1992).

31. Gushee, *Righteous Gentiles*, Kindle edition, location 2820.

32. Gushee, *Righteous Gentiles*, Kindle edition, location 2832.

33. Gushee, *Righteous Gentiles*, Kindle edition, location 2832; Michael, *Holy Hatred*, 17, 34.

34. Gushee, *Righteous Gentiles*, Kindle edition, location 2901.

35. See for example, Calvin's commentary on Isaiah, which states, "But because God is continually mindful of his covenant, and 'his gifts and calling are without repentence' [from Romans 11:29], Paul justly concludes that it is impossible that they shall not at length be collected along with the Gentiles that out of both 'there may be one fold under Christ' [from John 10:16]." See John Calvin, "Commentary on the Book of the Prophet Isaiah," in *Calvin's Commentaries*, translation by W. Pringle (Edinburgh: Calvin Translation Society, 1844–1856); reproduced Grand Rapids: Baker, 1999), 8:269. See also Gushee, *Righteous Gentiles*, Kindle edition, location 2901.

36. Gushee, *Righteous Gentiles*, Kindle edition, location 2866.

37. Gushee, *Righteous Gentiles*, Kindle edition, location 2877.

38. Sammetreuther, *Predigtmeditationen*, 164.

39. Paul Hinz, Sermon manuscript on Luke 17:11–19, 26 September 1943, Collected Sermons of Paul Hinz, EZA 766/38.

40. *Dietrich Bonhoeffer's Christmas Sermons*, edited and translated by Edwin Robertson (Grand Rapids: Zondervan, 2005), 123.

41. Bonhoeffer, *Christmas Sermons*, 123.

42. Bonhoeffer, *Christmas Sermons*, 123.

43. The following biographical sketch of Jan is largely based on Stroud's profile in *Preaching in Hitler's Shadow*, 118–120. The work is an edited collection of sermons and profiles of the pastors who delivered them. For more on Jan, see Conway, *Nazi Persecution of the Churches*, 375–376; and Barnett, *For the Soul of the People*, 142.

44. Conway, *Nazi Persecution of the Churches*, 375; and Stroud, *Preaching in Hitler's Shadow*, 123.

45. Martin Gilbert, *Kristallnacht: Prelude to Destruction* (New York: HarperCollins, 2006), 23.

46. See Barnett, *For the Soul of the People*, 139; Gilbert, *Kristallnacht*, 28–29, 118; and Richard Evans, *The Third Reich in Power* (New York: Penguin, 2005), 584.

47. Evans, *Third Reich in Power*, 581.

48. In fact, the true figure of those murdered may run between one and two thousand. See Evans, *Third Reich in Power*, 590.

49. See Gutteridge, *The German Evangelical Church and the Jews*, 188–189; Barnett, *For the Soul of the People*, 142; and Evans, *Third Reich in Power*, 581.

50. Translated and quoted in Gutteridge, *The German Evangelical Church and the Jews*, 188–189; original German in *Kirchliches Jahrbuch für die Evangelische Kirche in Deutschland, 1945–1948*, edited by Joachim Beckmann (Gütersloh: C. Bertelsmann, 1950), 275.

51. See for example Gerlach, *And the Witnesses Were Silent*; Barnett, *For the Soul of the People*; and Kershaw, *The Nazi Dictatorship*, 174.

52. Gerlach, *And the Witnesses Were Silent*, 147.

53. Julius von Jan, "O Land, Land, Land: Hear the Word of the Lord!" in Stroud, *Preaching in Hitler's Shadow*, 121.

54. Jan, "O Land, Land, Land," in Stroud, *Preaching in Hitler's Shadow*, 123.

55. Jan, "O Land, Land, Land," in Stroud, *Preaching in Hitler's Shadow*, 123.

56. Stoud, *Preaching in Hitler's Shadow*, 124. Thanks to Frank Biess for this helpful insight.

57. Jan, "O Land, Land, Land," in Stroud, *Preaching in Hitler's Shadow*, 124.

58. Gerlach, *And the Witnesses Were Silent*, 144.

59. The following biographical background is based on Stroud, *Preaching in Hitler's Shadow*, 119. See also Conway, *Nazi Persecution of the Churches*, 375–376; and Barnett, *For the Soul of the People*, 142.

60. *The Jews in the Secret Nazi Reports on Popular Opinion in Germany, 1933–1945*, edited by Otto Dov Kulka and Eberhard Jäckel, translated from the German by William Templer (New Haven, CT: Yale University Press, 2010), 445–446.

61. See Kulka and Jäckel, *The Jews and the Secret Nazi Reports*, 445–446.

62. Paul Hinz, Sermon manuscript on 1 John 4:16, delivered between 1941 and 1943, Collected Sermons of Paul Hinz, EZA 766/38.

63. The sermon is mistakenly labeled Matthew 28:46, but this verse does not exist. The quotation Forell uses is from Matthew 27:46.

64. Friedrich Forell, Sermon manuscript on Matthew 28:46, delivered on 20 March 1945, Papers of the Newcomers Christian Fellowship, University of Iowa Libraries, Special Collections, MSC 358, Iowa City, Iowa.

65. Marlis Steinert, *Hitler's War and the Germans: Public Mood and Attitude during the Second World War*, translated by Thomas de Witt (Athens: Ohio University Press, 1977); Walter Laqueur, *The Terrible Secret*; Kershaw, *Popular Opinion and Political Dissent in the Third Reich*; Mommsen, "What did the Germans Know about the Genocide of the Jews?", 187–221; Bankier, *The Germans and the Final Solution*; Mommsen and Ullrich, "'Wir haben nichts gewusst',": 11–46; Johnson and Reuband, *What We Knew*; and Bajohr and Pohl, *Der Holocaust als offenes Geheimnis*.

66. Johnson and Reuband, *What We Knew*, 39. Also, Laqueur argues that "news of the 'final solution' had been received in 1942 *all over Europe*" (emphasis added). See *The Terrible Secret*, 196.

67. Johnson and Reuband, *What We Knew*, 392.

68. See Bankier, *The Germans and the Final Solution*, 113; Johnson and Reuband, *What We Knew*, 396–397; Mommsen, "What did the Germans Know?" 206; and Laqueur, *The Terrible Secret*, 201.

69. Bankier, *The Germans and the Final Solution*, 113.

70. One should keep in mind that pastors who voiced criticism of the Nazi regime from the pulpit may not have actually written the criticisms in their sermons, or they may have destroyed their sermons after the fact.

71. Jeffrey Herf, *The Jewish Enemy: Nazi Propaganda during World War II and the Holocaust* (Cambridge, MA: Bellknap Press, 2006), 267.

72. Bajohr and Pohl, *Der Holocaust als offenes Geheimnis*, 128.

73. Bajohr and Pohl, *Der Holocaust als offenes Geheimnis*, 128.

74. Johnson and Reuband, *What We Knew*, 397.

75. Mommsen, "What did the Germans Know?" 192; and Kershaw, *Popular Opinion*, 360.

76. Kershaw, *Popular Opinion and Political Dissent in the Third Reich*, 364.

77. Mommsen, "What did the Germans Know?" 206, 209; and Bankier, *The Germans and the Final Solution*, 115.

78. Mommsen, "What did the Germans Know?" 213–214.

79. Mommsen, "What did the Germans Know?" 205; Bankier, *The Germans and the Final Solution*, 103; and Laqueur, *The Terrible Secret*, 208

80. Bankier, *The Germans and the Final Solution*, 115.

81. Mommsen, "What did the Germans Know?" 205; Bankier, *The Germans and the Final Solution*, 103; and Laqueur, *The Terrible Secret*, 208.

82. See Michael, *Holy Hatred*; Probst, *Demonizing the Jews*; and also Friedländer, *Nazi Germany and the Jews, Vol. 2*, 56.

83. Peter Fritzsche, *Life and Death in the Third Reich* (Cambridge: Harvard University Press, 2009), 119.

84. Fritzsche, *Life and Death in the Third Reich*, 119.

85. Alon Confino, *A World without Jews: The Nazi Imagination from Persecution to Genocide* (New Haven, CT: Yale University Press, 2014), 6.

86. Confino, *A World without Jews*, 5 and 14.

87. Confino, *A World without Jews*, 14.

88. Confino, *A World without Jews*, 5.

89. Confino, *A World without Jews*, 1–3.

90. Confino, *A World without Jews*, 8.

91. Michael, *Holy Hatred*, 16–19.

Chapter 9

Spying in God's House

A substantial problem in analyzing the significance of sermons is gauging their reception among the German people.[1] Then as today, most Christian parishioners do not reflect on the contents or merits of their pastors' sermons in diaries, letters to friends, or the editorial pages of newspapers. Yet in Nazi Germany, spies and informants routinely attended church services, listened attentively to sermons, noted anti-Nazi criticisms, and submitted reports through the Secret State Police (*Geheime Staatspolizei*, or Gestapo) and the Security Service (*Sicherheitsdienst*, SD), an intelligence agency.[2] The reports of the Gestapo and the SD provide us with a treasure trove of evidence to understand what specific expressions of opposition or dissent from within the walls of the German churches pricked Nazi ears. To date, historians of the Nazi state police apparatus have predominantly focused on the actions of clergymen and church leaders outside the walls of the church.[3] Yet Nazi state records give us an excellent indication of why the regime saw fit to spy on pastors within the walls of the church, and specifically as preachers of the gospel. Furthermore, they reveal the extent of Christian public opposition from the authority of the pulpit. My aim in this chapter is to clarify and nuance the Nazi regime's reception of sermons through the lens of the Gestapo and SD.

Historians such as John Conway, Victoria Barnett, and Wolfgang Gerlach have explored in-depth the responses of the clergy to the Nazi state, and furthermore, have expertly shown how the Nazi secret police harassed and arrested pastors for a variety of actions relating to their ministries, including illegally collecting church funds, criticizing Nazi leaders, reading intercessory lists (*Fürbittenliste*) of imprisoned pastors in worship services, and administering illegal seminaries, among other acts.[4] But scholars have not yet focused sufficiently on how the Nazi secret police perceived pastors' oppositional activity from behind the pulpit. Gestapo and SD records indicate that, indeed, the regime was concerned about the oppositional messages clergymen preached from the authority of the pulpit, in a Christian worship service, and in the context of the explication of Scripture.

It is important to emphasize again the limits to the clergy's opposition to the Nazi regime in their sermons. As far as I am aware, and as well might be expected, there is no evidence to suggest that pastors ever explicitly, from the pulpit, called for Hitler's removal from office or the overthrow of the National Socialist government. Such acts would have been exceedingly dangerous and would have merited immediate arrest. Likewise, pastors did not call for Germans to sabotage or otherwise fight against the German military or police state. Nor are there explicit calls for Christians to defy Nazi laws to come to the aid of persecuted Jews. In other words, my research supports the historiography that contends that the pastors did not go far enough in resisting the Nazi regime—especially as men who preached to a captive audience week after week—by discussing specific and concrete ways to undermine the Nazi regime and seek its eventual destruction.[5] Nevertheless, the comments as reported by the Gestapo and SD indicate that pastors occasionally and publicly sought to undermine Nazi leaders, ideology, and policies through the messages of their sermons.

Specifically, the Gestapo and the SD reports reveal concern about three fundamental criticisms pastors expressed from the pulpit. First, clergymen criticized Nazism as a "false ideology" that is contradictory to Christianity and detrimental to the German nation. This could even lead pastors to criticize the purveyors of this ideology, the Nazi leadership. Second, the Gestapo and SD reports indicate great concern when pastors condemned Nazi persecution of the German churches and its clergy. As discussed in chapter 6, this condemnation of Nazi persecution of the churches at the very least implicitly portrays the churches and clergy as righteous victims, and at the same time, paints the regime as anti-Christian and unjust. Lastly, the reports reveal concern when pastors expressed views in support of Jews or Judaism, especially in calling Jews the people of God and asserting that Judaism is the foundation of Christianity. Such expressions could only stoke sympathy for the Jewish people and inspire their support and protection. My purpose is not to present an exhaustive account of Gestapo and SD reports on pastors' sermons but rather to gain an understanding of the types of criticisms from the pulpit that might have concerned Germans most sensitive to politically charged comments. These Gestapo and SD reports present verbatim quotes by pastors from various confessions, all of which were of concern to the regime for undermining Nazi ideology and values.

I have widened the scope of this chapter to include not just Gestapo and SD records of Confessing Church pastors, but also clergymen in Catholic and various Protestant churches as well for a few significant reasons. First, the records do not always differentiate whether the clergyman in question was a member of the Confessing Church (or the PEL), or the leader of a neutral Protestant church or a Roman Catholic church. Second, one must cast a wide net to perceive the variety of messages the Nazi secret police responded to. And third, widening the scope reveals that the regime was concerned about sermons delivered throughout Nazi Germany, regardless of the denomination. The secret police were watching all the German churches, not just the Confessing Church. The evidence presented here indicates the regime kept a constant, watchful eye on a vast and diverse German institution.

The Gestapo and SD records include the agent's or informant's notes on the identity of the pastors, the specific comments made, and the pertinent dates and locations; however, they do not convey the spy's personal beliefs or reflections about the pastor's comments. The reports span the entirety of the Nazi era, from January 1933 to May 1945, and they are from all throughout Germany. The reports tend to focus on the comments of Protestant pastors more than the comments of Catholic priests. This may reflect the Nazi regime's concern about the inter-Protestant conflicts about Nazi intrusions in the Protestant churches, giving rise to the division between the pro-Nazi German Christian movement and the oppositional Confessing Church in 1933–1934. At the same time, the Catholic Church signed a Concordat with the Nazi regime in July 1933, unifying the German priesthood in its approach to the Nazi regime and also limiting Catholic influence in politics. Also, the reports tend to focus on Protestants more simply because Germans at the time were two-thirds Protestant, and Protestants usually preached lengthier sermons than Catholics.

The reports filed by the Gestapo and the SD provide revealing insights into how the Nazi regime viewed the work of the German churches and which actions it deemed offensive or criminal. The reports indicate simply that a pastor expressed criticisms of the Nazi regime from the pulpit, but not whether the Nazi dictatorship took any action as a consequence. Despite the limitations, these reports indicate which actions and comments the Nazi dictatorship found objectionable and the degree to which the regime was aware of pastors' oppositional comments from the pulpit.

It has been well documented that the Gestapo was a proactive and brutal force in policing Jews, communists, and anyone whom the regime deemed outside the *Volksgemeinschaft*, the national community.[6] Yet it was generally a reactive agency in policing ordinary German citizens; it depended on denouncements by citizens or by Nazi spies and informers to police those within the *Volksgemeinschaft*.[7] Informants notified the Gestapo of suspicious comments made in beer halls, workplaces, in stairwells and sanctuaries. In Nazi Germany, there was no such place as the private domain.[8] The clergyman had to conscientiously lead his congregation every Sunday, cognizant than any single member or casual visitor could report a suspicious comment to the Gestapo that very day. Given that hundreds, if not thousands, of sermon manuscripts survive, one can surmise that many or even most critical statements about the Nazi regime were purposefully made and not off-the-cuff remarks. They were made with the full knowledge that they could land the pastor in trouble with the Nazi regime.

We now know that ordinary German congregants, by and large, did not denounce their own priests or ministers.[9] Complaints about pastors' sermons came predominantly from Nazi informants critical of any expression of dissent. Eric Johnson has noted that this fact helps to "demonstrate that many Germans continued to take their religion seriously during the Nazi years and that Hitler never completely won over the hearts and minds of a considerable percentage of the German population."[10] The loyalty of most parishioners to their pastors underscores the importance of their sermons, especially when pastors offered criticisms of the Nazi state and its ideology and policies.

Hitler and the Nazi leaders understood the influence of the German churches and were justifiably concerned about dissident pastors. From the start of 1933, the SD considered the German churches—Catholic, Protestant, and smaller religious sects—to be serious ideological threats to the Nazi state, and thus established the Division of Political Churches, developing policies and procedures to spy on clergymen, even within the walls of the sanctuary.[11] By 1937, the Gestapo organized a division called IV-B to specifically investigate the churches, staffed by experts, including three ex-Catholic priests and one ex-Protestant minister.[12] Both the Gestapo and SD utilized *Vertrauensmänner* (or V-Men), contacts assigned to spy on dissenting clergy. The Gestapo required Confessing Church leaders to notify their offices of church meetings and activities, even allowing officers to attend and listen in.[13] The Gestapo network of spies and informers would report on pastors' sermons and identify religious dissidents. It should also be noted that it was rare for Gestapo officers to be stationed in small towns and communities; instead, the local regular police force often stepped in to do the work of the Gestapo.[14]

The Gestapo practice of spying on pastors and their preaching was well known by the clergy. Recalling the sermon that opened this study, Pastor Martin Niemöller preached on June 27, 1937, condemning Gestapo interference and harassment in the churches. Again, this sermon would be his last as a free man in Nazi Germany. He condemned not only the Gestapo's arrest of eight church leaders but also the spying of three agents who crashed his Friday communion service, just days prior, "to inform upon the activities of the community of Jesus."[15] Niemöller was arrested the next Tuesday and spent the rest of the Nazi period imprisoned or in a concentration camp.

One must keep in mind that the Gestapo played by two different rulebooks according to the individual or group under suspicion for actions against the Nazi state. Those deemed outside the *Volksgemeinschaft*—including Jews, the Roma and Sinti, and political dissidents—were as a matter of course brutalized and treated as subjects without rights. But this was not necessarily the case with ordinary German citizens. As historian Frank McDonough has argued, "Gestapo brutality is almost entirely absent in cases of denouncement involving 'ordinary' Germans, which reinforces the idea that while the Nazi terror system showed a brutal face towards a clearly defined set of opponents, it displayed a more professional and humane face to ordinary German citizens."[16] Given the status of pastors, including Confessing Church pastors, the Gestapo was very careful in proceeding with arrests and imprisonments of clergymen. In fact, "it was extremely rare for such cases to proceed to trial. Fair trials were the norm for Protestant clergymen, not the exception."[17] Hitler realized that measures against clergy had the potential to backfire and inspire popular opposition. Thus, arrests of dissenting clergy were typically meant to intimidate and harass, to manipulate the clergy into obedience, rather than to permanently harm or incarcerate.[18] Yet, as Barnett argues, "The Nazis reacted more brutally and decisively, however, when attacked publicly by the church, particularly when those involved were already at risk."[19] Examples include German pastors of Jewish descent or pastors who had a track record of critical comments against the regime.

Outside the walls of the sanctuary, the Gestapo and SD paid careful attention to the activities of dissenting clergy. Gestapo reports mention several "offensive" actions by pastors, including public criticisms of Hitler and other Nazi officials, the war effort, the persecution of the churches, and the "paganization" of Christianity in Nazi Germany. For example, one Gestapo report dated September 13, 1933, indicates a humorous but critical opinion from a former Nazi member, Pastor Heinrich Grüber of Templin. The report indicates that Pastor Grüber resigned his membership in the Nazi Party with the words: "The Nazis are similar to a beefsteak: brown on the outside and when one touches it, the red soup runs [*läuft die rote Suppe*]."[20] The offensive comment, "the red soup runs," refers to the perception that the Nazis had more in common with the Socialists (or the Left) than they cared to admit. In fact, by late 1933, Ernst Röhm, as the head of the Storm Troopers (*Sturmabeilung*, or SA), oversaw the immense expansion of the organization, even welcoming whole sections of the communist Red Front. Berliners called these units "beefsteak sections," a humorous epithet to indicate the SA was not as ideologically "pure" as they claimed.[21] Yet Grüber criticized the entire Nazi movement in this way.

The Gestapo reported instances when a pastor publicly criticized the Nazi leadership. The Gestapo took note when Confessing Church pastor Kurt Scharf commented at a meeting of the Pastors' Emergency League on December 12, 1933, that "a man like Baldur von Schirach" should not lead the youth of Germany (as the head of the Hitler Youth) because he believes that Hitler is Germany's Savior and Leader.[22] Likewise, a pastor named Lemke from Templin came under Gestapo scrutiny because he declared publicly, mostly likely in January 1934, that Hitler discouraged people from attending church and that National Socialism was a godless ideology.[23] While the Gestapo and SD were certainly concerned with the comments and actions of pastors outside the walls of the churches, they were particularly concerned with statements made from within the walls of the churches, to captive audiences, and by the authority vested in the pulpit.

AGAINST NATIONAL SOCIALISM AS A FALSE IDEOLOGY

Gestapo and SD reports demonstrate that the Nazi regime was indeed listening as pastors preached sermons, sitting in the pews and taking notes of subversive statements. Perhaps the most common criticism identified in the reports was that National Socialism was a pagan or anti-Christian ideology. This criticism could even lead the pastors to criticize Nazi leadership, the purveyors of Nazi ideology. One especially illuminating SD "Special Report" is dated March 1935, and written by the Chief of the Reich Main Security Office of the *Schutzstaffel* (SS).[24] The document is a compilation of criticisms against the Nazi regime made by pastors, the majority of whom belonged to the Pastors' Emergency League (PEL). Remarkably, the SS refused to characterize the PEL as oppositional, even though various PEL members criticized the regime in sermons (by the time this report was issued in March 1935, the PEL had become the Confessing Church). The report lists examples of pastors who preached against the Nazi worldview, Nazi leaders, the Nazi Party, and antisemitism.

The SD report tells of a pastor named Peterson from Pellworm who preached a sermon on April 3, 1934, in which he proclaimed, "The way to Jesus is without any attachment to the new Germany and is even opposed to the people and state . . . We must not even hesitate to go to the concentration camp for this truth."[25] This comment does not speak explicitly of Hitler, the Nazis, or National Socialism, but only of the "new Germany," which could only be understood by his congregation as a criticism of the Nazi regime as un-Christian or even anti-Christian. Another pastor named Töllner used common sense and a simple reading of the Bible to argue that love is from God, and hate and pride are from the devil. If this is the case, he argued, then national pride and national hate must be from the devil as well.[26] These are just two examples that illustrate the SD took note of pastors who criticized the Nazi worldview from the pulpit.

The report also mentions one example of a sermon critical of Nazism that demonstrates the blurred line between dissent and opposition in the pulpit. A pastor from Seebucknow named Kniess delivered a sermon at a funeral on August 8, 1934, in which he refused to give the Hitler salute, saying, "I have never yet greeted with 'Heil Hitler,' and I will not make this greeting. Salvation comes from God and not from men."[27] While Kniess did not deny obedience to the Nazi state or undermine Hitler's legitimacy as the temporal ruler of Germany, he asserted limits to Hitler's person and leadership, and thereby modelling sober submission to the governing authority. Yet, in doing so, Pastor Kniess undermined the National Socialist image of Hitler as a savior of Germany.[28] This concern for undue reverence or even worship of Hitler or the German nation is particularly significant. Furthermore, for a Christian to assert that other Christians "worship" Hitler was tantamount to charging them with idolatry for breaking the first commandment to worship God alone. Pastors who made this accusation of idolatry drew a line in the sand about how Christians ought to understand and relate to Hitler.

The Gestapo and SD reports also provide insights into how some pastors and priests felt about the Nazi propaganda machine and its apparent success in spreading a false ideology. One Gestapo report from Berlin on August 22, 1940, mentions a Catholic priest from Frankfurt am Main who made a connection between the Nazi leaders and false prophets. He said, "The modern false prophets work with the resources of modern mass persuasion. They use the stage, art, beautiful literature, and above all film. Beware of false prophets."[29] It is unclear where the priest made this statement—in a sermon or in another setting. Another Catholic priest from Nuremberg preached a sermon on July 14, 1940, in which he commented on the Nazi use of the radio to influence the German people. "What good is a two-hour victory on the radio against the Almighty God[?]"[30] Unfortunately, the report does not indicate the context of this comment, or what "victory" the priest refers to. These two examples illustrate that some priests, and presumably Protestant pastors as well, were well aware of the means the Nazis used to spread propaganda and warned congregants to listen with a discerning ear.

But more disturbing to the secret police were criticisms of Nazi Germany's war aims. A report from the Chief of the Security Police and the SD concerning the political attitudes of the churches and sects written on October 20, 1939, just a month after the German invasion of Poland, indicated concern that Confessing churches and other Protestant groups "portray the war as a consequence of atheism [*Gottlosigkeit*] in Germany," and that God's judgment is coming.[31] Likewise, one Berlin Gestapo report, dated April 22, 1940, indicates several pastors expressed critical remarks in their sermons that the Second World War was a punishment from God. An unidentified pastor from Ried went so far as to say, "The West is in for a bloodbath as the world has never seen (!)."³² The reporter's inclusion of the exclamation signals perhaps his disbelief that a pastor would say this publicly and that a "bloodbath" could possibly be in Nazi Germany's future. This report indicates that pastors viewed the war, even within the first year, as God's punishment, yet the objects of God's punishment varied, to include the Germans and "the West" more generally. These expressions drew the attention of the Gestapo and SD not only because they indicated defeatism and called into question the loyalty of the pastor, but they undermined the National Socialist tenet of the superiority of the "Aryan" and the qualifications of Hitler as the savior and Führer. These tenets would be rendered suspect or meaningless in a German "bloodbath" or defeat. It should be noted that these reports were made within the first seven months of the war, as German forces conquered Poland, Denmark, and Norway. These assertions about God's judgment or punishment were based on faith in God's justice, not on the daily news reports.

Clergymen's sermons contributed to a public conversation about the moral nature and truth claims of National Socialism, and it's clear that the Gestapo and SD were listening in to these conversations. The sermons that criticized Hitler, the Nazi leadership, or the superiority of the "Aryan" race or the German nation, undermined them as not worthy of worship or undue reverence, and thus de-legitimized the Nazi totalitarian claim to the individual.³³ These sermons served to redirect the allegiance and obedience of the Christian away from others and toward God. Furthermore, the sermons that criticized National Socialism as a morally corrupt ideology that elevated one people, one race, one nation, as intrinsically superior (thus denigrating all others), became oppositional to the priorities and policies of the Nazi dictatorship. These sermons publicly undermined the Nazi philosophy of governance and provided an alternative vision for governing society and the German nation.

AGAINST THE NAZI PERSECUTION OF THE GERMAN CHURCHES

The Gestapo and SD reports provide evidence that the regime was concerned about pastors' spreading word of Nazi persecutions against Christians and the German churches, particularly when the pastor cast the Nazi regime or its leaders as anti-Christian or neo-pagan. For example, Pastor Ulricht of Prenzlau delivered a sermon on January 1, 1934, nearly a year after the establishment of the Nazi regime, which connected the paganization of Christianity under the Nazi regime with the persecution of the churches and even Jews. He says,

Lord, come and see it, how your Christianity today is paganized [*verheidnischt wird*]. The true Christianity is gagged and suppressed. Man idolizes today great men who have achieved much, but the Christ who let himself be nailed to the cross, whom one forgets, he is no longer considered. Jesus Christ was also a Jew, yes indeed, but the faith teaches: Go into the world and make disciples of all the peoples, etc. If a Jew cannot be a German, so can he very well—and I stress this explicitly—be a good Christian.[34]

Ulricht criticizes not only the prevalence of a paganized faith that has excluded a Jewish Jesus, but also persecution and suppression of "true Christianity." Statements from the pulpit such as these caught the attention of the Gestapo as oppositional to National Socialism.

The case of the Confessing pastor Enke Hansse of Cologne is illustrative of Gestapo grave concerns about the Nazi regime's public portrayal as persecutors of Christians.[35] In a sermon Hansse delivered on September 30, 1937, he criticized the Nazi persecution of German pastors, specifically the bans on speaking and imprisonments. This persecution was so severe that, as he stated, "Children no longer [are] being taught in a Christian manner."[36] A Gestapo informant noted these comments, but no arrest was made nor interrogation conducted. Nevertheless, two years later he was denounced by a German citizen for conducting an illegal Confessing Church student examination on October 2, 1939. The Gestapo arrested and interrogated Hansse, who denied having anything to do with a Confessing Church examination. They took his word for it, closed the file, and let him go. The Gestapo proceeded carefully and cautiously when dealing with clergy, mindful of their influence in their communities.

Unsurprisingly, the Gestapo took note when pastors called special attention to individual clergymen who courageously stood up against Nazi persecution and faced imprisonment for anti-Nazi activities. Perhaps no other figure represented the unjust Nazi persecution of clergymen than Martin Niemöller, imprisoned in 1937 after continuous criticisms of the Nazi harassment and arrests of Christians. A report dated August 4, 1939, details the activity of a pastor named Gerhard Nierlich, who came to the attention of the Gestapo simply because he emphasized the case of Martin Niemöller while reading off a list of pastors imprisoned or in concentration camps.[37] He read this list of pastors immediately after his sermon. He noted that the Gestapo even arrested ten Jehovah's Witnesses in Soest for stuffing leaflets in mailboxes containing this witty rhyme,

> "Morgenrötchen, Morgenrötchen.
> Die Nazis backen kleine Brötchen.
> Forderung an die Bonzenpartei:
> Gebt uns Niemöller frei!"[38]

> (Little red dawn, little red dawn.
> The Nazis bake small rolls.
> Call on the bigwigs of the party:
> Give us Niemöller free!)

Leaflets with this rhyme were distributed on October 16, 1939, just weeks after the German invasion of Poland. Remembering the persecution of Niemöller and other imprisoned pastors became a way for preachers to expose the Nazi regime as the persecutors of Christians, even as anti-Christian, and in this way to undermine the people's perception of the Nazi state.

Occasionally, pastors even condemned the aggression and militarism of the National Socialist state. A Gestapo report from Berlin on February 19, 1940, just months into the Second World War, mentions a clergyman, a Catholic priest from *Kreise Deutsch-Krone*, who said of the recent German invasion of Poland: "It looks as if the campaign [*Feldzug*] against Poland was a robbery [*Raubzug*]!"[39] In this case, the clergyman was brought up on charges and faced a criminal proceeding for his outburst. The clergyman's clever wordplay revealed the corrupt morality of Germany's invasion of its neighbor to the east.

The sermons that criticized the Nazi persecution of Christians reveal the courage of the clergymen, but they also reveal in the pastors' voices a sense of betrayal that the regime—a supposedly Christian-friendly regime—could persecute good and decent German citizens.[40] One report recorded the comments of a pastor from the Poznan area, who said in a sermon dated August 24, 1942, "Our sons fight Bolshevism in Russia, and at home the church is persecuted and oppressed . . . The floods and food shortages last winter are God's punishment for the suppression of faith in Germany."[41] These comments highlight the hypocrisy of the popular belief that the Nazis are the defenders of German tradition (including Christianity) against the "godless" communists. It is not known what happened to this pastor.

While the Nazi regime may have pursued the formulation of a unified *Volksgemeinschaft*, this research indicates that pastors' sermons had the potential to undermine the regime and even divide the community, or at least to offer another narrative critical of the Nazi vision.[42] In the early 1930s, the Nazi regime offered the German people "a new improved version of national life," one that promised security and prosperity, and they did this through a variety of media, including radio, film, newspapers and magazines, and even advertising.[43] As Peter Fritzsche has argued, "Coordination was a process of dissolution *and* affiliation" (italics in original), and the Nazi propaganda machine was critical to inculcating the National Socialist vision.[44] The Nazi regime constantly reaffirmed this vision of a racial and ethnic community, which enabled it to effectively pursue policies of racial discrimination, deportation, mass killings, and war amid an approving German public.[45] Robert Gellately writes, "In attempting to forge that 'community,' which was based on a maddening logic of sameness, purity, and homogeneity, [the Nazis] and the German people got caught up in a murderous game of pillorying, excluding, and eventually eliminating unwanted social 'elements' and 'race enemies.'"[46] The press informed the German public about the concentration camps and antisemitic discrimination—the German public approved of these measures as a means to the fulfillment of the *Volksgemeinschaft*.[47] These sermons as reported by the Gestapo and SD reveal room to criticize this Nazi vision and to undermine national unity.

The critical remarks in these sermons undermined the regime and its leaders as unjust persecutors of the German churches and Christians, and thus destabilized their legitimacy as the God-instituted rulers of the state. This criticism asserts not only that the Nazi dictatorship was unjust in its treatment of its citizens, but that the leadership was in some sense anti-Christian and thus at odds with the tradition of the German Reformation. Furthermore, it calls into question Hitler's and many Nazi leader's claims to be Christians themselves or at least respectful of the Christian tradition.[48]

But again, one should not over-emphasize the oppositional nature of these sermons. The Gestapo and SD reports do not reveal sermons offering a sustained attack on Hitler, National Socialism, or the regime's policies. There are no calls for Germans to sabotage or otherwise fight against the regime, military, or secret police. Nor are there any sermons that call for organized and united action against the state. Instead, they are isolated comments in the context of pastors' theological reflections.

IN SUPPORT OF THE JEWS AND JUDAISM

Gestapo and SD reports indicate that the Nazi regime was deeply concerned when pastors defended Christianity's Jewish roots from the pulpit. Any connection to Judaism or the Jewish founders of the Christian faith was suspect. For example, one report describes how a pastor, the aforementioned Ulricht of Prenzlau, lamented the paganization of Christianity in the one year since the establishment of the Nazi dictatorship.[49] In his January 1, 1934, sermon, Ulricht drew a connection between the Christ whom the Nazis "forgot" and how the Jews were denied full participation in German life. "If a Jew cannot be a German, so can he very well—and I stress this explicitly—be a good Christian."[50] This statement not only condemns Nazi ideology and those who "forget" Christ, but at the same time the sermon connects into one community all individuals who desire to be Christian, regardless of ethnicity or nationality. Ulricht's statement caught the attention of the Gestapo because he claimed Jesus was a Jew, contrary to the pro-Nazi German Christian movement. Furthermore, he asserted that Jews can indeed be good Christians, even if Nazis declared they cannot even be good Germans. He is pointing out the absurdity of the Nazi position from a distinctly Christian point of view. Ulricht affirmed that German identity, in truth, is less important than Christian identity and that Christian identity is intricately tied to Jewish foundations.

Another Gestapo report mentions Pastor August Schäfer from Greetsiel who made a similar assertion nearly a month later in February 1934. Schäfer publicly repudiated the Aryan Paragraph saying, "the Jews are [God's] people as we are. Jesus and his Apostles had been Jews themselves."[51] The parish council, which was composed of National Socialists, later deposed Schäfer from his seat on the council because of such remarks.[52] The unequivocal assertion of the connection between Christian origins and Judaism directly contradicted Nazi conceptions of "Aryan" superiority. Ultimately, the Nazi concern with pastors affirming the Jewish foundations of Christianity rests on the belief in Aryan supremacy.

To Hitler and the Nazis, salvation cannot come from the Jews, for they are agents of corruption and destruction. To assert otherwise is a blatant contradiction of National Socialism. This is why the SD reported one Pastor Lindenmeyer for an "anti-state sentiment" when he wrote on a broadsheet in March 1935, "If it has however pleased God to reveal himself in the Jewish people, so should it also please us, that salvation is not of the Aryans, but as Christ says, is of the Jews."[53] The SD interpreted this religious conviction that salvation is of the Jews as an "anti-state sentiment" because it undermined Nazi racial ideology, which was the basis of the Nazi *Weltanschauung*.

A common theme found in the Gestapo and SD reports is that Christians and Jews have the same God, thus binding the two peoples together in a common religious tradition. For example, a Gestapo report from Berlin on December 1, 1939, relates that a Confessing Church pastor by the name of Kurt Eberle in Hundsbach (in the district of Kreuznach) was arrested because he said in a sermon, "The God of our Church is the Jewish God of Jacob, to whom I confess . . . In 1932, I stood in Saarbrücken together with 3000 faithful Protestants. Since that time, more and more are falling away from the Protestant faith."[54] This report is unique because it reports a rare instance of the Nazi regime actually arresting a pastor solely due to the content of a sermon. But what is more, the "offensive" remarks were not about Hitler or the Nazi leadership *per se*. Instead, the pastor was arrested for publicly acknowledging that the Christian God is the Jewish God and that Christianity is in decline in the Third Reich. The offense was in identifying the Jewish God as the Christian God, and that indeed Christianity owes much to Judaism. The assertion that Christians and Jews have the same God closely binds the two together as God's people, and this contradicts Nazi racial ideology that denigrates Jews as inferior and degenerate human beings.

Likewise, a brief Gestapo report on January 17, 1934, records the words Pastor Preising from Helsen, who, in a Bible study, raised eyebrows when he said, "All salvation comes from the Jews" (this sentence is underlined in the original report).[55] While Preising did not say this in a sermon, but rather a Bible study, it gives an indication of Gestapo concerns about the public discussion of the gospel message. His assertion about the Jews is the only one recorded in this report and, apparently, it was the main reason the Gestapo took notice of him. Pastor Preising simply publicly affirmed the chosen-ness of the Jewish people and that they are a source of blessing. The Gestapo took the time to spy on pastors who simply affirmed that the Jews and Christians had the same God and that God's salvation "comes from the Jews." The question is why would the Gestapo appear so concerned with a theological claims such as this? The answer is that National Socialism unequivocally asserts that the Jews are the source of evil and destruction. Contrary to Preising's assertion, the Nazi formula was essentially, "All corruption comes from the Jews." Preising's assertion directly opposes National Socialism, and thus the Gestapo's concern.

However, just because a pastor affirmed that the Jews are the people of God did not necessarily mean that his sermons were free of anti-Judaic tropes. A Gestapo report from the city of Hannover on January 26, 1934, gives an account of a sermon by Pastor Grotjahn in the town of Hary, in which he asserted that the Jews were the special people of God and that Jesus must be understood in a Jewish context. But in asserting that the Jews are the chosen people of God, he warns his fellow Germans that one must not "push racial idolization" like the Jews lest he face the same divine chastisement. The report quotes Grotjahn as saying,

> The cradle of Jesus stood in the middle of the Jewish people; the Jewish people was highly regarded by God . . . It is not good when a people push racial idolization (*Rassenvergötzung*), because even the Jewish people have pushed racial idolization, and were therefore scattered by God to the four winds. The Nordic people [*Das nordische Volk*] should not believe and think that they were preferred by God the Father, no, God is for all peoples the father and almighty.[56]

The example demonstrates the common occurrence of a pastor defending the Jewish foundation of Christianity and the Jewish-ness of Jesus, yet at the same time criticizing the Jews using anti-Judaic tropes. In this case, the pastor criticized the Jews for what he interpreted as their racial exclusiveness, or in other words, their "chosen-ness," and offered the Jewish diaspora as "proof" of divine punishment. This alone likely did not catch the attention of the Gestapo, but rather the assertion that the "Nordic people" were like the Jews as racial idolaters. Furthermore, Grotjahn argued that the "Aryans" were not the favored, or "chosen," of God, thus undermining the Nazi claim to the racial superiority of the "Aryan" race. Pastor Grotjahn remarkably uses an anti-Judaic trope (God's punishment of the Jews) to criticize the Nazis for the same crime the Jews supposedly committed, "racial idolization."

As has been previously shown, the leadership of the oppositional Confessing Church often compared Jews and Nazis in their views of race and Volk, so as to criticize the Nazi regime, its leadership, and National Socialism, especially after the mid-1930s. Pastors at times gave expression to their views of Jews to challenge Nazi racism. Historians such as Tal and Haynes have demonstrated that the Confessing Church leadership commonly voiced anti-Judaic tropes in anti-Nazi rhetoric.[57] This strategy to challenge the Nazi worldview emphasized that both Jews and Nazis were purveyors of a false ethno-nationalist identity, an approach that implicitly draws on the traditional antisemitic trop of "tribalism," the notion of the superiority of one's own racial or ethnic group over others.[58] As previously demonstrated, Confessing Church leaders made these same criticisms in sermons as part of worship services and not simply in the secular public sphere. Pastors utilized overt anti-Judaic tropes with implicit antisemitic overtones, in a religious context, to condemn a political system and its ideology.

Nevertheless, the pro-Jewish statements in pastors' sermons did not explicitly advocate resistance against the Nazi state or even unity with the German Jews experiencing Nazi persecution. Instead, they sought to make connections between Christians and Jews based on a common cultural and religious tradition. Statements like those from Lindenmeyer, Schäfer, Ulricht, and others, concerned the Nazi regime because the implication was that Christians who remain true to historic Christianity simply cannot join hands with the Nazis to de-Judaize the faith or the churches. The Gestapo and SD reports reveal that Christians in Nazi Germany were publicly struggling to maintain their historic Jewish foundations within the context of worship services. Furthermore, these sermons are evidence that the German churches became sites in German society where pastors (within narrow limits) could publically express anti-Nazi ideas and pro-Jewish sentiment simultaneously.

There is another reason why the Nazi regime would have been so concerned about pastors making these pro-Jewish statements. The sense of a shared religious tradition has the potential to cultivate a shared sense of community among Jews and Christians. While preaching a shared tradition will by no means inevitably serve to advance inter-religious dialogue and strengthen relationships, the potential is there. Gushee's research presented in *Righteous Gentiles* insightfully demonstrates that a commonly cited religious motivation for Christians to intervene was "a strong sense of religious kinship with

Jews as a people."⁵⁹ Among rescuers, there was often an acknowledged bond between Christians and Jews and gratitude for the Jewish tradition. This is one key reason why the Nazi police apparatus could not countenance Christians preaching these pro-Jewish statements. Every time preachers reminded their Christians parishioners that Jesus was Jewish, that Mary, the apostles, and all the prophets of Israel were Jewish—and that the faith of Jews is the foundation of the Christian faith—a building block was laid in constructing a bridge between Jews and Christians in Nazi Germany. And if such a bridge were built, National Socialism would lose its coherence, as one of its main pillars was the claim that Jews were racially inferior and a source of corruption in society. The Nazi regime could not countenance pastors claiming that Jews were spiritual cousins, the people of God, for this claim would undermine its ideological basis and threaten its stability. Thus, the Gestapo and the SD were understandably concerned when pastors preached on the Jewish foundations of Christianity. Such statements had the potential to undermine Nazi policies of Jewish exclusion, Aryanization, ghettoization, and extermination. Given this research, the Gestapo and the SD were right to be concerned when pastors preached on the Jewish foundations of Christianity. Such statements had the potential to undermine Nazi policies of Jewish exclusion, Aryanization, ghettoization, and extermination.

CONCLUSION

The Gestapo and SD reports offer us extraordinary insights into the critical messages pastors expressed from the pulpit under the Nazi regime. This research demonstrates that clergymen took advantage of the unique space of the sanctuary in Nazi Germany to voice opposition and to debate the spiritual problems that have led to the conditions of conflict, disunity, and compromise among Germans under the regime. And again, these are not the same expressions of dissatisfaction one would find in beer halls, universities, or factory floors. But more to the point, this research demonstrates that the Nazi regime expressed concern for these expressions of opposition, taking names and documenting perceived infractions. Thus, these reports present a unique glimpse into oppositional motivations one would perhaps hear only in the churches. After all, Christians in Germany might have had a variety of religious concerns about Nazi intrusions in the German Protestant churches, such as the problem of preserving the traditions and autonomy of the churches, combating racist and nationalist beliefs that undermined Christian teaching, and defending persecuted co-religionists.

The Gestapo and SD reports provided Hitler and the regime with critical information about popular opinion throughout Nazi society. The reports of pastors' pulpit criticisms corroborates the research of scholars such as Kershaw, Gellately, Johnson, and McDonnough, who have shown that ordinary German citizens offered significant criticisms of Hitler and Nazi policies, in a variety of contexts, even throughout the war.[60]

These sermons present evidence of three distinct criticisms of the Nazi regime, each expressed from the basis of religious conviction. First, they condemned National Socialism as a "false belief," and furthermore, one that supported the worship or undue reverence of false idols. Second, the sermons condemned Nazi or pro-Nazi supporters' persecution of the German churches and Christians, even portraying the Nazi persecutors as anti-Christian or pagan. And third, they criticized the Nazi de-judaization of Christianity and the churches. For some devout Christians, these religiously based criticisms might have tipped the balance against the Nazis and National Socialism. At the very least, the Gestapo and SD reports indicate the regime was concerned about these criticisms and their ability to undermine the German *Volksgemeinschaft*. Thus, they kept a close eye on opposition from behind the pulpit.

Yet the Gestapo and SD files do not often state what happened to the pastors, how the information was used, or if the information became part of a case against particular pastors. Remarkably, I have found only a couple instances of the Gestapo arresting a pastor after expressing criticism of the Nazi state.[61] Pastors might be harassed or arrested for a reputation of voicing critical comments about the Nazi regime, but the historical evidence suggests it was rare for a pastor to be arrested and incarcerated simply for making a critical comment from the pulpit. For example, the popular Dahlem pastor Martin Niemöller made frequent and extraordinary critical comments about the regime from 1933 to 1937 before he was finally incarcerated by the Gestapo. Likewise, as previously discussed, the ministries of Bonhoeffer, Vogel, and Schneider support this conclusion. This evidence indicates that the Gestapo treated ordinary Germans differently than they treated those deemed outside the *Volksgemeinschaft*, such as German pastors of Jewish descent. As long as pastors did not criticize the regime too often or too severely, the Gestapo and SD appears to have simply taken note and kept an eye on them. It should also be noted that the reports do not provide specific information about the sources of information, that is, whether sources were civilian informants or Gestapo spies. In short, more research is necessary to identify the individuals responsible for providing the Gestapo and SD with information, and also to determine the specific consequences for pastors who spoke out against the regime from the pulpit.

But can one trust the Gestapo and SD reports to accurately reflect what pastors actually said from the pulpits? Could they have fabricated these oppositional statements to cast dissenting pastors in a negative light, and thus legitimize action against them? While this is a possibility, the oppositional statements recorded by the Gestapo and SD correspond in kind and severity with the messages found in over 900 Confessing Church sermon manuscripts delivered by 95 pastors during the Nazi years, which I have examined for this study. The sermons themselves are the best corroboration of the evidence in the Gestapo and SD reports. The messages correspond to the same messages found in Gestapo and SD reports: the condemnation of Nazism as a false ideology, the criticism of Nazi persecution of Christians and the churches, and the challenge to Nazi antisemitism by supporting Jews as the chosen people of God and Judaism as the historical foundation of Christianity.[62]

This research suggests Gestapo and SD spies dutifully recorded the criticisms they actually heard from the pulpit. The Gestapo and SD reports reflect the same kinds of limited but publicly expressed statements of opposition found in Confessing Church sermons. Also, all the Confessing pastors' criticisms of the Nazi regime, its leadership, and ideology are framed in short, concise statements within a sermon on a biblical (not political) theme. The pastors' criticisms are not fully developed into sermons; rather they are always briefly stated in the larger context of a biblical story or theological reflection. This, too, corresponds to the evidence in the Gestapo and SD reports.

My analysis confirms the arguments of historians such as Hoffmann and Kershaw that the German churches were among the only institutions in Germany able to withstand Nazi "coordination" to the regime and its values, thus giving them a modicum of freedom to criticize the Nazi regime and its ideology.[63] These Gestapo and SD reports reveal just how concerned the Nazi regime was with this freedom. The evidence suggests that the German churches had the potential to become sites of criticism against the regime, its ideology, and its persecutions against Christians. But also, the churches could be sites of support and sympathy for Jews in Nazi Germany, a place where Christians could develop their imagination—based on common theological concepts and stories—to place themselves in the situations of persecuted Jews. Nevertheless, the occasional and limited nature of the criticisms was apparently insufficient to inspire significant action against the Nazi state or in support of persecuted Jews.

NOTES

1. This chapter has been previously published in *Church History and Religious Culture* (2018). It has been reprinted with permission.

2. The reports have been gathered from the Bundesarchiv in Berlin (BA), specifically the Papers of the Reichssicherheitshauptamt, and the published source from

editor Heinz Boberach, *Berichte des SD und der Gestapo über Kirchen und Kirchenvolk in Deutschland 1934–1944* (Mainz, 1971).

3. See Jacques Delarue, *Gestapo: A History of Horror* (New York, 2008), Kindle edition; Eric Johnson, *Nazi Terror: The Gestapo, Jews, and Ordinary Germans* (New York, 1999); Frank McDonough, *The Gestapo: The Myth and Reality of Hitler's Secret Police* (New York, 2017); and Robert Gellately, *The Gestapo and German Society: Enforcing Racial Policy 1933–1945* (New York, 1990).

4. See Barnett, *For the Soul of the People*; Conway, *The Nazi Persecution of the Churches, 1933–1945*; and Gerlach, *And the Witnesses Were Silent*.

5. See Barnett, *For the Soul of the People*; Gerlach, *And the Witnesses Were Silent*; Littell and Locke, *The German Church Struggle and the Holocaust*; Phayer, *The Catholic Church and the Holocaust*; and Spicer, *Resisting the Third Reich*.

6. Johnson, *Nazi Terror*, 373. See, for example, Andrew Stewart Bergerson, *Ordinary Germans in Extraordinary Times: The Nazi Revolution in Hildesheim* (Bloomington, 2004), 160–162; and Detlef Schmiechen-Ackermann, *Nationalsozialismus und Arbeitermilieus: Der nationalsozialistische Angriff auf die proletarischen Wohnquartiere und die Reaktion in den sozialistischen Vereinen* (Bonn, 1998), 639–642.

7. McDonough, *The Gestapo*; Johnson, *Nazi Terror*; and Gellately, *The Gestapo and German Society*.

8. See McDonough, *The Gestapo*, 129; and Gellately, *Backing Hitler*, Kindle location 1175–1193.

9. Johnson, *Nazi Terror*, 231. However, Jantzen provides evidence of a few cases where students denounced pastors who taught their religious classes in school or confirmation classes. See for example, Jantzen, *Faith and Fatherland*, 196–197.

10. Johnson, *Nazi Terror*, 231.

11. See Wolfgang Dierker, *Himmlers Glaubenskrieger: Der Sicherheitsdienst der SS und seine Religionspolitik 1933–1941* (Paderborn, 2002), 51–59.

12. McDonough, *The Gestapo*, 65; Delarue, *Gestapo*, Kindle Edition, location 6482.

13. Barnett, *For the Soul of the People*, 77.

14. Johnson, *Nazi Terror*, 47.

15. Niemöller, *Here Stand I!* translated by Jane Lymburn (New York, 1937), 226.

16. McDonough, *The Gestapo*, 158. See also Johnson, *Nazi Terror*, 283–284.

17. McDonough, *The Gestapo*, 66. See also Johnson, *Nazi Terror*, 227.

18. Barnett, *For the Soul of the People*, 83.

19. Barnett, *For the Soul of the People*, 83.

20. Gestapo Report on Pastor Heinrich Grüber: "Staatsfeindliches Verhalten evangelischer Geistlicher, v.a. der Bekennenden Kirche, 1934–1935," Papers of the Reichssicherheitshauptamt, BA R58/5679.

21. *Delarue, Gestapo*, Kindle edition, location 826.

22. Gestapo Report on Pastor Kurt Scharf: "Staatsfeindliches Verhalten evangelischer Geistlicher, v.a. der Bekennenden Kirche, 1934–1935." Papers of the Reichssicherheitshauptamt. BA R58/5679. Another similar comment was made by a superintendent from Insterburg named Federmann, who called the Hitler Youth leader Baldur von Schirach a "neo-pagan"; see Gestapo Report: "Beobachtung der

Vorläufigen Kirchenleitung der Deutschen Evangelischen Kirche, 1936–1937." R58/5670.

23. Gestapo Report on Pastor Lemke of Templin: "Staatsfeindliches Verhalten evangelischer Geistlicher, v.a. der Bekennenden Kirche, 1934–1935." Papers of the Reichssicherheitshauptamt. BA R58/5679.

24. Boberach, *Berichte des SD und der Gestapo*, 63–78.

25. Boberach, *Berichte des SD und der Gestapo*, 76.

26. Boberach, *Berichte des SD und der Gestapo*, 76.

27. Boberach, *Berichte des SD und der Gestapo*, 76.

28. Ian Kershaw, *Hitler: A Biography* (New York, 2008), Kindle edition, location 7203–7309.

29. Boberach, *Berichte des SD und der Gestapo*, 454.

30. Boberach, *Berichte des SD und der Gestapo*, 454.

31. Boberach, *Berichte des SD und der Gestapo*, 361. The report does not indicate the names of pastors behind this portrayal, but it does mention the Niemöller Office in Berlin-Dahlem.

32. Boberach, *Berichte des SD und der Gestapo*, 421.

33. Michael Burleigh, *The Third Reich: A New History* (New York, 2000), 252–255.

34. Gestapo Report on Pastor Ulricht: "Staatsfeindliches Verhalten evangelischer Geistlicher, v.a. der Bekennenden Kirche, 1934–1935," Papers of the Reichssicherheitshauptamt, BA R58/5679.

35. McDonough, *The Gestapo*, 65–66.

36. McDonough, *The Gestapo*, 65.

37. Gestapo Report on Pastor Gerhard Nierlich, dated August 4, 1939, Papers of the Reichssicherheitshauptamt, "Informationen des Geheimen Staatspolizeiamtes," BA R58/7010.

38. Boberach, *Berichte des SD und der Gestapo*, 352. Apparently, distributing leaflets in mailboxes was a modus operandi of the Jehovah's Witnesses. Johnson argues, "the majority of Witnesses brazzenly demonstrated their opposition to the Nazi regime by stuffing mailboxes and doorsteps with literature that pointed out specific instances of Nazi atrocities, cited Gestapo, police, and Nazi Party torturers by name, and called upon the German people to turn away from the false prophet Hitler and to place their faith in the true savior, Jesus Christ." Johnson, *Nazi Terror*, 239.

39. Boberach, *Berichte des SD und der Gestapo*, 401.

40. Point 24 of the Nazi Party platform stated the demand for the "freedom for all religious confessions in the state" and asserted that "the Party as such stands for positive Christianity." Matheson, *The Third Reich and the Christian Churches*, 1.

41. Boberach, *Berichte des SD und der Gestapo*, 720.

42. Ian Kershaw has argued that material conditions that affected people's everyday lives "provided the most continuous, and usually the most dominant, influence upon the formation of public opinion." Kershaw, *Popular Opinion and Political Dissent in the Third Reich*, 373. More recent research has indicated that the Nazi regime was largely successful in making the *Volksgemeinschaft* a reality. See Peter Fritzsche, *Germans into Nazis* (Cambridge, 1998) and *Life and Death in the Third Reich* (Cambridge, 2008); and Robert Gellately, *Backing Hitler*.

43. Fritzsche, *Life and Death in the Third Reich*, 37. See also Carolyn Birdsall, *Nazi Soundscapes: Sound, Technology and Urban Space in Germany, 1933–1945* (Amsterdam, 2012), 136.

44. Fritzsche, *Life and Death in the Third Reich*, 51; and Fritzsche, *Germans into Nazis*, 193–196.

45. Gellately, *Backing Hitler*, Kindle edition, location 6315.

46. Gellately, *Backing Hitler*, Kindle edition, location 6430.

47. Gellately, *Backing Hitler*, Kindle edition, location 304.

48. Steigmann-Gall, *The Holy Reich*, 3.

49. Gestapo Report on Pastor Ulricht: "Staatsfeindliches Verhalten evangelischer Geistlicher, v.a. der Bekennenden Kirche, 1934–1935," Papers of the Reichssicherheitshauptamt, BA R58/5679.

50. Gestapo Report on Pastor Ulricht, "Staatsfeindliches Verhalten evangelischer Geistlicher," BA R58/5679.

51. Gestapo Report on Pastor Ulricht, "Staatsfeindliches Verhalten evangelischer Geistlicher," BA R58/5679.

52. Gestapo Report on Pastor Ulricht, "Staatsfeindliches Verhalten evangelischer Geistlicher," BA R58/5679.

53. Boberach, *Berichte des SD und der Gestapo*, 77.

54. Boberach, *Berichte des SD und der Gestapo*, 376.

55. Gestapo Report on Pastor Preising: "Staatsfeindliches Verhalten evangelischer Geistlicher, v.a. der Bekennenden Kirche, 1934–1935," Papers of the Reichssicherheitshauptamt, BA R58/5679.

56. Gestapo Report on Pastor Grotjahn: "Staatsfeindliches Verhalten evangelischer Geistlicher, v.a. der Bekennenden Kirche, 1934–1935," Papers of the Reichssicherheitshauptamt, BA R58/5679.

57. Tal, "On Structures of Political Theology and Myth in Germany Prior to the Holocaust," 122; and Haynes, "Who Needs Enemies?" 350-367.

58. Haynes, "Who Needs Enemies?" 344-347.

59. Gushee, *Righteous Gentiles*, Kindle edition, location 2807.

60. Johnson, *Nazi Terror*; Kershaw, *Popular Opinion*; McDonough, *The Gestapo*; and Gellately, *Gestapo and German Society*.

61. For example, Pastor Eberle in Hundsbach was arrested for stating that the God of the Jews is the God of the Church as well.

62. It should be noted that pastors at times revealed anti-Jewish prejudice in their sermons, often at the same time as voicing comments in support.

63. See Hoffmann, *The History of German Resistance*, 13; Kershaw, *Hitler, the Germans, and the Final Solution*, 166.

Chapter 10

Conclusion

This study has examined the messages Confessing Church pastors preached to German communities of faith about the Nazi regime, its ideology, and the Jews and Judaism. The evidence demonstrates that the sermon was a prominent means by which Confessing Church pastors criticized the regime and its ideology and sought to reorient the perspectives and values of their congregants. My aim throughout this work has been to elucidate and nuance the nature of opposition within the Confessing Church from the pulpits. The sermon manuscripts reveal that Confessing Church pastors voiced limited opposition to the Nazi regime, its ideology, and its policies. By and large, the expressions of opposition served to defend the autonomy and identity of the German churches. The sermons reveal a conversation within the churches about how to address crucial concerns: the Nazi state's imposition of a false ideology, the persecution of Christians under the Nazi regime, and the denigration of Judaism and persecution of Jews. Sermons that addressed these fundamental points are evidence of the pro-active yet limited opposition of Confessing pastors. The critical sermons reveal a degree of freedom, even in wartime, to express criticism and oppose the Nazi state.[1]

The sermons that criticized National Socialism as a false ideology served to undermine the German peoples' adherence to this belief system. They portrayed National Socialism as a morally corrupt ideology that elevated one people, one race, one nation, as intrinsically superior (thereby denigrating all others), and thus, they became oppositional to the priorities and policies of the Nazi state. These sermons publicly undermined the Nazi philosophy of governance and provided an alternative vision for governing a society and nation. The messages had the potential to redirect the allegiance and uncritical obedience of the Christian away from Adolf Hitler and the Nazi state to God and God's kingdom.

The sermons that criticized the Nazi regime as an unjust persecutor of Christians and the German churches served to destabilize its legitimacy. This criticism asserted not only that the Nazi regime was unjust in its treatment of its citizens but that the leadership was in some sense anti-Christian and at odds with the tradition of the German Reformation. Furthermore, it called into question Hitler's and many Nazi leaders' claims to be Christians themselves or at least respectful of the Christian tradition.[2] These criticisms cast the pro-Nazi persecutors of Christians as enemies of God and the church, serving to reorient the perspectives of congregants listening to the sermons.

Confessing Church pastors occasionally used anti-Judaic tropes in their sermons, which could be understood to support Nazi claims about the inferiority of the Jews. These sermons reveal ambivalence among Confessing Church pastors about Judaism and the Jewish people and a millennia-long ingrained prejudice that came to the surface. Even when pastors wished to support the Jewish people and affirm the value of Judaism as the foundation of Christianity, embedded anti-Judaic theology in the churches confused what could have been a clearer message to the Christian faithful in Nazi Germany. Yet Confessing pastors often used these anti-Judaic tropes to critique or challenge the antisemitism of the Nazi regime, the German Christian movement, or Germans generally. Even Confessing Church heroes such as Niemöller and Hinz, for example, argued that both the Jews of ancient Israel and the Germans (and more specifically Nazis) of their own day had hardened their hearts; both are race-conscious and emphasize racial purity; and both are assured of their "chosen-ness" and divinely-bestowed superiority. These messages demonstrate that anti-Judaic expressions were not often simply extemporaneous comments or simply meant to denigrate Jews in German society, but that they were often utilized purposefully to criticize the Nazi regime and its ideology and racial policies.

The sermons that supported Jews and Judaism, or that condemned Nazi persecution of Jews, undermined Nazi racial ideology and policies. Confessing Church pastors affirmed that the Jews are the people of God and that Judaism is a foundation of Christianity that cannot be denied. The importance of these sermons as oppositional to the regime is reflected in the Gestapo and SD reports that identify pastors who supported Jews and Judaism in this way. This research underscores the potential of the sermon as a means to bind the Christian community of faith to the Jewish people, an instrument that was unfortunately not used sufficiently enough in Nazi Germany.

The sermons of the Confessing Church reveal limits to the opposition of Confessing Church pastors, as would be expected under Nazi totalitarianism. The pastors did not explicitly preach against Hitler's legitimacy as the Chancellor of Germany, and they did not argue against the Christian's subjection to the Nazi state as the governing authority. Nor are there explicit calls for Christians to defy Nazi laws to aid persecuted Jews. Nevertheless, the comments indicate that Confessing Church pastors infrequently but publicly sought to undermine Nazi leaders, ideology, and policies through critical messages in their sermons.

While the sermon manuscripts reveal limited opposition from the pulpits of the Confessing Church, it is entirely possible, and perhaps likely, that pastors offered dissent and opposition in various other ways that cannot be documented in the church records. A pastor could simply read a Scripture passage and repeat key words or phrases, or compel reflection with pregnant pauses, to admonish his congregation and encourage them to align their beliefs with their actions. For example, a pastor may base a sermon on Matthew 22:37–39, in which Jesus speaks to an expert in the law about the most important commandment. Jesus says, "'You shall love the Lord your God with all your heart and with all your soul and with all your mind.' And a second is like it: 'you shall love your neighbor as yourself.'" The pastor could repeat the word "love," changing his tone with each iteration to express emotion, or he could inflect his voice with empathy at the word "neighbor." The pastor could creatively use his voice in a myriad of ways when reading this text to express dissent or opposition to Nazi ideology and policies. One's voice can carry manifold meanings that sermon manuscripts simply cannot preserve. Thus, the sermons should be understood to reflect one facet of how Confessing Church pastors opposed the Nazi regime from within the walls of the sanctuary.

One may well argue that the true significance of this research is that it reveals that the vast majority of sermons did not, in fact, criticize or in any way oppose the Nazi state. As emphasized earlier, Confessing Church members were united only on a single point: they wanted the Nazi regime to stay out of the affairs of the German churches.[3] They were all committed to halting any National Socialist infringements into Christian theology and practice—this was a religious struggle. One might contend, in other words, that pastors were not interested in a political struggle but sought to unite to oppose Nazi efforts to undermine church autonomy. Based on this research one might conclude that Confessing pastors simply provided parishioners with a way to retreat from the political sphere in the Third Reich, and in doing so, that the churches actually discouraged dissent.[4]

This criticism is valid. Yet it is important to understand the degree and nature of opposition such as it was within the churches. The pastors never rallied parishioners to overthrow the regime or incited violence against the state or its officials—such acts would have been virtually inconceivable. Yet the pastors publicly criticized the regime on matters pertinent to their own ministries in the Protestant churches. They were concerned about Nazism as a false ideology in competition with Christianity, Nazi persecution of Christians, and the denigration of Judaism and the persecution of Jews.

The expressions of opposition were framed and bound by the genre of the sermon, which is based on Scripture, informed by tradition, and shaped by the other elements in the worship service. The pastors had to walk a fine line in expressing criticisms while at the same time maintaining the purpose of the sermon, which is to edify and convert listeners, to bring them closer to God and one another. To focus inordinately on criticisms of the state and its ideology in a sermon would potentially transgress the proper boundaries of the sermon. The pastor's job was to preach the gospel, not deliver diatribes, which meant conforming the message appropriately to the genre of a sermon in the setting of a worship service.

The history of preaching in Nazi Germany, and in the Confessing Church in particular, raises questions about how preachers understood their task in Nazi Germany. Bonhoeffer once wrote, "As a witness to Christ, the sermon is a struggle with demons. Every sermon must overcome Satan. Every sermon fights a battle."[5] His statement presupposes that the pastors recognized the "demons" to be overcome. This history of preaching raises the question of whether the pastors clearly recognized the "demons" in Nazi Germany to cast out, the "demons" that threatened the churches, the Jews, the German nation, European peoples, and the world. This research has shown that many Confessing pastors indeed recognized and publicly named some of these "demons" in the pulpit, specifically those the Nazi regime introduced into the churches, the false ideology and idol worship that sparked division and fueled the persecution of the churches. Yet the evidence also reveals a lack of consistent, explicit, and vigorous condemnation of the multitude of "demons" in Nazi Germany from the pulpit. Again, one cannot forget that pastors could have expressed dissent and opposition in a myriad of ways from the pulpit. Suggestive pauses, revealing hand gestures, and the rising and declining intensity of speech could add meaning and nuance—inferring dissent and opposition—that is not reflected in the historical record.

At the same time, this research raises questions about how pastors understood the power or ability of preaching to actually "struggle with demons," in Bonhoeffer's words. In the history of Christianity the clergy and religious have often been considered the "soldiers" of God, whose weapons to combat evil were not fashioned with iron or infused with gun powder. Rather, their weapons were prayer and the preaching of the gospel, a distinctive arsenal for combatting the "demons" of National Socialism. Yet this research indicates many pastors may not have sufficiently utilized the weapons at their disposal to combat the "demons" that lurked in Nazi Germany. The new school of homiletics that emerged in the early- and mid-1930s contributed to limiting the scope of the sermon, focusing the preacher's attention on Scripture alone rather than also on how Scripture challenged the community of faith in Nazi Germany. This research points to the need for pastors to balance a

Scripture-centric approach to preaching with a clear and incisive reflection and application of how the Scripture speaks to the challenges Christians face in the world. And again, there is more than one way to express criticism in a sermon—implicitly and explicitly. The history of preaching in the Confessing Church offers an illuminating glimpse into the ministries of pastors who struggled to preach Scripture effectively in a tumultuous time.

NOTES

1. This argument is in agreement with Barnett, *For the Soul of the People*, 55; and Scholder, *The Churches and the Third Reich,* vol. 2.
2. Steigmann-Gall, *The Holy Reich,* 3.
3. Barnett, *For the Soul of the People*, 5.
4. Special thanks to one of my anonymous reviewers for this critique.
5. Clyde Fant, *Bonhoeffer: Worldly Preaching, With Bonhoeffer's Finkenwalde Lectures on Homiletics* (Nashville, TN: Thomas Nelson, 1975), 133.

Selected Bibliography

1. ARCHIVAL SOURCES

Bundesarchiv, Berlin
    Staatsfeindliches Verhalten evangelischer Geistlicher, v.a. der Bekennenden Kirche, 1934–1935, R58

Evangelisches Zentrumarchiv, Berlin
Kirchenkamfarchiv, Bestand 50
    Berliner Predigten, 1937–1944
    Bruderrat Akten
    Bruno Benfey Akten
    Friedrich Forell Akten
    Ernst Gordon Akten
    Gerhard Harder Akten
    Peter Henselmann Akten
    Paul Hinz, Gesammelte Predigten
    Kirchenkampf in Fehrbellin, 1933
    Kirchenkanzlei: Arierparagraph, von September 1933 bis März 1934
        Kirchenkanzlei: Nichtarische Studenten der Theologie und Pfarrer von Juni 1936 bis Dezember 1939
    Erich Klapproth Akten
        Kurt Meschke Akten
        Nichtarische Geistliche Kirchengemeindebeamte, Gemeindevertreter usw., von Oktober 1933 bis Dezember 1952
        Carl-Günther Schweitzer Akten
        Werner Sylten Akten
Heinrich Vogel Akten
Evangelisches Landeskirchliches Archiv in Berlin, Bestand 14
Heinz-Hermuth Arnold Akten
Walter Augustat Akten
Friedrich Flemming Akten

Rudolf Friedberg Akten
Daniel Julius Koschade Akten
Carl Lommatzsche Akten
Paul Mendelson Akten
Fritz Stein Akten
Fritz Otto Richard Suderow Akten
Karl Richard Willi Süssbach Akten
Landeskirchliches Archiv der Evangelischen Kirche von Westfalen, Bielefeld (LKA EKvW)
Hans Ehrenberg Collection, W4891
Das Landeskirchenamt Archiv, *Düsseldorf* (LKA-D)
Peter Brunner Collections 7NL 006, 105/5812/0388
National Library of Scotland (NLS)
Franz Hildebrandt Collection, 9251.53/54
University of Iowa Libraries, Special Collections, Iowa City (UIL)
Newcomers Christian Fellowship Collection
Friedrich Forell Collection, MSC 358

2. PRIMARY SOURCES

Albertz, Martin. *Wen wollt ihr wählen?* Predigt über Josua 24:14–15, in der reform. Kirche zu Neuenhaus, Grafschaft Bentheim, am 7. März 1937. Wuppertal-Elberfeld: Köhler, 1937.

Anton, R. *Alles in Jesu Namen!* Predigt über Kol. 3:17. Berlin-Charlottenburg: Der Freie, 1937.

———. *Gelegen oder Ungelegen. Predigten.* Stuttgart: Schwabenverlag, 1947.

———, ed. *Nationale Feiertagspredigten und Ansprache.* Helingsche Verlagsanstalt Leipzig, 1935.

———. *Predigt in der Jesus-Christus-Kirche*, am Ostermontag, dem 29. März 1937. Wuppertal-Elberfeld: Köhler, 1937.

Bauer, Johannes. "Homiletik" in *Die Religion in Geschichte und Gegenwart: handwörterbuch in gemeinverständlicher Darstellung.* Herausgegeben von Friedrich Michael Schiele und Leopold Ischarnack. Dritter Band, Hesshus bis Lytton. Tübingen: Verlag von J.C.B. Mohr (Paul Siebeck), 1912.

Barth, Karl. *Drei Predigten.* Chr. Kaiser Verlag, 1934.

———. *The Epistle to the Romans*, translated from the sixth edition by Edwyn Hoskyns. New York: Oxford University Press, 1968.

———. *Evangelische Theologie im 19. Jahrhundert.* Zurich: Zollikon, 1957.

———. *Für die Freiheit des Evangeliums.* Chr. Kaiser Verlag, 1933.

———. *Fürchte dich nicht!* Predigten aus den Jahren 1934 bi 1948. München: Chr. Kaiser Verlag, 1949.

———. *Gesegnet ist der Mann . . . Predigt über Jeremia 17, 5–10*, gehalten in der Marktkirche zu Detmold, am 25. November 1934, abends 8 Uhr. - Rheinisch-Westfälischer Gemeindetag "Unter dem Wort," 1934.

———. *Homiletics*. Louisville, KY: Westminster/J. Knox Press, 1991.

———. *Predigt über Kol. 3, 1–4*, gehalten am Himmelfahrtstag 1937 im Münster zu Basel Reinhardt 1937.

———. *"So ihr bleiben werdet . . . " Predigt*, gehalten am 16. Juni 1946, Johannes 8:31. Frankfurt a.M.: Aussaat-Verlag, 1946.

———. *Wirf dein Anliegen auf den Herrn*. Psalm 55, 23; Predigt am 13. Juli 1947 in der Lukas-Kirche Hamburg-Fuhlsbüttel. Reich & Heidrich 1947.

———. *The Word of God and the Word of Man*. New York: Harper & Row, 1957.

Barth, Karl and Eduard Thurneysen, *God's Search for Man*, translated by George W. Richards, Elmer Homrighausen, and Karl Ernst. Edinburgh: T&T Clark, 1935.

Barth, Karl and Ed Thurneysen, eds. *Predigten aus Württemberg*. München: Chr. Kaiser Verlag, 1936.

Baumgärtner, Hans, ed., *Deutsches Christentum dargestellt in Predigt und Vortrag*. Nürnberg: Fr. Städler, 1937.

Boberach, Heinz, ed., *Berichte des SD und der Gestapo über Kirchen und Kirchenvolk in Deutschland 1934–1944*. Mainz: Matthias-Grünewald-Verlag, 1971.

Bodelschwingh, Friedrich von. *Lebendig und Frei: Predigten, 1. u. 2 Folge*. Bielefeld: Verlagshandlung der Anstalt Bethel, 1947.

Bonhoeffer, Dietrich. *Berlin: 1932–1933*. Dietrich Bonhoeffer Works, Vol. 12. Edited by Carsten Nicolaisen and Ernst-Albert Scharffenorth. Translated by Isabel Best and David Higgins. Minneapolis: Fortress Press, 2009.

———. *Conspiracy and Imprisonment: 1940–1945*. Dietrich Bonhoeffer Works, Vol. 16. Edited by Jørgen Glenthøj, Ulrich Kabitz, and Wolf Krötke. Translated by Lisa Dahill. Minneapolis: Fortress Press, 2006.

———. *The Cost of Discipleship*. Translated by R.H. Fuller. New York: Simon & Schuster, 1995.

———. *Ethics*. Translated by Neville Horton Smith. New York: Simon & Schuster, 1995.

———. *Letters and Papers from Prison, New Edition*. New York: Touchstone, 1997.

———. *London, 1933–1935*. Dietrich Bonhoeffer Works, Vol. 13. Edited by Hans Goedeking, Martin Heimbucher, and Hans-Walter Schleicher. Translated by Isabel Best. Minneapolis: Fortress Press, 2007.

———. *Theological Education Underground, 1937–1940*. Dietrich Bonhoeffer Works, Vol. 15. Edited by Dirk Schulz. Translated by Victoria Barnett, Claudia Bergmann, Peter Frick, and Scott A. Moore. Minneapolis, MN: Fortress Press, 2011.

Brandmeyer, Adolf, ed. *Kirchliche Verkünkigung unter Frauen und Müttern. Predigten, Ansprachen, Vorträge und Andachten.* Verlag Bertesmann Gütersloh, 1940.

Brandt, Theodore. *Der gehorsame Gottesdienst.* Predigt über Römer 12:1–2, in Dortmund in der St. Reinholdi-Kirche, am Januar 1937. Wuppertal-Elberfeld: Köhler, 1937

Breit, Thomas. *So kommt der Glaube aus der Predigt, das Prediger aber durch das Wort Gottes.* Predigt über Römer 10:17. München, Chr. Kaiser Verlag, 1936.

Brunner, Emil. *The Mediator: A Study of the Central Doctrine of the Christian Faith.* Philadelphia: Westminster Press, 1947.

Brunner, Peter. *Die Zehn Gebote Gottes.* Wuppertal-Barmen: Vollmer, 1945.

———. *Predigt über Lukas 22:35–38.* Wuppertal-Elberfeld: Köhler, 1937.

Buesing, W. Deutschhausen, H. Ehrenberg, F. Hildebrandt, H. Kramm, J. Rieger, C. Schweitzer, "Letter to the Editor," *The Times.* London, Saturday, 02 January 1943, Issue 49433.

Calvin, John. *Institutes of the Christian Religion.* Translated by Henry Beveridge. Peabody, MA: Hendrickson, 2008.

Delekat, Friedrich. *Ich glaube, darum rede ich. Glaubenszeugnis einer mitbekennenden Gemeinde: Zwölf Predigten.* Furche-Verlag, 1936.

———. *Von Advent bis Pfingsten. Zwei Prediten.* Dresden: Krause, 1934.

Descartes, René. *Meditations on the First Philosophy*, in Great Books of the Western World. Chicago: Encyclopedia Britannica, 1993.

Deutschland-Berichte der Sozialdemokratischen Partei Deutschlands (Sopade), Vierter Jahrgang 1937. Salzhausen: Verlag Petra Nettelbeck, 1980.

Dibelius, Otto. *Ausgerichtet auf Christus allein!* Predigt über Matth. 20, 1–19. Verlag "Der Freie," 1937.

———. *Das Hohelied der Christen auf die Liebe: eine Predigt*, gehalten am 3. April 1949 (Sonntag Judika) in der Berliner St. Marienkirche. Verlag Die Schöpfung, 1949.

———. *Deutschland in der Georgenkirche zu Eisenach.* Christlicher Zeitschriften-Verlag, 1948.

———. *Die Kirche und der Friede: eine Predigt*, gehalten am 1. Mai 1949 (Sonntag Miserikordias Domini) in der Berliner St. Marienkirche. Verlag Die Schöpfung, 1949.

———. *Im Namen Jesu Christi von Nazareth: eine Predigt*, gehalten am 3. Juli 1949. Sonntag nach Trinitatis - in der Berliner St. Marienkirche. Verlag Die Schöpfung, 1949.

———. *Liebe mit der Tat und mit der Wahrheit.* Festpredigt zum 90. Jahresfest des Ev. Johannesstifts, Berlin-Spandau am Himmelfahrtstag, 1948.

———. *Predigten.* Berlin-Dahlem: Verlag die Kirche, 1952.

———. *Um die Einheit der Kirche.* Predigt über Hes. 37, 15–22; Predigt am 11. Juli 1948 zur Eröffnung der Kirchen-Versammlung der Evangelischen Kirche in Deutschland. Berlin: Selbstverlag der EKD, 1961.

———. *Wie Christen wählen.* Predigt am Sonntag Exaudi über Apostelgesch. 1, 15–26. Verlag Der Freie, 1937.

———. *Wir sind Gottes Mitarbeiter.* Christlicher Zeitschriftenverlag, 1946.

Diem, Hermann. *Folge mir nach!* Predigt über Joh. 21:15–24, am 11 April 1937 in Ebersbach, a.d. Fils. Stuttgart: Verlag der Evang. Gesellschaft, 1937.

———. *Warum Textpredigt? Predigten und Kritiken als Beitrag zur Lehre von der Predigt.* München: Kaiser, 1939.

Döhring, Bruno. *Das Vaterunser mitten ins Leben hinein!* Eine Predigtreihe im Dom zu Berlin geh. Berlin: Beenken, 1938.

Ehrenberg, Hans. *Autobiography of a German Pastor*. London: Student Christian Movement Press, 1943.
———. *Drei Predigten*. Bochum: F.W. Fretlöw, 1937.
Falke, D. Robert, ed. *Wenn du glauben könntest? Ein Jahrgang Predigten für die Gegenwart über Zeit und Ewigkeit*. München: Verlag Paul Müller, 1939.
Fant, Clyde. *Bonhoeffer: Worldly Preaching, With Bonhoeffer's Finkenwalde Lectures on Homiletics*. Nashville, TN: Thomas Nelson, 1975.
Fendt, Leonhard. *Grundriss der Praktischen Theologie für Studenten und Kandidaten. Abteilungen 1–3. Grundlegung, Lehre von d. Kirche, vom Amt und von d. Predigt*. Tübingen: Mohr, 1949.
———. *Zur Predigt in der Kirche des Dritten Reichs*.
Fezer, Karl. *Das Wort Gottes und die Predigt* (1925). Stuttgart: Calwer Vereinsbuchhandlung, 1926.
———. "Predigt" in *Die Religion in Geschichte und Gegenwart: Handwörterbuch für Theologie und Religionswissenschaft*. In Verbindung mit Alfred Bertholet, Hermann Faber, und Horst Stephan. Herausgegeben von Hermann Gunkel und Leopold Ischarnack. Vierter Band, Mi-R. Verlag von J.C.S. Mohr (Paul Siebeck).
Fischer, Otto. "Arische Abstammung und Evangelische Pfarrer," in *Deutsches Pfarrerblatt* (October 31, 1933), 607–610.
Frick, Friedrich. *Predigt über Lukas 10:38–42*, in Bonn am 24. Januar 1937 in der Kirche zu Poppelsdorf. Wuppertal-Elberfeld: Köhler, 1937.
Gohl, Wilhelm, ed. *Kirchengebete, insbesondere Fürbittegebete für den Predigtgottesdienst und die Betstunde*. Chr. Kaiser Verlag, München, 1940.
Gollwitzer, Helmut. *Wir dürfen Ihren . . . Predigten*. Chr. Kaiser Verlag, 1941.
Gollwitzer Helmut und Eva Bildt. *Ich will Dir schnell sagen, dass ich lebe, Liebster: Briefe aus dem Krieg, 1940–1945*, herausgegeben von Friedrich Künzel und Ruth Pabst. Verlag C.H. Beck, 2008.
Gräber, Fr. *Zweierlei Hoffnung. Zwei Predigten. Eine Stimme aus der Kirche unter dem Kreuz*, Nr. 9. Essen: Freizeiten Verlang, 1935.
Grüber, Heinrich. *Leben an der Todeslinie. Dachauer Predigten*. Berlin: Kreuz Verlag, 1965.
Harder, Günther. *Predigt, Johannes 15:26- bis 16:1–4*, zur Eröffnung der 5. Preussensynode in Halle am 9. Mai 1937. Wuppertal-Elberfeld: Köhler, 1937.
———. Untitled sermon in Fehrbellin, am 30. Mai 1936. Berlin: Montanusdruck, 1936.
Harnack, Adolf von. *What is Christianity?* New York: Harper & Row, 1957.
Hein, Karl. *Predigt über Matth. 7:15–16*, am 22 Juli 1934. Wuppertal-Elberfeld: Köhler, 1934.
Heppe, Bernhard. *Predigt über Matth. 28:18–20*, Coelbe b. Marburg am 23. Mai 1937 in Bad Wildungen. Wuppertal-Elberfelt: Köhler, 1937.
Hesse-Elberfeld, H. Klugkist. *Mose sprach zu ihnen: Eure Brueder sollen in den Streit ziehen, und ihr wollt heir bleiben? Predigt über 4. Mose 32:6*, am Sonntag, dem 27. September 1936. Wuppertal-Elberfeld: Köhler, 1936.
———. *4. Mose 32:6–9, 13,14, und 16,17*. Wuppertal-Elberfeld: Köhler, 1936.

Hitler, Adolf. *Mein Kampf*. Translated by Ralph Manheim. Boston: Houghton Mifflin, 1971.
Hollweg, E. *Predigt über Ps. 118:15, 16, 22, 23*, am Ostersonntag, den 28. März 1937 in Wülfrath. Wuppertal-Elberfeld: Köhler, 1937.
Humburg, D. *Der Strom aus dem Heiligtum*. Predigt bei dem Bekenntnisgottesdienst in der Emmauskirche in Berlin am 21 Juni 1935. Mit einem Nachwort der "Deutschen Christen." Berlin-Steglitz: Eisemann, 1935.
Immer, Karl. *Konfirmationspredigt über Lukas 22:31–34*, am Sonntag, dem 14. März 1937, in der Gemarker Kirche. Wuppertal-Elberfeld: Köhler, 1937.
In Jesu Namen. Zwanzig Predigten. Siegen, Westfalen: Wilhelm-Schneider Verlag, 1937.
Iwand, Hans Joachim. *Nachgelassene Werke, Dritter Band*. München: Chr. Kaiser Verlag, 1963.
———. *In Namen Jesu. Amen*. Predigt zu St. Jordan, Neumark, über Hebraeer 13:12–14. Wuppertal-Elberfeld: Köhler, 1936.
Kalb, Heinrich. „Judenchrist—deutscher Christ?" in *Deutsches Christentum, dargestellt in Predigt und Vortrag*. Nürnberg: Fr. Städler, 1937.
Kampffmeyer, Karl ed. *Dein Wort ist Deiner Kirche Schutz. Predigten von der Kirche*. Göttingen: Vandenhoeck & Ruprecht, 1934.
Klein, D. Paul. *Das ewige Evangelium und das dritte Reich. Acht Volksmissions-Predigten*. Verlag des Evang. Vereins Kaiserslautern-Mannheim, 1934.
Kloppenburg, Heinz. *Predigt über Hebraeer 10:19–25*, am 2. Adventssonntag, den 6. Dezember 1936. Wuppertal-Elberfeld: Köhler, 1936.
Kolle, Erich, ed. *Traureden: für die geistliche Rede*. Verlag Bertelsmann Gütersloh, 1938.
Lempp, W. *Zwanzig Thesen über zeitgemässe Predigt*. Stuttgart: Verlag der Ev. Gesellschaft, 1937.
Lilje, Hanns. *Unser Gott kommt und schweiget nicht. Zehn Predigten*. Hannover: Verlag von Heinr. Fesche, 1936.
Luther, Martin. *Three Treatises*. Translated by Charles Jacobs, A.T.W. Steinhäuser, and W. A. Lambert. Philadelphia: Fortress Press, 1970.
Matheson, Peter, ed. *The Third Reich and the German Churches: A Documentary Account of Christian Resistance and Complicity During the Nazi Era*. Grand Rapids, MI: Eerdmans, 1981.
Müller, Eberhard ed. *Wahrheit und Wirklichkeit der Kirche. Vorträge und geistliche Reden gehalten auf der Deutschen Evangelischen Woche*, 26. bis 30. August 1935 in Hannover. Berlin: Furche-Verlag, 1935.
Müller-Hildenbach, Hermann. *Gemeinde in Not! Predigt über Apostelgeschichte 4:23–31*, zur Kirchenvisitation in der Kirche zu Klafeld. Wuppertal-Elberfeld: Köhler, 1937.
Niemöller, Martin. *Ach Gott vom Himmel sieh darein. Sechs Predigten*. München: Chr. Kaiser Verlag, 1946.
———. *Alles und in allen Christus! fünfzehn Dahlemer Predigten*. Warneck, 1935.
———. *Dachau Sermons*. Translated by Robert Pfeiffer. New York: Harper and Brothers, 1946.

———, ed. *Das Aufgebrochene Tor. Predigten und Andachten gefangener Pfarrer im Konzentrationslager Dachau.* Neubau Verlag, 1946.

———. *. . . dass wir an Ihm bleiben! Sechzehn Dahlemer Predigten.* Berlin: Verlag von Martin Warneck, 1935.

———. *Drei Konfirmationspredigten gehalten in Berlin-Dahlem 1936.* Berlin-Steiglitz: Eisemann, 1936.

———. *God is My Fuehrer, being the Last Twenty-Eight Sermons.* New York: Philosophical Library and Alliance Book Corp., 1941.

———. *Here Stand I!* Translated by Jane Lymburn. New York: Willett, Clark & Co., 1937.

———. *Letzte Predigt vor der Verhaeftung*, in *Was wuerde Jesus dazu sagen? Reden - Predigten - Aufsaetze 1937–1980.* Berlin: Union, 1980.

———. *Predigt*, gehalten in Berlin-Dahlem am 2. Pfingsttag, dem 17. Mai 1937. Wuppertal-Elberfeld: Köhler, 1937.

———. *Predigt über 1. Johannes 5:4–5*, "Unser Glaube ist der Sieg," gehalten am Reformationsfest, 3.11.1935 in der Jesus-Christus-Kirche zu Berlin-Dahlem. Eisemann, 1935.

———. *Predigt über 2. Korinther 5:19–21*, am 10. April 1936. Wuppertal-Elberfeld: Köhler, 1936.

———. *Predigt über Ps. 43 am Sonntag Judika 7.4*, 1935 in der Jesus-Christus-Kirche zu Berlin-Dahlem. Eisemann, 1935.

———. *Synodalpredigt*, gehalten in der St. Barbara-Kirche zu Breslau am 15. Dezember 1936, über Jesaja 40:1–8. Wuppertal-Elberfeld: Köhler, 1936.

Nietzsche, Friedrich. *Beyond Good and Evil: A Prelude to a Philosophy of the Future*, translated by Walter Kaufmann. New York: Vintage Books, 1989.

Oettingen, H. *Predigt über Lukas 12:32*, am 1. Januar 1937. Wuppertal-Elberfeld: Köhler, 1937.

Palmer, Christian. *Evangelische Homiletik.* Stuttgart: J.F Steinkopf'schen Buchhandlung, 1845.

Prater, [no first name]. *Religion und Offenbarung. Schriftenreihe um Evangelium und Kirche*, Heft 4. Leipzig: Verlag Arwed Strauch, 1934.

Quervain, Alfred de. *Das Gesetz Gottes. Predigten: die erste Tafel und die zweite Tafel.* Chr. Kaiser Verlag, 1935.

———. *Der Prediger unter dem Tore. Zwei Predigten.* Wuppertal-Barmen: Müller [no date].

———. *Die neue Schöpfung. Sechs Predigten über II. Kor. 4:16–5.* Elberfeld: Verlag der niederl. reform. Gemeinde, 1934.

Rietmüller, Otto. *Predigt über Matth. 13:45–46 auf dem 10 Jugendtag der Ev.-lutherischen Landeskirche Hannover*, am 8. September 1935. Hannover-Kleefeld: Buchdruckerei des Stephansstiftes, 1935.

Robinson, Edwin, ed. *Dietrich Bonhoeffer's Christmas Sermons.* Grand Rapids, MI: Zondervan, 2005.

Rüling, Josef. *In der Nachfolge Jesu Predigten nach dem Gang des Kirchenjahres.* Leipzig: Heinsius, 1936.

Sachsse, D. Eugen, *Evangelische Homiletik. Ein Leitfaden für Studierende und Kandidaten*. Leipzig: A. Deichert'sche Verlagsbuchhandlung Nachf., 1913.

Sammentreuther, Julius. *Predigtmeditationen über die Altkirchlichen Episteln und die Eisenacher (neuer) Evangelien*. München: Chr. Kaiser Verlag, 1936.

Sasse, Hermann. *Zeugnisse: Erlanger Predigten und Vortraege vor Gemeinden 1933–1944*. Herausgegeben von Friedrich Wilhelm Hopf. Erlangen: Martin Luther Verlag, 1979.

Scharf, Kurt. *Wartezeit. Predigt, gehalten in einer Bekenntnisstunde zu Friedrichsthal bei Oranienburg am Freitag vor Pfingsten, dem 14. Mai 1937*. Wuppertal-Elberfeld: Köhler, 1937.

Schlier, [no first name]. *Predigt über Lukas 2:25–33*, gehalten in der Immanuelskirche zu Barmen. Wuppertal-Elberfeld: Köhler, 1937.

Schlink, Edmund. *Bekennende Kirche und Welt. Das Christliche Deutschland 1933 bis 1945*. Dokumente und Zeugnisse. Tübingen: Furche Verlag, 1947.

———. *Predigt über Johannes 11:21–27*, am Sonntag Seeagesima 1937 in der Zionskirche zu Bethel. Wuppertal-Elberfeld: Köhler, 1937.

Schneider, Julius. *Der anwalt des deutsches Volkes*. Predigt über Roem 10:13–21, am 4. Juni 1935, auf der Synode in Augsburg. München: Chr. Kaiser Verlag, 1935.

———. *Ein Christ Predigt über Hermann von Bezzel*. Nürnburg-Zirndorf: Bollmann-Verlag, 1937.

Schneider, Margarete, ed. *Paul Schneider, Der Prediger von Buchenwald*, ed. Margarete Schneider. Neuhausen/Stuttgart: Hänssler, 1995.

Schöffel, S. *Wohin? Die Frage der Kirche*. Predigt über Joh. 6:68–69. Hamburg: Paul Hartung Verlag, 1935.

Schuler. D. *Ist die protestantische Kirche auf dem Wege nach Rom?* Freiburg: Verlag der Buchhandlung Wichernhaus, 1937.

Schwartz, Karl von. *Gottes Wort an Gottes Volk. Ein Jahrgang Predigten*. Braunschweig: Wollermann, 1933.

Smidt, Udo. *Dazu ist erschienen der Sohn gottes, dass er die Werke des Teufels zerstöre*. Predigt über Matth. 4:1–11. Wuppertal-Elberfeld: Köhler, 1936.

Soden, Hans von. *Wahrheit in Christus. Zwölf Predigten*, aus dem Nachlaß herausgegeben. Chr. Kaiser Verlag, 1947.

Solberg, Mary, ed. *A Church Undone: Documents from the German Christian Faith Movement 1932–1940*. Minneapolis, MN: Fortress Press, 2015.

Stählin, Wilhelm. *Der Kelch des Herrn und der Becher der Dämonen*. Predigt beim 120. Jahresfest des Evangelischen Missionsvereins Bremen-Stadt am Sonntag Rogate, 28. April 1940, über I Kor. 10:14–22. Bremen: Monatsblatt der Norddeutschen Missions-Gesellschaft, 1940.

Stein-Wilnsdorf, [no first name]. *Predigt über Jesiaja 40:26–31 am Sonntag Jubilate*, 18. April 1937. Wuppertal-Elberfeld: Köhler, 1937.

Stroud, Dean, ed. *Preaching in Hitler's Shadow*. Grand Rapids, MI: Eerdmans, 2013.

ten Boom, Corrie. *The Hiding Place*. Grand Rapids, MI: Chosen Books, 2006.

Thurneysen, Eduard. *Die Kraft der Geringen. Drei Predigten*. München: Chri. Kaiser Verlag, 1934.

Tolzien, Gerhard. *Du und deine Seele. Ein Jahrgang Predigten über die alten Evangelien des Kirchenjahres.* Zweiter Band. Schwerin: Verlag Friedrich Hahn, 1937.

Treplin, [no first name]. *Predigt über Matth. 12:46–50*, gehalten am 18. Juli 1937 in der Kirche zu Handemarschen, Schleswig-Holstein. Barmen: Presbyteriums der evang.-reform., 1937.

Trillhaas, Wolfgang. *Evangelische Predigtlehre.* München: Chr. Kaiser Verlag, 1935.

Vogel, Heinrich. *Auslegung des Johannesbriefs. 4. Lieserung, 1 Joh. 3:4–6.* Wilhelm Schneider-Verlag, Siegen und Leipsig.

———. *Auslegung des Philipperbriefs. 4. Lieserung, Phil. 2:4–8.* Wilhelm Schneider-Verlag, Siegen und Leipsig.

———. *Das Freijahr Gottes. Die Frohe Botschaft in Predigten.* Berlin: Verlag Haus und Schule, 1949.

———. *Der Name Gottes.* Predigt über 2. Mose 3:13–15, gehalten zum Trinitatisfest 1937 in der Kirche zu Dobbrikow. Barmen: Presbyteriums der evang.-reform, 1937.

———. *Kurze Instruction für einen soldaten Jesu Christ.* München: Chr. Kaiser Verlag, 1936.

Vogel, Heinrich und Wilhelm Gross. *Ars Crucis: Eine Predigt in Wort und Bild.* Berlin: Montanus, 1936.

Weber, Hermann. *Trübsal schafft Herrlichkeit, sieben Predigten.* Furche-Verlag, 1937.

Wehr, O. *Dein Wort ist die Wahrheit?* Predigt für Sonntag, den 22. August 1937 über I. Petrus 4:12–19. Siegen: Köhler, 1937.

Wurm, Theophil. *Auftrag, Not und Ziel der Kirche.* Predigt zur Eroeffnung der ersten Nationalsynode am 27. September 1933 in der Schlosskirche zu Wittenberg. Stuttgart: Verlag der Evang. Gesellschaft, 1933.

———. *Die Kraft des Wortes.* Predigt am Reformationsfest 4.11.1934 in der Stiftskirche zu Stuttgart über Hebr. 4:12–13. Verlag der Evang. Gesellschaft, Stuttgart.

———. *Der lutherische Grundcharakter der württembergischen Landeskirche.* Zum 70. Geburtstag 7.12.1938, vom Verin für württembergische Kirchengeschichte dargeboten. Verlag von Chr. Scheufele, Stuttgart.

———. *Der Sieg der Wahrheit.* Predigt am 4. Sonntag nach dem Erschungsfest 3.2.1935, über Joh. 4:15–26, im Münster in Ulm und in der Stadkirche in Blaubeuren. Verlag Dr. Karl Hoehn.

———. *Der Weg zur wahren Einheit.* Predigt über Apostelg. 2:1–18, am Pfingstfest, 20. Mai 1934, in der Marienkirche zu Reutlingen. Stuttgart: Verlag der Evang. Gesellschaft, 1934.

———. *Predigt über Joh. 8:21–30* in Tailfingen und Balingen am Sonntag Geragesimae 24 Februar 1935. Verlag der Evang. Gesellschaft, Stuttgart.

———. *Recht und Grenze der Tolerance in der Kirche.* Vortrag bei der Kirchlichen Woche in Stuttgart am 29.7.1939. Verlag der Evang. Gesellschaft.

———.

———. *Unser Hirte und Bischof.* Predigt über 1. Petri 2:21–25 am Sonntag Misericordias Domini in der Stiftskirche zu Stuttgart. Stuttgart: Verlag der Evang. Gesellschaft [no date].

———. *Wie vermeiden wir den Anstoss am Evangelium?* Predigt über Lukas 4:14–30 im Backnang und Waiblingen am 2. Sonntag nach dem Eischeinungsfest, 20.1.1935. Verlag der Evang. Gesellschaft, Stuttgart.

3. SECONDARY SOURCES

Ach, Manfred and Clemens Pentrop, *Hitlers "Religion."* Munich: Arbeitsgemeinschaft für Religions-und Weltanschauunsfragen, 1977.

Ahlers, Rolf. *The Barmen Declaration of 1934: The Archeology of a Confessional Text* (Toronto Studies in Theology). Lewiston, New York: Edwin Mellon Press, 1996.

Aichelin, Albrecht. *Paul Schneider: Ein radikales Glaubenszeugnis gegen die Gewaltherrschaft des Nationalsozialismus.* Gütersloh: Chr. Kaiser/Gütersloher Verlagshaus, 1994.

Anderson, George. *The Legend of the Wandering Jew.* Providence, RI: Brown University Press, 1965.

Babík, Milan. "Nazism as a Secular Religion," in *History and Theory* 45, no. 3 (Oct. 2006).

Bacharach, Walter Zvi. *Anti-Jewish Prejudices in German-Catholic Sermons*, Translated by Chaya Galai. Lewiston: Edwin Mellon Press, 1993.

Bajohr, Frank and Dieter Pohl, *Der Holocaust als offenes Geheimnis: Die Deutschen, die NS-Führung und die Allierten.* München: C.H. Beck, 2006.

Bankier, David. "The Confessing Church and Antisemitism," in *Betrayal: German Churches and the Holocaust*, edited by Robert P. Ericksen and Susannah Heschel. Minneapolis: Fortress Press, 1999.

———. *The Confessing Church, Conservative Elites, and the Nazi State, Texts and Studies in Religion* 28. New York: Edwin Mellen, 1986.

———. "Consent and Dissent: The Confessing Church and Conservative Opposition to National Socialism," in *Journal of Modern History* 59. March 1987: 53–78.

———. *The Germans and the Final Solution: Public Opinion under Nazism.* Cambridge, MA: Blackwell, 1992.

Barnett, Victoria. *For the Soul of the People: Protestant Protest against Hitler.* New York: Oxford University Press, 1992.

Baron, Lawrence. "The Holocaust and Human Decency," in *Humbolt Journal of Social Science*, vol. 13, no. 1/2, Humbolt University, 1986.

Bärsch, Claus-Ekkehard. *Die Politische Religion des Nationalsozialismus.* Munich: W. Fink, 1998.

Bäumgärtel, Friedrich. *Wider die Kirchenkampf-Legenden.* Neudettelsau: Freimund, 1959.

Behrenbeck, Sabine. *Der Kult um die toten Helden: Nationalsozialistische Mythen, Riten und Symbole.* Vierow: SH-Verlag, 1996.

Bentley, James. *Martin Niemöller*. New York: The Free Press, 1984.
Berben, Paul. *Dachau: The Official History, 1933–1945*. London: Norfolk Press, 1975.
Bergen, Doris. "Catholics, Protestants, and Antisemitism in Nazi Germany," in *Central European History*, vol. 27, (1994), pp. 329–348.
———. *Twisted Cross: The German Christian Movement in the Third Reich*. Chapel Hill, NC: The University of North Carolina Press, 1996.
———. *War and Genocide: A Concise History of the Holocaust*. New York: Rowman & Littlefield, 2003.
Berger, Peter. *The Heretical Imperative: Contemporary Possibilities of Religious Affirmation*. New York: Anchor Press, 1979.
Bergmeier, Horst J.P. and Rainer E. Lotz, *Hitler's Airwaves: The Inside Story of Nazi Radio Broadcasting and Propaganda Swing*. New Haven, CT: Yale University Press, 1997.
Besier, Gerhard and Gerhard Ringhausen, *Bekenntnis, Widerstand, Martyrium: Vom Barmen 1934 bis Plötzensee 1944*. Göttingen: Vandenhoeck & Ruprecht, 1986.
Bethge, Eberhard. *Dietrich Bonhoeffer: A Biography, Revised Edition*. Minneapolis, MN: Fortress Press, 2000.
Birdsall, Carolyn. *Nazi Soundscapes: Sound, Technology and Urban Space in Germany, 1933–1945*. Amsterdam: Amsterdam University Press, 2012.
Blackbourn, David. *History of Germany 1780–1918: The Long Nineteenth Century, Second Edition*. Malden, MA: Blackwell, 2003.
Block Gay and Malka Drucker, *Rescuers*. New York: Holmes & Meyer, 1992.
Boeselager, Philip Freiher von and Florence and Jerome Fehrenbach. *Valkryrie: The Story of the Plot to Kill Hitler, by Its Last Member*. New York: Vintage, 2011.
Borg, Marcus. *The Heart of Christianity: Rediscovering a Life of Faith*. New York: HarperOne, 2003.
Bosanquet, Mary. *The Life and Death of Dietrich Bonhoeffer*. New York: Harper & Row, 1968.
Brakelmann, Günter. *Hans Ehrenberg: Ein judenchristliches Schicksal in Deutschland*. Spenner, 1999.
Brandt, Richard. *The Philosophy of Schleiermacher: The Development of His Theory of Scientific and Religious Knowledge*. New York: Harper & Brothers, 1941.
Brilioth, Yngve. *A Brief History of Preaching*. Translated by Karl Mattson. Philadelphia: Fortress Press, 1965.
Browning, Christopher. *The Origins of the Final Solution: The Evolution of Nazi Jewish Policy, September 1939—March 1942*. Lincoln, NE: University of Nebraska Press, 2004.
Brunner, Emil. *Die Mystik und das Wort, Second Edition*. Tübingen: J.C.B. Mohr, 1928.
Buber, Martin. *Two Types of Faith*. Translated by Norman Goldhawk. New York: Harper and Brothers, 1961.
Bucher, Rainer. *Hitler's Theology: A Study in Political Religion*. Translated by Rebecca Pohl. New York: Continuum, 2011.
Burleigh, Michael. "National Socialism as a Political Religion, *Totalitarian Movements and Political Religions* 1, no. 2, (2000).

———. *The Third Reich: A New History*. New York: Hill and Wang, 2000.
Burleigh, Michael and Wolfgang Wippermann, *The Racial State: Germany 1933–1945*. New York: Cambridge University Press, 1991.
Burrin, Philippe. "Political Religion: The Relevance of a Concept," *History and Memory* 9, no. 1 (1997).
Busch, Eberhard. *Karl Barth: His Life from Letters and Autobiographical Texts*. Philadelphia, PA: Fortress Press, 1976.
Buttrick, David. *Homiletic: Moves and Structures*. Philadelphia: Fortress Press, 1988.
Carroll, James. *Constantine's Sword: The Church and the Jews*. New York: Houghton Mifflin Company, 2001.
Ceyer, Michael and John W. Boyer, eds., *Resistance against the Third Reich, 1933–1990*. Chicago: University of Chicago Press, 1994.
Clowney, Edmund P. *Preaching and Biblical Theology*. London: Tyndale Press, 1961.
Cochrane, Arthur. *The Church's Confession under Hitler*. Philadelphia: Westminster Press, 1962.
Cohn-Sherbok, Dan. *The Crucified Jew: Twenty Centuries of Christian Anti-Semitism*. Grand Rapids: Eerdmans, 1997.
Confino, Alon. *A World without Jews: The Nazi Imagination from Persecution to Genocide*. New Haven, CT: Yale University Press, 2014.
Conway, John. "The German Church Struggle: Its Making and Meaning," in *The Church Confronts the Nazis: Barmen Then and Now*, ed. by Hubert Locke. New York: The Edwin Mellon Press, 1984.
———. "The Historiography of the German Church Struggle," *Journal of Bible and Religion* 32, no. 3. July 1964.
———. *The Nazi Persecution of the Churches, 1933–1945*. Vancouver: Regent College Publishing, 1968.
———. "The Present State of Research and Writing on the Church Struggle," in *The German Church Struggle and the Holocaust*. Edited by Franklin Littell and Hubert Locke. Detroit: Wayne State University Press, 1974.
Cox, John M. *Circles of Resistance: Jewish, Leftist, and Youth Dissidence in Nazi Germany*. New York: Peter Lang, 2009.
Cresswell, Amos and Maxwell Tow. *Dr. Franz Hildebrandt: Mr. Valiant-for-Truth*. Macon, GA: Smyth & Helwys, 2000.
Cushman McGiffert, Arthur. *Protestant Thought before Kant*. London: Duckworth, 1911.
Dahm, Karl-Wilhelm. "German Protestantism and Politics, 1918–1939," *Journal of Contemporary History* 3, no. 1 (Jan. 1968), 29–49.
Dargan, Edwin Charles. *A History of Preaching, Vol. 1, From the Apostolic Fathers to the Great Reformers, A.D. 70–1572*. New York: Burt Franklin, 1968.
Dawidowicz, Lucy. *The War Against the Jews, 1933–1945*. New York: Holt, Rinehart and Winston, 1975.
Dawson, Jerry. *Friedrich Schleiermacher: The Evolution of a Nationalist*. Austin: University of Texas Press, 1966.
DeBona, Guerric. *Fulfilled in Our Hearing: History and Method of Christian Preaching*. New York: Paulist Press, 2005.

de Gruchy, John. *Daring, Trusting Spirit: Bonhoeffer's Friend Eberhard Bethge*. Minneapolis: Fortress Press, 2005.

———, ed. *Dietrich Bonhoeffer: Witness to Jesus Christ, The Making of Modern Theology*. Minneapolis, MN: Fortress Press, 1991.

Dietrich, Donald. *Catholic Citizens of the Third Reich*. New Brunswick, NJ: Transaction Books, 1988.

Dilthey, Wilhelm. *Das Leben Schleiermachers, Second Edition*. Edited by H. Mulert. Berlin: W. de Gruyter and Company, 1922.

Dorrien, Gary. *The Making of American Liberal Theology: Idealism, Realism, and Modernity, 1900–1950*. Louisville: Westminster John Knox Press, 2003.

Douglas, J.D., et al. *The Bible Dictionary, Second Edition*. Wheaton, IL: Tyndale, 1962.

———. *New Bible Dictionary, Second Edition*. Leicester: Inter-Varsity, 1982.

Dramm, Sabina. *Dietrich Bonhoeffer and the Resistance*. Translated by Margaret Kohl. Minneapolis, MN: Fortress Press, 2009.

Dumbach, Annette and Jud Newborn. *Sophie Scholl and the White Rose*. Oxford: One World, 2006.

Dunn, James, ed. *Jews and Christians: The Parting of the Ways, A.D. 70 to 135*. Grand Rapids, MI: Eerdman's, 1999.

Dwork, Debórah and Robert Jan van Pelt, *Holocaust: A History*. New York: Norton & Company, 2003.

Edwards Jr., O.C. *A History of Preaching*. Nashville: Abingdon Press, 2004.

Eltscher, Louis. *Traitors or Patriots? A Story of the German Anti-Nazi Resistance*. Bloomington, IN: iUniverse, 2013.

Ericksen, Robert. *Complicity in the Holocaust: Churches and Universities in Nazi Germany*. New York: Cambridge University Press, 2012.

———. *Theologians under Hitler: Gerhard Kittel, Paul Althaus and Emanuel Hirsch*. New Haven: Yale University Press, 1985.

Ericksen, Robert and Susannah Heschel. *Betrayal: German Churches and the Holocaust*. Minneapolis: Fortress Press, 1999.

———. "The German Churches Face Hitler," in *Tel Aviver Jahrbuch für deutsche Geschichte* 23. 1994.

Erickson, Millard. *Christian Theology*, Second Edition. Grand Rapids, MI: Baker, 1998.

Evans, Richard. *The Coming of the Third Reich*. New York: Penguin, 2003.

———. "Nazism, Christianity and Political Religion: A Debate," in the *Journal of Contemporary History* 42, no. 1 (January 2007).

———. *The Third Reich in Power*. New York: Penguin Press, 2005.

———. *The Third Reich at War*. New York: Penguin Press, 2009.

Fein, Helen. *Accounting for Genocide*. New York: Free Press, 1979.

Ferguson, Everett. *Backgrounds of Early Christianity, Second Edition*. Grand Rapids, MI: Eerdmans, 1993.

Ferguson, Sinclair, David Wright, and J. I. Packer, eds., *New Dictionary of Theology*. Downer's Grove: InterVarsity Press, 1988.

Fest, Joachim. *Plotting Hitler's Death: The Story of the German Resistance*, translated by Bruce Little. New York: Metropolitan, 1996.
Forsyth, P.T. *Positive Preaching and the Modern Mind*. New York: A.C. Armstrong and Son, 1907.
Foster Jr., Claude. *Paul Schneider: The Buchenwald Apostle: A Christian Martyr in Nazi Germany: A Sourcebook on the German Church Struggle*. West Chester, PA: West Chester University, 1995.
Friedländer, Saul. *Nazi Germany and the Jews: Volume 1, Years of Persecution, 1933–1939*. New York: HarperCollins, 1997.
———. *Nazi Germany and the Jews: Volume 2, The Years of Extermination, 1939–1945*. New York: Harper Perennial, 2008.
Frizsche, Peter. *Germans into Nazis*. Cambridge: Harvard University Press, 1998.
———. *Life and Death in the Third Reich*. Cambridge: Harvard University Press, 2008.
Galante, Pierre. *Operation Valkyrie: The German General's Plot against Hitler*. Cooper Square, 2012.
Gamm, Hans-Jochen. *Der braune Kult: das Dritte Reich und seine Ersatzreligion*. Hamburg: Rütten und Loening, 1962.
Gellately, Robert. *Backing Hitler: Consent and Coercion in Nazi Germany*. New York: Oxford University Press, 2001.
———. "Denunciations in Twentieth Century Germany: Aspects of Self-Policing in the Third Reich and the German Democratic Republic," in the *Journal of Modern History*, Vol. 68, No. 4, Practices of Denunciation in Modern European History, 1789–1989 (Dec., 1996), pp. 939–940.
———. *The Gestapo and German Society: Enforcing Racial Policy 1933–1945*. New York: Oxford, 1990.
Gentile, Emilio. "Fascism, Totalitarianism and Political Religion: Definitions and Critical Reflections on Criticism and Interpretation," translated by Natalia Belozentseva, in *Totalitarian Movements and Political Religions* 5, no. 3 (Winter 2004).
———. "Political Religion: A Concept and its Critics—A Critical Survey." Translated by Natalia Belozertseva, in *Totalitarian Movements and Political Religions* 6, no. 1 (June 2005).
———. "The Sacralization of Politics: Definitions, Interpretations and Reflections on the Question of Secular Religion and Totalitarianism." Translated by Robert Mallett. *Totalitarian Movements and Political Religions* 1, no. 1 (2000).
Gerlach, Wolfgang. *And the Witnesses Were Silent: The Confessing Church and the Persecution of the Jews*, Edited and Translated by Victoria J. Barnett. Lincoln: University of Nebraska, 2000.
Gibson, Scott. "Challenges to Preaching the Old Testament," in *Preaching the Old Testament*. Edited by Scott Gibson. Grand Rapids, MI: Baker Books, 2006.
Gilbert, Martin. *Kristallnacht: Prelude to Destruction*. New York: HarperCollins, 2006.
Gisevius, Hans Bernd. *To the Bitter End: An Insider's Account of the Plot to Kill Hitler, 1933–1944*. Translated by Richard and Clara Winston. New York: Da Capo Press, 1998.

Gitelman, Zvi, ed. *Religion or Ethnicity?: Jewish Identities in Evolution*. New Brunswick, NJ: Rutgers University Press, 2009.

Glatzer, Nahum. *Franz Rosenzweig: His Life and Thought, Third Edition*. Indianapolis, IN: Hackett, 1998.

Goldhagen, Daniel. *Hitler's Willing Executioners: Ordinary Germans and the Holocaust*. New York: Vintage Books, 1996.

———. *A Moral Reckoning: The Role of the Catholic Church in the Holocaust and its Unfulfilled Duty of Repair*. New York: Knopf, 2002.

Gonzalez, Justo. *A History of Christian Thought: From Augustine to the Eve of the Reformation*. Nashville: Abingdon Press, 1987.

Green, Joel, Scot McKnight, and I. Howard Marshall, eds., *Dictionary of Jesus and the Gospels*. Downers Grove, IL: InterVarsity Press, 1992.

Green, Lowell. *Lutherans against Hitler: The Untold Story*. Saint Louis: Concordia Publishing House, 2007.

Greenberg, Irving. "Cloud of Smoke, Pillar of Fire," in *Auschwitz: Beginning of a New Era?* Edited by Eva Fleischner. New York: KTAV, 1997.

Greenfeld, Liah. *Nationalism, Five Roads to Modernity*. Cambridge, MA: Harvard University Press, 1992.

Grenz, Stanley. *Theology for the Community of God*. Grand Rapids, MI: Eerdmans, 2000.

Gritzsch, Eric W. *Martin Luther's Anti-Semitism: Against His Better Judgment*. Grand Rapids, MI: Eerdmans Publishing, 2013. Kindle Edition.

Gushee, David. *Righteous Gentiles of the Holocaust: Genocide and Moral Obligation, Second Edition*. St. Paul, MN: Paragon House, 2003.

Gutteridge, R.T.C. *The German Evangelical Church and the Jews, 1879–1958*. New York: Harper & Row, 1976.

Habermas, Rebekka. "Piety, Power, and Powerlessness: Religion and Religious Groups in Germany, 1870–1945," *Oxford Handbook of Modern German History*. Edited by Helmut Walser Smith. New York: Oxford, 2011.

Hallie, Philip. *Lest Innocent Blood Be Shed*. New York: Harper & Row, 1979.

Hamerow, Theodore. *On the Road to the Wolf's Lair: German Resistance to Hitler*. Cambridge, MA: Harvard University Press, 1997.

Hancock, Angela Dienhart. *Karl Barth's Emergency Homiletic, 1932–1933: A Summons to Prophetic Witness at the Dawn of the Third Reich*. Grand Rapids, MI: Eerdmans, 2013.

Hasan-Rokem, Galit and Alan Dundes. *The Wandering Jew: Essays in the Interpretation of a Christian Legend*. Bloomington, IN: Indiana University Press, 1986.

Haynes, Stephen R. *The Bonhoeffer Legacy: Post Holocaust Perspectives*. Minneapolis, MN: Fortress Press, 2006.

———. *The Bonhoeffer Phenomenon: Portraits of a Protestant Saint*. Minneapolis, MN: Fortress Press, 2004.

———. "Who Needs Enemies? Jews and Judaism in Anti-Nazi Religious Discourse," in *Church History*, vol. 71, no. 2 (June 2002), pp. 341–367.

Heer, Friedrich. *Der Glaube des Adolf Hitler: Anatomie einer politischen Religiosität*. Munich: Bechtle, 1968.

Heinonen, Reijo. *Anpassung und Identität: Theologie und Kirchenpolitik der Bremer Deutschen Christen 1933–1945.* Göttingen, 1978.

Hellman, Peter. *Avenue of the Righteous.* Michael D. Ryan, ed. *Human Responses to the Holocaust.* New York: Edwin Mellon Press, 1981.

Helmreich, Enrst Christian. *German Churches under Hitler: Background, Struggle, and Epilogue.* Detroit: Wayne State University Press, 1980.

Herf, Jeffrey. *The Jewish Enemy: Nazi Propaganda during World War II and the Holocaust.* Cambridge, MA: Bellknap Press, 2006.

Hermle, Siegfried. "Predigt an der Front: Zur Tätigkeit der Kriegspfarrer im Zweiten Weltkrieg," in *Blätter für württembergische Kirchegeschichte.* Verlag Chr. Schleufele in Stuttgart, 2002.

Heron, A.I.C. *A Century of Protestant Theology.* Guildford, 1980.

Heschel, Susannah. *The Aryan Jesus: Christian Theologians and the Bible in Nazi Germany.* Princeton, NJ: Princeton University Press, 2008.

Hockenos, Matthew. *A Church Divided: German Protestants Confront the Nazi Past.* Bloomington, IN: Indiana University Press, 2004.

———. *Then They Came for Me: Martin Niemöller, the Pastor Who Defied the Nazis.* New York: Basic Books, 2018.

Hoffmann, Peter. *The History of the German Resistance, 1933–1945, Third Edition.* Ithaca: McGill-Queen's University Press, 1996.

Jähnichen, Traugott. "Von der 'Schwärmerei' zur 'Gegenreligion,'" Die Auseinandersetzung Ehrenberg smit dem Nationalsozialismus al seiner 'politischen Religion," in *Das Erbe des Theologen Hans Ehrenberg: Eine Zwischenbilanz.* Edited by Manfred Keller and Jens Murken. Dortmund: Titelbild, 2009.

Jantzen, Kyle. *Faith and Fatherland: Parish Politics in Hitler's Germany.* Minneapolis, MN: Fortress Press, 2008.

Johnson, Eric. *Nazi Terror: The Gestapo, Jews, and Ordinary Germans.* New York: Basic Books, 1999.

Johnson, Eric A. and Karl-Heinz Reuband, *What We Knew: Terror, Mass Murder, and Everyday Life in Nazi Germany, An Oral History.* Cambridge, MA: Basic Books, 2005.

Kaiser, Joachim-Christoph. "Kirchengeschichte des 20. Jahrhunderts, Teil A: Der Protestantismus von 1918 bis 1989," in *Ökumenische Kirchengeschichte*, Bd. 3. Edited by Hubert Wolf. Darmstadt, 2007.

Kershaw, Ian. *Hitler, 1889–1936: Hubris.* New York: W.W. Norton, 1999.

———. *Hitler, 1936–1945: Nemesis.* New York: W.W. Norton, 2000.

———. *Hitler, the Germans, and the Final Solution.* New Haven: Yale University Press, 2008.

———. *The Nazi Dictatorship: Problems and Perspectives, third edition.* New York: Arnold, 1993.

———. *Popular Opinion and Political Dissent in the Third Reich: Bavaria 1933–1945.* New York: Oxford University Press, 1983.

Kersting, Andreas. *Kirchenordnung und Widerstand: Der Kampf um den Aufbau der Bekennenden Kirche der altpreußischen Union aufgrund des Dahlemer Notrechts von 1934 bis 1937*, Heidelberger Untersucheungen zu Widerstand, Judenverfolgung und Kirchenkampf im Dritten Reich 4. Gütersloh: Christian Kaiser, 1994.

Kirk, Tim. *Nazi Germany*. New York: Palgrave, 2007.

Klemperer, Victor. *I Will Bear Witness: A Diary of the Nazi Years, 1933–1941*. New York: Modern Library, 1999.

———. *I Will Bear Witness: A Diary of the Nazi Years, 1942–1945*. New York: Random House, 1999.

———. *The Language of the Third Reich: A Philologist's Notebook*, translated by Martin Brady. New York: Continuum, 2008.

Koehne, Samuel. "Nazism and Religion: The Problem of 'Positive Christianity,'" in *Australian Journal of Politics and History* 60 (1) (2014), 28-42.

———. "Reassessing 'The Holy Reich': Leading Nazis' Views on Confession, Community and 'Jewish Materialism,'" in *Journal of Contemporary History* 48 (3) (2013), 423-445.

———. "Were the National Socialists a 'Völkisch' Party? Paganism, Christianity, and the Nazi Christmas," in *Central European History* 47 (4) (2014), 760-790.

Koonz, Claudia. *The Nazi Conscience*. Cambridge, MA: Belknap Press of Harvard University Press, 2003.

Kulka, Otto Dov and Eberhard Jäckel, eds. *The Jews in the Secret Nazi Reports on Popular Opinion in Germany, 1933–1945*. Translated from the German by William Templer. New Haven: Yale University Press, 2010.

Kulka, Otto Dov and Paul R. Mendes-Flohr, eds. *Judaism and Christianity under the Impact of National Socialism*. Jerusalem: The Historical Society of Israel and the Zalman Shazar Center for Jewish History, 1987.

Langmuir, Gavin. *History, Religion, and Antisemitism*. Berkeley: University of California, 1990.

———. *Toward a Definition of Antisemitism*. Berkeley: University of California, 1996.

Laqueur, Walter. *The Terrible Secret: An Investigation into the Suppression of Information about Hitler's "Final Solution."* London: Weidenfeld and Nicolson, 1980.

Larson, David. *The Company of Preachers: A History of Biblical Preaching from the Old Testament to the Modern Era*. Grand Rapids, MI: Kregel, 1998.

Latourette, Kenneth Scott. *A History of Christianity, Vol. 2, Reformation to the Present*. Peabody, MA: Prince Press, 1997.

Lazier, Benjamin. *God Interrupted: Heresy and the European Imagination between the World Wars*. Princeton, NJ: Princeton University Press, 2008.

Levine, Hillel. *Economic Origins of Antisemitism: Poland and Its Jews in the Early Modern Period*. New Haven, CT: Yale University Press, 1991.

Lewy, Günter. *The Catholic Church and Nazi Germany*. New York: Da Capo Press, 1964.

Lindemann, Albert S. and Richard S. Levy, *Antisemitism: A History*. New York: Oxford, 2010.

Lindemann, Gerhard. *"Typisch jüdisch": Die Stellung der Ev.-luth. Landeskirche Hannovers zu Antijudaismus, Judenfeindschaft und Antisemitismus 1919–1949*. Berlin: Duncker & Humblot, 1998, pages 310–438.

Littell, Franklin Hamlin. *The Crucifixion of the Jews*. New York: Harper & Row, 1975.

———. *The German Phoenix: How the German Churches' Resistance to Hitler Gave Birth to the Massive Lay Movements of the Kirchentag and the Academies*. New York: Doubleday & Company, 1960.

Littell, Franklin Hamlin and Hubert Locke, eds. *The German Church Struggle and the Holocaust*. Detroit: Wayne State University Press, 1974.

Locke, Hubert, ed. *The Church Confronts the Nazis: Barmen Then and Now*. New York: Edwin Mellon Press, 1984.

Lutherhaus Eisenach, *Wider Das Vergessen: Schicksale judenchristlicher Pfarrer in der Zeit von 1933–1945*. Herausgegeben vom Evangelischen Pfarrhausarchiv, 1989.

Maier, Hans. "Political Religion: A Concept and its Limitations," in *Totalitarian Movements and Political Religions* 8, no. 1 (March 2007).

———. "Political Religions and Their Images: Soviet Communism, Italian Fascism and German National Socialism," in *Totalitarian Movements and Political Religions* 7, no. 3 (September 2006).

Maier, Hans and Michael Schäfer, eds. *Totalitarismus und Politische Religionen: Konzepte des Diktaturvergleichs, 3 Volumes*. Paderborn: Schöningh, 1996, 1997, 2003.

Martin, Ralph and Peter Davids, eds. *Dictionary of the Later New Testament and Its Developments*. Downers Grove, IL: InterVarsity Press, 1997.

McGrath, Alister. *The Making of Modern German Christology, 1750–1990*. Grand Rapids, MI: Zondervan, 1994.

Meier, Kurt. *Die Deutschen Christen: Das Bild einer Bewegung im Kirchenkampf des Dritten Reiches*. Göttingen: Vandenhoeck & Ruprecht, 1964.

———. *Kirche und Judentum: die Haltung der evangelischen Kirche zur Judenpolitik des Dritten Reiches*. Halle [Saale]: Veb Max Niemeyer Verlag, 1968.

———. *Kreuz und Hakenkreuz: Die evangelische Kirche im Dritten Reich*. Munich, 1992.

Meyer, Beate (Hrsg.). *Die Verfolgung und Ermordung der Hamburger Juden 1933–1945, Geschichte. Zeugnis. Erinnerung*. Göttingen: Wallstein Verlag, 2006.

———. "Juedische Mischlinge": Rassenpolitik und Verfolgungserfahrung 1933–1945. Hamburg: Doelling und Galitz, 2002. 68–72

Michael, Robert. *Holy Hatred, Christianity, Antisemitism, and the Holocaust*. New York: Palgrave Macmillan, 2006.

Micklem, Nathaniel. *National Socialism and the Roman Catholic Church: Being an Account of the Conflict between the National Socialist Government of Germany and the Roman Catholic Church, 1933–1938*. New York: Oxford University Press, 1939.

Moeller, Robert G. *War Stories: The Search for a Usable Past in the Federal Republic of Germany*. Berkeley, CA: University of California Press, 2001.

Mommsen, Hans. *Germans Against Hitler: The Stauffenberg Plot and Resistance under the Third Reich*. Translated by Angus McGeoch. New York: I.B. Tauris, 2009.

———. "What did the Germans Know about the Genocide of the Jews?" in Walter H. Pehle, ed., *November 1938: From 'Kristallnacht' to Genocide*. New York: Berg, 1991, 187–221.

Mommsen, Hans and Volker Ullrich, "'Wir haben nichts gewusst': Ein deutsches Trauma," 1999 4 (1991): 11–46.

Mosse, George. *The Crisis of German Ideology: Intellectual Origins of the Third Reich*. New York: Grosset and Dunlap, 1964.

———. *Masses and Man: Nationalist and Fascist Perceptions of Reality*. Detroit, MI: Wayne State University Press, 1987.

———. *Nationalism and Sexuality: Respectability and Abnormal Sexuality in Modern Europe*. New York: Howard Fertig, 1985.

———. *The Nationalization of the Masses: Political Symbolism and Mass Movements in Germany from the Napoleonic Wars through the Third Reich*. New York: H. Fertig, 1975.

———. *Toward the Final Solution: A History of European Racism*. New York: Howard Fertig, 1985.

Murken, Jens and Manfred Keller, *Das Erbe des Theologen Hans Ehrenberg: Eine Zwischenbilanz*. Lit Verlag, 2010.

Nation, Mark Thiessen, Anthony Siegrist, and Daniel Umbel. *Bonhoeffer the Assassin? Challenging the Myth, Recovering His Call to Peacemaking*. Grand Rapids, MI: Baker, 2013.

Neuhäusler, Johann. *Kreuz und Hakenkreuz: Der Kampf des Nationalsozialismus gegen die katolische Kirche und der Kirchliche Widerstand.* München: Katholiche Kirche Bayerns, 1946.

The New Oxford Annotated Bible, Third Edition. Oxford University Press, 2001.

Niebuhr, Richard. *Schleiermacher on Christ and Religion*. New York: Scribner, 1964.

Niemöller, Wilhelm. *Kampf und Zeugnis der Bekennenden Kirche*. Bielefeld: L. Bechauf, 1948.

Nietzsche, Friedrich. *Beyond Good and Evil: A Prelude to a Philosophy of the Future*. Translated by Walter Kaufmann. New York: Vintage Books, 1989.

Niven, Bill, ed., *Germans as Victims: Remembering the Past in Contemporary Germany*. New York: Palgrave, 2006.

Noakes, Jeremy. "The Development of Nazi Policy towards the German-Jewish 'Mischlinge' 1933–1945," in *Leo Baeck Institute Yearbook*, vol. 34. New York, 1989.

Oden, Thomas. *Pastoral Theology: Essentials of Ministry*. New York: HarperCollins, 1983.

Old, Hughes Oliphant. *The Reading and Preaching of the Scriptures in the Worship of the Christian Church, Volume 6, the Modern Age*. Grand Rapids, MI: Eerdmans, 2007.

Oliner, Samuel and Pearl Oliner, *The Altruistic Personality: Rescuers of Jews in Nazi Europe*. New York: Free Press, 1988.

Petry, Christian. *Studenten aufs Schafott: Die Weisse Rose und ihr Scheitern*. Munich: Piper, 1968.

Peukert, Detlev. *Inside Nazi Germany: Conformity, Opposition and Racism in Everyday Life*. Translated by Richard Deveson. New Haven, CT: Yale University Press, 1987.

———. *The Weimar Republic.* Translated by Richard Deveson. New York: Hill and Wang, 1989.

Phayer, Michael. *The Catholic Church and the Holocaust, 1930–1965.* Bloomington, IN: Indiana University Press, 2000.

Pinson, Koppel. *Pietism as a Factor in the Rise of German Nationalism.* New York: Octagon Books, Inc., 1968.

Pois, Robert. *National Socialism and the Religion of Nature.* New York: St. Martin's Press, 1986.

Poliakov, Léon. *The History of Anti-Semitism, Vol. 1, From the Time of Christ to the Court of the Jews.* Translated by Richard Howard. New York: Vanguard, 1965.

Porter, S. E. "Peace, Reconciliation," in the *Dictionary of Paul and His Letters.* Downers Grove, IL: InterVarsity Press, 1993.

Prittie, Trence. *Germans against Hitler.* Boston: Little, Brown and Company, 1964.

Probst, Christopher. *Demonizing the Jews: Luther and the Protestant Church in Nazi Germany.* Bloomington: Indiana University, 2012.

Prolingheuer, Hans. "Der ungekämpfte Kirchenkampf 1933–1945—das politische Versagen der Bekennenden Kirche," in *Neue Stimme Sonderheft* 6 (1983): 3–34.

Pulzer, Peter. *The Rise of Political Anti-Semitism in Germany and Austria, Revised Edition.* Cambridge: Harvard University Press, 1988.

Redeker, Martin. *Schleiermacher: Life and Thought*, translated by John Wallhausser. Philadelphia: Fortress Press, 1973.

Redles. David. *Hitler's Millennial Reich: Apocalyptic Belief and the Search for Salvation.* New York: New York University Press, 2005.

Rees, Joseph. *Titus Bransma: A Modern Martyr.* Sidgwick and Jackson, 1971.

Robertson, E.H. *Christians against Hitler.* London: SCM Press, 1962.

Roggelin, Holger. *Franz Hildebrandt: Ein lutherischer Dissenter im Kirchenkampf und Exil* (Arbeiten zur Kirchlinchen Zeitgeschichte—Reihe B). Göttingen: Vandenhoeck & Ruprecht, 1999.

Rohls, Jan and John Hoffmeyer, *Reformed Confessions: Theology from Zurich to Barmen.* Louisville, KY: Westminster John Knox Press, 1998.

Rubenstein, Richard. *After Auschwitz: Radical Theology and Contemporary Judaism.* Indianapolis: Bobbs-Merrill, 1966.

Sautter, Reinhold. *Theophil Wurm: Bekenner und Kämpfer.* Stuttgart: Verlag Junge Gemeinde, 1954.

Schilling, S.P. *Contemporary Continental Theologians.* Nashville: Abington Press, 1966.

Schleunes, Karl. *The Twisted Road to Auschwitz: Nazi Policy toward German Jews 1933–1939.* Chicago: University of Illinois, 1990.

Schlingensiepen, Ferdinand. *Dietrich Bonhoeffer 1906–1945, Martyr, Thinker, Man of Resistance.* New York: T&T Clark, 2010.

Schmidt, Dietmar. *Martin Niemöller: Eine Biographie.* Stuttgart: Radius-Verl, 1983.

Schmied-Kowarzik, Wolfdietrich. "Streiflichter zum Dialog zwichen Franz Rosenzweig und Hans Ehrenberg," in *Das Erbe des Theologen Hans Ehrenberg, Eine Zwischenbilanz.* Edited by Manfred Keller and Jens Murken. LIT, 2009.

Scholder, Klaus. *The Churches and the Third Reich. Volume 1: Preliminary History and the Time of Illusions, 1918–1934.* Translated by John Bowden. Philadelphia: Fortress Press, 1987–1988.

———. *The Churches and the Third Reich. Volume 2: The Year of Disillusionment: 1934. Barmen and Rome.* Translated by John Bowden. Philadelphia: Fortress Press, 1987–1988.

———. *A Requiem for Hitler and Other New Perspectives on the German Church Struggle.* Philadelphia: Trinity Press International, 1989.

Schroeder, Steven. *To Forget It All and Begin Anew: Reconciliation in Occupied Germany, 1944–1954.* Lincoln, NE: University of Toronto Press, 2013.

Schuchalter, Jerry. *Poetry and Truth: Variations on Holocaust Testimony.* New York: Peter Lang, 2009.

Schumacher, Karl. *Theophil Wurm in den Krisen und Entscheidungen seiner Zeit.* Bad Cannstatt: R. Müllerschön, 1958.

Schwartz, Karl von. *Gottes Wort an Gottes Volk: Ein Jahrgang Predigten.* Braunschweig: Hellmuth Wollermann Verlagsbuchhandlung, 1933.

Sifton, Elizabeth and Fritz Stern, *No Ordinary Men: Dietrich Bonhoeffer and Hans Dohnanyi, Resisters against Hitler in Church and State.* New York: New York Review Books, 2013.

Skiles, William. "'The Bearers of Unholy Potential': Confessing Church Sermons on the Jews and Judaism," in *Studies in Christian-Jewish Relations* 11, no. 1, (2016), 1-29.

———. "Franz Hildebrandt on the BBC: Wartime Broadcasting to Nazi Germany" in the *Journal of Ecclesiastical History*, 74, no. 1 (January 2023), pp. 90-115.

———. "Protests from the Pulpit: The Confessing Church and the Sermons of World War II," in *Sermon Studies* 1, no. 1, (2017), 1-23.

———. "Spying in God's House: The Nazi Secret Police and Sermons of Opposition," in *Church History and Religious Culture*, 98 (2018), 425-447.

Smart, James. *The Divided Mind of Modern Theology: Karl Barth and Rudolf Bultmann, 1908–1933.* Philadelphia: The Westminster Press, 1967.

Smid, Marjike. *Deutscher Protestantismus und Judentum 1932/1933.* Munich: 1990.

Snoek, Johan. *The Grey Book: A Collection of Protests against Anti-semitism and the Persecution of the Jews, Issued by Non-Roman Catholic Churches and Church Leaders During Hitler's Rule.* New York: Humanities Press, 1970.

Snyder, Timothy. *Black Earth: The Holocaust as History and Warning.* New York: Tim Duggan Books, 2015.

———. *Bloodlands: Europe Between Hitler and Stalin.* New York: Basic Books, 2010.

Sonne, Hans-Joachim. *Die Politische Theologie der Deutschen Christen: Einheit und Vielfalt deutsch-christlichen Denkens, dargestellt anhand des Bundes für Deutsche Kirche, der Thüringer Kirchenbewegung "Deutsche Christen" und der Christlich-Deutschen Bewegung.* Göttingen, 1982.

Spicer, Kevin P. *Hitler's Priests: Catholic Clergy and National Socialism.* Dekalb, IL: Northern Illinios University Press, 2008.

———. *Resisting the Third Reich: The Catholic Clergy in Hitler's Berlin*. Dekalb, IL: Northern Illinois University Press, 2004.
Spotts, Frederic. *The Churches and Politics in Germany*. Middletown, CT: Wesleyan University Press, 1973.
Stassen, Glen and David Gushee, *Kingdom Ethics: Following Jesus in Contemporary Context*. Downers Grove, IL: InterVarsity Press, 2003.
Steigmann-Gall, Richard. "Christianity and the Nazi Movement: A Response," in the *Journal of Contemporary History* 42, no. 2. April 2007.
———. *The Holy Reich: Nazi Conceptions of Christianity, 1919–1945*. New York: Cambridge University Press, 2003.
———. "Nazism and the Revival of Political Religion Theory," in *Totalitarian Movements and Political Religions* 5, no. 3. 2004.
———. "The Nazis' 'Positive Christianity': a Variety of 'Clerical Fascism?'" in *Totalitarian Movements and Political Religion* 8, no. 2. June 2007.
Stein, Andre. *Quiet Heroes*. New York: New York University Press, 1988.
Steinert, Marlis. *Hitler's War and the Germans: Public Mood and Attitude during the Second World War*. Translated by Thomas de Witt. Athens: Ohio University Press, 1977.
Stern, J. P. *Hitler: The Führer and the People*. Berkeley: University of California Press, 1975.
Stott, John. *Between Two Worlds: The Art of Preaching in the Twentieth Century*. Grand Rapids, MI: Eermans, 1982.
Stowers, Stanely. "The Concepts of 'Religion,' 'Political Religion' and the Study of Nazism" in the *Journal of Contemporary History* 42, no. 1. Jan. 2007.
Stroud, Dean. *Preaching in Hitler's Shadow*. Grand Rapids, MI: Eerdmans, 2013.
Tal, Uriel. "Lutheran Theology and the Third Reich," in *Speaking of God Today*. Edited by Paul Opsahl and Marc Tannenbaum. Philadelphia, 1974.
———. "On Modern Lutheranism and Jews," in the *Year Book of the Leo Baeck Institute*. London: Secker & Warburg, 1985.
Tec, Nechama. *When Light Pierced the Darkness: Christian Rescue of Jews in Nazi-Occupied Europe*. New York: Oxford University Press, 1986.
———. *Resistance: Jews and Christians Who Defied the Nazi Terror*. New York: Oxford University Press, 2013.
Tent, James F. *In the Shadow of the Holocaust: Nazi Persecution of Jewish-Christian Germans*. Lawrence, KS: University Press of Kansas, 2003.
Thierfelder, Jörg. *Das Kirchliche Einigungswerk des württembergischen Landesbischofs Theophil Wurm*. Göttingen: Vandenhoeck und Ruprecht, 1975.
Thomas, Theodore. *Women against Hitler: Christian Resistance in the Third Reich*. Westport, CT: Praeger, 1995.
Tidy, Roger. *Hitler's Radio War*. London: Robert Hale, 2011.
Tiefel, Hans. "The German Lutheran Church and the Rise of National Socialism," *Church History* 41, no. 3. Sept. 1972.
Tillich, Paul. *A History of Christian Thought: From Its Judaic and Hellenistic Origins to Existentialism*, edited by Carl Braaten. New York: Harper and Row, 1968.

Veli-Matti, Kärkkäinen. *The Doctrine of God: A Global Introduction*. Grand Rapids, MI: Baker, 2004.

Vermes, Geza. *Christian Beginnings: From Nazareth to Nicea*. New Haven, CT: Yale University Press, 2014.

Vielhaber, Klaus, Hubert Hanisch, and Anneliese Knoop-Graf. *Gewalt und Gewissen: Willi Graf und die Weisse Rose, Eine Dokumentation*. Freiburg, 1964.

Vondung, Klaus. *Magie und Manipulation: ideologischer Kult und politische Religion des Nationalsozialismus*. Göttingen: Vandenhoeck und Ruprecht, 1971.

———. "National Socialism as a Political Religion: Potentials and Limits of an Analytical Concept," in *Totalitarian Movements and Political Religion* 6, no. 1. June 2005.

Webster, Ronald. "Eberhard Röhm und Jörg Thierfelder. Ein langer Weg von Breslau nach New York: Der Flüchtlingsseelsorger Friedrich Forell," in *Studien zur Kirchlichen Zeitgeschichte. Festschrift für Carsten Nicolaisen. Edited by Joachim Mehlhausen*. Göttingen: Vandenhoeck & Ruprecht, 1995, pages 315–22.

———. "German 'Non-Aryan' Clergymen and the Anguish of Exile after 1933," in *The Journal of Religious History*, 22:1. February 1998.

Weikart, Richard. *Hitler's Ethic: The Nazi Pursuit of Evolutionary Progress*. New York: Palgrave Macmillan, 2009.

———. *Hitler's Religion: The Twisted Beliefs that Drove the Third Reich*. New York: Regnery History, 2016.

Weintraub, Stanley. *Silent Night: The Story of the World War I Christmas Truce*. New York: Plume 2002.

Weiss, John. *Ideology of Death: Why the Holocaust Happened in Germany*. Chicago: Ivan R. Dee, 1996.

Wentorf, Rudolf. *Der Fall des Pfarrers Paul Schneider: Eine biographische Dokumentation*. Neukirchen-Vluyn: Neukirchener Verlag, 1989.

Wilson, John. *Introduction to Modern Theology: Trajectories in the German Tradition*. Louisville, KY: Westminster John Knox, 2007.

Wilson, Paul Scott. *Concise History of Preaching*. Nashville: Abingdon Press, 1992.

Wintzer, Friedrich. *Die Homiletik seit Schleiermacher bis in die Anänge der 'dialetischen Theologie' in Grundzügen* (Göttingen: Vandenhoeck & Ruprecht, 1969).

Wright, J.R.C. *'Above Parties,' The Political Attitudes of the German Protestant Church Leadership, 1918–1933*. New York: Oxford University Press, 1974.

Yahil, Leni. *The Holocaust: The Fate of European Jewry*. Translated by Ina Friedman and Haya Galai. New York: Oxford University Press, 1987.

Zabel, James. *Nazism and the Pastors: A Study of the Ideas of Three Deutsche Christen Groups*. Missoula, MT, 1976.

Zahn, Gordon. *German Catholics and Hitler's Wars*. New York: Sheed and Ward, 1962.

Zahrnt, Heinz. *The Question of God: Protestant Theology in the 20th Century*. New York: Harcourt, Brace 7 World, 1969.

Zimmermann, Wolf-Dieter and Ronald G. Smith, eds. *I Knew Dietrich Bonhoeffer*. Translated by Käthe Gregor Smith. New York: Harper & Row, 1966.

Index

Abraham, 192, 211–214, 230n12
Abwehr resistance, 190
Action T4, 137. *See also* euthanasia.
age of reason, 39
Ahab, King of Israel, 115–116
Althaus, Paul, 74–77, 119
ambivalence toward Jews, pastors,' 176, 182–183, 199, 211, 216, 229. *See also* incongruous messages about Jews and Judaism
anti-Judaic theology: in Biblical history, 174–178, 182, 198, 227; deicide by Jews, 178, 184–186, 194, 199; God-forsaken people, 191–194; moral failings and legalism of Jews, 184, 194–195, 199; and racial antisemitism, 181, 184. *See also* curse, Jews'; early church and Jews
antisemitism, 174, 176, 179–180. *See also* racism
Aquinas, Thomas, 38
Aristotle, 38
Aryan Paragraph, 34–35, 120; PEL/Confessing Church response to, 44, 182–184; pastors' criticism of, 220–221, 246. *See also* Sports Palace
Asmussen, Hans, 47
Augsberg Confession, 46, 75

autonomy and identity of church: church identity, 17–18, 47–51, 107, 124, 130, 218, 255; fight for, 4, 35, 45, 120, 154, 255, 257; and Nazi interference, 7–8, 13, 99, 147, 156; permitted by Hitler, 158. *See also* "coordination"; freedom to speak, pastors'
awareness of Jewish persecution, pastors,' 224, 226–227

Bacharach, Walter Zvi, 176
baptism, 35, 100, 102, 112n94, 196
Barmen Conference, 46–47. *See also* Barmen Confession
Barmen Confession, 25n90, 47–51, 154; and divine revelation, 92, 117; and obedience to state, 78, 119, 121; as platform for dissent/opposition, 117
Barth, Karl, 17, 41, 44–45, 107; and Barmen Confession, 47, 92; Church Dogmatics, 41; and creation of "new school," 80, 85–87, 89; *Der Römerbrief*, 42; "emergency homiletic," 92–93; and liberal Protestantism and divine revelation, 41–43, 58n94, 89–94; on orders of creation, 92; on preaching fundamentals, 90–91; on sacraments,

285

100–101; on sermon manuscript, 104–105; on sermon's purpose, 96–97; on Old Testament, 102–103; on role of sermon, 66–67, 71; *Theological Existence To-day*, 44, 97
Bauer, Johannes, 66–67, 90
Baumgärtel, Friedrich, 10; *Wider der Kirchenkampf-Legenden*, 10
Baumgärtner, Hans, 79
BBC. *See* British Broadcasting Corporation
"beefsteak sections," 239
Bertram, Cardinal Adolf, 137
Bethge, Eberhard, 190, 198
Bible, Hebrew. *See* Testaments, Old and New
Bible translations, 71
"binding" (*Bindung*) the gospel: and Confessing Church autonomy, 44, 51, 63–64; to nature and history, 37, 38, 40, 49, 161, 194; to sacraments, 102; to scripture, 94, 101, 107; to state (political theology), 76–78, 97, 107
bishop, Reichskirche, 34, 46, 88, 132–133
blood libel, 178
Bodelschwingh, Friedrich von, 25n83, 34, 88, 147, 184, 186
bomb plot of 20 July 1944, 127, 166
Bonhoeffer, Dietrich, 17, 86–87, 93; criticizing Nazism, 126, 129–131, 139–40n9, 148, 221; on divine revelation, 94; on Judaism, 159, 190–191, 196, 198, 205n93 and Old Prussian Council of Brethren, 93; on Old Testament, 103; on justice and redemption, 159, 163, 190–191; on orders of creation, 92; on sacraments, 100–101; on sermon manuscript, 105–106; on sermon's purpose, 98; on spiritual battle, 258; underground seminary, 116, 121, 148, 150, 170n65
Bormann, Martin, 149
Breit, Thomas, 47

British Broadcasting Corporation (BBC), 14, 25n84, 150, 165, 226, 230n4. *See also* suppression of media, Nazi
Bröckelschen, Otto, 48
"brown synod," 34
Brunner, Emil, 76
Brunner, Peter, 160–162, 179
Buber, Martin, 43
Busch, Wilhelm, 126

Calvin, John, 39, 42, 220, 232n35
Calvinism, 220
"campaign of terrorism and intimidation," 157
Catholic Church: Concordat, 8, 237; historiography, 176; Nazi persecution of, 134, 150, 158, 171n87; in "positive Christianity," 4–5; sermon statements about Nazis, 124, 241, 244
Chamberlain, Houston Stewart, 30–31; *Foundations of the Nineteenth Century (1899)*, 30
chosenness: by God (Judaism), 174, 191, 213–215, 219, 247; by race (Nazism), 177, 193, 215, 248
Christians and Jews, history between. *See* early church and Jews
Christian Social Party, 180
Church Struggle (*Kirchenkampf*), 8–9, 99–100; and Christian unity, 162–163; and Confessing Church disunity, 51, 53, 144; and divided congregations, 51–52, 137; historiography, 2–3, 9–11; as spiritual battle, 156; underlying theological controversy of, 28, 130. *See also* autonomy and identity of church; divine revelation; spiritual battle
Communism, 6, 29, 31–32
concentration camp: pastors sent to, 2, 133, 153, 162, 188; preaching in, 14,

25n84, 185, 188. *See also* Niemöller: persecution and arrest

Confessing Church (*die Bekennende Kirche*): in contrast to German Christian movement, 11, 38, 46–47; on divine revelation (*see under* divine revelation); emergence, 4, 46; finances (*see* finances in Confessing Church); membership (*see under* membership, church); organizational structure, 51–53. *See also* autonomy and identity of church; Barmen Conference; Pastors' Emergency League

"coordination": Barmen Confession and, 50; Church resistance of, 11, 43, 125, 170n65, 210, 251; of institutions, 32, 98, 244; of the Church, 34–35, 123, 127, 149, 154, 182. *See also* autonomy and identity of church

criticism, public. *See* dissent and opposition

curse, Jews', 174, 179, 186, 188–191, 247

Dahlemites, 53
DAP (German Workers' Party; *Deutsche Arbeiterpartei*), 29
Darwinism, Social, 30, 180
deicide, 178, 184–186, 194, 199
de-judaization, 50, 134, 219, 228; opposition to, 248, 250
democracy. *See* Weimar Republic
de Quervain, Alfred, 125
Deutsche evangelische Kirche. *See* German Evangelical Church.
Deutsche Völkskirche (German People's Church), 134
dialectical theology, 42
Dibelius, Otto, 121, 184
Diem, Hermann, 186
Dinter, Arthur, 134–135; *Die Sünde wider das Blut* ("The Sin Against the Blood"), 134

dissent, 13–14; through behavior, 241, 257–258; through faithful preaching, 92, 108n5, 125–127, 210–213; through reclamation of tradition, 117, 122–124; through word choice, 13–14, 117, 122, 124–125

dissent and opposition: sermon as a tool, 85–86, 92, 98, 108, 108n5, 125–127, 249, 255–258. *See also* autonomy and identity in church; dissent; opposition

divine punishment for Jews. *See* curse, Jews'.

divine revelation, 37–38; as central in Church struggle, 28–29; found in Hebrew Bible (Old Testament), 69, 102–104, 210–211, 213–214, 216–218; general revelation, evolutions in, 36–39, 65, 161; in liberal theology, 38–40, 64, 66–68; in Luther Reformation, 91; in "new school" neo–orthodoxy, 40–41, 86–87, 89–96; in PEL and Confessing Church, 17, 25n90, 43–44, 47–50, 63–64, 82n53; in political theology, 74–75, 77, 80; in *völkisch* theology, 64–65, 72–73, 128–132

early church and Jews, 177, 182, 191–192, 194–195, 218
Ebeling, Gerhard, 137–138
Eberhard, Rudolf, 128
Eberle, Kurt, 246
Ehrenberg, Hans, 145–146
elections, church (1933), 34–35, 44, 57n49, 60n122, 88, 130, 147
Elert, Werner, 74–76
Elijah, prophet, 115–116
encouragement from pulpit, 146, 151–152, 157, 159, 163, 166–167, 214–215
the Enlightenment, 39, 48, 65
"eternal Jew." *See* curse, Jews'
The Eternal Jew, 189

ethnic religion (*völkischen Religion*), 162. See also *völkisch* theology
eugenics, 42, 179
euthanasia, 137–138, 228
exile, 14, 25n84, 160, 164
existentialism, 43

Fendt, Leonhard, 90, 95–96
fettered gospel. See "binding" (*Bindung*) the gospel
finances in Confessing Church, 8, 21n41, 62–63n185, 52–53, 98, 147, 168n10, 206n103; Nazi interference in, 148, 157, 162–163, 171n88
Foreign Affairs, Office of, 134
Forell, Friedrich, 225
freedom to speak, pastors,' 92, 117, 224, 238–239, 243, 250–251, 255–256; due to church autonomy, 11, 18, 98, 219
Frick, Robert, 130
Fürbittenliste (intercessory lists), 8, 21–22n41, 147, 163, 235, 243

Galen, Clemens August von (bishop), 137
Gamaliel, Pharisee, 1
Garden of Gethsemane, 155
Geheime Staatspolizei (Secret State Police, Gestapo), 235
Geistchristliche Religionsgemeinschaft (Spiritual Christian Religious Community), 134
general revelation. See divine revelation
Gerlach, Wolfgang, 2, 117–118, 175, 235; *Als die Zeugen schwiegen* (*And the Witness Were Silent*), 2
German Christian Faith Movement (*Glaubensbewegung Deutsche Christen*), 3–6, 32–33; "The Guiding Principles of the Faith Movement of the 'German Christians,'" 33, 37; membership (*see under* membership, church). See also liberal theology; *völkisch* theology

German Evangelical Church (*Deutsche evangelische Kirche*), 4, 28, 33. See also Church Struggle
German Workers' Party (*Deutsche Arbeiterpartei*; DAP), 29
Gestapo, 151, 159, 237–239, 250–251
Gethsemane, 155
Gideon, 129
Gleichschaltung. See "coordination"
Gloege, Gerhard, 93
Gobineau, Joseph-Arthur de, 30–31; *An Essay on the Inequality of the Human Races* (1852), 30
God: as eternal Encourager, 146, 151–152, 157, 159, 163, 166–167, 214–215; as eternal Judge, 131, 146–147, 151–154, 157, 166–167, 174, 179, 242
Goebbels, Joseph, 98, 132, 226
Gogarten, Friedrich, 74–76
Gollwitzer, Helmut, 124
Göring (chief of Prussian secret police), 156
Grotjahn (pastor), 247
Grüber, Heinrich, 188, 239
Grundmann, Walter, 46
Grynszpan, Herschel, 222

Hansse, Enke, 243
Harnack, Adolf von, 105
"Heil Hitler," 122, 241. See also Nazi ideology: religious language
Herod, 159
Hertzberg, Wilhelm, 131
Herzberg, Hans, 217
Hildebrandt, Franz, 148, 150, 164–165, 168n15
Himmler, Heinrich, 140n25, 148, 157, 170n64
Hinz, Paulus (Paul), 135–137, 173, 191, 193, 212, 221, 224
Hirsch, Emanuel, 74
historiography, Church Struggle, 2–3, 9–11, 19n8

Index 289

history, Jews and Christians. *See* early church and Jews
Hitler: attempted assassination, 12; attitude toward Christianity, 5; attitude toward Jews, 29–30, 181, 209, 222; and the Church, 4, 33–34, 130, 149, 158–159, 238–240; and Martin Niemöller, 156, 185; political rise, 7, 29–31
Hitler salute (*Hitlergruß*), 122, 241. *See also* Nazi ideology: religious language
Hitler Youth. *See* youth programs
Holy Spirit: as agent of truth, 125–127, 136, 191; in baptism, 102; in preaching, 90–91, 95, 106, 111n62; in reformation, 116; as unifying agent in Church, 146, 164
hope, divine, 146, 151–152, 157, 159, 163, 166–167, 214–215
"hour of darkness," 155

identity of church. *See* autonomy and identity of church
incongruous messages about Jews and Judaism, 185–187, 188, 191, 247–248. See *also* ambivalence toward Jews, pastors'
informants, Nazi, 235, 237–238
Institute for the Study and Eradication of Jewish Influence on German Religious Life, 46, 112n100, 197, 216
intercessory lists. See *Fürbittenliste*
inter-Jewish conflict in early Church, 151, 191, 195
Isaiah, prophet, 122, 225
IV-B, 238
Iwand, Hans, 93, 209

Jacobi, Gerhard, 43
Jäger, August, 34, 154
Jan, Julius von, 222–224
Jeremiah, prophet, 151, 190, 223

Jesus: Aryanized, 46, 50, 134, 197; as basis for gospel, 38, 43–45, 47–48, 53, 80, 90, 92, 95, 129; calming sea, 132; and dissent/opposition, 77, 136, 138; highest Führer, 131; Jewish identity, 177, 219, 243, 247; and Old Testament, 68–69, 104, 218; persecution of, 155, 159, 184, 225; rejected by Jews, 174, 178, 184–186, 195, 216; in sacrament, 112n94; Shepherd and Protector, 152; walking on water, 132
"Jewish Christian Church," 46
"Jewish menace," 226. *See also* racism: in National Socialism
Jews and Christians, history between. *See* early church and Jews
Jezebel, Queen of Israel, 115–116
judgment of Nazis, divine, 131, 146–147, 151–154, 157, 166–167, 174, 179, 242

Kalb, Heinrich, 196
Kant, Immanuel, 39
Kerrl, Hans, 7, 156
Kershaw, Ian, 12–14, 227
Kierkegaard, Søren, 43
kinship, spiritual (Christians and Jews), 209, 218–219, 248
Kirchenkampf. See Church Struggle
Klemperer, Victor, 27
Kloppenburg, Heinz, 152–153
Kniess (pastor), 241
knowledge of God. *See* divine revelation
knowledge of Jewish persecution, pastors,' 224, 226–227
Koch, Erich, 123
Köster (pastor), 193, 216
Krause, Reinhold. *See* Sports Palace.
Kristallnacht (Night of Broken Glass), 15, 146, 209, 222–225, 228
Kube, Wilhelm, 33
Künneth, Walter, 156

law and gospel doctrine, 65, 74–76, 80

Leffler, Siegfried, 33
legalism, Jewish, 184, 194–195, 199
Lemke (pastor), 240
Lempp, Friedrich Wilhelm (Wilfried), 17, 86, 88; on divine revelation, 95; on obedience to state, 95; on Old Testament, 104; on orders of creation, 92; on sacraments, 101; on sermon as spiritual weapon, 98–99; on sermon's purpose, 88
Leutheuser, Julius, 33
liberal theology, 40–42, 66, 70, 72
love, Christian, 126, 151, 164, 245, 257; for Jews, 183, 220–222, 224
Lueger, Karl, 180
Luther, Martin, 64, 91; legacy in Confessing Church, 116, 118, 122–124; "Luther spirit" (*Luthergeist*), 45, 123, 130

Main Security Office of the *Schutzstaffel* (SS), 240
manuscript, sermon, 104–106
Marahrens, August (bishop), 163
Marr, Wilhelm, 179
martyrdom, Christian. See persecution of church
Mary and Martha, 135
Meiser, Hans, 154–155, 161
membership, church: Confessing Church, 52; German Christian movement, 35, 51; PEL, 44, 46
Minister for the Occupied Eastern Territories, Reich, 134
Ministry of Church Affairs, 7, 53, 156
Ministry of Culture, 34
Müller, Fritz, 63
Müller, Ludwig (Reich Bishop), 33–34, 46, 88, 132–133
"muzzling decree" (*Maulkorbgesetz*), 88–89

National Socialist German Workers' Party (NSDAP), 29
natural theology, 38–39

nazification of institutions. See "coordination"
Nazi ideology: alignment to Protestant groups, 8, 32–33; Hitler as savior and other idols, 17, 27–29, 50, 74, 78–80, 117, 129–133, 183; ideology, 3, 5, 8, 54n10; redefinition of Christian identity, 36; religious language, 6, 11, 13, 28, 31, 33, 122–125, 181; symbolism, 79, 128–131. *See also* Aryan Paragraph; Rosenberg, Alfred
neo-orthodoxy. *See* "new school" of homiletics
"neutrals," 4, 52
"new school" of homiletics: on divine revelation (*see* divine revelation); emergence, 85–87; on liturgy, 86; Old and New Testaments in, 68–70; on preaching's purpose and function, 90–91, 96–102, 125–127; prioritization of spiritual above political, 16, 89, 97. *See also* liberal theology
Niebergall, Friedrich, 72
Niemöller, Martin: on Church struggle and unity, 162; and Confessing Church, 92, 113n107; criticism of Nazis, 1–2, 120–121, 123–124, 135, 139n9, 153–156, 162–163, 188–190, 197, 238; and establishment of PEL, 4, 43, 63, 120; hope in Nazis, 1, 7–8; on Judaism and Jews, 184–186, 189–190; on obedience to state, 119–120; persecution and arrest, 1–2, 185, 238, 244
Niemöller, Wilhelm, 9; *Kampf und Zeugnis der Bekennenden Kirche*, 9
Nierlich, Gerhard, 243
Night of Broken Glass (*Kristallnacht*), 15, 146, 209, 222–225, 228
NSDAP (National Socialist German Workers' Party), 29
Nuremberg Laws (1935), 221

obedience to state, theology on: law and gospel doctrine, 65, 74–76, 80; limits of disobedience, 49, 119–121, 133–134; orders of creation doctrine, 35, 65, 75–77, 80, 92; two kingdoms doctrine, 4, 65, 74–78, 80, 83, 118. *See also* political theology
Office of Foreign Affairs, 134
Old Prussian Union: Confessing Church, 52, 93; *Reichskirche*, 34, 120
Operation Barbarossa, 190, 209
opposition, 10, 13, 15–16, 255–258; to antisemitism and Jewish persecution, 183, 210, 217–226, 229, 242–243, 245–249, 256; to church persecution, 147, 150–167, 242–245, 253n37, 255–256; to Nazi ideology and idolatry, 47–48, 98, 116–117, 123–124, 126, 128–137, 139, 147–148, 241, 242–243, 255n37, 255; to Nazi policies and actions, 117, 137–138, 183, 244, 255. *See also* autonomy and identity of church: fight for; surveillance, Nazi
orders of creation doctrine, 37, 65, 75–77, 80, 92
Ordinance for the Restoration of Orderly Conditions in the German Evangelical Church, 88–89
Operation 7 (*Unternehmen 7*), 190

Palmer, Christian, 69, 102
Pastors' Emergency League (*Pfarrernotbund*; PEL): first national synod, 44, 63; founding of, 4, 43–44, 46, 60n122, 63–64, 120; and Reich surveillance, 240. *See also* Confessing Church
Paul, apostle: on communion, 100; on evil and spiritual battle, 99, 135–136; on fettered gospel, 51, 64, 80; on God as ultimate authority, 131, 145, 159, 223–224; on Judaism and Jews, 173–175, 179, 192–195, 200n6, 217, 232n35; on knowledge of God (divine revelation), 40, 210; on obedience to government, 76–78, 118–120, 123; on persecution, 160–161, 163; on salvation, 188;
PEL. *See* Pastors' Emergency League
persecution of church, 235, 239; arrests (clergy), 34, 87, 116, 121, 133, 154, 162, 165, 183, 188, 224, 239, 243, 246, 254n60; concentration camp imprisonment (clergy), 2, 133, 146, 162, 188, 238; mass arrests (clergy), 8, 147–150; turning point, 158. *See also* Niemöller, Martin
persecution of Jews, 190, 197, 209, 215; Christian silence, 225; Christian support, 176, 188, 225; public awareness of, 224, 226–227. *See also Kristallnacht*
Peter, apostle, 84n86, 119, 130, 132
Peter, Rudolf, 49
Peterson (pastor), 240
Pfarrernotbund. *See* Pastors' Emergency League
Pharisees, 1, 187, 194–195, 218
Pietism, 40, 65
Pilate, 184
political theology, 74–80; in contrast to "new school," 107; in *völkisch* religion, 64, 92–94, 119;
"positive Christianity," 4–5, 134
preaching: in concentration camps, 184, 188: in exile, 160, 164–165, 225
preaching emergency, 87
preaching practices and customs, 70–73
Preising (pastor), 247
pro-Jewish Christian sentiments: affirmation of Hebrew Bible, 86, 102–104, 210–213; spiritual kinship, 209, 218–219, 248
propaganda, Nazi, 29, 46, 55n22, 98, 180, 189, 226, 241, 244
Psalms, 81n21, 104, 153, 157–158, 212–213

racial theology, 46

racial theory, 30
racism: in Europe, 180–181; in German Christian movement, 196–197, 199; in National Socialism, 181, 189, 192, 196, 226; scientific, 179. *See also* antisemitism
Rath, Ernst vom, 222
redemption for Jews, 214
Reichskirche: Confessing Church's separation from, 47–51; divided congregations, 51–52; establishment of, 3–4, 33–35, 120; fragmentation and disputes, 147, 149, 154–156; PEL response to establishment of, 44
religious antisemitism, *See* anti-Judaic theology.
rescue of Jews, 175, 190, 219–220, 248
resistance, 12–13
Röhm, Ernst, 239
romanticism, 40, 65
Rosenberg, Alfred, 132, 134, 135, 147; *The Myth of the Twentieth Century* (*Der Mythus des zwanzigsten Jahrhunderts*), 132, 134, 147

Sachsse, Eugene, 67
Sammentreuther, Julius, 122, 190, 194, 220
Sasse, Hermann, 93, 218
Schäfer, August, 246
Scharf, Kurt, 239
Schirach, Baldur von, 239
Schleiermacher, Friedrich, 40–41, 59n107, 65–66, 112n95; in contrast to "new school," 90–91, 103; *On Religion: Speeches to Its Cultured Despisers*, 40. *See also* liberal theology
Schmidt, Kurt Dietrich, 47
Schmitz, Otto, 93
Schneider, Paul, 131–133
Schnieber, Hans, 131
Schutzstaffel, Main Security Office of (SS), 240
Schwartz, Karl von, 186, 194, 214

SD. *See* Security Service
Secret State Police (*Geheime Staatspolizei;* Gestapo), 235
Security Service (*Sicherheitsdienst*; SD), 149, 235, 238–240, 242, 245, 250–251
Seggel, Hermann, 224
seven churches (book of Revelation), 162, 191
Social Darwinism, 30, 180
Social Democratic Party (*Sozialdemokratische Partei Deutschlands*; SPD), 6, 41, 121
sola scriptura, 46, 90, 118. *See also* divine revelation
special revelation. *See* divine revelation
spies and informants, 235, 237–238
spiritual awakening. *See* spiritual rejuvenation, hope in Hitler for
spiritual battle, 98–100, 135–137, 258; sermon as weapon, 86, 89, 106
spiritual rejuvenation, hope in Hitler for, 1, 7, 33, 65, 97
Sports Palace (*Sportspalast*): event, 45–47, 88; response from Vogel, 115–117, 118
SS (*Schutzstaffel*), 240
state church(es). *See Reichskirche*
Stoecker, Adolf, 73, 180
Storm Troopers (*Sturmabeilung*; SA), 239
Stroud, Dean, 125–127
"sub-humans," 198, 224
suppression of media, Nazi: publications and advertising, 151, 158; radio, 24n79, 165, 171n88
surveillance, Nazi, 250; criticism of church persecution, 236, 242–245; criticism of Nazi "false ideology," 236, 240–242; statements supporting Jews or Judaism, 236, 245–249. *See also* spies and informants

ten Boom, Corrie, 22
Ten Commandments, 125, 257

Testaments, Old and New: controversy, 216–218; Hebrew Bible, 86, 102–104, 210–213
theology of crisis (*Theologie der Krisis*), 42
Töllner (pastor), 240
Tower of Babel, 164
"tribalism," 189, 196, 248
Trillhaas, Wolfgang, 17, 86, 88–89; on divine revelation, 94–95; on Old Testament and Jews, 103–104; on orders of creation, 92; on sacraments, 101; on sermon manuscript, 106; on sermon's purpose, 97–98;
two kingdoms doctrine, 4, 65, 74–78, 80, 83, 118

Ulricht (pastor), 242, 245–246
underground seminary, 116, 121, 148, 150, 170n65
"unholy potential," 228
Untermenschen (sub-humans), 199, 224
Unternehmen 7 (Operation 7), 190

Vertrauensmänner ("V-men"), 238
"violent spirit" (*Gewaltgeist*), 116

Vogel, Heinrich, 115–116, 147, 157
völk, 45–46, 50, 74–76, 134
völkisch theology, 31–32, 45, 73; and divine revelation, 37–38, 65, 72. *See also* political theology
Völkseelsorge, 73, 92. *See also völkisch* theology
Völksgemeinschaft ("people's community"), 5; in Nazi ideology, 29, 31, 36, 92, 97; and persecution, 237–239, 245; in sermons, 125

"Wandering Jew." *See* curse, Jews'
Wehrmacht, 209, 224, 226
Weimar Republic, 5–7, 29, 31, 73
Weissler, Friedrich, 183
Weltanschauung, 135, 183, 246
White Rose group, 127, 166, 227
Wollermann, Hellmuth, 214
wolves, Nazis compared to, 132–133, 152–153, 158
Wurm, Theophil, 154–155, 161
WWI theology and disillusionment, 43, 72–74

youth programs, 88, 120, 239